Cayo Coco

Morón

ancti
píritus

Ciego de Ávila

CENTRAL CUBA – EAST

Florida

Nuevitas

Camagüey

Guáimaro

Las Tunas

Holguín

EASTERN CUBA

Baracoa

Bayamo

Manzanillo

Guantánamo

Santiago
de Cuba

Caribbean Sea

**Central
Cuba – West**
Pages 158–181

**Central
Cuba – East**
Pages 182–211

Western Cuba
Pages 136–157

Eastern Cuba
Pages 212–249

EYEWITNESS TRAVEL

CUBA

EYEWITNESS TRAVEL

CUBA

Produced by Fabio Ratti Editoria Srl, Milan, Italy

Project Editor Giorgia Conversi
Art Editor Paolo Gonzato

Editors Carla Beltrami, Barbara Cacciani,
Fernanda Incoronato, Alessandra Lombardi

Main Contributor
Irina Bajini

Other Contributors
Alejandro Alonso, Christopher Baker, Miguel A Castro Machado, Andrea G Molinari,
Matt Norman, Marco Oliva, Francesca Piana

Photographers
Heidi Grassley, Lucio Rossi

Cartographers
Laura Belletti, Oriana Bianchetti, Roberto Capra

Illustrators
Marta Fincato, Modi Artistici

English Translation
Richard Pierce

Dorling Kindersley Limited
Editor Fiona Wild
Consultant Emily Hatchwell
DTP Designers Jason Little, Conrad Van Dyk
Production Joanna Bull

Printed and bound in China

First American Edition 2002
17 18 19 20 10 9 8 7 6 5 4 3 2 1

Published in the United States by Dorling Kindersley Limited,
345 Hudson Street, New York, New York 10014

Reprinted with revisions 2004, 2007, 2009, 2011, 2013, 2015, 2017

Copyright © 2002, 2017 Dorling Kindersley Limited, London
A Penguin Random House Company

A catalog record for this book is available from the Library of Congress.

ISSN 1542-1554
ISBN 978-1-46546-032-5

Floors are referred to throughout in accordance with European
usage; ie the "first floor" is the floor above ground level.

MIX
Paper from
responsible sources
FSC™ C018179
www.fsc.org

The information in this DK Eyewitness Travel Guide is checked regularly.
At the time of going to press, changes to Cuba's foreign policy were taking place.
Every effort has been made to ensure that this book is as up-to-date as possible but
some information in this guide may have since altered. In addition, details such as
telephone numbers, opening hours, prices, gallery hanging arrangements and
travel information, are liable to change. The publishers cannot accept responsibility
for any consequences arising from the use of this book, nor for
any material on third party websites, and cannot guarantee that any website
address in this book will be a suitable source of travel information. We value
the views and suggestions of our readers very highly. Please write to:
The Publisher, DK Eyewitness Travel Guides, Dorling Kindersley, 80 Strand,
London WC2R 0RL, UK or email: travelguides@dk.com.

Front cover main image: Classic car on a street in Havana

◀ Driving along the Malecón, Havana

Contents

How to Use this Guide **6**

Ídolo de Tabaco, Museo
Montané, Havana *(see p105)*

Introducing Cuba

The altar of Santuario de San Lázaro, just
outside Havana *(see p121)*

Fishing boats moored at Nueva Gerona harbour on Isla de la Juventud *(see pp152–5)*

Pilgrimage destination, Basílica del
Cobre *(see p225)*

Guava paste and cheese

Flower at the Jardín Avenida del Paraíso,
Parque Baconao *(see pp238–41)*

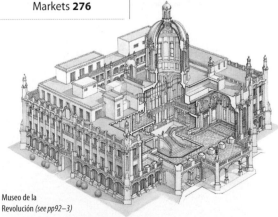
Museo de la
Revolución *(see pp92–3)*

HOW TO USE THIS GUIDE

This guide will help you to get the most out of your visit to Cuba by providing detailed information and expert recommendations. *Introducing Cuba* maps the island and sets it in its historic, artistic, cultural and geographical context. *Havana* and the four regional sections describe the most important sights, with maps, floor plans, photographs and detailed illustrations. Hotels and restaurants, together with night spots and shops, are described in *Travellers' Needs*, while the *Survival Guide* offers tips on everything from transport to phones and local currency.

Havana Area by Area

The centre of the city is divided into three areas, each with its own chapter. The last chapter, *Further Afield*, covers peripheral sights. All the sights are numbered and plotted on the *Area Map*. The detailed information for each sight is easy to locate because it follows the numerical order on the map.

A Locator Map shows where you are in relation to the other areas of the city.

All pages relating to Havana have the same coloured thumb tabs.

Sights at a Glance lists the sights in each chapter by category: Churches, Museums and Galleries, Streets and Squares, Historic Buildings, Parks and Gardens.

1 Area Map
All the major sights are numbered and located on this map. Those in the historic centre are also listed in the *Havana Street Finder* (see pp122–7).

2 Street-by-Street Map
This gives a bird's-eye view of the most important areas in each chapter.

Stars indicate the sights no visitor should miss.

Suggested routes are shown in red.

3 Detailed Information
The most important monuments and sights in Havana are described individually. Addresses, phone numbers, opening hours and information concerning guided tours and taking photos are also provided.

EASTERN CUBA

Granma · Holguín · Santiago de Cuba · Guantánamo

Cubans refer to the eastern part of Cuba as the Oriente, giving it an almost magical appeal. The landscape, stretching out towards Haiti and other Caribbean islands, is varied, with majestic mountains, magnificent coastlines and an area of arid desert, unusual in Cuba. The eastern cities, often rich in history, include Santiago de Cuba, host to one of Latin America's most famous carnivals.

1 Introduction to the Region
The landscape, history and character of each region are described here, showing how the region has developed over the centuries and what it has to offer to visitors today.

Cuba Region by Region

Apart from Havana, the island has been divided into four regions, each with a separate chapter: Western Cuba, Central Cuba – West, Central Cuba – East and Eastern Cuba.

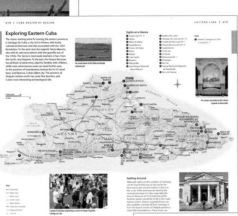

Exploring Eastern Cuba

2 Regional Map
This shows the road network and provides an illustrated overview of the whole region. All the interesting places to visit are numbered in the same order in which they are described, and there are also useful tips on getting around the region by car and by public transport.

Each region can easily be identified by its own colour coding.

3 Detailed Information on Each Sight
All the major cities and other top sights are described in detail. They are listed in order, following the numbering on the *Regional Map*. Within each town or city there is detailed information on important buildings and other sights.

The Visitors' Checklist
provides all the practical information you will need to plan your visit.

Boxes provide further information on the region: leading figures, legends, historical events, local flora and fauna, curiosities, and so on.

Castillo del Morro

4 Cuba's Top Sights
These are given two or more full pages. Historic buildings are dissected to reveal their interiors, while museums have colour-coded floor plans to help you locate their most interesting features, which are shown in photographs with captions.

INTRODUCING CUBA

DISCOVERING CUBA

The following tours have been designed to cover the best areas for experiencing the many pleasures of Cuba, while keeping long-distance travel to a minimum. First comes a two-day tour of the country's vibrant capital, Havana. Next, a five-day tour of Western Cuba gives you the chance to explore the lush mountains and valleys of the western peninsula before relaxing by the coast. These itineraries can be followed individually or combined to form a week-long tour. The country's rich historical past is explored in a one-week tour of central Cuba, which includes some of the country's best-preserved

provincial towns, landscapes, historic sites and coastal attractions. Finally, a one-week itinerary in the far east covers areas of both cultural interest and great natural beauty. Baracoa, Cuba's oldest city, is surrounded by coconut palms, chocolate and coffee bushes, and has 29 rivers running through it. One-time capital and second city, Santiago de Cuba is steeped in history and has a strong musical tradition, while Guardalavaca offers visitors the opportunity to relax and enjoy beautiful crystal-clear waters and pure white sands. Follow and combine your favourite tours, or simply seek inspiration.

Key

— Five Days in Western Cuba

— A Week in Central Cuba

— A Week in Eastern Cuba

0 km 50

0 miles 50

Five Days in Western Cuba

- Zipline through the eco-community of Las Terrazas

- Wander past steep *mogotes* and green tobacco fields in Valle de Viñales

- Snorkel the shallow reefs of María La Gorda

- Sniff the perfect cigar at the factory in Pinar del Río

- Admire 700 species of orchid at the gardens in Soroa

Valle de Viñales
Surrounded by mountains and punctuated by dramatic rock formations known as *mogotes*, this lush green valley offers spectacular scenery.

 Wall mural in Havana

A Week in Central Cuba

- Wander the colonial streets of maritime city Cienfuegos
- Explore the old *palacios* and ancient churches of perfectly preserved Trinidad
- Soak up the sun at Playa Ancón
- Hike to pools fed by tumbling waterfalls in the mountains at Topes de Collantes
- See the workings of a sugar plantation at Manaca Iznaga
- Pay your respects at Che Guevara's mausoleum
- Sail, swim or just relax at the resorts of Cayo Santa María

Playa Ancón
Just outside Trinidad, this pristine white beach stretches for 5 km (3 miles) and is surrounded by palm trees.

Punta Gorda
The former aristocratic quarter of Cienfuegos, stretched out along a thin peninsula, is home to many impressive 19th-century villas.

Cayo Santa María

Remedios

Sancti Spíritus

Golfo de Ana María

Guardalavaca

Holguín

Parque Nacional Alejandro de Humboldt
Playa Maguaná

Bayamo

El Yunque
Baracoa

Santiago de Cuba
La Farola

Basílica del Cobre
Costa Sur

Castillo El Morro
Guantánamo Naval Base (USA)

Baracoa
Located on the very eastern tip of the island, Baracoa is the oldest city in Cuba, and is surrounded by rainforest-covered hills.

A Week in Eastern Cuba

- Sip a *mojito* and enjoy the views over pretty Baracoa from Hotel El Castillo
- Climb flat-topped El Yunque or explore the rainforest in Parque Humboldt
- Laze on the shaded sands of Playa Maguana
- Motor over the winding mountain pass La Farola
- Get on the dance floor at Santiago de Cuba's Casa de la Trova
- Find out about the early struggles of the Revolution at Cuartel Moncada
- Join the pilgrims at the revered Basílica del Cobre
- Seek out the sun at the resorts of Guardalavaca

Baroque Catedral de San Cristóbal, Plaza de la Catedral, Havana

Two Days in Havana

Havana's stunning architecture, rich cultural traditions and vibrant nightlife make it one of the most alluring capitals in Latin America.

- **Arriving** Arrive and depart from Havana's José Martí International Airport, 17 km (11 miles) south of the city. The only transport into the centre is by official yellow Cubataxis.
- **Moving on** Domestic flights leave from neighbouring terminals. Car hire is available at the airport or in the city. Víazul's coach service terminal is in Nuevo Vedado.
- **Book ahead** Accommodation in Havana needs to be booked well in advance.

Day 1
Morning Havana is huge, but most of the main sights are found in **La Habana Vieja** (pp64–81), the historic Spanish colonial heart of the city, and in the nearby modern district of **Vedado** (pp100–9). Start your day in Old Havana at the Cuban Baroque **Palacio de los Capitanes Generales** (pp74–5). This former palace is now home to the city museum and holds a range of important historical artifacts. Then visit the robust **Castillo de la Real Fuerza** (p72). A 16th-century fortress built to

protect the city from pirates, it is now a shipwreck museum. Walk down Calle Oficios to one of the oldest squares in the city, colourful **Plaza Vieja** (p80), edged with arcades and historic buildings. You'll find cafés here, or walk on to pretty **Plaza de la Catedral** (pp66–7) for a relaxing lunch.

Afternoon Fast-forward 500 years to learn about Fidel Castro's exploits in the **Museo de la Revolución** (pp92–3), or admire avant-garde Cuban paintings and sculpture in the **Palacio de Bellas Artes** (p97). A block south of the art gallery, on the corner of Avenida de Las Misiones and O'Reilly, is the Art Deco **Edificio Bacardí** (p29), once home to the famous rum company. Take a bus to the other side of the harbour to the monumental castle museum **Del Morro** (p114), which features exhibits on the 1762 British attack on Havana.

Hire a classic car and motor along the **Malecón** (pp62–3), a serpentine ocean road that winds around the colonial centre. Drive up elegant **Paseo del Prado** (pp90–91) and out to the **Plaza de la Revolución** (pp106–7), Cuba's political and administrative centre. Look out for the **Memorial José Martí** (p107) and the colossal iron sculptures of revolutionary heroes Che Guevara and Camilo Cienfuegos on the façades of the ministry buildings (p106).

Day 2
Morning Finca La Vigía (p119) was the home of novelist Ernest Hemingway, where his belongings and beloved boat *Pilar* can be seen. Stop at **Cojímar** (p116), his old stomping ground, on your way back to Havana. This pleasant coastal town inspired his novel *The Old Man and the Sea*, and is a great place to enjoy a seafood lunch.

Afternoon Vedado is a leafy, arty entertainment district. Check out the **Hotel Nacional** (p102) – a sumptuous Art Deco hotel that has played host to numerous famous guests – before exploring the marble tombs of the illustrious dead at the **Necrópolis de Colón** (pp108–9). Follow up with a guided tour of the **Museo de Artes Decorativas** (p104), filled with porcelain and carpets, and home to an eye-popping pink Art Deco bathroom. Stay in Vedado for the evening – there are plenty of eating and drinking options in this hip, buzzing neighbourhood.

Arcaded colonial architecture in Plaza Vieja, Havana

To extend your trip...
Enjoy the white sand beaches of **Playas del Este** (p117) or explore the matinees, dance, cabaret and rumba venues of the city, such as the **Tropicana** (p113), or along **Callejón de Hamel** on Sundays (p95).

Five Days in Western Cuba

- **Airport** Fly to Havana's José Martí International Airport.
- **Transport** You will need to hire a car to complete this tour, although the Víazul coach service *(p303)* does stop at Las Terrazas, Pinar del Río and Viñales. It is essential to take the *Guía de Carreteras* map *(p304)* and fill the car up when you pass gas stations.
- **Booking ahead** It is important to book accommodation in advance, particularly in Las Terrazas and María La Gorda.

Day 1: Las Terrazas
Starting from Havana, drive an hour south to the lakeside eco-community of **Las Terrazas** *(p141)*. The area is renowned for its birdlife, remains of old coffee plantations and an organic vegetarian restaurant *(p273)*. Choose from one of several hiking trails or enjoy a zipline canopy tour. Spend the evening in Las Terrazas.

Day 2: Valle de Viñales
Head two hours south to the gloriously beautiful **Valle de Viñales** *(pp146–7)*. Stop at the viewpoint near Hotel Los Jazmines to soak up wonderful panoramas of the area, and then book a walking tour at the Visitors' Centre to amble amid the limestone stacks and tobacco fields. Retreat to one of the hotels in the area.

Day 3: Viñales and to the west
In the morning, explore the small town of **Viñales** *(p145)*, with streets of colonial houses bearing coloured columns and terraces furnished with rocking chairs. Alternatively, take an atmospheric boat ride through the **Cueva del Indio** and the underground San Vicente river *(p147)*. In the afternoon, drive three hours south to coastal retreat **María La Gorda** *(p150)* and take an evening dip in the sea. Stay the night in Hotel María La Gorda *(p258)*.

To extend your trip…
From Viñales, drive to Palma Rubia to catch the ferry to **Cayo Levisa** *(p141)*, a white sand arc with one beachfront hotel *(p258)*. Alternatively, drive to **Cayo Jutías** *(p140)*, where a restaurant and a parasol-filled beach greet visitors. The real draw, though, are the giant orange starfish found at the tip of the bay – accessed by a long, hot walk or by boat.

White sands at the edge of warm seas, María La Gorda

Day 4: María La Gorda
Spend the day snorkelling the Caribbean coral reef or sunbathing beneath palm trees on the pure white sand. Look out for the giant iguanas that roam the hotel grounds and beach. Stay the night in Hotel María La Gorda.

Day 5: Return via Pinar del Río and Soroa
The six-hour drive back to Havana can be broken up with a stop at **Pinar del Río** *(p144)* to take in the aroma of the tobacco factory on a guided tour (open on weekdays only). Closer to Havana, don't miss the opportunity to see the famous perfumed orchid gardens at **Soroa** *(p140)*.

Mural de la Prehistoria, painted by Leovigildo González on the side of a *mogote* in Valle de Viñales

A Week in Central Cuba

- **Airport** Fly to Havana's José Martí International Airport, 17 km (11 miles) south of the city.
- **Transport** This tour is most easily done with a hire car, which you can pick up at the airport. Víazul coaches travel to Cienfuegos and Trinidad.
- **Booking ahead** Book car hire ahead in high season (Dec–Feb, Jul and Aug). Book hotels and resorts in advance, as well as any coach travel.

Day 1: Cienfuegos
From Havana, drive four hours southeast along the A1 Autopista, turning south to Cienfuegos on the Caribbean coast. Wander the vast central square **Parque Martí** (p172) and marvel at the extraordinary interior of **Teatro Tomás Terry** (p172), a 19th-century theatre. Walk south along **Paseo del Prado** (p173), passing the columned arcades to the stunning mixture of colonial and 1950s architecture of **Punta Gorda** (p174). Have a drink here at the Moorish **Palacio de Valle** (p174), a private villa-turned-restaurant. Stay in Cienfuegos.

> **To extend your trip…**
> See the bird and marine life of the **Bay of Pigs** (pp168–71) in the Península de Zapata.

Day 2: On to Trinidad
Head out of Cienfuegos along the coastal road and visit the lush **Jardín Botánico Soledad** filled with exotic plants en route (pp176–7). Continue your journey, arriving in Trinidad in time for lunch. Either drive the 13 km (8 miles) to **Playa Ancón** (p196) to recline on the white sands, or just take time to wander the town in the pretty late-afternoon light – a photographer's dream. Visit the outstanding **Palacio Cantero** (p193) and climb the tower for excellent views of the town.

Day 3: Exploring Trinidad
Begin in the heart of the city at **Plaza Mayor** (pp186–7). Next to the imposing **Iglesia Parroquial de la Santísima Trinidad** (p188), the glorious **Palacio Brunet** (p189), which boasts furnishings from many wealthy families, is worth exploring. Afterwards, settle into the city's most famous bar, the **Canchánchara** (p186), known for its eponymous drink, then visit the handsome **Iglesia y Convento de San Francisco** (p193). Wind down for the day by listening to live performances in the **Casa de la Cultura** (p193) or **Casa de la Trova** (p282).

Day 4: Around Trinidad
Head north to the resort of **Topes de Collantes** (p195), set in the Escambray mountains, where visitors can enjoy walks to waterfalls and caves. Alternatively, travel to the steamy Caribbean coast to swim in the turquoise seas off **Playa Ancón** (p196), or take a catamaran out to **Cayo Blanco** (p196) for excellent snorkelling opportunities. Stay the night in Trinidad.

Day 5: Valle de los Ingenios and Guevara's mausoleum
Leave early, stopping at the **Manaca Iznaga Estate** (p197), a former sugar plantation in the **Valle de los Ingenios** (pp196–7), before passing through **Sancti Spíritus** (pp198–9). Drive west on the A1 to Che Guevara's mausoleum, the **Conjunto Escultórico Comandante Ernesto Che Guevara** (p180), conveniently

Iglesia Parroquial de la Santísima Trinidad in Plaza Mayor, Trinidad

located on the outskirts of Santa Clara. Head north from here to the white-sand paradise of **Cayo Santa María** (p181).

Day 6: Cayo Santa María
Spend your leisure time sunbathing, having a massage or cruising on a catamaran at this stunning, small, white-sand resort. Spend the night here.

Day 7: Return via Remedios
Enjoy your last morning of relaxation before heading back to Havana. Stop in the pretty town of **Remedios** (p181) and admire the lavish altar of the Iglesia de San Juan Bautista before driving the A1 back to the capital.

> **To extend your trip…**
> Visit **Matanzas**, the "Athens of Cuba", with its interesting historic centre (pp162–3).

Villas along Punta Gorda, Cienfuegos

For practical information on travelling around Cuba see pp302–7

A Week in Eastern Cuba

- **Airports** Transfer at Havana's José Martí International Airport to a domestic flight to Baracoa. Return to Havana from Holguín's airport.
- **Transport** To see all of the stops on this tour you will need to hire a car. Víazul coaches cover Baracoa, Santiago de Cuba, Guantánamo, Bayamo and Holguín as a single route.
- **Booking ahead** Buy coach tickets in advance and book car hire ahead in high season (Dec–Feb, Jul and Aug). Reserve accommodation well in advance during Santiago's two July festivals, and during high season in Bayamo.

The River of Honey, close to Baracoa

Day 1: Arriving in Baracoa
Having landed in **Baracoa** *(pp246–7)*, take time to wander the pretty streets of this historic city, which was, for a short time, the first capital of Cuba. Follow the road around the bay and climb a steep hill to the atmospheric **Hotel El Castillo** *(p262)* for fantastic views of the city. Finish the day with a cocktail on the swimming pool terrace.

Day 2: Exploring Baracoa
Visit the **Catedral de Nuestra Señora de la Asunción** *(p246)*, home to the wooden cross that, legend has it, was brought by Christopher Columbus on his first voyage to America. Afterwards, visit the **Fuerte Matachín** museum *(p247)*, which features exhibits relating to the history of the local area. Walk southeast along the town's beach to the delightful fishing village of **Boca de Miel** on the River of Honey. Return to Baracoa for the night.

Day 3: El Yunque and Playa Maguana
Either take a guided tour to climb the distinctive **El Yunque** mountain *(p248)* and enjoy extraordinary panoramic views of the coast, or visit the protected **Parque Nacional Alejandro de Humboldt** *(p249)*, a mountainous

rainforest, home to rare wildlife. In the afternoon, visit the white-sand beach of **Playa Maguana** *(pp248–9)*. Spend the night in Baracoa or Playa Maguana.

Day 4: Over La Farola Pass and past Guantánamo Bay
Set off early to drive over the spectacular mountain pass known as **La Farola** *(p243)*. Travel through the enormous cactuses of the **Costa Sur** *(p243)*, set against the midnight blue Caribbean sea, and drive past the perimeter fences of the US Naval base at **Guantánamo Bay** *(p243)*. Head on to Santiago de Cuba, and spend the evening salsa dancing at the **Casa de la Trova** *(p226)*.

Day 5: Santiago de Cuba
Start your city tour early with a trip to the **Museo Ambiente Histórico Cubano** *(p230)*, the Moorish home-turned-history

Statue of the revered Virgen del Cobre in the Basílica del Cobre

museum of Cuba's Spanish founder Diego Velázquez, before visiting the large **Catedral de Nuestra Señora de la Asunción** *(p231)*. Take a moment to watch the world go by from the city's most famous terrace at the **Hotel Casa Granda** *(p228)*, which overlooks the park. Walk east along Calle Heredia then south to see the eclectic artifacts at the **Museo Emilio Bacardí Moreau** *(p228)*. In the afternoon, visit the **Cuartel Moncada** museum *(p234)* to learn about Fidel Castro's rebel beginnings before taking a guided tour of the **Cementerio de Santa Ifigenia** *(p234)*, the last resting place of nationalist José Martí. Finish your day with a short walk in the smart **Vista Alegre** neighbourhood *(p235)*, where you can see how the upper classes once lived.

Day 6: On to Guardalavaca
On leaving Santiago de Cuba by car, either drive south for a tour of the impressive **Castillo del Morro** *(pp236–7)*, a 17th-century Spanish fortress built to protect Santiago de Cuba, or west to **Basílica del Cobre** *(p225)*, home to the venerated statue of Cuba's patron saint, La Virgen del Cobre. Drive west to Bayamo, and then north through Holguín to the aquamarine seas and white sands of **Guardalavaca** *(p219)*.

Day 7: Return via Holguín
Spend the morning sunbathing, sailing or snorkelling at one of the Guardalavaca resorts before driving the hour to Holguín airport for a flight back to Havana.

Putting Cuba on the Map

Washed by the Atlantic Ocean, the Caribbean Sea and the waters of the Gulf of Mexico, Cuba is the largest island in the Greater Antilles, situated just south of the Tropic of Cancer. It lies only 180 km (112 miles) from Florida and 210 km (130 miles) from Mexico, while Haiti and Jamaica are slightly less than 80 km (50 miles) and 140 km (87 miles) away, respectively. Cuba is not a single island, but a varied archipelago with a total surface area of 110,922 sq km (42,815 sq miles). Lying on an east-west axis, the main island, the elongated Isla Grande, is about 1,250 km (776 miles) long and 100 km (62 miles) wide on average. Around it are five archipelagos: Colorados, Sabana, Camagüey, Canarreos and Jardines de la Reina, consisting of thousands of *cayos* (keys and small islands). The largest minor island is Isla de la Juventud. Cuba has about 11 million inhabitants, 2,500,000 of whom live in Havana, the capital.

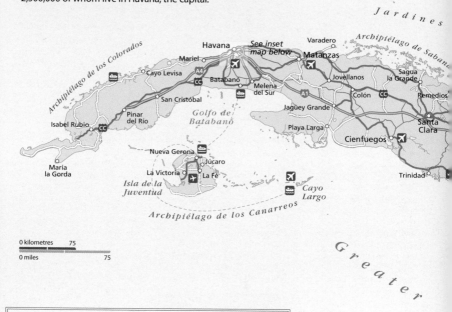

For keys to symbols *see back flap*

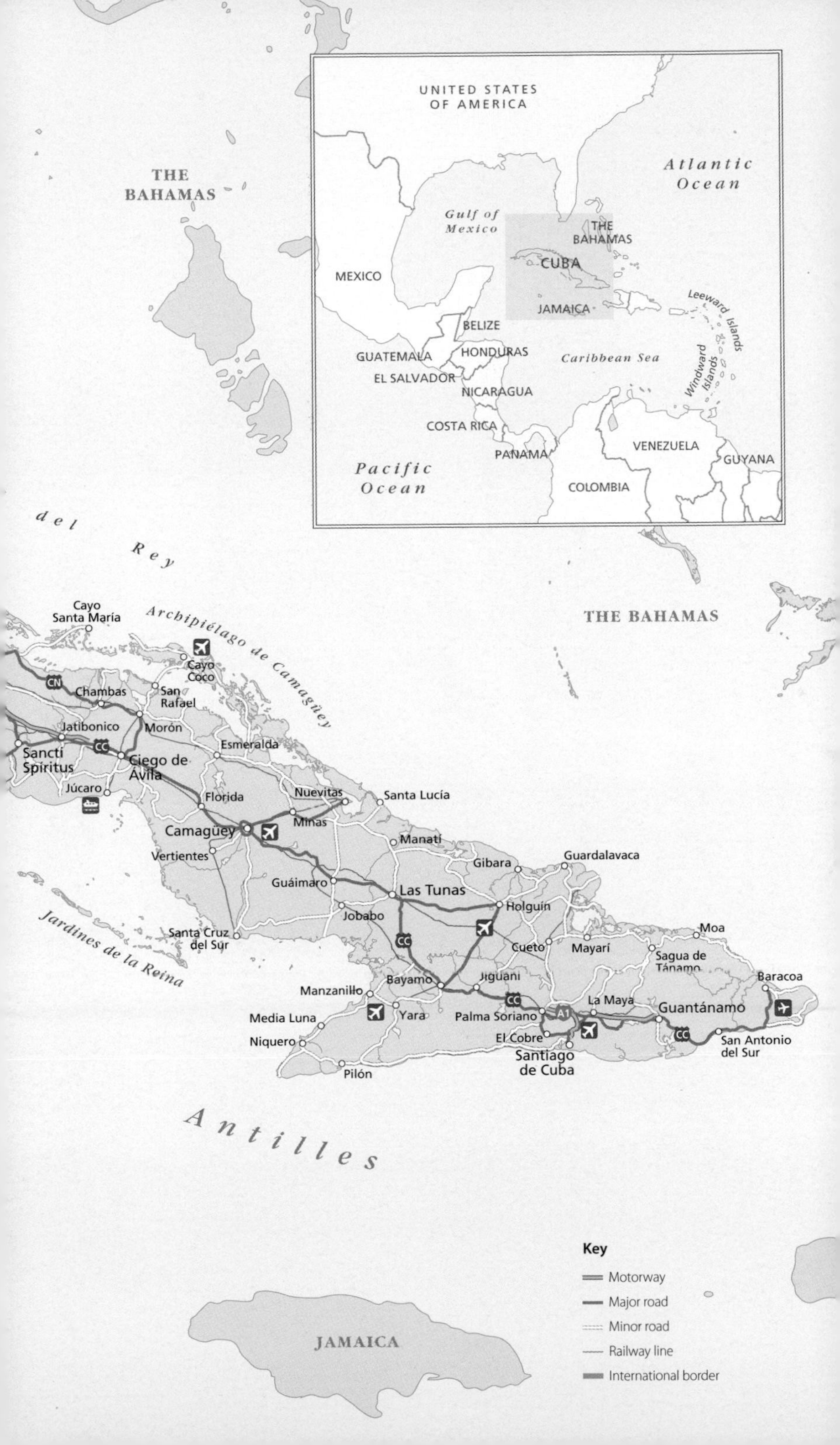

UNITED STATES
OF AMERICA

*Atlantic
Ocean*

THE
BAHAMAS

*Gulf of
Mexico*

THE
BAHAMAS

MEXICO

CUBA

JAMAICA

Leeward Islands

BELIZE

Caribbean Sea

GUATEMALA   HONDURAS

Windward Islands

EL SALVADOR

NICARAGUA

COSTA RICA

VENEZUELA   GUYANA

PANAMA

*Pacific
Ocean*

COLOMBIA

del

Rey

Cayo
Santa María

Archipiélago de Camagüey

THE BAHAMAS

Cayo
Coco

CN

Chambas   San
Rafael

Jatibonico   Morón

Esmeralda

Sancti
Spiritus   CC

Ciego de
Ávila

Júcaro

Florida   Nuevitas   Santa Lucía

Minas

Camagüey

Vertientes   Manatí

Guáimaro   Gibara   Guardalavaca

Jardines de la Reina

Santa Cruz
del Sur

Las Tunas   Holguín

Jobabo

Moa

CC   Cueto   Mayarí   Sagua de
Tánamo

Manzanillo   Bayamo   Jiguaní   Baracoa

Media Luna   Yara   Palma Soriano   La Maya   Guantánamo

Niquero   El Cobre   A1   San Antonio
del Sur   CC

Santiago
de Cuba

Pilón

A n t i l l e s

JAMAICA

Key

═══ Motorway

──── Major road

······ Minor road

──── Railway line

═══ International border

A PORTRAIT OF CUBA

Images of Cuba show hot sun and fields of sugar cane, tall palm trees and deep, clear-blue sea. Cuba is indeed all these things, but it is also a country with a deep-rooted, complex culture in which old traditions and new intellectual developments co-exist. It is a young and vital island, a place of music and colour, which, despite severe economic difficulties, has held on to its unique identity.

Cuba's identity owes a great deal to the fact that it is surrounded by sea as well as to its geographical position. It is sometimes called the "key to the Gulf" because of its strategic location between North and South America at the entrance to the Gulf of Mexico, and the island has been a crossroads since the beginning of the colonial period. As a result, by the mid-1500s, the island's population consisted of European settlers; Guanah-atebey, Siboney and Taíno Indians, the first of whom arrived in 3000 BC and survived struggles against the invaders, imported disease and hard labour; and thousands of black slaves, brought over from Africa. Up to the

abolition of slavery in 1886, the dominant culture was that of the conquering Spanish. However, by surreptitious means, the African slaves managed to preserve their songs, musical instruments and dances, introduced new spices and tastes to the local cuisine, and continued to worship their Yoruba gods (see pp26–7).

The result of this cross-fertilization is a surprising ethnic mosaic of white, black, people of mixed race and Asian (a Chinese community grew in Havana in the 19th century). The same mosaic characterizes Cuban culture too: the bringing together of vastly different traditions has produced a unique blend.

Colourful old buildings in a small street of Cuba

◀ Raising the Cuban flag, Havana

Playing dominoes, a national pastime

The Lifestyle

Cubans are generally hospitable, talkative and sociable, largely due to their tight-knit communities and collaborative culture. It is rare to pay even a fleeting social visit and not be offered refreshment. City neighbourhoods are built cheek to jowl, and people talk to one another from their balconies, or from the steps or pavement in front of their house.

The whole day can be spent outside, thanks to the perennial tropical summer. People spend a lot of time outdoors, chatting, playing dominoes, flirting, cycling around the streets alive with colour, voices and sounds, or simply sitting. Music is everywhere and is the soul of the island. Melodic thanks to the Spanish heritage, and dynamic due to the hypnotizing rhythm of Afro-Cuban percussion, religious and passionate at the same time, music is a vital part of daily life, like dance. Even the smallest Cuban town has a Casa de la Trova, a Cuban institution, where local bands play and young and old alike go to dance. Indeed, there is

no single designated venue for dancing in Cuba, and any excuse is good enough to improvise a party. One of the official celebrations is the *quinceañera*, the debut in society of 15-year-old girls, who get dressed up like elaborate prom queens for the occasion. Besides this lively, fun-loving side, Cubans have an equally strong domestic one, and love to spend time at home with the family, in front of the television or chatting from ever-present rocking chairs.

The Political System

The present Constitution of the Republic of Cuba, approved by 97.7 per cent of voters (in Cuba people can vote at the age of 16), was promulgated in 1976. In 1992 various amendments were introduced, including guarantees for foreign investments, some flexibility in foreign trade, more religious freedom, and the introduction of direct election by universal suffrage of deputies to the National Assembly. The Constitution states that Cuba is a socialist republic whose supreme governmental body is the National Assembly of People's Power (the equivalent of Parliament), elected by universal suffrage every five years.

A trio of musicians playing in the street

A 15-year-old girl preparing for her debut in society

Fidel Castro, the Líder Máximo, during a rally in Plaza de la Revolución

The Assembly in turn elects the State Council, the Council of Ministers, and the president of the State Council, who is the head of state and of the government, as well as the judges of the Supreme Court. There are also the Provincial and Municipal Assemblies of the People's Power (Poder Popular), through which the population expresses its wishes. Since the only political party is the Cuban Communist Party, which by law cannot propose candidates, the citizens directly elect their candidates. Lastly, there are many social organizations, to which most of the citizens belong. These groups are

Billboard with political propaganda along the Carretera Central

for young people (UJC), children (UPCJM), women (FMC), students (FEEM and FEU), trade unions (CTC) and small private farmers (ANAP). The largest of these groups consists of the Committees for the Defence of the Revolution (CDR), founded in 1960 to watch over neighbourhoods and tackle social issues.

Even as Cuba moves into a new phase of increased international relations and foreign investment in the country, pride in the achievements of the revolution remain strong. The hostile relationship with the US has eased, which was emphasized by a state visit from President Obama in 2016. Trade and travel restrictions between the two countries have loosened, however, the US embargo still continues to be in place. It remains to be seen how the introduction of piecemeal capitalism will affect the country in the long term.

The Economy

The most important factor in the Cuban economy is tourism. Since the late 1980s the island has opened up to foreign tourists, which has meant that the traditional flow of citizens from Eastern European countries has been replaced by

Waving Cuban flags at a rally

Varadero, one of the most popular resorts for international tourism

the arrival of tourists from western capitalist countries. The decision to make more of the nation's rich natural and architectural heritage to produce some degree of wealth was crucial for the economy. In reaction to the tourism boom, the uneasy dual economy of the Cuban peso and the convertible peso was set up. However, with those who work in tourism gaining access to higher earning opportunites than those who do not, a social divide

Machines used to harvest sugar cane

A popular toy made of wood and three wheels

has opened up. The state seeks to address this major change in the country's socio-economic balance through taxes and redistribution of wealth programmes. Other important factors in the local economy are the exportation of sugar, tobacco, and more recently, pharmaceuticals including vaccines.

Education and Children

José Martí, who was a poet , a man of letters and became a hero of national independence *(see p49)*, stated that the only way to be free was to be educated. The Cuban Revolution has not forgotten this motto and has staked much on fostering free public education. Thanks to the massive literacy campaign of 1961 *(see p56)*, illiteracy was almost completely eradicated within a short time. Today most of the island's people, more than half of whom are under 50 – that is, born since the Revolution – can read and write the official language, Spanish, and are also taught foreign languages. Throughout the country Casas de la Cultura, or cultural centres, act as venues for exhibitions, performing arts and even dance evenings. Child care is an important component of the nation's educational policy: the government has invested a great deal of effort and funds in the younger generations and is particularly keen on protecting children, who are safeguarded from the exploitation and sweatshop labour so common in many Latin American and developing countries. Children are well looked after in Cuba: they have the right to attend nursery schools and day-care centres and to education, physical education and recreational activities. All these services are free for everyone and generally of good quality.

Health

The achievements of the government in the field of health have raised the country to the level of the world's most industrialized nations. A great deal has been invested in providing hospitals and medical consultants throughout the island, in free medicine, and in concentrating on prevention (the nationwide vaccination of infants and children has virtually eliminated diseases common on the American continent) and medical research. Cuba has the lowest infant mortality rate and the second highest life-expectancy rate in Latin America. The health service,

Javier Sotomayor, the gold medallist in the high jump in the 1992 Olympics in Barcelona

which is free for everyone, is good despite restrictions imposed by the economic crisis. The presence of highly-trained Cuban doctors and the reduced costs of therapy and hospitalization have made the island a centre for "health tourism"; patients from many countries come here for specific treatments, especially for skin and stress problems.

Sports

Physical activity has always been encouraged by the government via a mass physical education programme and numerous specialist schools. As a result, sports standards are high, and Cuba has many Olympic champions. Baseball is the national sport (the Cuban team is one of the best in the world), and athletics, volleyball, basketball and boxing are also popular. Leading figures in sport include boxer Kid Chocolate (1910–88), successful in the US before the Revolution, high-jump champion Javier Sotomayor, Ana Fidelia Quirot, the 800m world champion in 1995 and 1997, Iván Pedroso, gold medallist in long-jump in Sydney 2000 and Mijaín López Núñez, the Olympic medalist who won gold for Greco-Roman wrestling in 2008, 2012 and 2016.

Boxing training in a Havana gym

Landscape, Flora and Fauna

The Cuban poet Nicolás Guillén once likened his native island to a green crocodile with eyes of stone and water. An aerial view would show the island stretching out in the Caribbean Sea and indeed covered with vegetation and patterned with rivers. Small islands and coral reefs lie just offshore in the sparkling blue sea. In the interior, the landscape is very varied, from plains of red earth to the *mogotes* outcrops of Viñales, from desert cactus to tropical forest. Protected reserves make up 22 per cent of the national territory. There are numerous species found only on Cuba, but no poisonous creatures.

Coral reefs, with their own distinct ecosystem *(see p151)*

Mountains

The most important ranges are the Sierra de los Órganos to the west, the Sierra del Escambray in the centre and the Sierra Maestra to the southeast. The latter is Cuba's principal range and includes Pico Turquino (1,974 m/ 6,475 ft), the highest peak in the country. The slopes are covered with forests of deciduous trees, pines and tropical plants, and by coffee and cocoa plantations.

Plains

Areas of plain occur throughout the island, but are particularly prevalent in the central regions – the provinces of Matanzas, Sancti Spíritus and Camagüey – and in the Pinar del Río area. The land is fertile and planted with sugar cane, palm trees, mangoes and citrus fruit, or left as grazing land for cattle.

Carpintero (carpenter) is the Cuban name for the woodpecker, which nests in tree trunks.

The *cartacuba* (Cuban tody) is an endemic species only a few centimetres long. It has colourful plumage.

The *tiñosa*, or turkey vulture, with its unmistakable red head, flies the plains in search of carrion.

The cattle egret follows grazing cows and feeds on insects, both those disturbed by ploughing and others on the cows' hides.

The *tocororo* (Cuban trogon) is the national bird. It shares its colours with the Cuban flag.

The so-called gulf fritillary is one of 190 species of butterfly in Cuba, about 30 of which are endemic to the island.

Flora

The Cuban landscape is characterized by the many varieties of palm tree *(see p177)*, together with the pine in the mountainous areas, and the ceibas in the plains. The *yagruma*, with large dark green and silvery leaves, is also widespread. Three important hardwoods are mahogany, cedar and *majagua*. Splashes of colour are added to the luxuriant green vegetation by flowering hibiscus, bougainvillea and *flamboyán* (royal poinciana). Numerous species of orchid grow here, as well as mariposa, Cuba's national flower.

A *flamboyán* (royal poinciana)

The mariposa, the national flower

The ceiba tree, sacred to Pre-Columbian peoples

Marshlands

The southern part of the island in particular has many lagoons and marshlands, often distinguished by mangrove swamps, and is rich in birdlife. The most important area is the Ciénaga (swamp) de Zapata, in the province of Matanzas *(see p170)*.

Pink flamingoes live in areas of brackish water from Cayo Coco to Zapata.

Buteogallus anthracinus gundlachi is an endemic hawk that feeds on crabs.

Mangroves develop an intricate root system under water. This habitat suits a diverse range of birds and fish.

Tropical Forest

The Sagüa-Baracoa mountain range in Eastern Cuba, under the influence of northeast trade winds, is one of the most biologically diverse areas in the Caribbean. Here, the heavy rainfall produces thick vegetation.

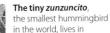

The tiny *zunzuncito*, the smallest hummingbird in the world, lives in protected or wooded areas like the Península de Zapata.

The black anolis lizard, a forest reptile, reacts to disturbance by inflating the white part under its throat.

The *Polymita picta*, an endemic species of snail that lives only in the Baracoa area, has a brightly coloured shell and feeds on plant parasites.

Santería

Different religions co-exist in Cuba as the result of its history. Both the Roman Catholicism of the Spanish conquerors and the practices imported by the African slaves have survived. The most widespread of the African faiths is Santería, also called Regla de Ocha. In order to be able to worship their gods despite the persecution of the Spaniards, Yoruba slaves, originally from Nigeria, merged their gods' identities with certain Roman Catholic saints. Pure Roman Catholicism today is not a widespread religion in Cuba (although there has been a resurgence since the 1990s), while Santería is strongly felt to be an important part of the national identity.

The batá, three conical drums of different sizes with two skins, accompany the most important Santería ceremonies.

The crown of Changó, the king of the *orishas*

Rituals are almost always performed in a domestic context (Santería has no temples as such). Rites are inspired by animistic spirituality, although there are elements that share similarities or even merge with Roman Catholicism.

Fresh fruit, including bananas, Changó's favourite

Santeros and **babalawos**, the Santería priests, foretell the future, the former by means of seashells, the latter through a complex system of divination that makes use of stones, seashells, seeds and coconut shells.

Agogó (traditional rattles), maracas and bells are played while greeting the gods.

An Altar for Changó

Altars are set up by Santería initiates on feast days, such as their "saint's birthday" (the initiation anniversary), and decorated with the attributes of the god to whom they are dedicated. They also contain elements belonging to other orishas, *such as cloth, devotional objects, flowers, fruit and other special foods.*

The Orishas

The main Santería god is Olofi, the creator divinity, similar to the God of Christianity but without contact with Earth. The gods who mediate between him and the faithful are the *orishas*, who listen to the latter's prayers. Each *orisha* has his own colour and symbols, as well as a ritual characterized by its type of dance, music and costumes: Oshún, for example, wears yellow clothes and loves honey, pale soft drinks and violins.

Obatalá, a hermaphrodite god, is the protector of the head as well as the chief intermediary between Olofi and humankind.

Oshún, the goddess of love, lives in rivers, and corresponds to the Virgen del Cobre (see p225).

The aspiring priest *(santero)* has to undergo a week of intense initiation ceremonies, and for an entire year has to dress in white and adhere to strict rules of behaviour.

The double-edged axe and sword are Changó's two warlike attributes.

The *batea* is a wooden receptacle containing natural elements in which the spirit of the god resides. Only the *santero* may open it.

The *pilón* is the large wooden mortar on which the *santero* sits during the week of initiation, and it is preserved as an object of worship.

Various objects – Christian, secular or even personal items – are set together on Santería altars. Here, three Madonnas are placed alongside plastic horses.

Elegguá is the first god to be greeted during ceremonies. He is represented by a stone made to look like a face, with two shells as eyes, and is usually placed behind a believer's front door.

Fresh flowers are always placed on the altars of the *orishas*: red ones for Changó, yellow ones for Oshún, and white ones for Obatalá.

Candles

A basket of offerings is on display during ceremonies. The money is used to buy objects of worship.

Other Afro-Cuban Religions

Among the African cults practised in Cuba, two others are also significant: Palo Monte (or Las Reglas de Congo), in which herbs and other natural elements are used for magical purposes, and Abakuá, more of a mutual aid secret society, for men only. The former, introduced to Cuba by Bantu-speaking African slaves from the Congo, Zaire and Angola, is based on the cult of the dead. The faithful, called *paleros*, perform rites that are sometimes macabre and even verge on black magic. A region between Nigeria and Cameroon was the birthplace of the Abakuá cult. In celebrations the participants, disguised as little devils *(diablitos)*, dance and play music. The *diablito* has become part of Cuban folklore.

Yemayá, sea goddess and mother of *orishas*, wears blue. Capable of great sweetness and great anger, she is linked with the Virgen de Regla *(see p116)*.

Changó is the virile and sensual god of fire and war who adores dancing and corresponds to St Barbara.

An Abakuá *diablito* with his typical headdress

Architecture in Cuba

Formal architecture in Cuba began in the colonial period. For the entire 16th century all efforts were concentrated on building an impressive network of fortresses; then came the first stone-built *mudéjar*-style houses, which replaced simple wooden dwellings with tiled roofs. The 18th century was a golden age of civic architecture, characterized by the Baroque style imported at a late stage from Europe, which in turn made way for Neo-Classical buildings in the 19th century. The mixture of styles typical of the *fin de siècle* was followed, in 1900–30, by Art Deco, a forerunner of the 1950s skyscrapers. Ugly prefabricated buildings characterize the post-1959 era, with some notable Brutalist exceptions.

The courtyard was a typical feature of colonial architecture and the centre of domestic life. Above, the Conde de Jaruco's Havana residence *(p80)*.

The 17th Century

The tropical climate, with high temperatures and heavy rain, influenced the local architecture. Many private homes had thick walls, tiled roofs and windows protected by shutters.

A typical wooden ceiling at Calle Tacón 4, in Havana

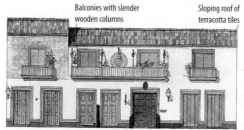

Balconies with slender wooden columns

Sloping roof of terracotta tiles

The house at Calle Obispo 117–19 *(p76)*, with its characteristic central courtyard and wooden balconies, shows a clear Spanish influence in the structure itself and in the building techniques used.

The 18th Century

More rooms were added to houses with a central courtyard, more houses were built, and some wonderful examples of civic architecture were created. Three highlights of light Cuban Baroque in Havana are the Palacio de los Capitanes Generales *(pp74–5)*, Palacio del Segundo Cabo *(p70)* and Havana Cathedral *(p68)*. Trinidad also has many 18th-century colonial buildings.

The mezzanine, a structural element introduced in the 1700s

The arcade on the ground floor, which was the external equivalent of the inner courtyard, was an 18th-century innovation. As trade increased, mansions like this housed growing numbers of servants, who lived in the lower part of the building.

Stained-glass windows

Arches supported by columns and pilasters distinguish 18th-century buildings.

Limestone façade

Palacio de los Capitanes Generales is a typical Cuban Baroque mansion, with thick stone walls, an abundance of arches, columns, porticoes and balconies, and a large central courtyard with dense vegetation.

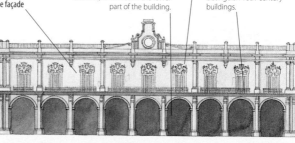

An elegant arched *mediopunto* window

Mediopunto

These half-moon, stained-glass windows were created in the mid-18th century to protect houses from the glare of the tropical sun. They became popular in the 1800s, when mansion windows were decorated with glass set into a wooden frame. The original geometric motifs were later replaced by others drawing inspiration from tropical flora and fauna.

The 19th Century

The widespread use of porticoes with columns and lintels, wrought iron and decoration inspired by Classical antiquity or the Renaissance, is the distinguishing feature of 19th-century Cuban Neo-Classical architecture. Grilles across windows and shutters helped air to circulate inside (previously the central courtyard performed this function). Buildings that best represent Cuban Neo-Classicism are the Palacio de Aldama in Havana *(p88)* and the Teatro Sauto in Matanzas *(p162)*.

Wrought- or cast-iron grilles

Ionic pilasters

Shutters and *mediopuntos* protected rooms from bright light.

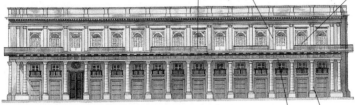

Palacio de Aldama, designed by Manuel José Carrera in 1840 for the wealthy Don Domingo de Aldama, is the most important Neo-Classical building in Havana. Rejecting Baroque exuberance, it echoes the austerity and purity of line of Classical architecture.

Doric columns

In the portico the arch is replaced by the lintel.

Bridging the 19th–20th Centuries

The architectural value of many Cuban cities derives from the mixture of different styles. This is seen in buildings such as the Neo-Moorish Palacio de Valle in Cienfuegos *(p174)*, the Capitolio in Havana *(pp86–7)*, and at Paseo and Calle 17, Havana's so-called "millionaires' row", with splendid mansions such as the Casa de la Amistad, built in 1926 *(p103)*.

Detail of the façade of the Palacio Guasch, Pinar del Río *(p144)*

Palacio de Valle in Cienfuegos, designed by the Venetian architect Alfredo Colli in 1912 for Acisclo del Valle, combines Moorish and Venetian Gothic elements with references to Beaux Arts forms – a typical example of the eclectic style's use of a range of prevailing architectural motifs and elements.

The 20th Century

The early 20th century saw the construction of a few examples of Art Nouveau and Art Deco buildings, paving the way for the major urban development that took place in Havana in the 1950s. This period witnessed the building of some very tall, modern skyscrapers and hotels such as the Riviera and the Habana Libre (then called the Habana Hilton, *p102*). In parallel with this came the rise of a style that was reminiscent of Rationalist architecture.

Edificio Bacardí (1930) in Havana, designed by E Rodríguez Castells, R Fernández Ruenes and J Menéndez, is a splendid example of Art Deco. It is clad in granite and limestone, with enamelled motifs.

Painting in Cuba

The history of Cuban painting can be divided into three basic stages. The first began in 1818 with the foundation of the San Alejandro Fine Arts Academy, run by Jean-Baptiste Vermay, a French Neo-Classical painter. The second began over a century later, in the 1930s, when, thanks to great artists such as Wifredo Lam, René Portocarrero and Amelia Peláez, a movement influenced by the European avant-garde created a universally comprehensible idiom that expressed the unique essence of Cuban identity. Thirdly, after 1959, as part of a programme of art education that promoted avant-garde artists, the National School of Art and the Institute for Advanced Art Studies were founded. Cuban painting has always brimmed with vitality and painters of recent generations have achieved international recognition, helped by shows like the Havana Biennial.

Víctor Manuel García, one of the fathers of modern Cuban art, created the archetypal *Gitana Tropical* (1929).

Wifredo Lam (1902–82), lived for a while in Europe and worked with Pablo Picasso in Paris. He developed a new pictorial language that went beyond national boundaries. He painted extraordinary pictures such as *La Jungla* (The Jungle), now in the Museum of Modern Art, New York, *La Silla (see p97)*, and *The Third World* (1966), seen here, which cast a dramatic light on the elements in Cuban religions.

Amelia Peláez (1897–1968) blended still life motifs with the decorative elements in Cuban colonial architecture such as stained glass and columns, as seen here in *Interior with Columns* (1951).

René Portocarrero (1912–86) expressed the essence of Cuba through a Baroque-like vision of the city, painting domestic interiors and figures of women, as in *Interno del Cerro* (1943). He made use of bold colour and was influenced by the European avant-garde and Mexican mural painting.

Raúl Martínez (1927–95) and Guido Llinás were leading exponents of the abstract art movement that came to the fore in the 1950s–60s and later adopted the Pop Art style in representations of current-day heroes, as exemplified by *Island 70* (1970) by Raúl Martínez, seen here.

Alfredo Sosabravo (b. 1930) – a painter, illustrator, engraver and potter – tackles the themes of nature, man and machines with an ironic twist. A leading figure, he has been active since the 1960s, together with Servando Cabrera Moreno, a Neo-Expressionist, Antonia Eiriz, a figurative artist, and Manuel Mendive, whose subject is Cuba's African heritage.

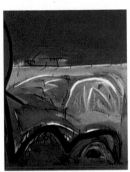

Flora Fong (b. 1949) – along with Ever Fonseca, Nelson Domínguez, Pedro Pablo Oliva, Tomás Sánchez and Roberto Fabelo – represents a strand of 1970s painting, which tended towards abstraction without quite losing sight of objective reality. Her *Dimensiones del Espejo* is seen here.

Graphic Art

Graphic design, which first flourished during the colonial period, when it was used in the sugar and tobacco industries, with time became an independent art form, with the creation of prestigious periodicals such as *Social*. During the 20th century the growing importance of marketing produced different types of graphic art. In the 1960s, in the wake of the enthusiasm for the victorious Revolution, well-designed graphic posters became a natural part of the main political and cultural campaigns, and designs became ever more sophisticated. Use of graphic art is still very visible in Cuba's towns and cities and at the roadside all over the island.

26 DE JULIO-XVII ANIVERSARIO.

Poster by Alfonso Prieto for July 26 celebrations

Ceramics

In 1950, the Cuban ceramicist and former physician Juan Miguel Rodríguez de la Cruz brought together a group of leading painters, including Wifredo Lam, René Porto-carrero and Amelia Peláez, in Santiago de las Vegas, near Havana, so that they could all work on ceramic designs. This marked the beginning of a new artistic genre in Cuba that today ranges from crockery to sculpture, and also includes installations and works for home interiors. Wonderful examples of Cuban ceramics can be found in the Hotel Habana Libre (see p102).

Decorated plate, Havana Ceramics Museum

Cuban Literature

A frequent theme in the literature of Cuba has always been the question of national identity, and the genre has evolved with a marked interest in social problems and questions about reality. The works of the great 20th-century Cuban authors are regarded as classics, and younger authors are beginning to attract attention on the international scene. The Revolution was a golden era for publishing, because production costs for books were very low. However, the trade was plunged into sudden crisis in the early 1990s and many publishers are only now slowly regaining their former status. Every year Havana plays host to an International Book Fair, a major literary event involving authors and publishers from all over the world.

An expressive portrait of the great Cuban poet Nicolás Guillén

The 19th Century

The birth of Cuban literature is usually dated from *Espejo de Paciencia*, an epic poem written in the early 1600s by Silvestre de Balboa, originally from the Canary Islands. However, truly national literature only began to emerge in the 19th century, with the call for an end to slavery and for Cuban independence from Spain.

Among the literary figures of that time, various names stand out. Father Félix Varela (1788–1853) was an eclectic philosopher and patriot who wrote a pamphlet extolling the "need to stamp out the slavery of the blacks on

Félix Varela, writer-philosopher

La Edad de Oro, José Martí's children's periodical

the island of Cuba, which would also be in the interests of their owners". José María de Heredia (1803–39) was a romantic poet who introduced the American landscape into New World literature and was forced to live in the US and Mexico because of his nationalist stance. Gertrudis Gómez de Avellaneda (1814–73), another romantic, lived for a long time in Spain and defended the black population in her novel *Sab*. Cirilo Villaverde (1812–94) was a patriot and author of *Cecilia Valdés*, a famous abolitionist work which was made into a *zarzuela* (operetta) in the 20th century by the Cuban composer Ernesto Lecuona.

However, the towering figure in the 19th century was the great José Martí (1853–95), an intellectual, journalist and author who expressed his nationalist ideas in elegant literary form (*Ismaelillo* and *Versos Sencillos* are his best-known works), and became a leading exponent of Latin American modernism.

Another figure in this movement was Julián del Casal, a decadent, symbolist writer. The premature deaths of these two brought the development of innovative literature to a halt.

The 20th Century

The leading interpreters of 20th-century Cuban literature were the poet Nicolás Guillén (1902–89) and the novelist Alejo Carpentier (1904–80), both of whom were sent into exile because of their opposition to Gerardo Machado's regime and their fierce criticism of Batista's dictatorship.

Guillén, who was of mixed race, spoke for the black population, exposing among other things the brutal working conditions of the *macheteros*, the labourers who cut sugar cane on the plantations. After Castro's victory, Guillén was proclaimed as "national poet" and asked to head UNEAC, the Cuban writers and artists' union. Taking as his starting point the rhythms of dance and traditional musical genres such as *son (see p34)*, grafted onto the classical Spanish octosyllable, Guillén's stylistic studies gave rise to bold experiments as early as 1931 in works like *Songoro Cosongo, poemas mulatos*.

Alejo Carpentier, an architect, musicologist and writer acutely aware of the

José Lezama Lima

realities of Cuba's situation, was one of the most original and innovative authors in 20th-century world literature. Using a blend of irony and respect, he gave voice to the myths of his country, anticipating the destructuring of the post-modern novel. Among his major works are *The Kingdom of This World*, *The Lost Steps*, *Concierto Barroco* and *The Age of Enlightenment*.

Two other leading figures of the same period are the dramatist Virgilio Piñera (1912–79), a reformer, who had a marked taste for experimental theatre, and José Lezama Lima (1910–76), a poet of elegance, also a novelist and chief editor of the magazine *Orígenes*. From 1944 to 1956 this leading periodical printed works by the best Cuban writers and artists of the time. It became one of the key publications in Latin America. Lima is internationally known as the author of *Paradiso* (1966).

Alejo Carpentier

CONCIERTO BARROCO

A famous novel by Alejo Carpentier (1974)

In general, the literary scene in revolutionary Cuba has been characterized by creative fervour, in poetry and in novel-writing. Among the "veterans", people who lived through the experience from the outset, mention should be made of the poets Eliseo Diego, Cintio Vitier, Pablo Armando Fernández and Fina García Marruz; and the novelists Félix Pita Rodríguez, Mirta Aguirre, and Dulce María Loynaz. The works of Loynaz were not published in Cuba until the late 20th century, just before her death.

These authors were followed by the younger writers Miguel Barnet, Antón Arrufat, López Sacha and César López, committed writers in favour of the Revolution.

Among the anti-Castro authors writing in exile, the leading name was the late Guillermo Cabrera Infante (1929–2005), whose works include *Infante's Inferno* and *Three Trapped Tigers*.

Author Dulce María Loynaz, pictured in her twenties

Contemporary Writers

Present-day authors worthy of mention include Abel Prieto, former Minister of Culture, a brilliant and perceptive author of several novels, including *The Cat's Flight*. Another name is Abilio Estévez, a dramatist and novelist of extraordinarily expressive intensity, with a lyrical and visionary tone. Marylin Bobes and Mirta Yáñez both write from the feminist angle. Senel Paz wrote the story that inspired the film *Strawberry and Chocolate*; and detective-story writer Leonardo Padura is known abroad for a quartet of mystery novels set in Havana.

Cuban Cinema

The founding of the Instituto Cubano del Arte y la Industria Cinemato-gráficos (ICAIC) in 1959 virtually marked the birth of cinema in Cuba. The aim of this institution was to disseminate motion picture culture throughout the country, and thus encourage the formation of Cuban directors, to work on documentary films in particular. Fostered by the revolutionary government, Cuban cinema experienced a golden age in the 1960s and has been evolving ever since. Today Havana is the capital of new Latin American cinema thanks to the annual film festival organized by ICAIC. The Fundación del Nuevo Cine Latinoamericano, which also runs the Escuela Internacional de Cine film school, is based in San Antonio de los Baños.

Among Cuba's many directors, who include Julio García Espinosa, Manuel Octavio Gómez and Pastor Vega, there are three outstanding names: Santiago Alvarez, who has made fine documentaries; Humberto Solás, the late director of the classic *Lucía* and of *Cecilia*; and the late Tomás Gutiérrez Alea, who found fame abroad in 1993 thanks to *Fresa y Chocolate* (*Strawberry and Chocolate*), which he made with Juan Carlos Tabío, which courageously dealt with the themes of homosexuality and dissent.

Poster for the film *Strawberry and Chocolate*

Music and Dance

Anything can be used to make music in Cuba: two pieces of wood, an empty box and a tyre rim are enough to trigger an irresistible rhythm anywhere and at any time of day – on the bus, on the beach or in the street. There are top classical music composers and interpreters, but it is popular music – a fusion of Spanish melodies and African rhythm – that is the very essence of Cuba. The success enjoyed by mambo and cha-cha-cha in the 1950s was followed by the worldwide popularity of *son*, rumba and salsa. Dance, too, is an essential part of life here. No one stays seated when the music starts: feet and hands start to move with the rhythm, and bodies sway and rock.

Compay Segundo (1907–2003), the famous *son* singer and songwriter

Salsa is dance music which maintains the rhythmic structure of *son* while adding new sounds borrowed from jazz and other Latin American genres.

The guitarist is often also the accompanying voice, while the solo singer plays a "minor" percussion instrument such as the maracas or *claves*.

Traditional maracas are made from the fruit (gourd) of the *güira* tropical tree.

Bongò

Double bass

Tres

Son

This genre is a type of country music that originated in Cuba in the 19th century, a blend of African rhythm and Spanish melody, which then greatly influenced Latin American music as a whole. In around 1920 son *began to be played in towns in Eastern Cuba, where, along with other genres, it produced the* trova tradicional, *a ballad-style song with guitar.*

The Musicians

Ernesto Lecuona

Three great 20th-century composers and musicians are pianist Ernesto Lecuona (1896–1963), Ignacio Villa (or "Bola de Nieve"), and Pérez Prado, in whose orchestra Benny Moré sang *(see p175)*. In the 1920s there was the star Rita Montaner and the Trío Matamoros, the top *trova* band in Santiago. Others were Sindo Garay, a bolero writer, and César Portillo de la Luz, a founder of *feeling* music in the 1960s. Contemporaries include the *salsero* Issac Delgado and Afro-Cuban jazzman Chucho Valdés.

Bola de Nieve (1911–71), or "snowball", is the stage name that Rita Montaner gave to her pianist Ignacio Villa. This husky-voiced musician also wrote and sang very moving love songs.

Dámaso Pérez Prado (1922–89), the king of mambo, became an international success with his orchestra in the 1950s.

Guaguancó, a fast rumba, enacts a breezy battle between a man and woman who tries to parry his insistent advances. In effect, this dance is a thinly disguised simulation of the sexual act.

The voice was the original element of the rumba, which began as song. The percussion instruments, the basis of this musical genre, were added at a later stage.

A *batá* covered with canvas and seashells

Tumbadora or conga

Cuban Musical Instruments

Claves

Tres

Güiro

There are several exclusively Cuban musical instruments. Among the stringed instruments are the *tres*, a small guitar, always used in *son* bands, with three pairs of metal strings, and the *requinto*, another small, high-pitched guitar that is used in trios to play melodic variations.

Typical Cuban percussion instruments are the *tumbadora*, a tall wooden and leather drum played with the hands, which is used in all musical forms, including jazz; the *bongó*, two small round drums; the *claves*, two wooden cylinders played by striking them against one another; the *güiro*, the gourd of the güira fruit which is stroked with a small stick; and the *marímbula*, a rarely used small piano.

Rumba

The African soul of Cuban music, the rumba originated in the warehouses of Matanzas as a voice of rebellion against slavery and segregation. It then became a form of political satire and social criticism, as well as the poignant expression of an unhappy love affair. Columbia is country-style solo dance, while yambú *and* guaguancó *are the urban varieties, with dance rhythms that are sensual and dynamic, or sad and slow.*

Los Van Van have dominated the Cuban musical scene for over 30 years and are world-famous for their new rhythms and sounds (they invented a new genre, the *songo*).

Silvio Rodríguez, a singer and songwriter who defends the ideals of the Cuban Revolution, founded the Nueva Trova with Pablo Milanés *(right)* in the late 1960s, revitalizing the style and repertory of the *trova,* a rural musical genre.

Buena Vista Social Club, Wim Wenders' film (1998), brought into the limelight traditional *son* interpreters over 80 years old, such as the late guitarist and singer Compay Segundo, the late pianist Rubén González, and the late singer Ibrahim Ferrer.

Cuban Cigars

The cigar is an inextricable part of Cuba's culture, history, and even, for some, its essence. It is known that cigars were used by the indigenous Indians. After Columbus's voyage, tobacco, regarded in Europe as having therapeutic qualities, was imported to Spain. However the first smokers were imprisoned, because people believed that cigar smoke produced diabolical effects. Even so, tobacco grew in popularity and was later exported to other European nations, where government agencies were set up to maintain a monopoly over the product. After the Revolution, the US embargo had a serious effect on the international sale of cigars *(puros)*, but since the 1990s the fashion for cigar smoking has given a boost to sales.

Tobacco *(cohoba)* was used by Cuban Indians during religious rites to invoke the gods. They either inhaled the smoke through a tubed instrument or smoked the rolled leaves.

The *tripa* is the inside, the "core" of the cigar with the filler leaves. In handmade cigars, the *tripa* consists of tobacco leaves which have been selected in order to obtain a particular flavour.

The *capa* is the wrapper leaf on the outside of the cigar. It gives it its smooth, velvety look as well as its colour.

The head (or top part of the cigar) is cut off before smoking.

Foot

The *capote* is the binder leaf that holds the inner part together and keeps it compact.

The Parts of a Cigar

Cigars can be either handmade or machine-made. With handmade cigars the inside consists of whole tobacco leaves, while machine-made cigars are made up of leaves that are blended and then shredded.

Brand Names

There are 33 brands of Cuban cigar on the market today. Below are four, each represented by a *marquilla*, or label, which is placed on the cigar box to identify the brand. Some designs have not changed since first marketed.

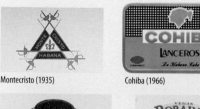

Montecristo (1935)

Cohiba (1966)

The *anillo*, the band that goes around the central part of the cigar and bears its brand name, has a curious history. It is said that in the 18th century, Catherine the Great of Russia, a heavy smoker, had her cigars wrapped with small bands of cloth so they would not leave stains on her fingers. Her eccentricity soon became fashionable. The first commercial cigar band was produced in 1830 by the manufacturers Aguila de Oro. Above is a band produced by the Cuban cigar-maker Romeo y Julieta in 1875.

Cuaba (1996)

Vegas Robaina (1997)

How Cigars are Made

Cigar manufacturing is a real skill that Cubans hand down from generation to generation. This sequence of photographs shows how Carlos Gassiot, a highly skilled torcedor *(cigar roller), makes a cigar, from selecting the loose tobacco leaves to the final touches.*

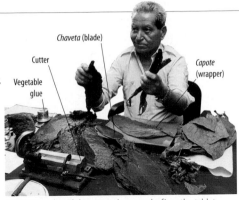

Chaveta (blade)

Cutter

Vegetable glue

Capote (wrapper)

1 Having placed the *capote* (wrapper leaf) on the tablet, the *torcedor* chooses the filler leaves he wants to use for the core of the cigar: three leaves from different parts of the plant – *seco*, *volado* and *ligero* (see p143).

2 He begins to roll (*torcer* in Spanish, hence the term *torcedor*) the leaves. The *capote* is wrapped around the filler leaves selected for the *tripa*, which in turn is covered by the *capa*, which is smooth and regular. This determines the appearance of the cigar.

3 Once the wrapping is complete, the final touches are added. First the wrapper leaf is worked until it is completely smooth. Then comes the trimming. The cigar tip is finished off by wrapping the end with a last tobacco leaf.

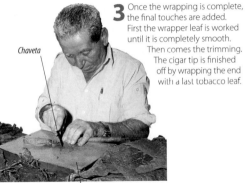

Chaveta

Tableta (tablet)

Gauge

4 Once the cigar is finished, the *torcedor* checks its diameter with a special gauge stamped with the various standard sizes established for every kind of cigar. The same instrument is also used to measure the pre-established length, after which the cigar is cut to this size using the cutting machine.

The Shape and Size

Cigars are made in different sizes (heavy, standard or slim ring gauge) and shapes (they may be regular or tapered, *figurado*). Fatter cigars tend to have a fuller flavour, which connoisseurs prefer. The best hand-rolled Cuban cigars benefit from ageing, like fine wine.

Cuaba Exclusivo, *figurado* cigar

Trinidad Fundador, regular-shaped cigar

CUBA THROUGH THE YEAR

Because of its tropical climate, Cuba does not really have a high or low season, although officially, peak season is from December to the end of March and in July and August, when hotel rates are higher and flights are packed. Except for the peak of summer, when temperatures can be searingly hot, and September and October, when hurricanes are most likely, any month is suitable for a visit. It is warm at the beach even in winter, because the *frentes fríos* (cold fronts) generally last only a couple of days and even then the temperature hardly ever drops below 10°C (50°F). The cooler, drier months from November to March are the best for sightseeing. Thanks to the climate, and the Cubans' love of music and cultural events, there are open-air concerts, festivals, and religious and folk festivities all year round. However, the most interesting and eventful months are July, during Carnival, and December, when the festivities in Remedios and Havana's famous cinema festival takes place.

Spring

During this season there is an escalation of dance and theatre performances, and the welcome but irregular art fair Bienal de La Habana. The beaches are crowded, but mainly with visitors – the Cubans usually go to the seaside only in summer.

March
Festival Internacional de la Trova Pepe Sanchéz, Santiago *(Mar)*. A celebration of Cuban *trova* music in all its forms. This festival attracts both Cuban and international performers.

April
Taller Internacional de Teatro de Títeres, Teatro Papalote, Matanzas *(Apr)*. Performances by leading puppet theatres, with seminars, conferences and workshops. Other workshop spaces include the Teatro Sauto and Galería Provincial de Artes Plásticas "Pedro Esquerré". See www.atenas.cult.cu.
Festival Internacional del Cine Pobre, Gibara *(Apr)*. An international festival of low budget movies held in the small town and well attended by locals and foreigners. Next staged 2018. See www.festival cinepobre.cult.cu.

May
Primero de Mayo *(1 May)*. Rallies, marches and parades in every city in Cuba. The most important one takes place, of course, in Havana, where the citizens gather in Plaza de la Revolución for speeches and patriotic songs.
Romerías de la Cruz de Mayo *(3 May)*. The townsfolk of Holguín process up to La Loma de la Cruz, a hilltop that dominates the northern end of the town. A mass is held at the wooden cross, followed by a lively party.
Feria Internacional Cubadisco (International Record Fair), Pabellón Cuba, Havana *(mid-May)*. Records on display and for sale; conferences and concerts.
Bienal de La Habana *(May–Jun)*. A highly respected art fair, which despite its name, is staged every three years. It welcomes local and international artists. More than 100 artists from 45 countries congregate in Havana, enlivening the city with workshops, performances and exciting gallery shows. Next staged November 2018. See www.bienal habana.cult.cu.
La Huella de España, Gran Teatro and other venues, Havana *(May–Jun)*. Celebrating Cuban culture of Spanish derivation: concerts, classical dance, flamenco and theatre.

A batá player

The First of May Parade in Plaza de la Revolución, Havana

Average Daily Hours of Sunshine

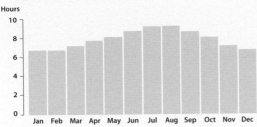

Hours

Sunshine
This chart shows the average daily hours of sunshine in Cuba. In the winter the days are short: at 6pm the sun has already set. In the summer the sun is strong and you should protect your skin and wear a hat and sunglasses, even if only taking a short stroll in town.

Summer

There are various festivals and festivities during the summer months, especially in Havana and Santiago. Regular open-air concerts are held along the Malecón in Havana, particularly in the square known as the Piragua, which is transformed into an open-air dance floor (free of charge). If you plan to include the Carnival in your visit, book accommodation well in advance in Santiago.

June
Ernest Hemingway International Billfishing Tournament, Marina Hemingway, Havana (early Jun). Fishermen compete for trophies in this annual tag-and-release event.
Festival Boleros de Oro, Santiago, Morón, Havana (mid-Jun). String of concerts by the best Cuban and international performers of bolero songs plus various lectures. See www.uneac.org.cu.

Walking on stilts in Morón during the Fiesta del Gallo

Encuentro de Bandas de Concierto, Plaza de la Revolución, Bayamo (1–15 Jun). Outdoor concerts by national and international bands; lectures, workshops.
Fiesta del Gallo, Morón (end of Jun). A parade including walking *gigantes* through the town based on the theme of the cockerel, which is symbolic here.
Jornada Cucalambeana, Encuentro Festival Iberoamericano de la Décima, Las Tunas (end of Jun). The most important festival of Cuban rural culture. Includes concerts and performances by poets, musicians and *repentistas* (improvisers). Lectures and literary meetings, exhibits of local handicrafts and theatre also feature.

July
Fiesta del Fuego, Santiago de Cuba (first half of Jul). Annual festival celebrating the music, poetry, figurative art, religions and history of the Caribbean nations. Meetings, shows, exhibits, concerts, poetry readings and festivities throughout the city, culminating on the last night with the *Quema del Diablo* – the burning of an effigy of the Devil.
Havana Carnival (Jul–Aug). A parade of floats in the city streets, going from the Hotel Nacional to Calle Belascoaín, and live music performances by *comparsas* (processional groups who prepare all year long) in various parts of the city. At weekends, free concerts are held at the Piragua. The parades can be viewed from a grandstand.

A group of dancers from a Havana *comparsa* ready for Carnival

Santiago Carnival, Santiago de Cuba (week leading up to 26 Jul). Parades along the city streets and live music performed by *comparsas*. For the most important parades there is a grandstand for spectators. Afternoons are filled with children's parades; adult floats start parading at 10pm. During the day, food and drink stalls are set up in various *repartos* of the city such as Sueño and along La Trocha, where "peso beer" is doled out to the crowds from giant vats.
"26 de julio" (held every year in a different city). The official commemoration of the attack on the Moncada barracks (see p234), with a speech by President Raúl Castro and other political leaders in the main square of a Cuban city, accompanied by concerts and by children who recite poetry.

August
Havana International Rap Festival, Havana (Aug). The cultural home of rap in Havana, Alamar, hosts performances and workshops of Cuban hip-hop and rap, as well as screenings of realted movies.

Average Monthly Rainfall

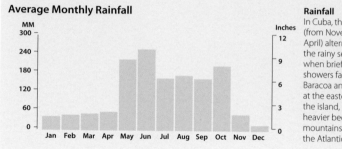

Rainfall
In Cuba, the dry season (from November to April) alternates with the rainy season, when brief but heavy showers fall. In the Baracoa and Moa area at the eastern tip of the island, rainfall is heavier because the mountains block the Atlantic winds.

Autumn

After the August heat, when everything to do with work seems to slow down, life starts to pick up again. In autumn the schools reopen and work returns to a normal rhythm. The number of tourists – Europeans in particular – decreases.

September

Fiesta de la Virgen del Cobre, El Cobre, Santiago de Cuba *(8 Sep)*. On the feast-day of the Virgin there is a surge in the regular pilgrimage to this site from all parts of the island. The statue of the Virgin is borne in procession through the streets. **Matamoros Son**, Santiago *(Sep)*. A biennial festival given over to son *(see p34)*.

October

Festival Nacional de Teatro de Camagüey, Camagüey *(Oct)*. A national theatre competition dedicated to Gertrudis Gómez de Avellaneda *(see p32)*, with the added participation of various foreign companies.
Days of Cuban Culture, countrywide *(10–20 Oct)*. Cubans celebrate their history and Cuban and Afro-Cuban culture. The main day is October 20th, in commemoration of the first day that the national hymn was sung in Bayamo. Literature, children's shows, film, arts and music all play their role.

Fiesta de la Cultura Iberoamericana, Holguín *(second half of Oct)*. A festival given over to Spanish culture, with concerts, exhibitions, festivities and lectures.

International Fishing Tournament Jardines del Rey, Marina Cayo Guillermo *(mid–late Oct)*. A fishing tournament in Cayo Guillermo, a favourite fishing ground of author Ernest Hemingway. Anglers can win prizes in exchange for caught sailfish and blue marlin. Contact Naútica Marlin Jardines del Rey, tel (33) 301 323.

Alicia Alonso performing at the Teatro García Lorca

Festival Internacional de Ballet de La Habana, Alicia Alonso, Gran Teatro and Teatro García Lorca, Havana *(Oct–Nov, biennial)*. A wide-ranging survey of classical ballet, organized by the Ballet Nacional de Cuba headed by Alicia Alonso. Famous international artists take part as well. Next staged 2018. See www.balletcuba.cult.cu.

November

Festival de Teatro de La Habana, Havana *(Nov)*. This biennial theatre festival features a wide range of performances, including opera, dance, puppet theatre, street shows and pantomime. Theoretical aspects of theatre are also discussed.
Festejos de San Cristóbal de La Habana *(Nov)*. Festivities and concerts to commemorate the foundation of Havana.
Festival de Raíces Africanas

Hurricanes

Hurricanes form when masses of hot air with low central pressure move upwards in a spiral, pulling cold air in towards the centre from the surrounding atmosphere. They cause high tides, extremely strong winds, and very heavy and persistent rainfall resulting in floods. The areas most vulnerable to these storms are the coasts, areas with little surface drainage, the valleys, the mountain areas and the cities. Most of the natural disasters in Cuba in the last 100 years have been caused by these storms. Hurricane Sandy struck the east of the island with devastating effect in 2012. Over 15,000 homes were destroyed in Santiago de Cuba and 11 people died. Agriculture was also severely affected throughout the region. It was one of the costliest hurricanes to ever hit Cuba. September and October are the most likely months for Caribbean hurricanes to occur.

Satellite photograph of Hurricane Gustav over Cuba

Average Monthly Temperature

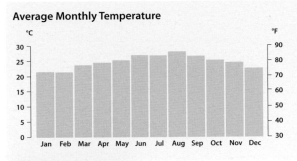

Temperature
The chart covers the entire island. In practice, Eastern Cuba, especially the Santiago area (except for the mountainous zones) is hotter. On the *cayos* the annual temperature range varies little. The humidity level goes from 81 per cent in summer to 79 per cent in winter.

A dancer performs in traditional Afro-Cuban costume

"Wemilere", Guanabacoa *(Nov)*. A festival of folk events, with a closing prize-giving ceremony.
Festival Cuba Danzón, Teatro Sauto, Matanzas *(second half of Nov)*. Performances by *danzón* orchestras and dancers, courses and conferences.
Baila en Cuba, Havana *(late Nov)*. Dance classes, workshops and seminars on Cuban salsa.
Festival Internacional de Música Contemporánea de La Habana, Havana *(late Nov)*. Contemporary classical, choral and electro-acoustic music as well as the work of young Cuban composers. World premiers and lectures. See www.musicacontemporanea.cult.cu.

Winter

The most active season of the year from a cultural point of view, with many top conferences and festivals, the majority held in the capital. The events calendar is not generally disrupted by the holiday season; although Christmas has grown steadily in popularity since it was

reintroduced in 1998. New Year's Day is usually celebrated at home with the family or with close friends, rather than being the focus for public events.

December

Festival Internacional del Nuevo Cine Latinoamericano, ICAIC, Havana *(first half of Dec)*. This is the most important cinema festival and competition of the year, attracting famous international guests. The main cinemas in the capital present screenings of the Latin American films in the competition, as well as retrospective Cuban and international filmmakers. See http://www.habanafilmfestival.com.
Fiesta a la Guantanamera, Guantánamo *(first half of Dec)*. Performances of, and lectures on, Afro-Cuban religion. Visits to the French *cafetales* (old coffee plantations) and the stone zoo.

The Feria Internacional del Libro logo

Festival Internacional del Nuevo Cine Latinoamericano poster

Día de San Lázaro, Santiago de Las Vegas, El Rincón *(16–17 Dec)*. The faithful and the sick come on pilgrimage to the church of Rincón; many come from Havana on their knees.
Parrandas de Remedios, Remedios *(8–24 Dec)*. Cuba's most popular folk festival begins with a children's parade and ends with floats, and lavish fireworks on Christmas Eve *(see p181)*.
Festival Internacional Jazz Plaza *(mid-Dec)*. The greats of world jazz celebrate alongside organiser Chucho Valdés.
Feria Internacional de Artesanía (FIART), Pabexpo, Havana *(Dec)*. Handicrafts fair. Stands from different countries; meetings and lectures.

February

Feria Internacional del Libro, Fortaleza de San Carlos de La Cabaña *(Feb–Mar)*. Book fair featuring a different nation each year. New Cuban and foreign publishing initiatives presented and sold. Round tables, poetry readings and concerts. See http://feriadellibro.cubaliteraria.cu.

National Holidays

New Year's Day/ Liberation Day (1 Jan)

Labour Day (1 May)

National Rebellion Day (26 July)

Start of First War of Independence (10 Oct)

Christmas Day (25 Dec)

THE HISTORY OF CUBA

First inhabited in Pre-Columbian times, Cuba was later conquered by the Spanish, who ruled here for four centuries. The island gained independence in 1898, only to come under the virtual control of the US, with the help of dictators Machado and Batista. The Revolution, headed by Fidel Castro, Raúl Castro, Camilo Cienfuegos and Che Guevara, who defeated Batista on 1 January 1959, was a turning point for the country. The new political system achieved major social results and Cuba is now finally emerging from decades of isolation.

Before the arrival of the Spanish, Cuba was inhabited by three Amerindian ethnic groups: the Guanajatabey, Siboney and Taíno. The first were gatherers who lived in caves. The Siboney, hunters and fishermen, left behind the most interesting Pre-Columbian rock paintings in the country – more than 200 pictures in the caves of Punta del Este on Isla de la Juventud *(see p155)*. The Taíno were farmers and hunters thought to be from present-day Venezuela, and their culture, the most advanced of the three, achieved a primitive form of social organization.

On 28 October 1492, Christopher Columbus landed in Cuba during his first voyage of discovery in the New World *(see p218)*. He named it "Juana" in honour of the king of Spain's son, but the natives continued to call it "Cuba". Columbus also revisited the southern Cuban coastline on his second voyage (1493–96), and fourth, and ultimate, voyage (1502–04). From 1510 to 1514 Diego Velázquez de Cuellar, upon commission from Columbus's son, set about annexing the island to Spain. This proved to be a straightforward enterprise, because the Indians put up little resistance, with the exception of a few episodes. The chief Hatuey led a rebellion in 1511–12, but was taken prisoner and burnt at the stake *(see p223)*.

Diego Velázquez then turned to colonization. He founded the city of Baracoa, first capital of the island, in 1511; San Salvador (present-day Bayamo) in 1513; San Cristóbal (the original Havana), Santísima Trinidad (Trinidad) and Sancti Spíritus in 1514; and Santiago de Cuba and Santa María del Puerto del Príncipe (present-day Camagüey) in 1515. The indigenous population was decimated despite vigorous defence by Friar Bartolomé de las Casas, so-called "Protector of the Indians", and the Spanish soon had to import slaves from western Africa to fulfil the need for labour on the sugar plantations that criss-crossed the island. Later, dissatisfied with the lack of gold in Cuba, the Spanish began to use the island both as a base from which to conquer other American territory, as well as a port of call for ships taking the riches of the New World back to Spain.

Before 1492 Cuba inhabited by Guanajatabey, Siboney and Taíno Indians		*Diego Velázquez de Cuellar*		**1512** Indian resistance leader Hatuey is killed by the Spanish	**1514** San Cristóbal (now Havana), Santísima Trinidad (Trinidad) and Sancti Spíritus founded
Pre-Columbian age	**1490**		**1500**		**1510**
Bust of Columbus, Museo de la Revolución, Havana		**28 October 1492** Christopher Columbus lands on the island	**1510** Diego Velázquez de Cuellar begins conquest of Cuba **1511** Foundation of Baracoa, first city in Cuba		**1515** Foundation of Santiago de Cuba and Santa María del Puerto del Príncipe (Camagüey)

◀ Detail from the painting *Siempre Che* (Che Forever) by Raúl Martínez

Pirates and Buccaneers

By the mid-1500s the population of Cuba had dwindled considerably because the indigenous Indians had been virtually annihilated by forced labour and diseases, and the Spanish had left for other parts of the New World in search of gold. However, the island was still important, strategically, as one of the defensive bastions of the Spanish colonies in America against the expansionist policies of France, Britain and the Netherlands.

Havana, the chief dock for vessels transporting treasure from America to Spain, soon drew the attention of pirates, who were plying the Caribbean Sea by the second half of the 16th century. In 1555, the French buccaneer Jacques de Sores sacked and burned Havana, triggering the construction of an impressive fortification system. Pirate raids became more and more frequent in the 17th century. The first buccaneers were French, then came the turn of the British (including Francis

The French buccaneers led by Jacques de Sores sacking the city of Havana

Drake and Henry Morgan) and the Dutch, who attacked Spanish galleons loaded with treasure as well as the Cuban ports.

In order to deprive Spain of her colonies, France, Britain and the Netherlands joined in the "corsair war" – essentially state-sanctioned piracy – by financing attacks on Spanish merchant ships. The Spanish crown took several measures to defend its possessions, but to no avail. In 1697 the Ryswyk Treaty signed by Spain, France and Britain finally put an end to this unusual war in the West Indies.

Henry Morgan, the British buccaneer

In the meantime Havana had become the new capital of Cuba, thanks to its well-protected bay, and the constant ebb and flow of men and precious cargo imparted a vitality unknown to most of the other cities in the New World. However, the rest of the island was isolated from this ferment, even though agriculture was developing rapidly as the Spanish encouraged the large-scale cultivation of sugar cane and tobacco, which soon became desirable commodities in Europe (see p36). Cuba, a major hub of maritime traffic, was compelled to trade only with the parent country, Spain. Within a short time the island became a haven for smuggling, which was a boost for the island's economy, stimulating the exchange of Cuban sugar and tobacco for the products of the Old World.

The Brief British Dominion

Although in the 17th century the Cuban population, concentrated around Havana, had increased with the arrival of Spanish

---

16th-century Spanish galleon

1586 Havana again risks being attacked by Francis Drake's British buccaneers

1555 Havana sacked and burned by French buccaneers under Jacques de Sores

The coat of arms of Havana: the key of the Gulf, with its fortresses

1607 Havana becomes the island's capital

1550   **1600**   **1650**

The British fleet taking Havana in the summer of 1762

settlers and African slaves, in the early 18th century the island was still a minor colony. In the summer of 1762 Havana was conquered by the British under the leadership of George Pocock and Lord Albemarle, who ruled for about a year. However, even in this short period the British occupation changed the economic and social organization of the island. The trade restrictions imposed by Spain were abolished, and Cuba began to trade openly with British colonies in North America. The slave trade grew, with Africans being used as labourers on the sugar cane plantations. As a result of the Treaty of Paris, drawn up in 1763, Havana was returned to the Spanish in exchange for Florida.

The Rise of National Identity

The 18th century marked the birth of a Creole aristocracy. These people, Cuban born of Spanish descent, commissioned the fine buildings which can still be seen today, and led a colonial lifestyle based on a combination of local, Indian and African traditions. In the early 19th century, a cultural movement promoted by the intellectuals de Heredia, Varela and Villaverde *(see p32)* aimed at establishing a Cuban national identity. Spain, forced to recognize the independence of other American colonies, eventually granted some freedom to Cuba, but then gave the island's governors dictatorial powers. Years of revolts, which the Spanish subdued mercilessly, then ensued. However, the new Creole middle class no longer had vested interests in the Spanish crown, and was determined to gain independence for the island.

The new Havana middle class taking a carriage ride

1697 The Treaty of Ryswyk ends the "corsair war" in the West Indies

1762 The British attack and occupy Havana

1830 Cuba replaces Haiti as the world's leading producer of sugar

1700

1750

1800

1763 The Treaty of Paris marks the end of British occupation and Havana is given back to the Spanish

Captain General Luís de las Casas, governor of Cuba 1790–96

1837 First Cuban railway line opens, beginning at the port of Havana

Sugar, Slaves and Plantations

At the beginning of the 19th century the Cuban sugar industry was booming, thanks to the growing demand for sugar in Europe and America. The growth of the industry was made possible by the labour of slaves brought from Africa in their greatest numbers from the late 18th to the early 19th centuries. About one million men and women were brought to Cuba, and by around 1830, black Africans, including slaves and legally-freed slaves, made up more than half the population of Cuba. The island became the world's leading sugar manufacturer, overtaking Haiti, and the industry continued to thrive after the abolition of slavery. Life on the sugar plantations therefore became a key feature of the island's history and life.

Bells marked the daily routine of life in the *ingenio*: at 4:30am the Ave Maria was played to wake the workers; at 6am the assembly marked the beginning of work proper. At 8:30pm the last bell sounded to announce bedtime.

Storehouses, stables and cattle sheds were built around the *ingenio* area.

The sugar refining area stood in the original core of the sugar factory, the *trapiche* or mill.

Cimarrones were runaway slaves who hid in the mountains or forests to avoid the *rancheadores*, whose job it was to find and capture them, dead or alive. These fugitives organized frequent revolts, which were almost inevitably suppressed with bloodshed.

The first stretch of railway on the island, which actually preceded the introduction of trains in Spain, was inaugurated in 1837 to transport sugar cane to the port of Havana.

Slaves were used in all phases of sugar manufacture, and not only as field labourers. This old illustration shows the *sala de las calderas*, where the cane juice was boiled before being refined.

Carlos Manuel de Céspedes, the owner of an estate near Manzanillo, freed his slaves on 10 October 1868, thus triggering the Cuban wars of independence. In his manifesto he asked for the abolition of slavery.

The dances and music that are thought to have given rise to the rumba *(see p35)* were performed in the *ingenio*, accompanied by the drumming of *cajones*, wooden boxes used to transport goods. Every year on 6 February the plantation owners allowed their slaves to celebrate their origins by dancing in the streets dressed in traditional costumes.

The *barracones* (the slaves' dormitories) were rectangular buildings divided into small rooms and with only one grilled door.

The Ingenio

The sugar factory (ingenio) was in reality an agro-industrial complex, in the middle of which stood the owner's house. This was usually an elegant building, often embellished with arches and wrought-iron grilles. The sugar factory owner would stay here during the long inspection periods. The batey, an Amerindian term used to describe collectively all the buildings on an ingenio, included a sugar cane mill, refinery rooms, a distillery, an infirmary, stables and cow sheds, vegetable gardens, storehouses, and the slaves' barracones, or sleeping quarters.

The ethnologist Fernando Ortiz (1881–1969) was the first person to seriously analyze the social condition of the black Cubans, emphasizing the cultural bonds with African traditions.

A Cultural Melting Pot

Symbol of the Abakuá religion

The *ingenio* was a place where landowners, farmers and slaves, white and black, men and women, had to live and work together. The African slaves came from different ethnic groups and spoke different languages, but they managed to keep their religious practices alive by meeting in the *cabildos* (mutual aid associations), where they continued to pray to their gods, "concealing" them in the guise of Roman Catholic saints *(see pp26–7)*. The Spanish themselves ended up assimilating elements of the very traditions they had been trying to suppress. Present-day Cuban music and dances were widespread in the *batey*, and the original songs and literature constantly refer to the *ingenio*, since it was here that the cultural crossover, typical of Cuba, evolved.

The Ten Years' War and the Abolition of Slavery

On 10 October 1868, at his La Demajagua estate *(see p223)*, the landowner Carlos Manuel de Céspedes launched the *grito de Yara* (war-cry from Yara), calling upon his fellow Cubans to rebel against Spanish rule. After conquering Bayamo, the rebels set up a revolutionary government and chose Céspedes as President of the Republic. On that occasion, the Cuban national anthem was sung for the first time. The new republic, however, was short-lived. The Spanish came back with a vengeance and the rebels – known as *mambises* (villains) – responded with the famous "machete assaults". In the meantime, the struggle had spread to other provinces, but differences among the rebels certainly did not help the cause.

The Ten Years' War – during which the first Cuban constitution was written (1869) – ended in 1878 with the Treaty of Zanjón, at which the rebels capitulated. Some revolutionaries rejected this agreement; one was General Antonio Maceo, who was forced into exile.

There followed the so-called "*guerra chica*", a brief conflict that resulted in the official abolition of slavery in 1886 (slave trade had in practice been prohibited since 1880). Cuba was the last American colony to abolish slavery. It was in this period that trade relations with the US developed.

General Maceo, who was exiled in 1878

Resumption of Hostilities and the End of the War

Towards the end of the 1800s, despite the rebellions, living conditions on the island had remained basically the same and none of the promised reforms had been enacted. In 1892, the Cuban intellectual José Martí (1853–95), in exile in the US, made a major contribution to the struggles that would follow: he founded the Partido Revolucionario Cubano, which united the Cuban forces in favour of independence.

The war against Spanish repression resumed on 24 February 1895. The leading figures were Martí – the real author and coordinator of Cuba's struggle for independence, who died in battle on 19 May, Máximo Gómez (recruited by Martí himself, who went to Santo Domingo to meet him) and Antonio Maceo. These last two had already distinguished themselves in the Ten Years' War. There was an escalation in the war and Spain sent reinforcements, but the situation was already out of control. Gómez and Maceo extended the war from the east to the west, gradually liberating the island. Not even the arrival of the Spanish general Valeriano Weyler, who was granted extraordinary powers, did any good: the war had taken a decided turn for the worse for the Spanish.

On 15 February 1898, when the Cubans had practically won, the American cruiser *Maine*, officially sent to the bay of Havana to protect US citizens and property in Cuban territory, exploded mysteriously, causing the death of about 250 marines. The US accused Spain of being responsible

Máximo Gómez

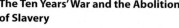

Road sign for La Demajagua, Céspedes' estate

10 February 1878 The Treaty of Zanjón marks the capitulation of the rebels and the end of the Ten Years' War (1868–78), the first stage in the struggle for independence

| 1870 | 1875 | 1880 | 1885 |

10 October 1868 From Yara, Carlos Manuel de Céspedes launches the "cry" that triggers the revolt

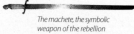

The machete, the symbolic weapon of the rebellion

1886 Formal abolition of slavery

The US battlecruiser *Maine* in Havana Bay in 1898, with the Castillo del Morro on the right

for the tragedy and, with public opinion on their side at home, intervened in the war. On 3 July the US Navy defeated the Spanish fleet, with the obvious intent of taking part in the peace treaty. On 10 December the Treaty of Paris – which involved Spain and the US, but not Cuba – marked the end of Spanish colonial dominion in America. On 1 January 1899 the last Spanish governor, Jiménez y Castellanos, officially handed the keys of Havana to US general John Brooke. From this point onwards, Cuba became inextricably linked with the United States.

US Supervision

In February 1901 the Constituent Assembly approved the first Cuban constitution and Tomás Estrada Palma was elected president. However, the delegates were forced to accept the Platt Amendment, formulated by US senator Orville Platt and added to a bill in Congress. Officially this provision aimed at safeguarding peace on the island, but its underlying purpose was to sanction the right of the US to intervene in Cuban affairs and to supervise trade relations between Cuba and other nations. In addition, the US was granted the right to establish naval bases on the island, including the one at Guantánamo in Eastern Cuba, which it still leases *(see p243)*.

Although formal independence was granted to Cuba on 20 May 1902, in the years that followed, American involvement in the local economy increased and, on the pretext of safeguarding their citizens and investments, the US sent marines to the island on many occasions.

José Martí

In 1895, when he died in battle at Boca de dos Ríos, José Martí was only 42. Despite this, he had had years of experience of living in exile and revolutionary struggle, besides writing a number of poems, articles and essays that would be the envy of a veteran author. Martí was born in Havana in 1853 to Spanish parents. By the time he went to secondary school he was already participating in anti-Spanish conspiracies. This activity led to his being deported in 1868, and exiled in 1878, after which he lived in the US, Spain, Mexico, Guatemala and Venezuela. As an essayist and journalist, Martí was known for his vigorous style. He was also a modernist poet *(see p32)*. He was an activist, a great politician and a sensitive interpreter of the impulses of the human soul.

José Martí, a national hero

1895–8 José Martí heads resumption of hostilities against the Spanish

15 February 1898 Explosion of the battlecruiser *Maine*

25 February 1901 First constitution

Tomás Estrada Palma, first president of Cuba

1890

1895

1900

1892 José Martí, in exile in the US, founds the Partido Revolucionario Cubano

19 May 1895 José Martí dies in combat

7 December 1896 Antonio Maceo dies in combat

10 December 1898 Paris Treaty marks end of Spanish dominion and beginning of American control

20 May 1902 Cuba obtains formal independence

The Early Period of the Republic

In its first 25 years, the Cuban Republic was headed by various presidents who did relatively little for the country. The second incumbent, José Miguel Gómez, who was nicknamed *tiburón* (shark), is at least to be credited for having introduced free public education and freedom of association and speech, as well as the separation of Church and State, and laws regarding divorce. In the early 1900s, sugar cane production increased to the point where sugar became virtually the only crop grown, and several new sugar factories were built. Havana, especially in the 1920s, saw the development of entire urban areas.

However, in general, independence had not really benefited the population at large, and protest demonstrations, repressed with force, began to increase. The first trade and student unions were set up, and in 1925 the Cuban Communist Party was founded. The leading figure in the party was the Marxist intellectual Julio Antonio Mella, leader of the Havana student movement and key to Latin American left-wing politics. Mella was arrested in Cuba but then freed because of the massive demonstrations that took place after he went on hunger strike; he was then sent into exile in Mexico. However, on 10 January 1929, Mella was assassinated in Mexico City by hired killers in the pay of the dictator Gerardo Machado. He became a national hero.

A popular uprising against the corrupt, inefficient government of Gerardo Machado

The Marxist intellectual Julio Antonio Mella

Gerardo Machado's Regime

In 1925 Gerardo Machado became president of Cuba, later changing the Constitution so he could rule for a further term, which he did with iron force until 1933. This period was marked by violence and tyranny; the people demonstrated their discontent by means of continual strikes, and the situation worsened with the Great Depression. A long general strike and the loss of the support of the army forced Machado to flee to the Bahamas on 12 August 1933.

After a brief period of progressive government, from early 1934 onwards there were various presidents who were little more than puppets, placed there by Sergeant Fulgencio Batista – who himself became president from 1940 to 1944. From 1934 to 1940 various social reforms came into being: the Platt amendment was revoked, women were allowed to vote, an 8-hour working day was instituted, and a new constitution was enacted.

1907 Birth of Independent Colour Party, which demands equality between whites and blacks

1910–20 Architectural boom in Havana

1925 Gerardo Machado becomes president

1929 Economic crisis

| 1905 | 1910 | 1915 | 1920 | 1925 | 1930 |

29 September 1906 Intervention of US Marines, who police Cuba until 1909

Havana railway station (1912)

1925 Founding of Cuban Communist Party

Batista's Dictatorship

After World War II the Orthodox Party led by Eduardo Chibás became popular, supported by the more progressive members of the middle class. This party might have won the election that was to take place on 1 June 1952, but on 10 March Fulgencio Batista staged a coup. Protest demonstrations followed, consisting mostly of students, which were ruthlessly repressed. The university was then closed. Batista's government, having the official support of the US, abandoned its initial populist stance and became an out-and-out violent dictatorship indifferent to the needs of the Cuban people. Vast areas of land were sold to American and British firms, and the money was pocketed. As the dictator's cronies became rich, the population became poorer, and the country more and more backward. Cuba was becoming a "pleasure island" which held an overpowering fascination, especially for Americans.

By the 1950s Cuba was famous for glamour – its music and cocktails, its prostitutes, cigars, drinking and gambling, and the sensational tropical life attracted mafiosi and film stars, tourists and

Fulgencio Batista (left) with American vice-president Richard Nixon

businessmen. However, there was a high price to pay: Cuba had not only become a land of casinos and drugs, it had also fallen into the hands of the American underworld, which ran the local gambling houses and luxury hotels, used for money laundering.

The Cuban Revolution

After Batista's coup, a young lawyer, Fidel Alejandro Castro Ruz, an active student leader who associated with the Orthodox Party, denounced the illegitimacy of the new government to the magistracy, without effect. Since peaceful means did not work, on 26 July 1953, Castro and a band of rebels made an unsuccessful attempt to capture the Moncada army barracks at Santiago (see p234). He was one of the few fortunate surviving rebels and was tried and sentenced to imprisonment in the Presidio Modelo, on Isla de Pinos (now Isla de la Juventud). Thanks to an amnesty, he was freed two years later and went into exile in Mexico, where he set about organizing the revolutionary forces, and was joined by a young Argentine doctor, Ernesto "Che" Guevara. This famous collaboration proved to be decisive for the success of the Revolution. In 1959, after years of armed struggle, the island was freed from previous dictatorships (see pp52–5).

Dancers at the Tropicana in the 1940s

12 August 1933 At night, Machado flees with a load of gold to the Bahamas	**1940–4** Fulgencio Batista obtains presidential mandate thanks to a coalition of forces		**1953–9** The Revolution liberates Cuba from the Batista dictatorship
1935	1940	1945	1950	1955

January 1934 Start of a period with a series of puppet presidents manoeuvred by the Cuban Army sergeant Fulgencio Batista

Sergeant Fulgencio Batista

10 March 1952 Coup d'état by Fulgencio Batista

The Cuban Revolution

In exile in Mexico after the attack on the Moncada army barracks, on 25 November 1956 Fidel Castro left for Cuba on the yacht *Granma* with 81 other revolutionaries, including Che Guevara and Raúl Castro. Three days later, after landing, they were attacked by Batista's troops. Only a few escaped to the Sierra Maestra, where they began to organize their guerrilla war. The miserable living conditions of the people and ever-increasing corruption and repression lent impetus to their struggle. The rebel army, which included farmers, students, women and regular army deserters, defeated Batista's troops after two years of fighting.

The attack against the Moncada barracks took place on 26 July 1953. The rebels took advantage of the Carnival festivities to make a move in the dead of night, but the attack ended in failure.

Santa Clara was the scene of the battle that marked the triumph of the Revolution. After the rebels' victory, Batista fled to Santo Domingo (31 December 1958).

Havana was occupied by Che Guevara's guerrillas, while Fidel Castro entered Santiago de Cuba (1 January 1959).

Key

- ‒ ‒ Raúl Castro's march
- ‒ ‒ Che Guevara's march
- ‒ ‒ Camilo Cienfuegos' march

Havana • Matanzas •

• Pinar del Río

Cienfuegos • Santa Clara •

Isla de la Juventud

Sierra del Escambray was reached by Che Guevara after an exhausting march; his men were without food or shoes and extremely weary but they were victorious (October 1958).

Radio Rebelde was the guerrillas' radio station, set up in the Sierra Maestra by Che Guevara in February 1958. Its programmes were listened to avidly all over the island.

The Phases of the War

The advance of two columns of guerrillas from the Sierra Maestra – one led by Che Guevara and Camilo Cienfuegos to the west (October 1958), the other by Raúl Castro bound for Guantánamo – marked the climax of the revolutionaries' struggle. After the battle of Santa Clara and the taking of the city by Guevara's troops at the end of December, Batista escaped to Santo Domingo. On 1 January 1959 victory was declared by the revolutionaries.

The Landing of the *Granma* in Cuba took place on 2 December 1956. Due to some problems at sea, the yacht landed on 2 December and not 30 November as planned. Three days later they were attacked by Batista's troops. Those captured were killed, while the survivors (including Fidel and Raúl Castro) took refuge in the Sierra Maestra.

Young women, including Haydée Santamaría, Celia Sánchez and Vilma Espín, participated actively in the revolutionary war. After Havana was captured, they were entrusted with guarding strategic points.

Fidel Castro entered Havana on 8 January 1959 and on 16 February was elected prime minister. At the time the president was Manuel Urrutia, elected after Batista's escape. The revolutionary government immediately abolished racial discrimination and reduced rents and the cost of electricity.

0 kilometres 75
0 miles 75

On the Sierra Maestra, Cuba's largest mountain range, the rebels organized guerrilla warfare, recruiting soldiers from among the population (above, Fidel Castro recruiting farmers). The strategy was to ambush Batista's troops and take their supplies and weapons.

• **Camagüey**

Holguín •

Playa Las Coloradas was where the *Granma* landed on 2 December 1956.

• **Bayamo**

Santiago de Cuba •

• **Guantánamo**

The attack at La Plata, a military barracks, was the rebels' first success (17 January 1957).

In the Sierra Maestra Fidel Castro, Che Guevara and the other survivors of the *Granma* worked out a strategy of guerrilla warfare with a growing number of *barbudos*, students, army deserters and reinforcements sent by the urban branch of the Movimiento 26 de Julio.

At Santiago de Cuba the rebel movement won an important victory on 17 January 1957.

October 1953 Fidel Castro condemned to 15 years' imprisonment in Presidio Modelo

30 November 1956 Bloody repression of revolt at Santiago

Che Guevara

31 August Che and Cienfuegos leave east to conquer central regions

1 January Che and Cienfuegos enter Havana; Castro, Santiago

| 1953 | 1956 | | 1958 | 1959 |

26 July 1953 Attack on Moncada barracks

15 May 1955 Fidel Castro freed, goes to Mexico in exile

Castro leaving prison

2 December 1956 Landing of *Granma*

1956–8 Guerrilla war in Sierra Maestra

24 February Radio Rebelde set up

31 December Santa Clara falls, Batista flees

8 January Castro enters Havana in triumph

The Heroes of the Revolution

The success of the Revolution can be partly explained by the moral stature of the heroes who headed it, and partly by the unity of the movement – an entire population was determined to obtain freedom. After their triumphal entrance into Havana, the revolutionary leaders were entrusted with the task of realizing their objectives: the reorganization of the country's agriculture, afflicted with large landed estates and monoculture; the battle against illiteracy and unemployment; industrialization; the construction of homes, schools and hospitals. Fidel Castro became Prime Minister and Che Guevara was appointed Minister of Industry and president of the National Bank. The Revolution continued, with its heroes and ideals.

Ernesto "Che" Guevara was an Argentinian who met Castro in Mexico. Unpretentious, straightforward and ascetic, and an uncompromising idealist, he believed the Third World could be freed only through armed rebellion *(see p180)*.

The straw hats worn by the *barbudos* were those commonly used by farmers.

Camilo Cienfuegos, a commander whose courage was legendary, was a direct, spontaneous person with a great sense of humour. He played a crucial role in the armed struggle, but took part in the government only for a brief period. On 28 October 1959, while flying back from Camagüey after arresting guerrilla commander Hubert Matos, who had betrayed the Revolution, Cienfuegos' small plane disappeared and he was never seen again.

Horses were the most common means of transport used by the revolutionaries.

Frank País (seen here with his mother and fiancée), head of the Movimiento 26 de Julio, was entrusted with organizing a revolt in Santiago de Cuba that would coincide with the landing of the *Granma* on 30 November 1956. But because of the delay in the landing the revolt was repressed. País died in Santiago during the armed revolt, in an ambush set up by the chief of police.

Raúl Castro, Fidel's brother, currently President of Cuba, was one of the few survivors of the landing of the *Granma*. He was a commander in the guerrilla war and became a member of the government, adopting a radical stance. As Minister of Defence he signed, with Khrushchev, the agreement for the installation of the nuclear missiles in Cuba that caused the 1962 crisis.

Fidel Castro with Juan Almeida (left), one of the strategists of revolutionary guerrilla warfare. Castro, a great orator and political strategist, the *Líder Máximo* and an uncompromising patriot, personified the Cuban state. As poet Nicolás Guillén wrote, "he accomplished what José Martí had promised". Born on 13 August 1926 in Mayarí in Eastern Cuba, the son of Spanish immigrants, he studied with the Jesuits and took a degree in law. He began to fight for the cause while at university.

The Cuban flag, used after the wars of independence, has the colours of the French Revolution. The three blue stripes represent the old provinces of the island.

The Barbudos

The rebels were referred to as barbudos (bearded men) because during their time in the mountains they all grew long beards. A large number of farmers joined their famous marches. This photograph, taken by the Cuban photographer Raúl Corrales, expresses the dynamic team spirit of the Revolution.

Guillermo García Morales was one of the first Cuban farmers to join the revolutionary war of the Movimiento 26 de Julio. A guerrilla in the Sierra Maestra together with Castro, he was named Commander of the Revolution for his distinguished service.

Celia Sánchez Manduley espoused the revolutionary cause at an early age and fought in the Sierra Maestra. Considered Fidel Castro's right-hand "man" and companion, after 1959 she filled important political positions. Celia died of cancer in 1980, while still young.

Eradicating Illiteracy, Agricultural Reform

One of the first acts of the revolutionary government was a campaign against illiteracy, initiated in 1961: thousands of students travelled throughout the countryside, teaching the rural population to read and write. Che Guevara, who during the guerrilla warfare in the mountains had encouraged his men to devote some time to study, participated in the campaign. In a short time illiteracy was eradicated.

The next step was agrarian reform, which began with the abolition of ownership of large landed estates, especially those in foreign (in particular American) hands. US landholdings were drastically reduced. This marked the beginning of hostilities between the two countries. In October 1960 the US declared an economic boycott that blocked the export of petroleum to Cuba and the import of Cuban sugar. After nearly two years of growing tension, Cuba secured closer economic and political ties with the Soviet Union, Eastern Europe and China. In the meantime, the struggle against counter-revolutionary guerrillas in the Sierra del Escambray continued.

Marines arriving at the US naval base of Guantánamo during the missile crisis

Participants in the campaign against illiteracy in 1961

embargo against Cuba, which heralded a boycott by most other countries in the Americas (except Mexico and Canada). These countries also severed diplomatic relations with the island, as the US had done. The result was the establishment of even closer ties between Cuba and the communist world. A year later, when the US discovered the presence of nuclear missile sites in Cuba, President Kennedy ordered a naval blockade around the island and demanded that the missile installations be dismantled immediately. At the height of the crisis, with the world poised on the brink of nuclear war, the Soviet president Nikita Khrushchev ordered the missiles to be taken back to the USSR.

The Embargo and Missile Crisis

On 17 April 1961 a group of Cuban exiles and mercenaries trained by the CIA landed at Playa Girón, in the Bay of Pigs, to invade the island. But the attack failed because, contrary to the expectations of the US, Cuban civilians did not rise up against Castro (see p171). Eight days later President Kennedy declared a trade

From the Zafra Campaign to the Emigration of the "Marielitos"

During the early stages, the government had aimed to create as much diversity in the economy as possible. However, in 1970, in order to inject life into the flagging economy, all efforts were concentrated on

1961 17 April: landing at Bay of Pigs; US embargo begins on 25 April

1991 The Soviet Union withdraws troops and technicians

1962 Missile crisis

1965 Only legal political party is the Cuban Communist Party

1975 First congress of the Cuban Communist Party

1990 Beginning of the Período Especial

1960   1970   1980   1990

1961 3 January, diplomatic relations with the US are broken

Armored tank

1970 The zafra campaign

1967 Death of Che Guevara

1980 125,000 Cubans emigrate from the small harbour at Mariel

Rations coupon booklet

promoting the *zafra* (sugar cane harvest) campaign. A target was set of ten million tons, but in the end only 8,500,000 were harvested. In the same period some Latin American countries resumed diplomatic relations with Cuba. While the Revolution had achieved a great deal in social terms, the country's economic problems had by no means been resolved. 1980 saw the emigration of 125,000 Cubans, the so-called *marielitos* – named after the small harbour of Mariel, near Havana, where they set off for Miami.

The Período Especial

The dismantling of the Berlin Wall in 1989 and the subsequent collapse of Communism in Eastern Europe deprived Cuba of economic partners. The suspension of Soviet aid was a crippling blow for the Cuban economy, and triggered a crisis that the government faced by imposing a programme of austerity. In 1990 the island went through one of the most difficult phases in its history, the Período Especial. Many sectors of industry came to a standstill due to a lack of fuel, imports were reduced, interruptions in the

Empty shelves in a shop during the crisis period

Pope John Paul II meets Castro during his visit to Cuba

supply of electricity and water became part of everyday life, food rations were reduced and wages were lowered. In 1991 the Soviet Union also withdrew its troops and technicians. The economic crisis continued to worsen until 1994.

Into the 21st Century

To counter the Período Especial the government began to encourage foreign investment, limited private enterprise was allowed and the US dollar became legal tender. A significant sign of change was Pope John Paul II's visit to Cuba in 1998. The 2000s saw a massive influx of tourism but still the economy remained precarious; the US dollar was later withdrawn. Raúl Castro replaced his ailing brother Fidel as president in early 2008 and introduced social and economic reforms, but the economy remained strained. In 2010 Raúl Castro began releasing political prisoners incarcerated since 2003, and Fidel reappeared after a four-year absence from the public stage. As the economy continued to sink, Raúl Castro announced that 500,000 workers would be laid off by the state, ameliorating their predicament with new self-employment rules allowing many more Cubans to work for themselves and start their own businesses – a sea change in state-run Cuba. At the end of 2014, a push towards normalizing trade relations with the US began and restrictions against US citizens travelling to Cuba were suddenly eased. The country is bracing itself for enormous change.

1996 In November, Castro visits Pope John Paul II in the Vatican

2000 1,774,000 tourists visit Cuba in one year

2008 Raúl Castro becomes President of the Cuban Council of State

Seaside tourism

2014 President Raúl Castro and President Barack Obama announce plans to ease travel and trade restrictions between Cuba and the US

2000   **2010**   **2020**

1998 Pope John Paul II's visit to Cuba (21–25 January), a significant turning point

1996 The Helms-Burton law tightens economic embargo

2008 Hurricanes Gustav and Ike hit Cuba and are the costliest storms in recent history

2006 July: Castro is taken seriously ill and his brother, Raúl, becomes Acting President

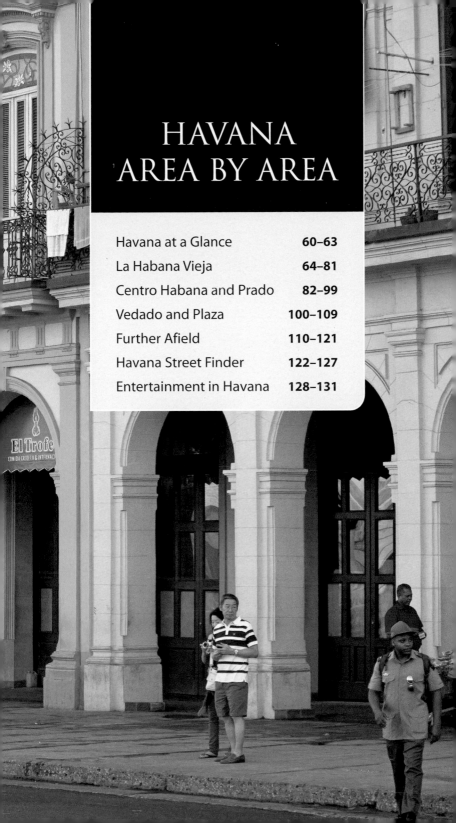

HAVANA
AREA BY AREA

Havana at a Glance

Havana is a lively, colourful capital city, full of bustle and entertainment, with some splendid architectural gems from the colonial period and beyond, and numerous other sights. The city alone is worth the trip to Cuba. Many attractions are concentrated in three quarters: La Habana Vieja (Old Havana), Centro Habana and Vedado. In the following pages La Habana Vieja, the colonial centre within the old city walls, is described first, followed by Centro Habana and the area known as Prado. The western part of the city is covered in the chapter called Vedado and Plaza. For map references for major sights in Havana, refer to the Street Finder *(see pp122–7)*.

HAVANA

```
0 kilometres          1
0 miles               1
```

MALECÓN

AVENIDA DE LOS PRESIDENTES

LINEA

MALECÓN

PASEO

23

VEDADO AND PLAZA
(see pp100–109)

LINEA

23

DE

ZAPATA

CALZADA

PASEO

Necrópolis de Colón *(see pp108–9)* is Havana's city cemetery as well as a national monument. Many famous people are buried here, often in striking tombs, and the site has become a place of pilgrimage for many.

Memorial José Martí *(see p107)* in Plaza de la Revolución is one of the symbols of Cuba. The white marble statue of the great patriot forms a focal point for national celebrations.

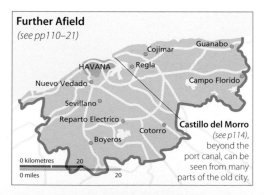

Further Afield
(see pp110–21)

Guanabo

Cojímar

HAVANA   Regla

Nuevo Vedado

Campo Florido

Sevillano

Reparto Electrico

Cotorro

Castillo del Morro
(see p114), beyond the port canal, can be seen from many parts of the old city.

Boyeros

```
0 kilometres    20
0 miles         20
```

◀ Façades painted in vivid pastels along the Paseo del Prado

Catedral de San Cristóbal *(see p68)* has a Cuban Baroque façade, with undulating lines, convex surfaces and columns which set off the brightly coloured rose window. The church dominates Plaza de la Catedral, which is surrounded by exquisite 17th–18th-century colonial buildings.

Museo de la Revolución *(see pp92–3)* is housed in the former presidential palace. In front stands the tank used by Fidel Castro in the 1961 Battle of the Bay of Pigs.

MALECÓN

SAN LÁZARO

CALZADA DE INFANTA

PADRE VARELA

ZANJA

PASEO DE MARTÍ

AVENIDA DEL PUERTO

AVENIDA DE LAS MISIONES

LA HABANA VIEJA *(see pp64–81)*

CENTRO HABANA AND PRADO *(see pp82–99)*

MÁXIMO GÓMEZ

AVENIDA BÉLGICA

AVENIDA DEL PUERTO

ALZADA DE AYESTARÁN

CALZADA DE INFANTA

ARROYO

Capitolio *(see pp86–7)* is a facsimile of Washington, DC's own Capitol. The two bronzes that flank the entrance are the work of the Italian sculptor Angelo Zanelli.

Palacio de los Capitanes Generales *(see pp74–5)* is probably the best example of 18th-century Baroque architecture in Havana. Its richly decorated marble entrance by the Italian sculptors Gaggini and Tagliafichi was added in 1835.

The Malecón

No other place represents Havana better than the Malecón, and no other place thrills tourists and locals so much. This seafront promenade winds for 7 km (4 miles) alongside the city's historic quarters, from the colonial centre to the skyscrapers of Vedado, charting the history of Havana from past to present. The busy seafront boulevard is lined with many attractive buildings, but it is the overall effect that is striking – and the Bay of Havana looks truly spectacular at sunset. In addition, the Malecón means tradition and religion to the people of the city: offerings to the gods (see p27) are thrown from the parapet into the sea.

Locator Map
See Street Finder pp122–7.

① **The Caryatid Building** is one of the most important structures in the first stretch of the Malecón. Built in the early 20th century, it was named after the Art Deco-style female figures that support the entablature of the loggia.

② **The area between Prado and Calle Belascoaín**, which has been scrupulously restored, is known for its pastel buildings. In the same part of the street, at No. 51, is the "Ataud" (the coffin), a 1950s skyscraper whose name derives from the shape of its balconies.

Varied decoration

Balconies with Neo-Moorish decorative patterns

Architecture

The Malecón is lined with buildings whose pastel hues have faded in the sun and salty air, as well as early 20th-century structures, often with two or three storeys and a loggia on the upper floor, in a mix of different architectural styles.

Edificio Focsa

③ **The Monument to the Victims of the Maine** was built in 1926 in memory of the sailors who died when the American warship *Maine* exploded in the Bay of Havana in 1898 (see p49). It stands in one of the wide stretches of the avenue on the edge of Vedado.

Hotel Nacional

④ **Between Calle 23 and Calle G** is the stretch of the Malecón that borders the Vedado quarter to the north. Dominated by Havana's tallest buildings, this is the seafront of the capital city.

On stormy days the waves break against the rocks and crash over the sea wall onto the street. Children love it when this happens. Storms are also a source of inspiration for followers of *Santería*, who view it as the wrath of Yemayá, the sea goddess *(see p27)*.

Fishing on the Malecón is a popular pastime among the locals. Others are playing music, strolling, or simply sitting on the low wall and watching the horizon.

Atmosphere

The Havana seafront is especially magical at sunset, when the colours of the buildings are accentuated. The Malecón is at its busiest on Sundays, when the Habaneros who cannot get to the Playas del Este flock here.

Young people love to walk along the Malecón, which is lined with 19th- and early 20th-century buildings.

The striking setting of the Malecón, facing the sea and with the city behind it, makes it a popular place for romantic young couples. There is also the occasional single person on the lookout for female or male companionship.

A Walk by the Ocean: The History of the Malecón

On 4 November 1901, the US authorities then occupying Cuba planned the Malecón as a tree-lined, pedestrian promenade to begin at the Castillo de la Punta. However the strong wind and rough sea obliged the engineers to change their original project and it was an American engineer named Mead, and Frenchman Jean Forestier, who came up with a more practical plan. In 1902 the open space in front of the Prado was completed with a municipal bandstand. Hotels and cafés were built near the old city, while bathing facilities were concentrated in Miramar. In 1919 the Malecón stretched as far as Calle Belascoaín, and in 1921 as far as Calle 23. It soon became a fast link between the old and modern cities – so much so that in the 1950s it was virtually abandoned by pedestrians. Today, despite the traffic, its original function has been partly revived.

The Malecón in the early 1900s

LA HABANA VIEJA

The historic heart of Havana, which was declared part of the "cultural heritage of humanity" by UNESCO in 1982, is the largest colonial centre in Latin America. After three centuries of neglect, restoration work under the direction of Eusebio Leal Spengler, the *historiador de la ciudad* (Superintendent of Cultural Heritage), is reviving the former splendour of this district. La Habana Vieja is characterized by Hispanic-Andalusian architecture, vitalized by the tropical sun and lush vegetation. Time seems to stand still here but nonetheless the zone does not give the impression of being a museum. The restoration programme is not limited to monuments and major buildings, but also includes old shops and ordinary houses. The aim is to ensure the revival of both the beauty of La Habana Vieja and its original vitality and everyday activities.

Sights at a Glance

Museums and Galleries
2 Museo de Arte Colonial
13 Museo del Ron
18 Casa Natal de José Martí

Historic Buildings
3 Seminario de San Carlos y San Ambrosio
4 La Bodeguita del Medio
5 Castillo de la Real Fuerza
6 El Templete
8 *Palacio de los Capitanes Generales pp74–5*

Historic Streets and Squares
7 Calle Oficios
9 Calle Obispo
10 Casa de la Obra Pía
11 Casa de Africa
12 Plaza de San Francisco
14 Alameda de Paula
15 Plaza Vieja

Churches and Monasteries
1 Catedral de San Cristóbal
16 Iglesia del Espíritu Santo
17 Iglesia de Nuestra Señora de la Merced

See also Street Finder, pp122–7, map 4

0 metres 300
0 yards 300

◀ Belfry of Basílica Menor de San Francisco de Asís, rising above Plaza de San Francisco   **For keys to symbols** *see back flap*

Street-by-Street: Plaza de la Catedral

Dominated by the elegant profile of its church, Plaza de la Catedral is one of the symbols of La Habana Vieja. In 1592, the Zanja Real, the city's first aqueduct (and the first Spanish aqueduct in the New World), reached the square. Water was channelled from the Almendares river, 11 km (7 miles) away. The Zanja Real was built to provide water to ships docking in the harbour, as well as to local residents. A 16th-century plaque in the square marks the spot where the Zanja Real was located. In the 18th century the aristocratic buildings and present-day Cathedral were built here. Plaza de la Catedral is an unmissable attraction for anyone visiting the historic centre, with women in colonial costume who stroll under the arcades and read fortunes, and a bar-restaurant where you can relax in the shade and listen to music.

A woman in colonial costume on the Cathedral steps

Former entrance to the seminary

Centro Wifredo Lam, housed in an 18th-century palazzo, promotes contemporary art with exhibitions and lectures.

CALLE SAN IGNACIO

CALLE EMPEDRADO

❸ Seminario de San Carlos y San Ambrosio
The modern entrance of this 18th-century building echoes the Baroque decorative motifs of the Cathedral.

Palacio de los Marqueses de Aguas Claras was built in the second half of the 18th century. In the 1900s it housed the París Restaurant and then the offices of the Banco Industrial. It is now a bar-restaurant, El Patio, with tables in the inner courtyard as well as in the picturesque square.

Key

— Suggested route

| 0 metres | 40 |
| 0 yards | 40 |

Casa de la Condesa de la Reunión, a 19th-century building surrounding a splendid courtyard, is the headquarters of the Alejo Carpentier Foundation. This well-known 20th-century Cuban writer *(see p33)* set his novel *Siglo de las Luces* here.

❹ ★ La Bodeguita del Medio
This restaurant and bar is legendary thanks to the writer Ernest Hemingway, who came here to drink *mojitos*.

❶ ★ Catedral de San Cristóbal
The Baroque façade of this church, declared a national monument, is considered one of the most beautiful in the Americas.

Locator Map
See Street Finder, pp122–7, map 4

Palacio del Conde Lombillo (1746) is home to the *Historiador de La Habana*, which hosts temporary exhibitions of photographs, paintings and lithographs.

Palacio de los Marqueses de Arcos, built in the 1700s, houses an art gallery where handicrafts and prints are on sale. The building was once the main post office and the original letter box is still visible on the outside wall.

Plaza de Armas (see pp70–71)

CALLE TACÓN

CALLE EMPEDRADO

CALLE MERCADERES

PLAZA DE LA CATEDRAL

CALLEJÓN DEL CHORRO

CALLE SAN IGNACIO

❷ ★ Museo de Arte Colonial
Dating from 1720, this is one of the city's finest examples of early colonial domestic architecture. It houses an exhibition of colonial furniture and objects.

The Taller Experimental de Gráfica (1962) holds theoretical and practical courses in graphic art for Cubans and foreigners, and houses a Gallery of Engravings.

❶ Catedral de San Cristóbal

Calle Empedrado 156. **Map** 4 E2.
Tel 7861 7771. **Open** 9am–5pm Mon–
Sat, 9am–noon Sun. 🕆 8am & 6pm
Tue & Thu, 8am Fri, 10:30am Sun.

Construction of the Catedral de San Cristóbal (Cathedral of St Christopher) began in 1748 under the supervision of Jesuit priests. They were, however, expelled from Cuba following conflict with the Spanish crown, meaning the church was finished by Franciscans in 1777. It became a cathedral after the collapse of the old Parroquial Mayor *(see p74)*, which was caused by the explosion of a ship in the nearby port.

In 1789, present-day San Cristóbal was consecrated as Catedral de la Virgen María de la Inmaculada Concepción, and the small square where it stands gained its current status. In 1796 it was renamed Catedral de San Cristóbal de La Habana, because, according to popular belief, from that year until 1898 it housed the relics of Christopher Columbus himself. A plaque to the left of the pulpit tells the same story, though there is no official historical record.

The architecture is in keeping with other Jesuit churches throughout the world: a Latin cross layout, chapels on the sides and to the rear, the nave higher than the side aisles. The Cuban Baroque façade is grandiose, with two large,

The austere nave of Catedral de San Cristóbal

asymmetrical bell towers and an abundance of niches and columns, which Cuban author Alejo Carpentier described as "music set in stone".

In comparison, the Neo-Classical interior is rather disappointing. Large piers separate the nave from the aisles, which have eight chapels. The largest one is the Sagrario chapel; the oldest (1755), designed by Lorenzo Camacho, is dedicated to the Madonna of Loreto and contains quaint, tiny houses used as *ex voto*s.

The three frescoes behind the high altar are by Giuseppe Perovani, while the original wooden and plaster ceiling, demolished and then rebuilt in 1946–52, was the work of Frenchman Jean

Statue of St Christopher

Baptiste Vermay, who founded the San Alejandro Fine Arts Academy *(see p30)*. The high altar was created by Italian artist Giuseppe Bianchini in the 1800s. To the right is a huge wooden statue of St Christopher, carved by the Seville sculptor Martín de Andújar in 1636. The legs are out of proportion with the trunk, as they were cut in order to allow the statue to pass through the portal.

On 16 November, the saint's feast day, a solemn mass is held here, during which the faithful, who have to stay quiet during the service, file past the statue to silently ask for his blessing. This blessing is given as long as worshippers do not utter a word until they have left the church.

Pope John Paul II in front of the Cathedral

Pope John Paul II's Visit

Pope John Paul II visited Cuba from 21–25 January 1998 *(see p57)*. This event was of great historical significance to Cuba, having officially been an atheist state after the 1959 revolution until the government allowed greater religious freedom in the early 1990s. It was greeted with enthusiasm not only by Roman Catholics, but by virtually the entire population. The visit was broadcast on television and the government also officially recognized Christmas Day as a holiday for the first time since 1969. On 25 January the "Celebration of the Word" was held in the Cathedral, during which the Pope met Cuban priests and held an audience with the faithful in Plaza de la Revolución. The trip paved the way for future papal visits by Pope Benedict XVI in 2012 and Pope Francis in 2015.

❷ Museo de Arte Colonial

Calle San Ignacio 61. **Map** 4 E2.
Tel 7862 4458. **Open** 9:30am–5pm
Tue–Sun. 🅿 🅲 Note: fee for
photography may apply.

This 18th-century mansion,
built by Don Luis Chacón,
governor of Cuba, has been
the home of a fascinating
museum dedicated to colonial
art since 1969. The building is
a fine example of a colonial
residence and is constructed
around an elegant courtyard.

The 12 rooms on the ground
floor and first floor contain
furniture, chandeliers, porcelain
and other decorative pieces
from various 18th–19th-century
middle-class and aristocratic
houses in Havana, in which
European, Creole and colonial
traditions are combined.
Besides a remarkable collection
of furniture made of tropical
wood, the museum has an
exceptional collection
of stained-glass
windows *(medio-
punto)*, typical
of Cuba's
Creole crafts-
men *(see p29)*.

There is also a
thirteenth room where exhibitions of contemporary art
and crafts inspired by colonial
art are held. During the week
the museum organizes tours
for school children and leisure
activities for the elderly in
the area.

❸ Seminario de San Carlos y San Ambrosio

Tacón e/ Chacón y Mercaderes . **Map**
4 E2. **Tel** 7862 6989. **Open** 9am–4pm
Mon–Sat (courtyard only). **Closed**
1 Jan, 26 Jul, 10 Oct, 25 Dec.

This building was erected by
the Jesuits in the mid-18th
century to house a seminary
first founded in 1689. Famous
Cuban patriots and intellectuals
studied here. One of them was
Padre Félix Varela (1788–1853),
who laid down the theoretical
bases for the Cuban war of
independence *(see p32)*.

Colonial furniture in the Museo de
Arte Colonial

There is also an old portal
on Calle San Ignacio, built
in the Churrigueresque style
which was common in Spain
and her colonies in this period.

The large central courtyard
is the only one of its kind in
Cuba: it has galleries on
three levels, the
first with simple
columns, the
second with
double
columns,
and the third
with plain
wooden piers.

The lavishly decorated
inner stairway leading to the
first floor has trapezoidal
motifs instead of the more
common arch, and fine black
mahogany banisters. The

Museo de Arte Colonial: an arched
mediopunto window

seminary has now moved to
a new home in Guanabacoa,
and the old seminary building
contains a Catholic cultural
centre, Centro Cultural
Católico de La Habana.

❹ La Bodeguita del Medio

Calle Empedrado 207. **Map** 4 E2. **Tel**
7867 1374. **Open** noon–midnight daily.

Standing exactly at the halfway
point in a typical small street
in old Havana, a few steps
away from the Cathedral, La
Bodeguita del Medio (literally,
"little shop in the middle") has
become a big attraction.

The place was founded in
1942 as a food shop. A bar
serving alcoholic drinks was
added, and the place became
a haunt for intellectuals, artists
and politicians. Today it is no
longer a shop but a bustling bar
at the front serving shots of rum
and Cuban cocktails and a good
restaurant hidden in the back
offering typical Creole dishes.
The walls are plastered with
photographs, drawings, graffiti
and visitors' autographs,
including those of famous
patrons such as the singer Nat
King Cole, poets Pablo Neruda
and Nicolás Guillén, and the
writers Gabriel García Marquez,
Alejo Carpentier *(see p33)*, and
Ernest Hemingway, who was
a regular here.

La Bodeguita del Medio with its memento-covered walls

Street-by-Street: Around Plaza de Armas

The elegant, spacious Plaza de Armas is lined with Baroque buildings, giving it a delightful colonial atmosphere, and is enlivened by the occasional passing performance of street dancers. The plaza was built in the 1600s to replace the old Plaza Mayor, the core of Havana's religious, administrative and military life, and up to the mid-1700s it was used for military exercises. After its transformation from 1771–1838, it became a favourite with rich Havana citizens and popular as an area for carriage rides. Following years of careful restoration work, the square now attracts throngs of visitors and locals, many of whom simply gather here to sit and relax.

Palacio del Segundo Cabo (1776), the former residence of the Spanish lieutenant governor, is now the home of a Cuba-Europe cultural exchange centre.

Plaza de la Catedral (see pp66–7)

CALLE TACÓN

CALLE O REILLY

CALLE MERCADERES

CALLE OBISPO

CALLE OBRAPÍA

❽ ★ Palacio de los Capitanes Generales
This fine Baroque palace, now the Museo de la Ciudad, was built for Cuba's old colonial rulers. A statue of Columbus stands in the courtyard, beneath towering royal palms.

Hotel Ambos Mundos

Former Ministerio de Educación

Farmacia Taquechel

❾ ★ Calle Obispo
Like an open-air museum of colonial architecture, this street is lined with buildings of interest dating from the 16th–19th centuries, including old pharmacies and historic shops.

❿ Casa de la Obra Pía
This large 17th-century mansion is well-known for its elaborate Baroque doorway, which was sculpted in Spain.

For hotels and restaurants in this area see p256 and p270

❺ ★ Castillo de la Real Fuerza

This 16th-century castle, with its broad moat and characteristic angular ramparts, is the oldest military construction in Havana. The Giraldilla, symbol of the city, stands in its entrance.

Locator Map
See Street Finder, pp122–7, map 4

Calle Enna is Havana's narrowest and shortest street. It was named after a general active in the colonial period.

❻ ★ El Templete

This Neo-Classical building, shaded by a majestic ceiba tree, evokes memories of the city's foundation.

CALLE O-REILLY

AVENIDA DEL PUERTO

PLAZA DE ARMAS

CALLE BARATILLO

CALLE OFICIOS

CALLE JÚSTIZ

Hotel Santa Isabel is in the former home of the Conde de Santovenia, built between the 18th and 19th centuries and comprehensively restored *(see p256)*.

La Casa de los Arabes housed the city's first school in the 17th century.

❼ Calle Oficios

This perfectly restored colonial street houses a number of shops and museums, including a vintage car museum.

0 metres	60
0 yards	60

Key

— Suggested route

Stairway leading to the battlements, Castillo de la Real Fuerza

❺ Castillo de la Real Fuerza

O'Reilly e/Tacón y Avenida del Puerto. **Map** 4 F2. **Tel** 7864 4490. **Open** 9:30am–5pm Tue–Sun.
Note: fee for photography may apply.

This fortress (castillo) was built in 1558–77 to protect the city from pirate attacks, following a raid by the French buccaneer Jacques de Sores in 1555, in which the original fort was destroyed and Havana devastated (see p44). But despite its moat and thick walls, the castle soon proved to be quite inadequate as a defensive bulwark because of its poor strategic position, too far inside the bay. The castle then became the residence of governors, military commanders and leading figures, as well as a safe place to store treasures brought from America and en route to Spain. In 1634, a weathervane known as La Giraldilla was placed on the lookout tower, which soon became the symbol of Havana. The original is on display in the entrance and a copy has been placed on the tower. In 1851, part of the fortress's façade was demolished to enable Calle O'Reilly to be extended to the waterfront. This street was named for Alejandro O'Reilly, an Irishman who became a Spanish military commander in the 18th century and who advised King Carlos III of Spain on improving Havana's defences after the British invasion of 1762.

Today, the Castillo houses a shipwreck museum with displays of artifacts, jewels and a large model of the naval ship *Santísima Trinidad*.

La Giraldilla

There are various theories as to the meaning of the bronze weather-vane sculpted by Gerónimo Martín Pinzón in 1630–34 and modelled on the one crowning La Giralda in Seville. Some people say it is the symbol of victory, others think it is the personification of Seville, the final destination of ships going to Europe. But others say the statue represents Inés de Bobadilla, wife of the Spanish governor Hernando de Soto. According to legend, she spent hours gazing at the horizon, waiting for her husband to return from his exploration of Florida and other parts of the US (in vain, since he died on the banks of the Mississippi). This is said to be the reason why the statue was placed on the highest point of the fortress dominating the port entrance.

The tower with its copy of the 17th-century weathervane

❻ El Templete

Plaza de Armas, Calle Baratillo y O'Reilly. **Map** 4 F2. **Open** 9am–5pm Tue–Sun. **Closed** 1 Jan, 1 May.

Small and austere, this Neo-Classical building, resembling a temple, stands on the spot where, according to legend, the city of San Cristóbal de La Habana was founded in 1599. Here, under a leafy ceiba – a tropical tree considered sacred by all the natives of Central America – the first meeting of the local government (the cabildo) and the first mass reputedly took place. A majestic ceiba tree still stands in front of El Templete, although it is not the original. Next to it is

Castillo de la Real Fuerza, with its drawbridge, entrance, moat and Giraldilla tower (left)

the Columna de Cacigal, a column named after the governor who ordered its construction in 1754.

El Templete, completed in 1828, was modelled after a monument in the Basque town of Guernica in northern Spain. Inside are three enormous canvases by Jean-Baptiste Vermay *(see p30)*, depicting scenes from the history of Havana: the local authorities inaugurating the building, the first *cabildo*, and the first mass, which was celebrated by Bishop Juan José Díaz Espada y Land, who blessed the city as part of the ceremony.

The First Mass, one of Vermay's paintings in the Templete

❼ Calle Oficios

Map 4 F2.

This is one of the capital's oldest streets, branching out from the city's roots in the Plaza de Armas, and is among only four Havana streets in existence from the end of the 16th century. It was originally a link between the military centre of Plaza de Armas and the commercial and harbour activities centred around Plaza San Francisco. Together with Calle Obispo, this is one of the most atmospheric streets in Old Havana and should be toured slowly (don't miss the many interesting façades which predominantly date from the 18th and 19th

centuries). Today, the buildings are occupied by a number of shops, hotels and restaurants.

The street is split in two by the Plaza de San Francisco. North of the plaza is No. 16, the 18th-century **Casa de los Arabes**. It displays 18th- and 19th- century Hispanic-Arab bronzes, fabrics, rugs and furniture: the largest ethnographic display of Arab objects in Cuba, evidence of the presence of an old Lebanese, Syrian and Palestinian colony on the island. The building also houses the only mosque in Cuba. The small prayer hall is beautifully inlaid with mother-of-pearl.

South of Plaza de San Francisco, tucked away down Calle Churruca, is the **Coche Mambí**, a handsome green-and-white train coach dating from 1900. For several decades from 1912, it was the official railroad accommodation for successive presidents of Cuba. Visitors can step inside to look

The Casa de los Arabes patio, with narrow balconies and a Moorish-style fountain

closely at the plush reception, dining rooms and lounge, with their dark wood panelling, and the neatly fitted bedroom and kitchen.

🏛 **Casa de los Arabes**
Tel 7861 5868. **Open** 9am–5pm Tue–Sat, 9am–1pm Sun.

🏛 **Coche Mambi**
Open 9:30am–5:30pm Tue–Sat, 9:30am–1pm Sun. 🖼

Havana's Indoor Arts Market

The Almacenes San José, a vast crafts market, opened in 2009 as part of the revitalization of the harbour area of Old Havana. In a restored warehouse just south of the cruise-ship docks, the Almacenes San José is a one-stop shopping centre for handmade Cuban arts and crafts. The space is enormous, and the number of stalls can seem overwhelming, but it's a useful place to pick up souvenirs. Search around and there are some gems to be had, and most stall holders are not averse to bartering. The second-hand book and

Paintings of classic cars and Che Guevara for sale at the craft market, Almacenes San José

curio market that sprung up in Plaza de Armas during the 1990s is expected to move to the upper floor. The vast beer hall and restaurant, the Antiguo Almacén de la Madera y el Tabaco, is next door.

⓿ Palacio de los Capitanes Generales

Construction of this palace, a splendid example of Cuban Baroque (see p28), took from 1776 to 1791. It was commissioned by the governor Felipe Fondesviela and designed by engineer Antonio Fernández de Trebejos y Zaldívar. The Palacio originally housed the Chapter House and the governor's residence as well as a house of detention, which until 1834 occupied the west wing. The seat of the Cuban Republic in 1902, the building became the Museo de la Ciudad (City Museum) in 1967, but the original structure of the sumptuous residence and political centre has not been altered. The complex as a whole offers an overview of the history of Havana, from the remains of the old Espada cemetery and Parroquial Mayor church to mementos from the wars of independence.

★ Hall of Flags
This hall contains objects from the independence wars, including the flag of Céspedes (see p46).

The Cabildo Maces
Considered the first major example of Cuban goldsmithery, these maces, by Juan Díaz (1631), are on display in the Sala del Cabildo, the room where local town council meetings were held in the governor's palace.

★ Christ of Humbleness and Patience
Once carried through the streets in processions, this 18th-century devotional wooden statue is, in the fashion of the time, naturalistically painted with glass eyes and real hair to increase its dramatic impact on the faithful.

KEY

① **The White Room** has on display the escutcheons of Bourbon Spain and the city of Havana, and is decorated with 18th- and 19th-century Meissen porcelain.

② **The stained-glass windows** brighten the grey of the piedra marina, a limestone encrusted with coral fossils.

③ **The Espada Cemetery Room** has relics from the first city cemetery, founded by Bishop Juan José Díaz de Espada in 1806. They include the tomb of the French artist Vermay (see p30).

④ **The portico pavement**, made of china pelona, a hard, shiny stone, dates from the 18th century.

Leather Cannon
Taken from the Cuban independence fighters by the Spanish army in 1873, this makeshift weapon – a lead pipe wrapped in horsehide – was loaded with whatever projectiles were at hand, from shrapnel to stones.

Gallery

The monumental gallery, which overlooks a large, leafy courtyard, features a collection of busts of illustrious figures, the work of the Italian sculptor Luigi Pietrasanta in the early 1900s.

VISITORS' CHECKLIST

Practical Information
Plaza de Armas, Calle Tacón, e/
O'Reilly y Obispo. **Map** 4 E2.
Tel 7861 2876, 7861 5062. **Open**
9:30am–4pm Tue–Sun. 🎥 📷 📷
Note: fee for photography applies.

Throne Room

Modelled on the large salon in the Palacio de Oriente in Madrid, this room was originally built for a Spanish monarch, but never used. It was restored in 1893 for the visit of Princess Eulalia of Bourbon.

★ Salón de los Espejos

The end of Spanish rule was proclaimed in 1899 in this light-filled salon with its 19th-century Venetian mirrors, and in 1902 the first president of the Republic of Cuba took office here.

Casa del Agua la Tinaja, vendor of purified well water

❾ Calle Obispo

Map 4 E2.

The liveliest and most characteristic street in Old Havana is like a long, narrow bridge linking the two architectural souls of the historic centre, the colonial and the Art Nouveau-eclectic. At one end is the Plaza de Armas, the Cuban Baroque heart of the old city, while at the other is Avenida de Bélgica and the famous El Floridita restaurant, which mark the start of the more modern district. The street is called Calle Obispo because in the past the city bishop (obispo) resided in the building situated on the corner of Calle Oficios.

Old filter, Taquechel pharmacy

Thanks to the restoration work promoted by the Oficina del Historiador de la Ciudad, headed by the charismatic Eusebio Leal Spengler, aimed at salvaging the best buildings in the old area, Calle Obispo has retained the elegance, vivacity and colours of the colonial period. Street lighting makes for enjoyable evening strolling.

A plaque on the left-hand side of the Palacio de los Capitanes Generales bears quotations made by the great Cuban patriot José Martí concerning Garibaldi's stop at Havana. Opposite is the small shop window of the **Casa del Agua la Tinaja**, which for centuries has been dispensing well water purified by very old but still quite efficient ceramic filters. Next door, **La Mina** restaurant serves food and cocktails outdoors and brightens up the whole block with live traditional music (see p270).

Among the most fascinating shops in this part of the street is the old pharmacy called **Taquechel**, which sells cosmetics and natural and homeopathic products, all created and produced in Cuba. Quaint shelves boast a pretty collection of 17th- and 18th-century glass and Italian majolica jars, as well as alembics and antique pharmaceutical and medical objects. No. 117–19 is the oldest house in Havana (see p28).

One of the major sights in the street is the restored **Hotel Ambos Mundos**

An old letter box at No.115

(see p256). This charming, eclectically decorated hotel is rich in literary memories. The writer Ernest Hemingway stayed here for long periods from 1932 to 1939 (see p118), and began writing his famous novel For Whom the Bell Tolls in room 511.

Towards the end of the street, near the small Obispo y Bernaza

Wooden "azul avana" blue doors of the colonial house at No. 117

square, there are more modern shops offering everything from embroidered shirts to books.

Next is **El Floridita** restaurant (see p270), known as "the cradle of the daiquirí". It was here, in the 1930s, that barman Constante (his real name was Constantino Ribalaigua) perfected the original cocktail mixed by Pagluchi (see p269). The new-style daiquirí, a blend of white rum, lemon, sugar and a few drops of maraschino and ice, was devised with the help of Ernest Hemingway, who was a regular. Today, in El Floridita's luxurious interior, besides Constante's classic cocktails you can feast on lobster and shellfish in the company of a bust of the great novelist. It was sculpted by Fernando Boada while Hemingway was still alive.

Typical majolica jars on the shelves of traditional pharmacy Taquechel

The upper gallery of the Casa de la Obra Pía, with its frescoed walls and polished wood balustrade

⑩ Casa de la Obra Pía

Calle Obrapía 158, esq. Mercaderes.
Map 4 E2. **Tel** 7861 3097.
Open 9:15am–4:45pm Tue–Sat,
9am–12:30pm Sun. **Closed** 1 Jan, 26
Jul, 10 Oct, 25 Dec.

Calle Obrapía (literally Charity Street) was named after this mansion, whose own name commemorates the pious actions of Martín Calvo de la Puerta y Arrieta, a wealthy Spanish nobleman who took up residence here in the mid-17th century. Every year he gave a generous dowry to five orphan girls for them to use to get married or enter a convent. A century later the residence became the home of Don Agustín de Cárdenas, who was given the title of marquis for taking Spain's side in 1762 during the British occupation of Havana (see p45). In 1793 new decoration, and the elaborate arch leading to the loggia on the first floor, were added to the building.

La Casa de la Obra Pía is regarded as one of the jewels of Cuban Baroque architecture, and its luxurious salons were used for young noblewomen to make their debut in society. Visitors

CALLE DE LA OBRA-PIA

Majolica tile street sign for Calle de la Obrapía

can appreciate its bygone opulence in the upper rooms, which have been decorated with colonial furnishings and decorative ware.

The mansion also houses a small museum of sewing machines, a reconstruction of Alejo Carpentier's study and an art gallery.

At the corner of Calle Obrapía and Calle Mercaderes is the **Casa de México**, a cultural centre that shows the close links between Mexico and Cuba. It has a library with more than 5,000 books and a museum displaying handmade glass, silver, fabric, terracotta and wooden objects. Lastly, on the other side of the street is the **Casa de Guayasamín**, named after the Ecuadorean painter whose works are on display.

Palo Monte objects (see p27), Casa de Africa

⑪ Casa de Africa

Calle Obrapía 157, e/ San Ignacio y Mercaderes. **Map** 4 E2. **Tel** 7861 5798.
Open 9:30am–5pm Tue–Sat,
9am–1pm Sun. **Closed** 1 Jan, 26 Jul,
10 Oct, 25 Dec.

Opposite the Casa de la Obra Pía is a 17th-century building that was rebuilt in 1887 to accommodate a family of plantation owners on the upper floor, and a tobacco factory, worked by slaves, on the ground floor. It is appropriate that the building is now a museum containing more than 2,000 objects linked to the history of sub-Saharan Africa and the various ethnic groups that were taken to Cuba on slave ships. Many of these items belonged to the ethnographer Fernando Ortíz, a specialist in the African roots of Cuban culture. Together with the section on religion, which includes objects from Afro-Cuban religions (see pp26–7), there are instruments of torture used on the slaves, batá drums, and paintings of plantation life. The museum also has a well-stocked library.

⓬ Plaza de San Francisco

Map 4 F2. Basílica Menor de San Francisco de Asís: **Tel** 7862 9683. **Open** 9:30am–6:30pm daily. **Closed** 1 Jan, 1 May, 26 Jul, 10 Oct, 25 Dec. 🅰 📷

Bordering the port, this picturesque square has an Andalusian character and evokes images of a distant age when galleons loaded with gold and other cargo set sail for Spain. In the middle of the square is the **Fuente de los Leones**, modelled on the famous fountain in the Alhambra in Granada. This work by the Italian sculptor Giuseppe Gaggini was donated in 1836 by the fiscal superintendent, Don Claudio Martínez de Pinillos, the Count of Villanueva, and for many years it supplied the ships docked here with drinking water.

The original commercial nature of the area can be seen in two buildings: the Aduana General de la República (the old customs house), built in 1914, and the **Lonja del Comercio** (the former stock exchange, 1908), with a dome crowned by a statue of Mercury, god of commerce. Restored in 1995, this building houses the offices of some of the top foreign firms now operating in Cuba.

The most important building in the square, however, is the **Basílica Menor de San Francisco de Asís**, built in

The Fuente de los Leones, Plaza de San Francisco

1580–91 as the home of the Franciscan community and partly rebuilt in the 1700s. The three-aisle interior has a Latin cross layout and contains some paintings by unknown 18th-century Cuban artists and a wooden statue of St Francis dating from the same period, again by an unknown artist. The basilica also has the remains of major Havana citizens, from the Marquis González, who died during the British siege of 1762, to José Martín Félix de Arrate, an illustrious historian of the colonial period. Because of its exceptional acoustics, this church has been converted into a concert hall for choral and chamber music every Saturday at 6pm *(see p129)*.

Attached to the church is a large, 42-m (138-ft) high bell tower. Originally a statue of St Francis of Assisi stood on the top, but it was badly damaged by a cyclone in 1846.

In the cloister and rooms of the adjacent monastery, which dates back to 1739, is a museum of holy art with 18th–19th-century missals, a collection of votive objects made of precious metals, and 16th–18th-century majolica and ceramics.

⓭ Museo del Ron

Calle San Pedro 262. **Map** 4 F3. **Tel** 7861 8051. **Open** 9:30am–5:30pm Mon–Thu, 9am–4:30pm Fri–Sun. 🅰 📷 🅿 💻

The manufacture of Havana Club, the most famous brand of Cuban rum, is displayed here with visuals and models that explain the production process of the spirit described as the "cheerful child of sugar cane" by Cuban writer and journalist Fernando Campoamor, a friend of Ernest Hemingway. The organized tours begin in the colonial courtyard of the Havana Club Foundation. After watching a brief film on the history of sugar cane and its cultivation, visitors are taken through rooms with exhibits that explain the fermentation, distillation (in a room with old alembics), filtration, ageing, blending and bottling processes. In the central hall is a fascinating model of an *ingenio (see pp46–7)*, or sugar plantation, which also includes a miniature steam train. Tours end in a bar where visitors can relax and sample three-year-old rum. The street-front bar also serves excellent cocktails and often has live music; it is open from 9am to midnight. The shop sells rum, glassware and various souvenirs.

Logo of the Havana Club Foundation

Interior of the basilica of San Francisco, now used for chamber music concerts

Cuban Rum

The history of rum dates back to the early 1500s, when an impure distillate was first obtained from sugar cane. With the arrival of Don Facundo Bacardí *(see p232)*, a new technique of distillation was introduced, and Cuban rum *(ron)* went on to enjoy international success. Rum is part of everyday life in Cuba: a constant companion at parties and festivities, the main ingredient in cocktails, and an offering that is frequently given to the gods of *Santería*. Rum-making begins with the main by-product of sugar, the sticky amber paste called molasses, which is diluted with water and fermented using special yeasts. The "must" thus obtained is then distilled and filtered to produce an eau de vie. Purified water and pure alcohol are then added 18 months later to produce Silver Dry, a young, clear rum.

Distillation, which used to be effected by means of alembics *(left)*, is now carried out by using a series of connected tubes in which the molasses vapour is channelled until it condenses and is transformed into a colourless liquid that is then aged in special barrels.

The *mezcla* process is carried out under the expert guidance of a master taster and consists of mixing the new rum with other rums. Once blended, the rum rests for a few weeks in special vats until the right balance of taste and aroma is obtained.

Special oak barrels are used for the ageing process which takes at least three years. With time the rum becomes richer in colour and more full-bodied, like the seven-year añejo. The temperature, humidity level and ventilation in the ageing cellars are carefully regulated.

The Types of Rum

Besides Silver Dry, which is normally used in cocktails, the market offers rum aged for three years (carta blanca), *five years* (carta oro), *and seven years* (añejo), *or even longer. Old rum, which is the most highly prized, should be drunk neat and at room temperature, while* carta blanca, *which is the most commonly seen, can be used in many ways and is often drunk with ice. There are assorted brands of Cuban rum, not all of which are internationally known like Havana Club.*

Silver Dry   Carta Blanca   Carta Oro   Añejo

The cloister of the convent of Santa Clara, filled with tropical plants

⓮ Alameda de Paula

This short waterfront promenade, built in the 18th century and later restored, forms part of the rebirth of the Havana bayside area. Lined with trees, benches and balustrades, the promenade is marked at its southern end by the Iglesia de Paula. This small church once served as the chapel of a 17th-century hospital. Today, it functions as a classical music concert venue. Across the road is Havana's largest craft market, the Antiguo Almacenes San José.

Near the market is the **Museo Automóvil** (Automobile Museum), located in a waterfront warehouse. It boasts an eclectic selection of cars, such as a 1927 Chevrolet Capitol, a 1924 Dodge, and four Harley Davidson motorbikes. There is also a Bel-Air Chevrolet that once belonged to Che Guevara.

🏛 Museo Automóvil
Avenida del Puerto. **Tel** 7863 9942.
Open 9:30am–5pm Tue–Sat,
9am–1pm Sun. **Closed** 1 Jan. 🈲 🖪

⓯ Plaza Vieja

Map 4 E3.

This square was laid out in 1559 and was originally called Plaza Nueva (New Square). In the 19th century, after the widening of Plaza de Armas and the creation of other urban areas, it lost its role as the city's main public square and was renamed Plaza Vieja. From the 1950s to the 1990s it was a car park, but it has now been restored to its original appearance.

The plaza is surrounded by arcades and a number of historic buildings from four different centuries. The most important of these is the **Casa del Conde Jaruco**. This was the home of the Countess de Merlin, a Cuban romantic novelist who became a French citizen and also wrote a travel book about Cuba. The edifice of the building is a fusion of Baroque and Spanish Moorish styles. While parts of the house are inaccessible due to structural issues, the Galería Diago on the ground floor has a small art and poster shop.

Next door are two 17th-century buildings, and at the corner of Calle Muralla and Calle Inquisidor is the eye-catching Art Nouveau Hotel-Palacio Cueto. It was first built as a hotel in 1908, then later turned into apartments and is now being restored as a five-star hotel. Diagonally opposite is the Centro de Desarollo de las Artes Visuales (Center for the Development of Visual Arts), one of the main venues of the Bienal de La Habana (see p38).

A fountain designed in 1796 stands in the middle of the square. It bears the crest of the city and of the Count of Santa Clara, then the city's governor. Nearby are a camera obscura, an important photo gallery and a high-tech planetarium.

Façade of Casa del Conde Jaruco, with typical *mediopunto* stained-glass windows on the first floor

The nave of the Iglesia de la Merced, illuminated by small light bulbs

⑯ Iglesia del Espíritu Santo

Calle Cuba esq. Picota. **Map** 4 E3. **Tel** 7862 3410. **Open** 9am–noon Tue–Sun, 3–6pm Tue, Thu & Sat, 3–5pm Wed & Fri. 🖾 ✝ 5pm Thu & Sat, 10:30am Sun.

The Church of the Holy Ghost (Espíritu Santo) is of historical importance as one of the oldest Roman Catholic churches in Havana. It was built in 1637 by freed African slaves. Thanks to a papal bull and a royal decree from Carlos III, in 1772 it acquired the exclusive right to grant asylum to all those persecuted by the authorities.

From an architectural standpoint, the building's most striking feature is the tower, which is almost as tall as the one on the Basilica of San Francisco (see p78). The church was radically rebuilt in the 19th century, retaining its Hispanic-Arab look only in the characteristic double pitch roof. The main chapel was built by Bishop Jerónimo Valdés in 1706–29.

Close by is the domed, white Catedral Ortodoxa Nuestra Senora de Kazán (Avenida del Puerto, e/ Sol y Santa Clara). It was built in 2008 to commemorate Cuban-Russian friendship.

⑰ Iglesia de Nuestra Señora de la Merced

Calle Cuba 806, esq. Habana. **Map** 4 F3. **Tel** 7863 8873. **Open** 8am–noon, 3–5pm daily. ✝ 9am Thu–Tue.

Construction of this church began in 1637 but ended only in the following century, while the lavish decoration of the interior dates from the 19th century. The church is popular among those who follow *Santería*, or local Afro-Cuban religion (see pp26–7). According to the beliefs of this cult, Our Lady of the Merced corresponds to a Yoruba divinity known as Obatalá, principal figure among the gods and the protector of mankind, who imparts wisdom and harmony.

On the Catholic saint's feast day, 24 September, *Santería* followers come dressed all in white – the colour associated with Obatalá.

⑱ Casa Natal de José Martí

Calle Leonor Perez 314, e/ Egido y Picota. **Map** 4 E4. **Tel** 7861 3778. **Open** 9:30am–4:30pm Tue–Sat, 9:30am– 12:30pm Sun. **Closed** 1 Jan, 1 May, 26 Jul, 10 Oct, 25 Dec. 🖾 🗂

This modest 19th-century building in the Paula quarter became a national monument thanks to the special historic importance attached to José Martí (see p49), who is the object of great patriotic veneration. The author and national hero, who died in combat on 19 May 1895 during the wars of independence against the Spanish, was born here in 1853. After his death, his mother Leonor Pérez lived in the building, and when she died it was rented to raise money to bring up her grandchildren. In 1901, it was purchased by the municipality after city-wide fundraising, and was turned into a museum in 1925, but government funding only became sufficient with the advent of Fidel Castro.

The house has been restored beautifully, and visitors can view furniture, paintings, and first editions of the writer's works. There are also objects of great historic value such as the inkpot

Portrait of José Martí by Herman Norman in Casa Natal de José Martí

and ivory pen used by Generalissimo Máximo Gómez and José Martí to sign the *Manifesto de Montecristi*, which officially marked the beginning of the war against Spain. Everyday objects are also on display, such as the penknife Martí had in his pocket when he died, and the album with dedications and signatures from friends during his wedding to Carmen Zayas-Bazán.

CENTRO HABANA AND PRADO

Centro Habana has the air of an impoverished aristocrat – a noble creature whose threadbare clothes belie a splendid past full of treasures. This varied quarter developed beyond the city walls (which ran parallel to present-day Avenida Bélgica and Avenida de las Misiones) during the 1800s and was initially built to provide housing and greenery for the citizens. Most of the construction took place after 1863, when the walls began to be demolished to make more land available. The work was finally completed in the 1920s and 30s, when French architect Forestier landscaped the area of the Paseo del Prado, the Parque Central, the Capitolio gardens and Parque de la Fraternidad.

Sights at a Glance

Historic Buildings
1 Hotel Inglaterra
3 Capitolio pp86–7
5 Real Fábrica de Tabacos Partagás
6 Palacio de Aldama
8 Castillo de San Salvador de la Punta

Historic Streets and Plazas
4 Parque de la Fraternidad
7 Paseo del Prado pp90–91
15 Avenida Carlos III
16 Callejón de Hammel
17 City Walls

Quarters
13 Barrio Chino

Theatres
2 Gran Teatro de La Habana

Churches
10 Iglesia del Ángel Custodio
14 Iglesia del Sagrado Corazón

Museums
9 Museo Nacional de la Música
11 Museo de la Revolución pp92–3
12 Museo Nacional de Bellas Artes pp96–9

See also Street Finder, pp122–7, maps 3 & 4

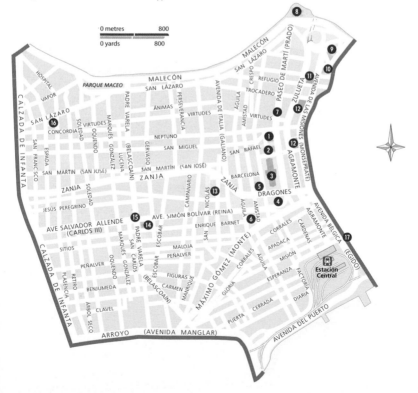

◀ The Capitolio, once the seat of Cuba's government – and soon to be again   **For keys to symbols** *see back flap*

Street-by-Street: Around the Parque Central

Lying on the border of the old city and Centro Habana, between the Capitolio and the Prado promenade, the Parque Central was designed in 1877 after the old city walls were demolished. A statue of Isabella II was put in the middle of the square but was later replaced by one of José Martí. The park is surrounded by 19th- and 20th-century monumental buildings and adorned with palm trees. It is the heart of the city centre and a popular meeting place. Towards evening, when the air is cooler, people gather here to talk until the small hours of the night about baseball, music and politics.

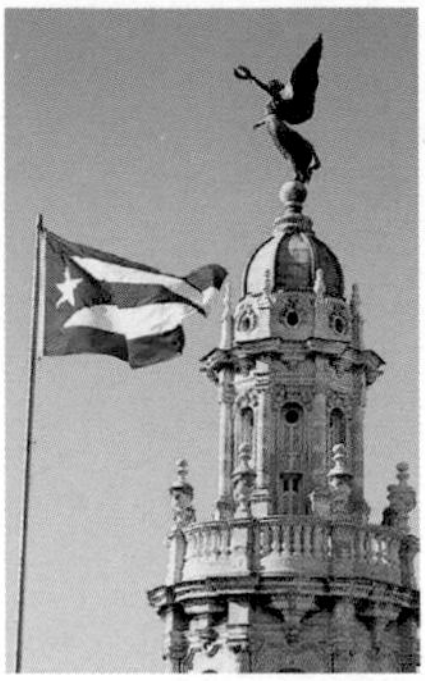

❷ ★ Gran Teatro de La Habana
With one of its rooms named after the great Spanish poet, García Lorca, who stayed in Havana for a few months in 1930, the theatre is a mixture of influences with slender, angular towers.

REAL FABRICA DE TABACOS
FLOR DE TABACOS
PARTAGAS
HABANA
CIFUENTES Y Cª

❺ Real Fábrica de Tabacos Partagás
This elegant red and cream-coloured building is home to a prestigious cigar factory.

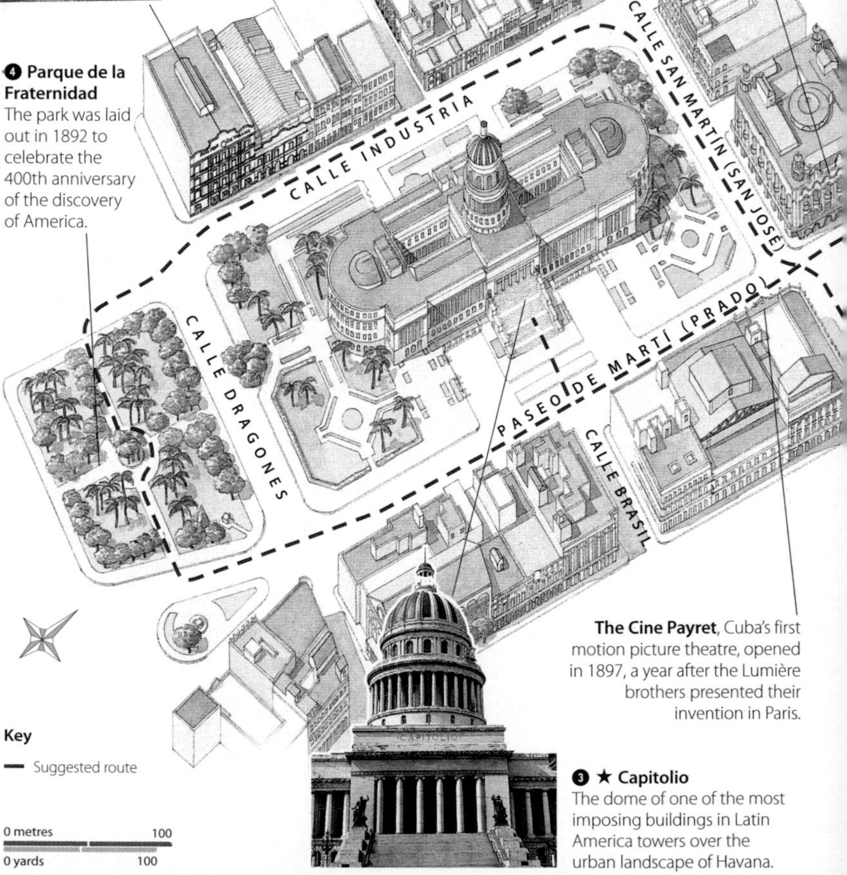

CALLE INDUSTRIA
CALLE SAN MARTÍN (SAN JOSÉ)
CALLE DRAGONES
PASEO DE MARTÍ (PRADO)
CALLE BRASIL

❹ Parque de la Fraternidad
The park was laid out in 1892 to celebrate the 400th anniversary of the discovery of America.

The Cine Payret, Cuba's first motion picture theatre, opened in 1897, a year after the Lumière brothers presented their invention in Paris.

❸ ★ Capitolio
The dome of one of the most imposing buildings in Latin America towers over the urban landscape of Havana.

Key

— Suggested route

0 metres 100
0 yards 100

For hotels and restaurants in this area see pp256–7 and p271

❶ ★ Hotel Inglaterra
This historic hotel has retained its 19th-century atmosphere. Despite the British name, the architectural elements and decoration are clearly Spanish-inspired.

Locator Map
See Street Finder, pp122–7, map 4

Calle San Rafael, known as *Boulevard*, is a narrow street for pedestrians only. Up to the 1950s it was famous for its luxury shops and boutiques.

The Iberostar Parque Central is modern but its design blends in well with the surroundings *(see p257)*.

❼ ★ Paseo del Prado
This avenue, the locals' favourite for strolling, is lined with lovely buildings with carefully restored arcades.

CALLE NEPTUNO

PARQUE CENTRAL

CALLE SAN RAFAEL

The statue of José Martí, Cuba's national hero, was sculpted in Carrara marble in Rome by José Vilalta y Saavedra and inaugurated on 24 February 1905 by Generalissimo Máximo Gómez.

The Manzana de Gómez, a 19th-century building, was once a major commercial centre. It is due to open as a five-star hotel in 2017.

The Centro Asturiano, with the characteristic towers on its corners, was designed by Spanish architect Manuel del Busto and opened in 1928. It is home to the Museo de Bellas Artes' international art collection *(see pp96–9)*.

The Hotel Plaza, built in the 19th century as a private residence, became a hotel in 1909. It was frequented by great artists of the time, from Isadora Duncan to Enrico Caruso and Anna Pavlova.

❶ Hotel Inglaterra

Paseo de Martí (Prado) 416, esq. a San Rafael. **Map** 4 D2. **Tel** 7860 8594.
Ⓦ **hotelinglaterra-cuba.com**

Although this hotel is built in the style of late 19th-century Havana Neo-Classical architecture, its soul is *mudéjar* (Moorish): the fine ochre, green and gold majolica tiles of the interior were imported from Seville, the foyer is decorated with Andalusian mosaics, and the wooden ceilings are reminiscent of Moorish inlay. Plus, one of the columns in the *salón-café* bears a classical Arabic inscription: "Only Allah is the victor". The Hotel Inglaterra dates from 1875, when a small hotel merged with the lively Le Louvre night spot and its adjacent ballroom. The pavement outside the hotel, known as the "Louvre sidewalk", was an animated meeting point for Havana liberals. It was here that the young José Martí *(see p49)* advocated total separation from Spain, as opposed to more moderate liberal demands for autonomy. General Antonio Maceo, a hero of the wars of Cuban independence, prepared plans for insurrection in this hotel.

Among many illustrious guests were the great French actress Sarah Bernhardt and the Russian ballet dancer Anna Pavlova.

❷ Gran Teatro de La Habana

Paseo de Martí (Prado) y San Rafael. **Map** 4 D2. **Tel** 7861 7391. 🖼 🎫
9am–5pm Tue–Sat, 9am–1pm Sun.
Note: fee for photography may apply.

One of the world's largest opera houses, Gran Teatro de La Habana is part of the monumental Palacio del Centro Gallego (1915), designed by Belgian architect Paul Belau to host the social activities of Havana's large and affluent Spanish community.

The magnificent façade is decorated with four sculpture groups by the Italian sculptor Giuseppe Moretti, depicting Charity, Education, Music and Theatre. The building lies over

❸ Capitolio

A symbol of the city, the Capitol (Capitolio) combines the elegance of Neo-Classicism with Art Deco elements. Inaugurated in 1929 by the dictator Gerardo Machado, it is a loose imitation of the Washington DC Capitol, but is even taller. It stands in an area once occupied by a botanical garden and later by the capital's first railway station. The home of government until 1959, the Capitol has seen major historic events: in 1933 the police fired on a crowd gathered here during an anti-Machado demonstration. The building is currently being restored in preparation for a return to its role as the seat of the Cuban government.

The staircase of honour, originally reserved for MPs

National Library of Science and Technology

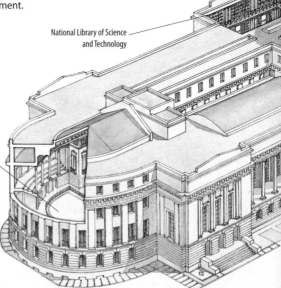

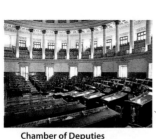

Chamber of Deputies
The Chamber still has its original furnishings and is decorated with bas-reliefs by the Italian artist Gianni Remuzzi.

Façade of the former Centro Gallego building, now home to the Gran Teatro

the foundations of the Teatro Nuevo or Tacón. From 1837 to the early 20th century this was the venue for performances by world-famous artists, including the Austrian ballet dancer Fanny Essler, who made her debut here in 1841. In the mid-19th century Antonio Meucci, the inventor of the "talking telephone", worked here as a stagehand, and his invention was patented in the US, thanks to the support of the Gran Teatro's impresario.

The theatre was inaugurated on 22 April 1915 with a performance of Verdi's *Aida*, and became a stage for great dramatic occasions. Sarah Bernhardt performed here in 1918, and the pianist Arthur Rubinstein the following year. Cuban composer Ernesto Lecuona and the great Spanish guitarist Andrés Segovia have also appeared.

In 1959 the Gran Teatro, though continuing as a concert hall and theatre, became the "home" of Alicia Alonso, the great Cuban ballet dancer. She founded the Ballet Nacional de Cuba, the dance company responsible for organizing the famous Festival Internacional de Ballet de la Habana (see p40 and p129). After two years of meticulous renovation the theatre reopened in 2016 and now looks particularly magnificent at night when the exterior is majestically illuminated.

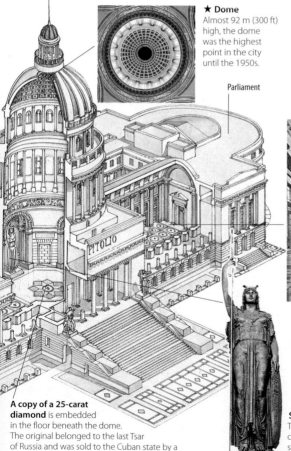

★ **Dome**
Almost 92 m (300 ft) high, the dome was the highest point in the city until the 1950s.

Parliament

A copy of a 25-carat diamond is embedded in the floor beneath the dome. The original belonged to the last Tsar of Russia and was sold to the Cuban state by a Turkish jeweller. It was stolen and, mysteriously, later turned up on the President's desk.

VISITORS' CHECKLIST

Practical Information
Paseo de Martí (Prado), esq. a San José. **Map** 4 D3. **Tel** 7864 9168. **Closed** for restoration.
Note: fee for photography applies.

★ **Salón de los Pasos Perdidos**
This sumptuous hall, with fine marble floors and gilded lamps, takes its name ("Hall of Lost Steps") from its unusual acoustics.

Statue of the Republic
This work, cast in Rome and covered with 22-carat gold leaf, stands 17 m (56 ft) high and weighs 49 tons. It is the third tallest statue in the world.

❹ Parque de la Fraternidad

Map 4 D3.

The spacious area of greenery behind the Capitol was called Campo di Marte (Parade Ground) in the 19th century, because it was near the Paseo Militar, used frequently for army drill. As the Parque de la Fraternidad (since 1928), it commemorates Cuba's common roots with the other people of the Americas, with monuments to major figures such as the Argentine José de San Martín, the Venezuelan Simón Bolívar, and US president Abraham Lincoln.

In the middle of the park is a gate with a plaque bearing an exhortation by José Martí: "It is time to gather and march together united, we must go forward as compact as the silver in the depths of the Andes. Peoples unite only through bonds of friendship, fraternity and love." Beyond the gate is a monument to American friendship and solidarity: a large ceiba – a tree sacred to both the Amerindians and the African slaves taken to the New World – planted here around 1920.

In front of the square is a white marble fountain, sculpted in 1831 by Giuseppe Gaggini. The fountain is known as the "Fuente de la India" or "La Noble Habana" – an allegorical representation of the city.

Nowadays the Parque de la Fraternidad is usually full of old American cars, most of which operate as private taxis.

The Fuente de la India symbolizing Havana

Façade of the Partagás cigar factory with its prominent pediments

❺ Real Fábrica de Tabacos Partagás

Calle Industria 524. **Map** 4 D3.
Tel 7879 1404. **Closed** for restoration; call for more information. 📷 🎥
🏠 💻 ✉️

Cuba's largest cigar factory, with its Neo-Classical façade, is a good example of 19th-century industrial architecture. It was founded in 1845 by the ambitious Catalan businessman Jaime Partagás Ravelo. However, he never revealed the sources of his tobacco leaves or how they were processed. The only information that survives is that he was the first person to use wooden barrels to ferment the leaves in order to heighten the aroma.

Neon sign at the Partagás cigar factory

With the profits made from his high-quality cigars, Partagás bought a plantation in the province of Pinar del Río. He wanted to oversee all aspects of the cigar-making process personally, from growing the plants to the placing of a wrapper leaf around the filler and binder leaves rolled by the *torcedor (see p37).* However, Partagás was assassinated in mysterious circumstances and the project failed.

His factory was then purchased by another shrewd businessman, Ramón Cifuentes Llano.

Dozens of people work in the aroma-filled interior. Nowadays, there is no longer someone reading aloud to alleviate the monotony of the work by entertaining and educating the workers, as was the case in the 19th century (Partagás himself introduced this custom to Cuba). However there is a loudspeaker that alternates reading passages with music and news on the radio. Connected to the factory is La Casa del Habano, an excellent shop with a back room that is used for sampling cigars.

❻ Palacio de Aldama

Avenída Simón Bolívar (Reina) y Máximo Gómez (Monte). **Map** 3 C3. **Closed** to the public.

This mansion *(see p29)* was designed by Manuel José Carrera and built in the middle of the 19th century, having been commissioned by the rich Basque industrialist Domingo de Aldama y Arrechaga. He had to depend on his influential friends in order to obtain permission to build his residence in front of the Campo di Marte, or Parade Ground, which was reserved for military and administrative buildings. The monumental grandeur of this Neo-Classical building, considered the finest example of 19th-century architecture in Cuba, is still striking. The mansion is now the seat of the Instituto de Historia de Cuba. Sadly, it is not officially open to the public, but upon request the porter allows visitors to go into the courtyard to admire the impressive marble staircases, Baroque arches, splendid wrought iron with Imperial motifs and the two inner gardens with fountains made of Carrara marble.

The monument to General Máximo Gómez

❼ Paseo del Prado

See pp90–91.

❽ Castillo de San Salvador de la Punta

Malecón y Paseo de Martí (Prado). **Map** 4 D1. **Tel** 7860 3196. **Open** 10am–6pm Wed Sun.

A modest fortified block on the west bank of the port entrance, this fortress *(castillo)* played a crucial role in the past as part of the defence system of the capital. Today, it is a modest three-room museum comprising naval-themed exhibits along with displays on the history of the fortress. Designed by Giovanni Bautista Antonelli, Juan de Tejeda and

Cristóbal de Roda and built in 1590–1630, it was part of the city's first line of defence, together with the much larger Castillo de los Tres Reyes del Morro on the other side of the bay. A large floating chain of wooden and bronze rings, an ingenious device added by the Italian engineer Antonelli in the late 16th century, connected the two fortresses. It was stretched tightly as soon as an enemy ship was sighted, to block access to the port. In the open space in front of the Castillo are the three cannons to which the chain was tied.

The adjacent open space across the road has several monuments that are more important historically than artistically. In the middle is the equestrian statue of Generalissimo Máximo Gómez, the hero of the wars of independence, by Italian sculptor Aldo Gamba (1935). Behind this, a dilapidated chapel is used daily for stamp exhibitions and history lectures. It originally belonged to the Real Cárcel prison, where José Martí was kept for 16 years for subversive activities against the Spanish crown. Some cells still stand, as does a section of the wall against which some medical students were executed on 27 November 1871 as punishment for rebelling against Spanish rule. A cenotaph in their honour stands in the Columbus cemetery *(see p108).*

The Museo de la Música, an example of eclectic architecture

❾ Museo Nacional de la Música

Calle Capdevila 1, e/ Habana y Aguiar. **Map** 4 E1. **Tel** 7861 9846, 7863 0052. **Closed** for restoration until August 2017.

The building (1905) that houses the National Music Museum is a mixture of different styles, a perfect example of 20th-century eclectic architecture. It was the residence of a family of opera lovers, whose guests included such illustrious figures as the great Italian tenor Enrico Caruso and the Spanish poet Federico García Lorca.

The museum was founded in 1971, and contains the largest collection of traditional musical instruments in Cuba, gathered by the ethnologist Fernando Ortiz, a pioneer in the study of Cuba's African roots. Besides the most complete collection of African drums in the world, there is the piano of singer and composer Bola de Nieve *(see p34)* and 40 guitars used by legendary figures of 20th-century Cuban music, such as the Trío Matamoros and Sindo Garay. Also on show are gramophones and phonographs, photos and famous composers' original manuscripts. In the foyer is a music stand with the score of the Bayamo, the Cuban national anthem. Visitors can consult specialist Cuban and foreign periodicals, as well as the archive of rare musical documents.

The Castillo de la Punta ramparts and the Morro fortress behind

❼ Paseo del Prado

The most picturesque boulevard in Havana is popular in the daytime for a gentle stroll and gossip in the shade of the trees, and at sunset is one of the locals' main haunts. The Marquis de la Torre had the Paseo laid out in 1772 outside the city walls, and it rapidly became the favourite spot for city aristocrats to take their carriage rides. Bands were positioned in five spots along the boulevard to play for their enjoyment. The Paseo was used for military and carnival parades in the 19th century, when the paving was redone. In 1927 the French architect Forestier designed the Prado as we see it today: it was widened and lined with bronze lions and marble benches.

Lions
Eight imposing bronze lions, symbolizing Havana, were added to the boulevard in 1927, together with the marble benches.

Neo-Moorish Building
The building at the corner of Calle Virtudes, richly decorated and with *mudéjar* arches, shows many architectural influences and is typical of Havana.

Hotel Sevilla
This historic hotel is a homage to Moorish architecture: the façade and hall decoration are *mudéjar (see p28)* in style. The ten-storey tower was added in 1917.

Palacio de los Matrimonios
Named after the civil weddings celebrated on the first floor, this Neo-Baroque building was inaugurated in 1914 as the Casino Español.

KEY

① **Casa del Científico** was the residence of José Miguel Gómez, second President of the Republic of Cuba.

② **Dr Carlos Finlay**, who discovered that mosquitoes spread yellow fever, lived here.

③ **The Art Deco Teatro Fausto** was built in 1938 over the foundations of an old theatre of the same name.

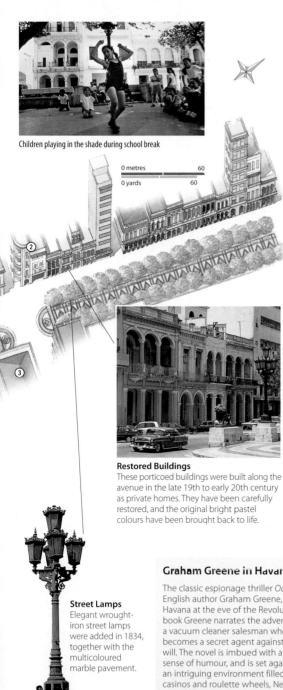

Children playing in the shade during school break

0 metres 60
0 yards 60

Restored Buildings
These porticoed buildings were built along the avenue in the late 19th to early 20th century as private homes. They have been carefully restored, and the original bright pastel colours have been brought back to life.

Street Lamps
Elegant wrought-iron street lamps were added in 1834, together with the multicoloured marble pavement.

⑩ Iglesia del Ángel Custodio

Calle Compostela 2, esq. Cuarteles.
Map 4 D2. **Tel** 7861 0469.
Open 8:30am–6pm Mon–Fri, 8:30am–noon Sun. ⛪ 9am Mon, Fri & Sun, 5pm Tue–Thu.

Built in 1693 on the Peña Pobre or "Loma del Ángel" hill as a hermitage and then transformed into a church in 1788, today the Neo-Gothic Ángel Custodio looks rather too white and unreal as a result of vigorous "restoration".

Standing in a key position between the former presidential palace (now the Museo de la Revolución) and the old town, it exudes literary references. The 19th-century Cuban novelist Cirilo Villaverde *(see p32)* used the Loma del Ángel hill as the setting for his story *Cecilia Valdés* about the tragic love affair between a Creole woman and a rich white man.

Félix Varela *(see p32)* and José Martí *(see p49)* were both baptised in this church.

The bell tower and spires of the church of Ángel Custodio

Graham Greene in Havana

The classic espionage thriller *Our Man in Havana* (1958), by the English author Graham Greene, is an excellent description of Havana at the eve of the Revolution. In the book Greene narrates the adventures of a vacuum cleaner salesman who becomes a secret agent against his will. The novel is imbued with a dry sense of humour, and is set against an intriguing environment filled with casinos and roulette wheels, New York skyscrapers and decadent Art Nouveau villas, cabarets and prostitution. The Hotel Sevilla is a constant presence in the background.

Graham Greene (1904–91)

⓫ Museo de la Revolución

The idea of putting the Museum of the Revolution in the former presidential palace of the dictator Fulgencio Batista was clearly symbolic. Designed by the Cuban architect Rodolfo Maruri and the Belgian architect Paul Belau, the building was inaugurated in 1920 by Mario García Menocal, and it remained the residence for all subsequent presidents until 1965. The building has Neo-Classical elements, and was decorated by Tiffany of New York. It contains works by the leading Cuban decorators of the early 1900s and by sculptors such as Juan José Sicre, Esteban Betancourt and Fernando Boada. The museum features documents, photographs and memorabilia presenting an overview of the Cubans' struggle for independence from the colonial period on, focusing in particular on the 1959 Revolution – from the guerrilla war to the Special Period in the 1990s.

Statues of Che Guevara and Camilo Cienfuegos
These life-size wax statues depict the two heroes in combat.

Granma Memorial

The large glass and cement pavilion in the tree-lined plaza behind the museum contains the yacht *Granma* (named after its first owner's grandmother). In 1956, this boat brought Fidel Castro and some of his comrades from Mexico to Cuba to begin the armed struggle against Batista *(see p52)*. There are also objects and vehicles relating to the invasion of the Bay of Pigs (1961), remains of an American spy plane shot down in 1962 during the missile crisis, and the delivery truck that was used by revolutionaries to attack the palace in 1957.

The remains of a plane

For hotels and restaurants in this area see pp256–7 and p271

The Dome
The inside of the dome, visible from the staircase, consists of multicoloured ceramics. It includes four panels, decorated by Esteban Valderrama and Mariano Miguel González, against a gold leaf background.

VISITORS' CHECKLIST

Practical Information
Calle Refugio 1, e/ Avenida de las Misiones y Zulueta. **Map** 4 D2.
Tel 7862 4091. **Open** 9am–8pm daily (last entry 4:15pm).

★ Salón de los Espejos
Lined with vast mirrors (espejos), the reception hall of the former presidential palace has ceiling frescoes by Cuban painters Armado Menocal and Antonio Rodríguez Morey.

KEY

① **The side wing** of the palace was home to Batista's office.

② **The third floor** contains photos and memorabilia from colonial times to 1959.

③ **The second floor** displays the President's desk, the Council of Ministers and memorabilia from 1959 to the present day.

④ **The tall windows** are similar to those in the Gran Teatro de La Habana, and were designed by the same architect, Paul Belau.

⑤ **The terrace** opposite the Salón de los Espejos has a fine view of the Bay of Havana.

Entrance

★ Main Staircase
The monumental staircase, which leads to the first floor, still bears marks of the bullets shot here on 13 March 1957, during an attack by some revolutionary university students on a mission to kill Batista. The dictator managed to save his life by escaping to the upper floors.

⑫ Museo Nacional de Bellas Artes

See pp96–9.

⑬ Barrio Chino

Map 3 C3.

The Chinese quarter of Havana, the Barrio Chino, which now occupies a small area defined by Calles San Nicolás, Dragones, Zanja and Rayo, developed in the 19th century. In its heyday, in the early 1900s, there was a cultural association performing plays and operas, and a casino. The colourful streets were full of vendors of fritters and other Asian specialities, and people came to buy the best fruit and freshest fish in the city.

Today, all the Chinese shops are concentrated in the so-called Cuchillo de Zanja area (the intersection of Zanja and Rayo), a mixture of the oriental and the tropical; the architecture, however, is not particularly characteristic, except for the quarter gate,

The austere interior of Iglesia de la Caridad

which has a pagoda roof. Another, much more impressive Ming and Ching-style portico was erected in 1998 at the corner of Calle Dragones and Calle Amistad. It is almost 19 m (62 ft) wide and was donated to Cuba by the Chinese government.

The Barrio Chino is also home to the **Iglesia de la Caridad**, dedicated to Cuba's patron saint *(see p225)*. The church also has a popular statue, a Virgin with Asian features, brought here in the mid-1950s.

The Chinese Community in Havana

The first Chinese arrived in Cuba in the mid-1800s to work in the sugar industry, and they were treated like slaves. The first to gain their freedom began to cultivate small plots of land in Havana. In one of these, near the present-day Calle Salud, they grew Cuba's first mangoes, which were an immediate, spectacular success. Chinese restaurants began to appear in the area after the second wave of Chinese immigrants arrived from California (1869–75), armed with their American savings. Without losing any of their cultural traditions, the Chinese community has become assimilated into Cuban society, accepting and sharing the island's lot. A black granite column at the corner of Calle Linea and Calle L remembers the Chinese who fought for Cuban independence.

Entrance gate to Barrio Chino, the Chinese quarter in Havana

⑭ Iglesia del Sagrado Corazón

Avenida Simón Bolívar (Reina) 463. **Map** 3 B3. **Tel** 7862 4979. **Open** 7:30am–6pm Mon–Sat, 8am–noon & 3–5pm Sun. ☐ 8am & 9am daily. ☑ ☑

With its impressive bell tower, 77 m (253 ft) high, the Church of the Sacred Heart can be seen from various parts of the city. It was designed in the early 1900s by the Jesuit priest Luis Gorgoza and consecrated in 1923, and is a rare example of the Neo-Gothic style in Cuba.

Dominating the façade is a figure of Christ resting on three columns decorated with a capital depicting the parable of the prodigal son. The interior has elaborate stained-glass windows narrating the life of Christ and a wealth of stucco-work and pointed arches. A Byzantine-style Sacred Heart with sculptures of saints and prophets is on the high altar.

Entrance to the Iglesia del Sagrado Corazón, with its statue of Christ

⑮ Avenida Carlos III

(Avenida Salvador Allende) **Map** 3 B3.

Laid out in 1850 during redevelopment under the supervision of Captain Miguel de Tacón, this boulevard (official name Avenida Salvador Allende) was designed to allow troops and military vehicles to go from the Castillo del Príncipe – built on the Aróstegui hill in the late 1700s – to their parade ground in the present-day Parque de la

Callejón de Hamel, famous for its exotic and colourful murals

Fraternidad. The middle section of the boulevard was reserved for carriages, while the two side avenues with their benches, trees and fountains were for pedestrians. First named Alameda de Tacón or Paseo Militar, it was renamed Avenida Carlos III in honour of the Spanish king who encouraged Cuban commerce and culture in the 18th century.

One of the most curious buildings on the street is the Grand National Masonic Temple, with a globe on the roof, built in the mid-1900s.

⓰ Callejón de Hamel

Map 3 A2.

This street in the working-class Cayo Hueso quarter is a curious open-air Afro-Cuban sanctuary. Its name derives from a legendary French-German resident called Fernando Hamel, a wealthy arms dealer-turned-merchant, who took the entire quarter under his wing. The colourful, 200-m (656-ft) mural here, for which the street is now famous, is the work of native painter Salvador González. He wanted to pay homage

to his varied cultural roots by representing all the religious cults and movements of African origin that are still active in Cuba, hence the many symbols, writings, and images of African gods and Abakuá devils (see p27). He began this enormous project in 1990.

This alley has everything: from small shops selling hand-crafted religious objects to a *Nganga*, the large cauldron-like pot which forms the basis of Palo Monte, the religion of former Bantu slaves from the African Congo. On Sundays Callejón de Hamel becomes the venue for rumba shows, popular with the locals and tourists alike.

Representation of Oshún, the goddess of love

⓱ City Walls

Avenida del Puerto **Map** 4 D5.

The old colonial city of San Cristóbal de La Habana was encircled and fortified by a 9-m (30-ft) high wall with nine bastions and a moat. Construction began in 1671 and took over a century to complete, finishing in 1797.

Once finished, the gates were closed every evening and access to the bay was blocked by a chain. Cannon shots were fired every night from a ship anchored in the bay, informing the inhabitants that the gates were closing. By the early 19th century, the city was expanding so fast that finally in 1863 the walls had to be torn down. Today, the best remaining sections are opposite the Museo de la Revolución and by the train station.

Remaining section of the old City Wall near Estación Central

⑫ Museo Nacional de Bellas Artes

The National Fine Arts Museum was founded on 23 February 1913 thanks to the efforts of the architect Emilio Heredia, its first director. After frequent moves, the collections eventually found a definitive home in the block once occupied by the old Colón market. The original design was changed when the arcades of the building were demolished and in 1954 the new Palacio de Bellas Artes was inaugurated, a Rationalist building with purely geometric lines designed by the architect Rodríguez Pichardo. The museum is now divided between two buildings: the original palacio dedicated to Cuban art, and the Centro Asturiano, by the Parque Central, dedicated to international art.

Locator Map
See Street Finder, p127, map 4

Virgin and Child
This triptych by Hans Memling (1433–94) exemplifies the vivid style and masterful spatial construction that made this artist one of the great masters of Flemish painting.

Sagrada Familia
The *Holy Family* by the Spanish artist Bartolomé Esteban Murillo (1618–82), who enjoyed great fame during his lifetime, is a calm, meditative scene.

Centro Asturiano
European painting and sculpture, together with the collection of ancient art, are on display in the Centro Asturiano, designed in 1927 by the architect Manuel del Busto.

★ Panathenaean Amphora
This terracotta amphora in the black figure style is one of the most important pieces in the museum's collection of ancient Greek vases, which once belonged to the Count de Lagunillas.

★ **La Habana en Rojo** (1962)
Havana in Red is part of a long series that René Portocarrero dedicated to the capital. This painting in particular expresses the passionate Baroque spirit that characterizes all of Portocarrero's work.

The permanent collection
is displayed in chronological order on the first and second floors.

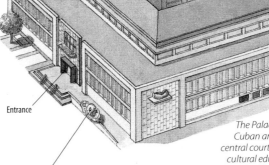

Entrance

Palacio de Bellas Artes

The Palace of Fine Arts is entirely given over to Cuban art. Sculptures line the perimeter of the central courtyard, which houses service rooms for cultural education, the auditorium, library, shop and café. The two upper floors feature galleries divided into three sections: colonial, academic and 20th-century art (divided into decades from the 1930s to the 1990s).

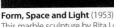

Form, Space and Light (1953)
This marble sculpture by Rita Longa, at the museum entrance, is characterized by a fluid concept of volume. Two male figures create a harmonious counterpoint.

★ **La Silla** (1943)
One of several fine works in which Wifredo Lam combines Cubism and Surrealism and adds a distinctively Cuban stamp: a Cubist chair with a vase on it is set in the magical context of the jungle.

Exploring the Museo Nacional de Bellas Artes

During the reassessment of many of Cuba's cultural institutions after 1959, a large number of works were added to the original museum collection – the result of the confiscation of property that had been misappropriated. The collection was divided into two sections: Cuban and international art. The first consists of paintings, prints, drawings, and sculptures; the second has paintings, sculptures and drawings primarily from Europe, the US and Latin America, with some works dating from the Egyptian to the Roman age.

Clotilde en los Jardines de la Granja by Joaquín Sorolla

Centro Asturiano (International Art)

The building, designed in 1927 as the home of the collection of international art, has maintained its original architectural elements, with furnishings, iron grilles, stained-glass windows and chandeliers. Besides the gallery, the place also has communal areas for the public, study rooms, a book shop, café, a video room and an auditorium.

The collection of international art comprises paintings and sculptures displayed in specific sections. These include the Middle Ages, Italy, Germany, Flanders, the Netherlands, Great Britain, France and Spain. There are also works from various European schools, the United States and Latin America.

Head of the god Amon, ancient Egyptian sculpture

Among the finest works in the collection are the Flemish paintings and the 19th-century Spanish pictures, including one by Joaquín Sorolla: *Entre Naranjos* (1903). In this the artist depicts a banquet in the countryside, using the play of the figures, light and shadow to create an Impressionist-like atmosphere. The same can be said of the movement of the water and the garden in the background in *Clotilde en los Jardines de la Granja*, which is a portrait of the artist's wife. Other Spanish artists represented are Murillo and Zurbarán. Then there are works by Constable, Bouguereau and Van Mieris.

The Italian collection includes a group of landscape paintings, including one by Canaletto: *Chelsea College, Rotunda, Ranelagh House and the Thames* (1751), in which the painter brilliantly renders the atmosphere of London. There is also a scene of Venice by Francesco Guardi, *The Lagoon in front of the Fondamenta Nuove*, a youthful work with the delicate rendering that characterized his later production. Other Italian works are *St Christopher* by Jacopo Bassano (c.1515–92), *Alpine Landscape with Figures* by Alessandro Magnasco (1667–1748), and *The Spinstress* by Giovanni Battista Piazzetta. *The Reception of a Legation* by Vittore Carpaccio (1490) has a rigorously symmetrical composition.

The ancient art section is also fascinating: Greek, Roman and Egyptian works, as well as Mesopotamian, Phoenician and Etruscan finds. The 5th-century BC Greek amphora and the Fayoum portraits are especially interesting.

Palacio de Bellas Artes (Cuban Art)

The permanent exhibition of 18th–21st-century Cuban art offers a complete overview of works by individuals and schools, and highlights the leading trends in each period. The temporary exhibition of prints and drawings, as well as of paintings, adds variety and

One of the many views that Canaletto painted of London

richness to the permanent collection, which has works by the great masters of contemporary Cuban art.

Two of the major figures are painter Wifredo Lam (*La Silla*, 1943) and sculptor Agustín Cárdenas, who were both influenced by the European avant-garde and African art. The free play of volumes in the wooden sculpture *Figure*, less than 1 m (3 ft) high, expresses to the full the African-derived sensuality that informs Cárdenas's style.

Cuban art in the 19th century, characterized by its technical skill, is represented by the portraits of Guillermo Collazo, an academic and painter, and landscapes by the Chartrand brothers. Other artists with an academic background are Armando García Menocal and Leopoldo Romañach, a painter and lecturer at the Academy.

The pioneers of modern Cuban art are particularly interesting. One of these is Víctor Manuel García, an exceptional landscape painter who conveys peaceful atmospheres with silently flowing rivers and figures with sinuous movements. García is the creator of the "mestizo" archetype: *Gitana Tropical* (Tropical Gypsy, 1929) includes a figure of a woman against the background of a

El Malecón by Manuel Mendive, an extraordinary Naive painting

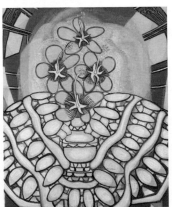

Figure (1953) by Augustín Cárdenas

barren landscape, which has become a symbol of Cuban painting *(see p30)*. There are several works by Amelia Peláez, who revived the still-life genre by merging Cubism and specifically Cuban motifs; among these are *Naturaleza Muerta sobre Ocre*, executed in 1930 in Paris, and *Flores Amarillas*, a mature work that marks a return to more simple compositions after a "Baroque" period.

El Rapto de las Mulatas (1938), by Carlos Enríquez, is a dream-like "tangle" of human figures, horses and landscape that echoes the classical theme of the rape of the Sabine women. It is considered emblematic of Cuban painting and of this artist's oeuvre. The sensuality of the human bodies and the tropical atmosphere in this work provide a key to the interpretation of the motifs of traditional art.

The chronological display of works illustrates the development of Cuban art. In the 1950s there was a move away from figurative art, as seen in the work of Guido Llinás and Hugo Consuegra. After the

victory of the Revolution in 1959, Cuban art embraced extremely varied styles. Servando Cabrera first took guerrillas as his subject and then made an erotic series. Antonia Eiriz was a particularly powerful Neo-Expressionist, and Raúl Martínez began with abstract art and then absorbed elements of Pop Art.

Another renowned contemporary artist is Manuel Mendive who, in embracing Cuba's African heritage, searches for the hidden depths of existence. *El Malecón* (1975), one of his most significant works, depicts the city's famous promenade as if it were an almost sacred site where people mingle with African gods. The style here is at once naive and sophisticated.

Of the leading artists of the 1970s there are works by Ever Fonseca, Nelson Domínguez, and illustrator Roberto Fabelo, who has a very unique style. Among the younger artists (all graduates of the historic San Alejandro Academy and Escuela Nacional de Arte), Tomás Sánchez, with his archetypal landscapes, and José Bedia, with his bold installations, stand out. The artists who continue to emerge on the Cuban art scene – thanks to the Biennial Art Fair – exhibit their works in the many temporary shows.

Of the considerable number of works in its possession, the museum now exhibits many paintings, drawings, prints and sculptures.

Flores Amarillas (1964), a still life dating from Amelia Peláez's mature phase

VEDADO AND PLAZA

The unusual grid plan of Vedado was the design of the engineer Luis Yboleón Bosque in 1859. It called for pavements 2-m (6-ft) wide, houses with a garden, and broad straight avenues. The name Vedado ("prohibited") arose because in the 1500s, in order to have full view of any pirates approaching, it was forbidden to build houses and streets here. In the late 19th and early 20th century the quarter was enlarged, becoming a prestigious residential area for many of the city's leading families. Vedado has two different roles. It is Havana's modern political and cultural centre, with the city's main hotels, restaurants, shops, theatres, cinemas, offices and ministries; and it is also a historic quarter with a wealth of gardens and old houses with grand colonial entrances. Plaza de la Revolución, the venue for major celebrations, is the political centre of Havana and the whole of Cuba, as well as a highly symbolic place.

Sights at a Glance

Museums and Galleries
3 Museo de Artes Decorativas
5 Museo Napolcónico

Historic Buildings
2 Casa de las Américas
4 Universidad de La Habana
6 Quinta de los Molinos

Monuments
8 Memorial José Martí p107

Streets and Squares
7 Plaza de la Revolución

Cemeteries
9 Necrópolis de Colón pp108–9

Walks
1 A Walk through Vedado pp102–3

See also Street Finder, pp122–7, maps 1 & 2

Key

• • • Walk pp102-3

● A Walk through Vedado

This walk takes in the broad avenues which are typical of Vedado, providing a taste of the district's odd architectural mix of 1950s high-rises and crumbling Neo-Classical mansions. There is only one museum on this route (Vedado has few conventional attractions), leaving you free to simply stroll and look around. Calle 23, modern Havana's most well-known street, is the main reference point for the walk. The most famous section is the first few blocks, known as La Rampa.

The Hotel Habana Libre, with the mosaic *La Fruta Cubana* (1957)

The Hotel Nacional viewed from the Focsa tower

Key

• • • Suggested route

| 0 metres | | 300 |
| 0 yards | | 300 |

Malecón

The stretch of the Malecón where this walk begins is dominated by the headland occupied by the Hotel Nacional ①. This gem of Art Deco architecture opened in 1930 (see p257). Many famous guests have stayed here including Winston Churchill, Fred Astaire, Buster Keaton and Walt Disney. The hotel park offers lovely views across the bay.

La Rampa

Head briefly south to reach La Rampa (the first rising stretch of Calle 23 between the seafront and Calle N). Modern and lively, lined with offices, restaurants and bars with old-fashioned neon signs, La Rampa would pass for a typical 1950s street were it not for the façade of the Ministry of Sugar (or AZCUBA) with its revolutionary mural and

the "futuristic" Pabellón Cuba, which hosts exhibitions. This part of the walk is accompanied by the unmistakable profile of the Edificio Focsa ②, a sky-scraper built in the 1950s.

This route also takes you by a small open-air crafts market and the Centro de Prensa Inter-nacional, which caters to foreign journalists.

Calle 23

In the middle of the park at the corner of Calle 23 and L is the Coppelia ice-cream parlour ③, a large glass and metal building (1966). This classic location in Havana was made famous by Tomás Gutiérrez Alea's film *Strawberry and Chocolate (see p33).*

Coppelia is the most popular ice-cream parlour in the city (hence the queues).

On the other side of Calle 23 is the impressive Tryp Habana Libre (see p257), with a tiled mural by renowned Cuban artist Amelia Peláez. The hotel first opened in 1958, and a year later was requisitioned from the Americans and became Fidel Castro's headquarters. Inside are two mosaics by Portocarrero and Sosabravo (see pp30–31). At the intersection with Calle J is the Parque El Quijote ④, a tree-filled area with a modern statue of a nude Don Quixote on horseback by Sergio Martínez. Further along Calle 23 the buildings lessen in height and are more varied in style.

The statue of Don Quixote by Sergio Martínez (1980)

Itinerary

① Hotel Nacional
② Edificio Focsa
③ Coppelia
④ Parque El Quijote
⑤ Museo de la Danza
⑥ Casa de la Amistad
⑦ ICAIC

The long queue for the Coppelia ice-cream parlour

VISITORS' CHECKLIST

Practical Information
Departure: Hotel Nacional.
Arrival: corner of 23 y 12.
Length: 3.5 km (2 miles).
Where to eat: Coppelia ice-cream parlour, Casa de la Amistad, one of the bars at the corner of 23 y 12. Plan stops and museum visits for the (hot) middle of the day. Museo de la Danza: **Tel** 7831 2198. **Open** 10am–5pm Tue–Sat. **Closed** 1 Jan, 1 May, 26 Jul, 25 Dec.

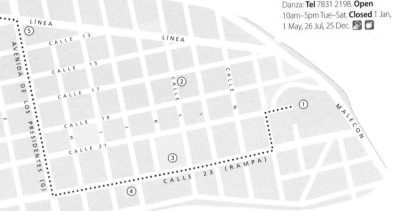

Avenida de los Presidentes

The tour continues by turning right at Calle G (Avenida de los Presidentes), a wide, tree-lined avenue with luxurious 19th- and 20th-century French-style buildings. In the middle of the street are benches and flower beds. Behind the statue of Simón Bolívar is the junction with Calle Línea.

Calle Línea

The first street to be laid out in the Vedado quarter owes its name to the tramline (*línea*) that once ran from here to the historic centre. Calle Línea also has many French-style buildings as well as colonial houses with stained-glass windows.

The restored building at the corner of Calle G is the Museo de la Danza ⑤, run by the legendary ballerina Alicia Alonso, founder of the Ballet Nacional (*see p87*). The only dance museum in Latin

Alicia Alonso's shoes, Museo de la Danza

America, it has mementos of famous dancers who have visited Cuba, drawings of stage sets, historic photos and works by contemporary artists.

Paseo

Continue along Calle Línea to the junction with one of the loveliest streets in Havana: Calle Paseo, which is like a long, thin park running up to the Plaza de la Revolución (*see p106*). It is lined with elegant buildings with splendid gardens: mostly ministries and public administration offices. The Casa de la Amistad ⑥, at No. 406 between Calle 17 and 19, is a cultural centre with a bar and restaurant, and part of a lavish Art Deco building given by the wealthy Pedro Baró to his mistress Catelina Lasa, grande dame of Havana high society. They were forced to flee to Europe by the scandal caused by their affair, but returned in 1917, when Lasa managed to get a divorce from her first husband.

23 y 12

Continue on Calle Paseo back to Calle 23, six blocks away from the busy central intersection where this walk ends. A sculpture of Fidel with the Granma revolutionaries has an inscription declaring that on 16 April 1961, on the eve of the American invasion at the Bay of Pigs (*see p171*), Fidel Castro announced that the Cuban Revolution was Socialist.

At Calle 23 y 12 there are restaurants, bars, shops and cinemas like the Chaplin Cinematheque and the Cuban Institute of Cinematographic Arts and Industry (ICAIC) ⑦ (*see p33*), which has a contemporary art gallery.

The permanent poster exhibition in the ICAIC building

The Art Deco building that is the home of the Casa de las Américas

❷ Casa de las Américas

Calle 3ra, esq. G. **Map** 1 C1. **Tel** 7838 2706, 7838 2707. **Open** 10am–4pm Mon–Fri. **Closed** 1 Jan, 1 May, 26 Jul, 10 Oct, 25 Dec. 🅦 **casa.cult.cu**

On the Malecón, beyond the Monument to the Victims of the *Maine (see p62)*, there is a kind of secular temple, with a bell tower but no cross. This is the Casa de las Américas, a cultural institution, which was built in just four months after the triumph of the Cuban Revolution. Haydée Santamaría, one of the heroines of the struggle, founded the Casa with the aim of promoting exchanges among artists and writers on the American continent.

The centre features Arte Nuestra América, the most comprehensive collection known of Latin American painting and graphic art from the 1960s to the present.

❸ Museo de Artes Decorativas

Calle 17, 502. **Map** 2 D2. **Tel** 7832 0924. **Open** 9am–4:45pm Tue–Sat. **Closed** 1 Jan, 1 May, 25 Dec. 🎨 🎟 Note: fee for photography applies.

The wonderful Museum of Decorative Arts is housed in the former residence of one of the wealthiest Cuban women of the 20th century: the Countess de Revilla de Camargo, sister of José Gómez Mena, the owner of the Manzana de Gómez *(see p85)*. The mansion was built in 1927, and is well worth a visit for its French Rococo-Louis XV furnishings, as well as for the inner gardens.

The collection reveals the sophisticated and exotic tastes of the ruling classes and wealthy collectors of the colonial period. Major works of art here include two paintings by Hubert Robert, *The Swing* and *The Large Waterfall at Tivoli*, and two 17th-century bronze sculptures in the foyer.

The main hall on the Louis XV-style ground floor has 18th-century Chinese vases, Meissen porcelain, a large Aubusson carpet dating from 1722 and paintings by French artists.

A bedroom on the ground floor holds a collection of Chinese screens, while the Countess's room features a secretaire that once belonged to Marie Antoinette.

Last but not least is the pink marble Art Deco bathroom, which should not be missed.

Chinese porcelain, Museo de Artes Decorativas

❹ Universidad de La Habana

Calle 27 de Noviembre (Jovellar) y Ronda. **Map** 2 F2. Museo Antropológico Montané: Felipe Poey Bldg, Plaza Ignacio Agramonte. **Tel** 7877 4221. **Open** 9am–2pm Mon–Fri. **Closed** 1 Jan, 1 May, 26 Jul, 10 Oct, 25 Dec.

The University of Havana was founded under the auspices of a papal bull in 1728 and was initially housed in the Dominican monastery of St John Lateran, in the heart of La Habana Vieja. In 1902, a few days after the proclamation of the Cuban Republic, it was transferred to the Vedado area to a site which had been utilized as an explosives store in the colonial period.

The new university, housed in various buildings, was built between 1906 and 1940. In front of the main entrance, now the venue for concerts, is the Alma Mater, the symbol of Havana University. This statue, of a woman with

The Neo-Classical foyer of the Museo de Artes Decorativas

The austere façade of the University of Havana, with the statue of the Alma Mater at the top of the staircase

her arms outstretched in a gesture of welcome, was cast in 1919 in New York by the Czech sculptor Mario Korbel. It was installed at the top of the broad granite stairway that forms the entrance to the complex in 1927. The grand entrance to the university overlooks Calle San Lázaro, which broadens out into an open space where the ashes of Julio Antonio Mella are kept *(see p50)*.

In the Science Faculty, the Felipe Poey Museum of Natural History is open to visitors. Of much greater interest, however, is the **Museo Antropológico Montané**, in the Mathematics Department. Founded in 1903, this museum has exceptional Pre-Columbian archaeological finds from Cuba, such as the Idolo de Tabaco found on the eastern tip of the island, the Idolo de Bayamo, one of the largest stone sculptures in the entire Caribbean area, and the Dujo de Santa Fe, a wooden ceremonial seat.

The oldest building on the hill is the Great Hall, with an austere façade behind which are allegorical paintings by Armando Menocal. The hall itself contains the old University of San Gerónimo bell, used to convene the professors, and the remains of Félix Varela *(see p32)*, brought to Cuba in 1911 from Florida, where the Cuban intellectual had died.

➎ Museo Napoleónico

Calle San Miguel 1159, esq. a Ronda. **Map** 2 F3. **Tel** 7879 1412, 7879 1460. **Open** 9:30am–5pm Tue–Sat, 9:30am–noon Sun. 🎫 📷

The surprising presence of a Napoleonic museum in Cuba is due to the passion of a sugar magnate, Julio Lobo. For years he sent his agents all over the world in search of Napoleonic mementos. In 1959, when Lobo left Cuba, the Cuban government bought his collection.

Every room in this curious museum contains fine examples of imperial-style furniture as well as all sorts of surprising Napoleonic memorabilia, including one of the emperor's teeth and a tuft of his hair. There are two portraits, one by Andrea Appioni, painted in Milan during Napoleon's second Italian campaign, and another by Antoine Gros. There is also his death mask, cast two days before Napoleon's death by Francesco Antommarchi, the Italian physician who had accompanied him to the island of St Helena and who later settled in Cuba.

The restored mansion itself was built in the 1920s by Oreste Ferrara, counsellor to the dictator Gerardo Machado, who furnished it in a Neo-Florentine Gothic style.

Idolo de Tabaco, Museo Montané

➏ Quinta de los Molinos

Avenida Carlos III (Salvador Allende) e/ Infanta y Calle G. **Map** 2 F3. **Tel** /8/3 6510. **Open** 10am–noon Tue, Thu & Sat. 🎫 📷 in Spanish only.

A typical 19th-century villa in the Vedado quarter, the Quinta de los Molinos offers a verdant retreat amid the bustle of the city. It was built as the summer residence of the captains-general in 1837. The villa stands in a leafy area with two tobacco mills *(molinos)*. Built by the royal decree, the mills were operated from early to mid 19th-century, and were powered by the waters of the city's aqueduct system.

Following an ambitious restoration project, the rambling grounds around the villa are now home to the lush botanical gardens, which are crisscrossed with pathways. The gardens contain a wealth of plant life, including many indigenous Cuban species. A colourful butterfly house is also located at the rear end of this oasis.

A stained-glass window in the Quinta de los Molinos

A parade in front of the Ministerio del Interior, Plaza de la Revolución

❼ Plaza de la Revolución

Map 2 E5.

Plaza de la Revolución has been Cuba's political, administrative and cultural centre since 1959. The square was designed in 1952 under the Batista regime, and most of the buildings visible today also date from the 1950s. What had been known as the Plaza Cívica was renamed Plaza de la Revolución following Fidel Castro's victory in 1959.

Though it does not distinguish itself by its architecture or design, the square is nonetheless an important place to visit because of its historic and symbolic importance. It was the venue for the first mass rallies following the triumph of the Revolution and of the festivities for the campaign against illiteracy in 1961.

Since 1959, military parades and official celebrations have often attracted crowds of more than a million people. During these events the area fills with people, and the speakers take their place on the podium next to the statue of José Martí, at the foot of the obelisk.

On the morning of 30 September 2015, Pope Francis celebrated mass from this podium together with thousands of worshippers.

🏛 Ministerio del Interior
Calle Aranguren.

A huge bronze wire sculpture of Che Guevara, completed in 1995, stretches up the façade of the Ministry of the Interior, where the guerrilla fighter had his office in the early 1960s. This striking and symbolic image was inspired by the world-famous photograph taken by the press photographer Alberto Korda *(see p180)*. The façade is illuminated at night.

🏛 Museo Postal Cubano
Ave Rancho Boyeros y 19 de Mayo. **Tel** 7881 5551. **Open** 8am–4:30pm Mon–Fri. **Closed** 1 Jan, 1 May, 26 Jul, 10 Oct, 25 Dec. 🎫 📷 Note: fee for photography may apply.

This fascinating postal museum has occupied a small corner of the building of the Ministry of Informatics and Communications since 1965. A steel wire sculpture of revolutionary commander Camilo Cienfuegos *(see p54)*, added in 2009 and much like the one of Che Guevara, hangs on the ministry's façade.

The museum illustrates the last two centuries of Cuban history through the medium of stamps, from the end of the colonial period to the years following the fall of the Berlin Wall, including the wars of independence, and figures like Machado, Batista and Che Guevara.

The most curious item on display is a fragment of a "postal missile". In 1939, a group of Cubans decided to use a missile for "express airmail deliveries" from Havana to Matanzas, but the crude device exploded a few minutes after "take-off".

The Teatro Nacional seen from Martí's memorial

🏛 Palacio de la Revolución
Calle Martí.

The former Ministry of Justice (1958) behind the Martí Memorial now houses the offices of the Council of State, the Council of Ministers and the Central Committee of the Communist Party. It was here that Fidel Castro received Pope John Paul II on 22 January 1998.

The elegant wooden card-index files in the Biblioteca Nacional

🏛 Biblioteca Nacional José Martí
Plaza de la Revolución. **Tel** 7855 5442. **Open** 8:15am–6:15pm Mon–Fri, 8:15am–4:15pm Sat. 📷 Call ahead to reserve, 7881 7657. 📷

The José Martí National Library has over two million books and is particularly strong in the humanities. The United States embargo, plus the Special Period crisis, have slowed the development of a library computerization programme, but all services are being modernized.

🎭 Teatro Nacional
Paseo y 39. **Tel** 7878 0771.

Built with a striking convex façade, the National Theatre is Cuba's most important cultural complex. It was inaugurated in June 1959. There are two auditoriums: the Avellaneda, with a seating capacity of 2,500, and the Covarrubia, which seats 800 and has a mural by Cuban artist René Portocarrero *(see p30)*. Theatre programmes include lectures, courses, theatre festivals, guitar and jazz concerts, and ballet. There is also a nightclub, Café Cantante *(see p129)*, and a piano bar with live shows.

❽ Memorial José Martí

Work on this monument in the middle of the Plaza de la Revolución began in 1953, on the 100th anniversary of the birth of Cuba's national hero. The memorial was finished in 1958. It consists of a 109-m (358-ft) tower representing a five-pointed star and is built of grey marble from the Isla de la Juventud. At the foot stands a huge statue of José Martí in a meditative pose. The actual Martí Memorial is in the interior of the base, which also houses the Sala de Actos, an auditorium used for concerts, lectures and poetry readings.

★ Panorama
On clear days, the *mirador* on top of the tower, the highest point in Havana, affords views covering the entire city and stretching out to the sea.

A lift goes to the top of the tower, which reaches a height of 139 m (458 ft) – the monument stands on a hill 30 m (100 ft) above sea level.

VISITORS' CHECKLIST

Practical Information
Plaza de la Revolución. Map 2 E5.
Tel 7882 0906. **Open** 9:30am–4:30pm Mon–Sat.
Note: fee for photography applies.

★ The Memorial
Two rooms contain manuscripts, portraits and mementos of Martí; the third room describes the history of the monument and the square, while a fourth puts on contemporary art exhibitions. The mural in the lobby features the patriot's thoughts.

Statue of José Martí
The 18-m (59-ft) high, white marble statue, carved on site by Juan José Sicre, is surrounded by six half columns.

❾ Necrópolis de Colón

Havana's monumental Columbus Cemetery is one of the largest in the world, occupying an area of 56 ha (135 acres) with 53,360 plots, where some two million people have been buried. It was designed in the 1860s by the Spanish architect Calixto de Loira, who based the layout on the rigorously symmetrical plan of Roman military camps. It was built between 1871 and 1886. Because of its many sculptures and monuments in different styles – from eclectic to the boldest expressions of contemporary art – the Necrópolis has been proclaimed a national monument. However, although it is full of fascinating funerary art, it is still the cemetery for and of Havana's citizens. People come here to visit their loved ones or simply to stroll around.

Mártires del Asalto al Palacio Presidencial
This avant-garde memorial (1982) honours the students killed during their attack on Batista's Presidential Palace in 1957.

★ La Piedad de Rita Longa
This delicate marble bas-relief pietà adorns the black marble tomb of the Aguilera family, which was built in the 1950s.

KEY

① Tomb of the author Alejo Carpentier (1904–80)

② Chapel of the Six Medical Students

③ The Pantheon of Catalina Lasa *(see p103)* was commissioned by her second husband, Juan Pedro Baró, who had her embalmed and brought from Paris to Havana.

④ La Milagrosa

⑤ The Osario General, an ossuary built in 1886, is one of the cemetery's oldest constructions.

⑥ Panteón de los Prelados

⑦ The Falla Bonet Pantheon is a truncated grey granite pyramid with a statue of Christ by the Spanish sculptor Mariano Benlliure.

⑧ Tomb of Generalissimo Máximo Gómez *(see p48)*

★ Main Entrance
The statue in Carrara marble of the three theological virtues, Faith, Hope and Charity, was sculpted in 1904 by the Cuban artist José Villalta de Saavedra in "Neo-Romantic" style.

Fuerzas Armadas Revolucionarias Monument (1955)
This pantheon houses the heroes of the Revolutionary Armed Forces.

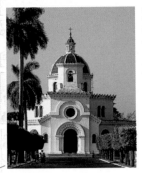

Capilla Central
Built in the late 1800s in the middle of Avenida Colón, the cemetery's main avenue, this chapel contains frescoes by the Cuban artist Miguel Melero.

★ **Monumento a los Bomberos**
This monumental homage to the 25 fallen firefighters of a fire that occurred in 1890 in the Isasi hardware store was designed by Spanish architects Agustín Querol and Julio Zapata.

A mother placing flowers on the statue of La Milagrosa

La Milagrosa

"The Miraculous One" is the tomb of Amelia Goyri de la Hoz, who died in childbirth in 1901, along with her baby. She was only 24. In keeping with the custom of the time, she and the child were buried together. According to popular legend, a few years later the tomb was opened and she was found intact, holding her baby in her arms. This "miracle", and the fact that the bereaved husband went to her tomb every day and never turned his back to it, made Amelia a symbol of motherly love. She became the protector of pregnant women and newborn children, and her tomb is a pilgrimage site for future mothers, who ask for her blessing and leave without turning their back to the tomb. The statue placed at the tomb in 1909 is by José Villalta de Saavedra.

FURTHER AFIELD

Beyond the city of Havana, sights of interest are rather more scattered. The Miramar quarter lies to the west of the city, and the Castillo del Morro and Fortaleza de La Cabaña defence fortresses – evidence of Havana's strategic importance – are physically separated from the city to the east, but linked to it historically. Cubans are enthusiastic beachgoers and the long golden beaches at Playas del Este, east of Havana, are especially popular at the weekend. Among the sightseeing highlights are the favourite haunts of Ernest Hemingway including Finca La Vigía, the villa where he wrote some of his best novels, and the fishing village of Cojímar.

Sights at a Glance

Museums
⑩ Finca La Vigía

Monuments and Churches
❸ Castillo del Morro
❹ San Carlos de La Cabaña
⑬ Santuario Nacional de San Lázaro

Parks and Gardens
⑪ Parque Lenin
⑫ Jardín Botánico Nacional

Beaches
❾ Playas del Este

Towns and Suburbs
❺ Casablanca
❻ Regla
❼ Guanabacoa
❽ Cojímar

Historic Places
❷ Tropicana

Walks
❶ A Walk through Miramar (pp112–13)

Key
▨ Historic centre
▭ Motorway
▬ Major road
═ Minor road
— Railway

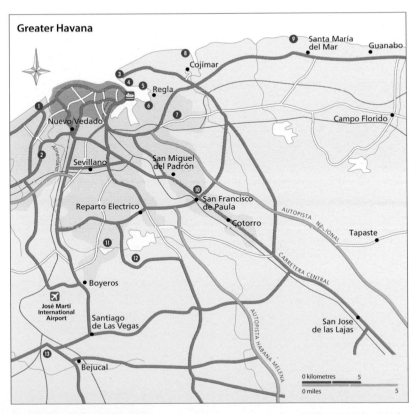

Greater Havana

Santa María del Mar · Guanabo · Cojímar · Regla · Campo Florido · Nuevo Vedado · San Miguel del Padrón · Sevillano · San Francisco de Paula · Reparto Electrico · Cotorro · Tapaste · AUTOPISTA NACIONAL · CARRETERA CENTRAL · Boyeros · José Martí International Airport · Santiago de Las Vegas · San Jose de las Lajas · AUTOPISTA HABANA MELENA · Bejucal

0 kilometres 5
0 miles 5

◀ Looking out to sea from the Castillo del Morro

For keys to symbols see back flap

❶ A Walk through Miramar

Miramar is the most elegant part of Havana – as it was before the Revolution, when the city's richest inhabitants lived here. Life in this quarter revolves around the Avenida 5, a broad, tree-lined avenue flanked by splendid early 20th-century villas that are now home to embassies and institutions. Administratively, Miramar belongs to the municipality of Playa, as does the adjacent Cubanacán quarter, where many foreign embassies are located.

Looking down Avenida 5, the main avenue in Miramar

The compact but imposing Fuerte de la Chorrera

Arriving from Vedado

This walk begins at the Fuerte de Santa Dorotea de la Luna en la Chorrera fort ①, a national monument. The fort, designed by Giovanni Bautista Antonelli and built in 1645, was crucial to the city's defence system (see p114) for over 200 years. Alongside the fort is Restaurante 1830 ②, a salsa venue and restaurant in a house that once belonged to Carlos Miguel de Céspedes, Minister of Public Works for President Machado.

Along Avenida 5 (Quinta Avenida)

From here, follow the northernmost tunnel under the Almendares river to reach Avenida 5, a broad, tranquil avenue with shrubs and benches in the middle. On both sides of it are large, imposing mansions built in the early decades of the 20th century and many Art Deco and eclectic-style houses, most of which were abandoned by their owners after Fidel Castro took power. The Cuban government has turned many of these buildings into ministries, embassies and even orphanages (an example is the one-time residence of the former President of the Republic Grau San Martín at the corner of Calle 14). At the corner of Quinta Avenida and Calle 2 is the restored Casa de las Tejas Verdes (House of the Green Tiles) ③,

Itinerary

① Fuerte de Santa Dorotea de la Luna en la Chorrera
② Restaurante 1830
③ Casa de la Tejas Verdes
④ Iglesia de Santa Rita
⑤ Acuario Nacional

0 metres 400
0 yards 400

Key

• • • Suggested route

VISITORS' CHECKLIST

Practical Information
Point of departure: Fuerte de la Chorrera, Malecón.
Length: 5 km (3 miles).
Stops: Mesón La Chorrera, Calle Calzada 1252, before the tunnel; Bar Tabarish, Calle 20, No. 503 e/ 5 y 7, 7202 9188.

which is now a centre devoted to architecture. The house and garden are open for guided visits during the week. Further down the Avenida, at the corner of Calle 26, is the modern Iglesia de Santa Rita ④, with three distinctive tall arches on its façade. Pop in to see the statue of St Rita by Cuban sculptress Rita Longa, to the left of the entrance. Walk up Calle 28 to Avenida 3 ("tercera"). Turn left to continue the walk along Avenida 3, taking in the stylish architecture, and then turn right to walk one block up to Avenida 1.

The Seafront

Avenida 1 ("primera") lacks the liveliness and fascination of the Malecón, but the water is clear and there are peaceful spots for sunbathing, such as Playita 16 (at the end of Calle 16). At the corner of Calle 60 is the unmistakable pale blue building housing the Acuario Nacional ⑤, the city aquarium. Here, large saltwater tanks reproduce an assortment of Caribbean and ocean habitats. About 3,500 specimens represent 350 different species of sea fauna. The most spectacular section is the tank of *Tursiops truncatus* dolphins, more commonly known as bottle-nosed dolphins. Dolphin shows are also performed here at regular intervals. The aquarium complex is open from 10am to 6pm every day except Monday.

Statue by Rita Longa, Church of Santa Rita

Emerald green Casa de las Tejas Verdes, designed by architect José Luis Echarte in the 1920s

The early 20th-century Fountain of the Muses at the Tropicana

❷ Tropicana

Calle 72 e/ 41 y 45, Marianao.
Tel 7267 0110.

The most famous nightclub in Cuba, America and perhaps the world is located in the outskirts of Havana, in the Marianao district. Many legendary figures of the 20th century have performed here, including Josephine Baker, Bola de Nieve, Rita Montaner and Nat King Cole.

The Tropicana was originally a farm estate belonging to Mina Pérez Chaumont, the widow of a wealthy man named Regino Truffin. In the 1930s she transformed her property into a vast nightspot with a restaurant and casino featuring extravagant floor shows with lavish costumes. The nightclub opened on 31 December 1939.

Perhaps surprisingly, given the change of regime, the Tropicana is still alive and kicking. Fortunately, the trees in the original estate were left intact, so that today the Tropicana stands in the middle of an extraordinary tropical forest. At night, floodlights illuminate the palm trees, partly hidden by clouds of artificial smoke. A reminder of the Tropicana's golden age is the enormous "Bajo las Estrellas" ballroom. With its capacity of 1,000 it is one of the largest of its kind.

At the main entrance is the Fountain of the Muses (1952). The garden's statue of a ballet dancer, by Rita Longa (1952), is now the symbol of the club.

Río Almendares

The Almendares river is no longer crystal-clear, but it must have been cleaner in the past, because in the 17th century a Spanish bishop called Almendáriz came to Havana in bad health and fully recovered after a stay along its banks. The river's name was changed from Casiguaguas to Almendares in the bishop's honour. Along its west bank, by the Calle 23 bridge from Vedado, is the Parque Almendares, an area filled with tropical plants and vegetation.

Thick vegetation in the Parque Almendares, Havana's "forest"

Castillo del Morro, situated on a rocky headland at the entrance to the bay of Havana

❸ Castillo del Morro

Carretera de la Cabaña, Habana del
Este. **Tel** 7862 0617. **Open** 9am–
6pm daily. 🦽 🚻 🚹 🏪 🚻

Construction of this fortress,
which was designed by the
Italian military architect
Giovanni Bautista Antonelli,
began in 1589 at the
request of the
governor, Juan de
Texeda. The function
of the Castillo de los
Tres Reyes del Morro
(its full title) was to
detect the approach
of any enemy (pirates
especially). Various
treasures of the
New World were
regularly concen-
trated in the port when ships
were docked in Cuba on their
voyage to Spain, and it was
necessary to protect them.

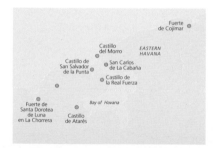

The old lamp in the
Morro lighthouse

The original lighthouse on the
"Morrillo", the highest point of
the hill, was rebuilt several
times, until General Leopoldo
O'Donnell ordered a new one
to be built in 1845. This still
stands today. It is made of
stone, and has its original lamp,
the rays of which shine for a
radius of 30 km (20 miles).
Today the fortress and
the neighbouring La
Cabaña fortification
(see below) form the
**Parque Histórico-
Militar Morro
Cabaña**. Many tourists
and locals come
here to admire
the outlook, as the
fortress affords a
magnificent view
of the city and port of Havana.
Access to the castles is
through an impressive gallery,
where plaques indicate the

spot where the British opened
a breach in 1762, allowing them
to take the Morro and all of
Havana after a 40-day siege.

On the northern side of the
complex is the Plataforma de
la Reina, with defence walls and
a flight of steps leading to the
upper terrace. From here visitors
can gain an overall view of
the fortress.

❹ San Carlos de La Cabaña

Carretera de la Cabaña, Habana del
Este. **Tel** 7862 0617. **Open** 9am–
10pm daily. 🦽 🚻 🚻

After the British conquest of
Havana in 1762, it was 11
months before the Spaniards
regained the capital. The
bitter experience of foreign
occupation convinced them
of the need to fortify the hill

Havana's Defences

Havana was the most important port in the New
World in the 1700s. It was a highly prized target
for enemies and pirates because of its extremely
favourable strategic position in the Caribbean,
and it was also the most fortified city in any
Spanish colony. Beyond the maritime canal
affording access to the Bay of Havana were the
two large fortresses of Morro and Cabaña. These
two, together with the castles of Real Fuerza,
Punta, Atarés and Príncipe and the city walls,
constituted for centuries the city's impressive
defence and attack system. From the outlying
forts of Cojímar and La Chorrera, to the east
and west respectively, any enemy approach
could be sighted.

dominating the port in a more effective manner, so, on 4 November 1763, construction work began on the new Cabaña fortress. No fewer than 4,000 men laboured on the project, including Mexican and Indian prisoners transported from the Yucatán peninsula in conditions of semi-slavery.

The new fortification cost 14 million pesos, a sum so large that, according to an old legend, when King Carlos III of Spain was informed of the expense, he asked for a spy-glass and reputedly commented: "Such an expensive construction should be visible from Madrid."

La Cabaña, which extends for more than 700 m (2,300 ft) along the entrance canal of the bay, is a huge 10-ha (25-acre) polygon designed in keeping with the principles of French military schools, but with detailing by the Spanish engineer Silvestre Abarca. With its crown-shaped plan, it is considered a fine example of a bastion-type defence fortification.

A visit to the fortress offers a variety of experiences. The fortress's central thoroughfare leads up to the Baluardo di San Ambrosio bastion and the Terraza de San Agustín, where the poet Juan Clemente Zenea was executed for his separatist ideas in 1871. In the same area some Soviet nuclear missiles, left over from the 1962 Cuban Missile Crisis *(see p56)*, are on display.

Entrance to the de La Cabaña parish church, which stands in the fortress parade ground

The **Museo Monográfico** illustrates the history of the fortress through documents and photographs. The **Museo de Armas y Fortificaciones** is a military museum. However, the one museum not to miss is the **Comandancia del Che**: on 3 January 1959 the *barbudos* (as Castro and his bearded revolutionaries were known) occupied La Cabaña and set up their headquarters in the 19th-century building that was once the residence of the Spanish military governor. Today it is a museum containing various items that belonged to Che Guevara, including his weapons, glasses and camera. The revolutionary's original office, which has been left intact, is also open to visitors.

The Cañonazo

Every evening, at 9pm exactly, the picturesque "Cañonazo" ceremony is held in the La Cabaña fortress. On the hour, a volley of cannon shots is fired by a group of young soldiers of the Revolutionary Armed Forces, dressed in 18th-century uniforms. This theatrical ceremony is interesting from the historical point of view: in the colonial period, a volley of cannon shots was fired at the end of each day to tell citizens that the city gates were closed and access to the bay had been blocked by a chain *(see p89)*.

The Cañonazo ceremony, a commemoration in historic costume

❺ Casablanca

from Muelle de Luz, La Habana Vieja, every 15 mins; 7794 5466.

This fishing village was built in the 1700s on the other side of the Bay of Havana from the city. Casablanca is best known for the huge Cristo de la Habana, an 18-m (60-ft) tall white marble statue of Christ, which looms over the village. The work of the Cuban sculptress Jilma Madera (1958), it was commissioned by President Batista's wife, Marta. She had made a vow that she would finance a large statue of Christ if her husband survived the attack by students on the presidential palace in 1957, during which he risked his life. The statue was completed a week prior to the Revolution. It can be seen from many parts of the city and is familiar to all Cubans.

The colossal Cristo de La Habana

❻ Regla

Havana. ⬛ 43,000. 🚢 from Muelle de Luz, Habana Vieja, every 30 mins; 7697 7473.

Regla lies on the east coast of the Bay of Havana, a few minutes by ferry from Muelle de Luz. The town was founded in 1687 and over the years grew in economic importance as a fishing port and centre for huge sugar warehouses. In the 19th century freed slaves settled in Regla, and there is still a strong Afro-Cuban culture here today.

The church of **Nuestra Señora de la Virgen de Regla** was built here in 1687. A modest structure, it stands on a small hill from which there are scenic views of the bay. The humble

Interior of the Regla church with its ornate high altar

interior includes an ornate golden altar into which is incorporated the figure of the dark-skinned Virgin.

The Liceo Artístico y Literario was opened by José Martí in 1879 with a famous speech on Cuban independence.

❼ Guanabacoa

Havana. ⬛ 115,000. 🚌

After its foundation in 1607, this town became an obligatory port of call for the slave traffic, which explains its fame as a city associated with Afro-Cuban culture. Its name, of Indian origin, means "land of many waters": there are several springs in this area which at one time encouraged wealthy Habaneros to build homes here. Today, Guanabacoa is proud of its colonial houses and of having been the birthplace of three leading 20th-century Cuban musicians: pianist and composer Ernesto Lecuona, singer Rita Montaner, and *chansonnier* Ignacio Villa, better known as Bola de Nieve.

The *Mano Poderosa* in the Guanabacoa Municipal Museum

Guanabacoa has several interesting churches. Of these, the **Ermita de Potosí** in particular is well worth a visit. Built in 1644, it is one of the oldest and most original colonial period churches.

The interesting **Museo Municipal de Guanabacoa**, located in a well-restored colonial house, illustrates the history of the town.

The dominant figure is that of Pepe Antonio, the local hero in the struggle against the British in the 18th century. The museum places particular emphasis on the *Santería* and Palo Monte religions and on the rituals of the Abakuá cult *(see p27)*. An impressive piece in this section is the *Mano Poderosa*, a multicoloured wooden sculpture that stands approximately 1-m (3-ft) high. According to legend, the sculpture belonged to a woman who was able to make contact with the dead. Traditional Afro-Cuban dance is sometimes held in the courtyard.

🏛 Museo Municipal de Guanabacoa
Calle Martí 108, e/ Quintín Banderas y E V Valenzuela. **Tel** 7797 9117. **Open** 9am–5pm Tue–Sat, 9am–1pm Sun. 🖼 📷

❽ Cojímar

Havana. ⬛ 20,100.

A charming village with one-storey wooden houses – often with a garden, small porch and courtyard at the back – Cojímar was once inhabited only by fishermen. Now there are also many elderly people, including writers and artists, who have chosen to leave the capital for a more peaceful life.

In the 1950s however, there was only one author to be seen on the streets of Cojímar: Ernest Hemingway. Many of the local fishermen were his friends and he liked to play dominoes and

La Virgen de Regla

The Virgin of Regla has been the patron saint of fishermen and Havana since 1714. The Neo-Classical sanctuary dedicated to her contains an icon of a dark-skinned Virgin holding a white child that the faithful call "La Negra". The icon's origins are not known but one legend suggests it acquired its colour while being taken across the Black Sea. The statue was brought from Spain by a hermit in 1696, and in the 1900s was watched over by a certain Panchita Cárdenas, whose modest home next to the church is now open to worshippers. For followers of *Santería* the Virgen de Regla is also Yemayá, the patroness of the sea and mother of all men, to whom food, flowers, candles and sweets are offered. On her feast day (8 Sep) the icon is borne through the town.

La Virgen de Regla, the protector of fishermen

The 17th-century fort at Cojímar

drink rum while listening to their stories. He made this village the setting for his famous novel *The Old Man and the Sea*.

In the small square named after Hemingway there is a monument featuring a bust of the author – a faithful copy of the one in El Floridita *(see p76)*. It is here thanks to the author's fishermen friends, who donated anchors, hooks and tools to pay for the casting.

Nearby, on the seafront, is a small fort, which was built as the easternmost defence point of Havana in 1646. It was designed by Giovanni Bautista Antonelli, architect of the Castillo del Morro *(see p114)*.

Cojímar is also the home of Hemingway's favourite restaurant, La Terraza *(see p272)*. It makes much of its connection with the author, and photos of him adorn the walls. However, the restaurant is as elegant and well-run as it was during Hemingway's time. The cocktail lounge has a splendid wooden bar and is an ideal spot to enjoy a drink.

❾ Playas del Este

Havana.

Havana is one of the few cities in the world to have sizable beaches only a 20-minute drive from the city centre. The Playas del Este consist of a stretch of about 10 km (6 miles) of fine sand and crystal-clear water, easy to reach via a good, fast road, with hotels, villages and tourist facilities. The beaches can offer a good compromise for people who want to spend some of their holiday at the seaside during their visit to Havana. Bear in mind, however,

that this area is also a popular haunt of *jineteros (see p292)*, though in places security guards have been drafted in to deter them.

Arriving from central Havana, the first beach is **Bacuranao**, a peaceful spot and a favourite with families. However, the loveliest place on the riviera is **Santa María del Mar**. It has the best beach, lined with pine and coconut trees, as well as some hotels and sport facilities, and is therefore very popular with tourists. **Guanabo** is more traditional, with small houses, restaurants and shops; at weekends this is the liveliest place along the coast when Habaneros arrive by the hundred. The Bajo de las Lavanderas, close to the shore, is a delight for scuba and skin divers, and deep-sea fishing trips can be arranged at the **Marlin Punto Náutico** kiosks on the beaches.

A small island, **Mi Cayito**, lies at the mouth of the Itabo river. There are fine views from Mirador Bellomonte.

One of the Playas del Este beaches popular with Havana residents

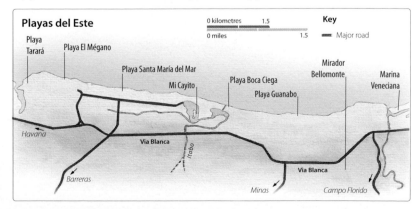

Playas del Este

Playa Tarará
Playa El Mégano
Playa Santa María del Mar
Mi Cayito
Playa Boca Ciega
Playa Guanabo
Mirador Bellomonte
Marina Veneciana

Havana
Via Blanca
Itabo
Via Blanca

Barreras
Minas
Campo Florido

0 kilometres 1.5
0 miles 1.5

Key
━ Major road

Ernest Hemingway in Cuba

The great American author fell in love with Cuba on his first visit in 1932, attracted initially by the marlin fishing. It was not until 1939, however, that Hemingway decided to move to the island, initially settling down in the Ambos Mundos hotel in Old Havana *(see p256)*. Having decided to stay on, he found a quiet villa outside the city in which to write, Finca La Vigía, where he lived at first with journalist Martha Gellhorn (whom he married in 1940). His bond with Cuba lasted 20 years, through the Batista period and the beginning of the Revolution, and longer, in fact, than his relationship with Martha Gellhorn. Hemingway's last wife, Mary Welsh (married in 1946), joined the writer in Cuba and lived with him at Finca La Vigía. The villa is now a museum *(p119)*. He eventually returned to the US in 1960, a year before his suicide.

Hemingway wrote his most famous novels in Cuba. He was at Finca La Vigía in 1954 when he found out that he had received the Nobel Prize. "This prize belongs to Cuba, since my works were created and conceived in Cuba, with the inhabitants of Cojímar, of which I am a citizen." With these words, Hemingway placed the prize at the foot of the Virgen del Cobre *(see p225)*.

A lover of cocktails, Hemingway was a regular at La Bodeguita del Medio *(see p69)* and El Floridita *(see p76)*. Both bars were a stone's throw from his room on the fifth floor of the Ambos Mundos Hotel. The writer helped to invent the daiquirí.

The Sea and Fishing

Hemingway loved the sea and was passionate about swordfish and marlin fishing. He practised the sport with great commitment and courage – not on a luxury yacht, but on a small fishing boat, the famous Pilar – together with a fisherman, Gregorio Fuentes, who also became a good friend. The boat was moored at the picturesque village of Cojímar.

Ernest Hemingway

Martha Gellhorn

Gregorio Fuentes

A marlin fishing tournament is held every year at the Hemingway Marina.

⑩ Finca La Vigía

Calle Vigía y Stheinhard, San
Francisco de Paula, Havana.
🚋 San Francisco de Paula.
Tel 7692 0176. **Open** 10am–
4:30pm Mon–Sat. 🗲 🗲 🗲 🗲
Note: fee for photography may apply.

At San Francisco de Paula, on
the outskirts of Havana, is the
only residence Ernest Hemingway ever had outside the US.
He lived here, in the periods
between his various foreign
trips, for almost 20 years.

The villa, built in 1887 to a
design by Catalan architect
Miguel Pascual y Baguer, was
bought by Hemingway in 1940.
It was made a public museum
in 1962, as soon as news of the
writer's suicide in the US reached
Cuba. To protect the interior,
visitors are not allowed inside,
however the rooms can be
viewed through the windows
and doors to the garden, which
are thrown open but roped off,
except on rainy days.

Everything in the villa is in the
same meticulous order as it was
in when Hemingway lived here.
There is his library with its more
than 9,000 books; various
hunting trophies from African
safaris hanging in the living
room; personal possessions, such
as his weapons and typewriter,
and valuable artworks, including
a ceramic plate by Picasso.

Two curious features in the
garden are the pet cemetery
(Hemingway had about 50 cats
during his lifetime) and the

The façade of Finca La Vigía, surrounded by tropical vegetation

Pilar, the author's fishing boat,
which was transferred from
Cojímar to the museum and
placed in a specially built
pavilion in the former tennis
court. The *Pilar* was a comfortable and fast boat made
of black American oak, and
the author loved ploughing
through the waves on fishing
expeditions with his friend

Gregorio Fuentes. During
World War II he used it to
patrol the sea north of Cuba,
on the lookout for Nazi
submarines that were trying
to sink ships laden with sugar
intended for the Allied troops.

Environs
Near Hemingway's villa is the
village of **Santa María del
Rosario**, founded in 1732
by Count Don José Bayona y
Chacón on the estate of his
large sugar factory. A real gem
here is the church of the same
name (it is also known as
Catedral de los Campos de
Cuba), notable for its splendid
mudéjar ceilings.

The church was designed
in 1760–66 by architect José
Perera. The austere façade is
reminiscent of the Spanish
missions in the western US,
while the interior contains some
unusually lavish elements, such
as the extravagantly gilded high
altar, and paintings attributed
to Nicolás de la Escalera, one
of Cuba's early artists.

The living room of Hemingway's villa, with hunting trophies on the walls

For hotels and restaurants in this area see p258 and p272

⑪ Parque Lenin

Calle 100 y Cortina de la Presa, Arroyo Naranjo, Havana. **Tel** 7643 1165. **Open** 10am–5pm Wed–Sun. 🖼 🖥 🚂 ExpoCuba: **Tel** 7697 4252 (train info 7644 2721). **Open** 9am–5pm Wed–Sun. 🐾 Parque Zoológico Nacional: **Tel** 7643 8063. **Open** 9:30am–3:15pm Wed–Sun. 🐾

The impressive monument to Lenin designed by Lev Korbel

Lenin Park, 20 km (12 miles) south of Central Havana, occupies an area of 1,840 acres (745 ha). It was created in the 1970s as an amusement park for children and an area of greenery for a city in continuous expansion.

In the same period, thanks to an initiative by Celia Sánchez, Castro's personal assistant during the Revolution, the Russian architect Lev Korbel designed the vast monument honouring the Soviet leader. The statue of Lenin, which weighs 1,200 tons and is 9 m (30 ft) high, was completed in 1982 under the supervision of Antonio Quintana Simonetti, who also designed the park.

The most enjoyable way of getting around Parque Lenin is to take the narrow-gauge train which follows a route of 9.5 km (6 miles) in 45 minutes, making several stops. Call ahead to check that the train is running. The train's old steam engines were used in previous years by Cuba's sugar factories to transport sugar cane. Open carriages allow passengers to admire the scenery. The park is popular with Habaneros, who love to walk among the palm, cedar, pine and araucaria trees. There is also a freshwater aquarium, stables, outdoor cinema, art gallery, swimming pools, café and the Las Ruínas restaurant. The latter occupies a 1960s building that incorporates the crumbling walls of an old plantation house.

Environs

Near the park, among gardens and tree-lined paths, is the largest exhibition centre in Cuba, **ExpoCuba**, which stages various exhibitions and shows all year round. In autumn the pavilions are occupied by the famous Feria Internacional de La Habana, which offers an overview of Cuba's economic and socio-political life. From Parque Lenin it is also easy to reach the 840-acre (340-ha) **Parque Zoológico Nacional,** where animals live freely in various natural habitats, often without cages. The savannah area is populated with zebras, hippopotamuses, giraffes and antelopes. Another area is the habitat of lions.

⑫ Jardín Botánico Nacional

Carretera del Rocío km 3, Calabazar, Arroyo Naranjo (Havana). **Tel** 7697 9159. **Open** 9am–4pm daily. **Closed** 1 Jan, 26 Jul, 25 Dec. 🐾 🍽

This enormous 1,500-acre (600-ha) botanical garden, set in an area of woods and cultivated fields, contains plants

The tranquil Japanese Garden, part of the Jardín Botánico Nacional

from all over the world. These are on display to the public and are also studied by specialists. The huge gardens are divided into geographical zones – Cuba, America, Africa, Asia and Oceania. The Caribbean section, which takes up one-fifth of the garden, has 7,000 flowering plants, half of which are unique to Cuba. There are also curiosities such as the Archaic Woods and the Palmetum. The former has plants descended from species that thrived in ancient geological eras, such as the *Palma corcho*, a fossil species that can still be found in the Pinar del Río region. The Palmetum has a large collection of palm trees from all tropical latitudes.

A must is the cactus area near the entrance. However, the most interesting part of this rather sparse park is the Jardín Japonés, a Japanese garden with artificial waterfalls and a pond with a gazebo. It was donated to Cuba by the local Asian community in 1989.

Another fascinating sight here is the orchid garden, with numerous varieties.

The Sanctuary of San Lázaro at El Rincón

⓭ Santuario Nacional de San Lázaro

Calzada de San Antonio km 23, El Rincón, Santiago de las Vegas (Havana). **Tel** 7683 2396. **Open** 7am–7pm daily. 🕈 9am & 5pm Mon–Sat, 11am & 4pm Sun. 🎏 Feast Day of St Lazarus, 17 Dec.

This sanctuary, dedicated to St Lazarus, the patron saint of the sick, lies in the small village of El Rincón, outside Santiago de las Vegas. It is next to an old lepers' hospital, which now specializes in dermatology.

In Afro-Cuban religions Lazarus corresponds to Babalú Ayé. Both saints are represented in folk iconography as old men in tatters and covered with sores. In the case of the African saint, the skin disease was supposedly punishment from Olofi, the father of all the gods *(see p26)*, for the saint's adulterous and libertine past.

On 17 December, the simple white sanctuary welcomes thousands of worshippers, many of whom have crawled or walked on their knees from Havana. They flock here to make vows or ask St Lazarus (called *milagroso* or "the miraculous one") to intercede for them. The pilgrims light candles, leave flowers and make offerings at the sanctuary's altars. The worshippers also bring dogs.

The water from the fountain to the right of the sanctuary, considered miraculous by believers, is used to cure diseases and ease pain.

Italo Calvino and Cuba

Santiago de las Vegas, most famous for its San Lázaro sanctuary, was also the birthplace of the great Italian novelist Italo Calvino (1923–1985). His father Mario was an esteemed agronomist who went to Cuba in 1918, following his appointment as director of the Estación Experimental de Santiago de las Vegas. This experimental field station covered 123 acres (50 ha) of land and employed 100 university graduates and 63 office workers. While in Cuba, Mario Calvino found ways of making genetic improvements to sugar cane and introduced new plants, including pumpkin and lettuce. He also worked on tobacco, corn and sorghum, while his wife Eva wrote articles exhorting Cuban women to emancipate themselves and acquire new dignity through education and training. When the Calvino family returned to San Remo in Italy, they took not only a son who would become a great writer, but also mango, avocado, flamboyant, cherimoya and even sugar cane seeds, which they cultivated at the San Remo Experimental Agriculture Station. In 1964 Italo Calvino was named a member of the jury for the Casa de las Américas prize *(see p104)* and visited Cuba, where he returned to his birthplace and also met Che Guevara.

Author Italo Calvino, born at Santiago de las Vegas

The altar of St Lazarus with flowers left by worshippers

HAVANA STREET FINDER

The page grid shown on the *Area by Area* map below shows the parts of Havana covered by maps in this section. All map references in this guide refer to the maps in the *Street Finder* section. Addresses are indicated in keeping with the system used in Cuba so that people will understand your requests for information. The street name plus the house number is followed by either "e/" (*entre*, or "between") and the names of the two streets between which the address you want is located, or "esq." (*esquina*, or "corner") followed by the name of the crossroad where the address is located. Knowing the cross streets is essential, as many roads in Havana are very long.

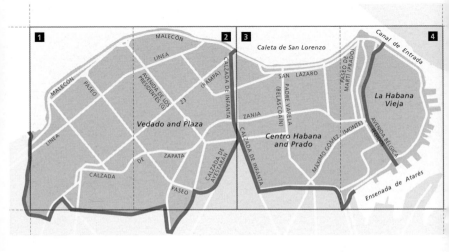

0 metres 700
0 yards 700

Cuban Street Names

Since many streets changed name after the revolution, some have both an official name and an unofficial, more commonly used one. Where this occurs in this guide, the latter is followed by the former in brackets.

In Vedado the streets are divided into neat 100-m (109-yd) long blocks or *cuadras*. The grid layout of the streets here is easy to follow. The streets parallel to the seafront are named with odd numbers, while the cross streets are indicated either with letters (from A to P), east of Paseo, or even numbers, west of Paseo. Street signs in the form of small stone blocks give coordinates at every corner.

Tile street sign in
La Habana Vieja

Scale of Maps

0 metres 300
0 yards 300

Key

- ▢ Major sight
- ▢ Place of interest
- ▢ Other buildings
- ℹ️ Tourist information
- ➕ Hospital
- 🚓 Police station
- ✝️ Church
- 🚌 Coach station
- 🚆 Train station
- ⛴️ Ferry

Street Finder Index

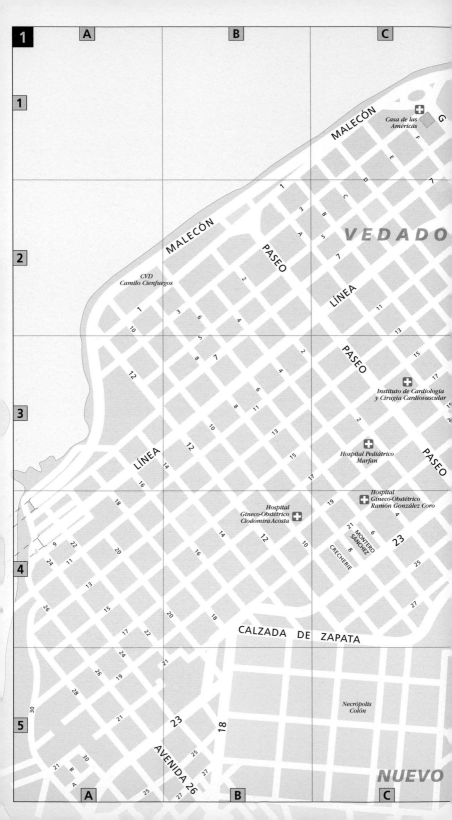

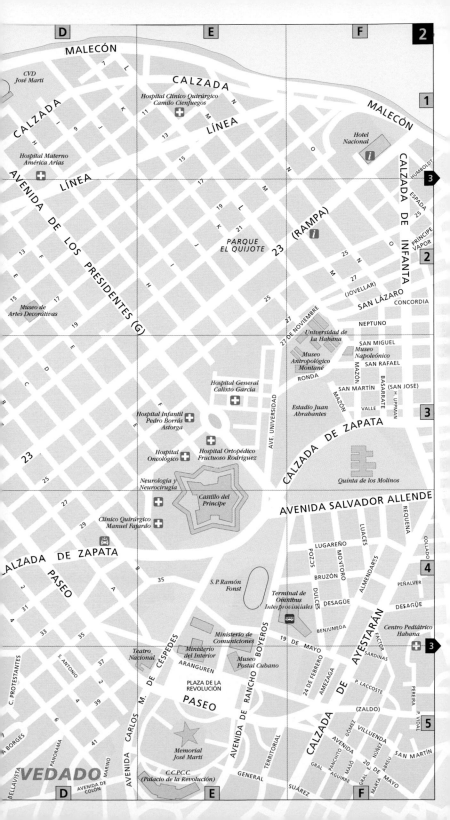

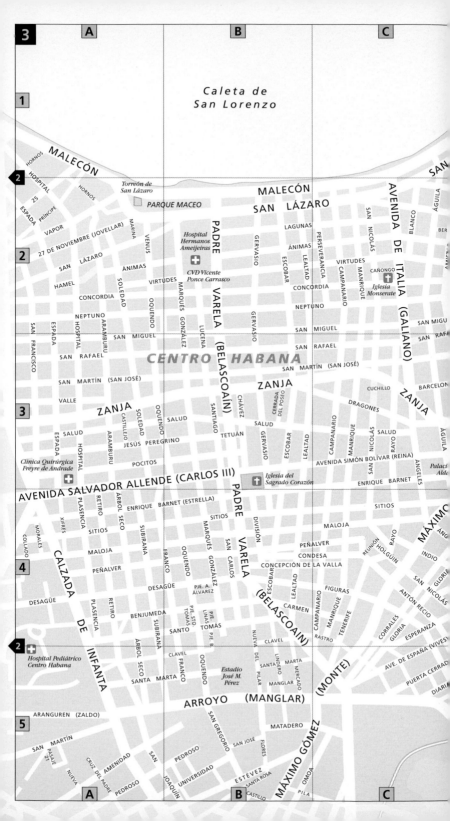

ENTERTAINMENT IN HAVANA

The lively, pleasure-loving capital of Cuba offers entertainment to suit visitors of all ages and tastes. Theatres, cinemas and concert halls are active year-round, while the city's annual ballet, cinema and jazz festivals draw admirers from afar. Havana has the biggest and best nightclubs in the country, offering all kinds of music from salsa and jazz to bolero to rap. The cabaret scene is world-class. You can dance 'til dawn in the discos, while those who prefer more traditional entertainment can investigate the neighbourhood Casas de la Trova or Casa de la Cultura. The bar scene is starting to pick-up as old pre-Revolution stalwarts compete with new, hipper venues, which have started opening as the economic climate improves.

Cuba's National Symphony Orchestra

Information

The airport, hotels and travel agents all distribute information brochures. The elusive *Cartelera,* a biweekly newspaper, and the online *Cuba Absolutely* events publication provide addresses of nightclubs and other venues, with details of shows. The *Granma* daily lists major events, which are also broadcast on Cubavisión (channel 6) on Thursdays at 10:05pm. Visitors can tune in to Radio Taíno (93.3FM), which broadcasts in Spanish and English.

Havana's thriving underground scene requires seeking out. The corner of Calles 23 and L (outside Cine Yara) is a good spot to find out about impromptu parties and shows – especially for the gay scene. Consult http://promociones.egrem.co.cu for all Casas de la Música.

Buying Tickets

To avoid long queues for festivals and other major events, visitors can purchase tickets in advance from the venue's ticket office, from tourist agencies in the hotels or through **Paradiso: Promotora de Turismo Cultural**.

Tickets for cabaret shows at the world-famous Tropicana nightclub and Cabaret Parisien can be obtained at the tour bureaus of any tourist hotel. For smaller shows and events, you will need to stand in line on the day or night of the performance.

Theatre

Theatre has a long and illustrious tradition in Havana, though the range of offerings has been severely curtailed for political reasons since the Revolution. The Festival Internacional del Teatro, held every two years, offers both mainstream and experimental theatre, and some companies, such as El Público, have their own venues. Havana's most important and active theatres are located mostly in the Vedado quarter and are presented exclusively in Spanish.

The Teatro Nacional de Cuba, a complex with several auditoriums *(see p106),* often hosts major international companies, while the large **Teatro Karl Marx** puts on the city's biggest events. The **Teatro Hubert de Blanck** specializes in contemporary drama, while the **Teatro Mella** has a more varied programme, as does the restored **Teatro José Martí**. The **Teatro Trianón** and **Teatro El Sótano** are committed to presenting experimental theatre. The **Café Teatro Brecht** shows alternative plays.

Cuban comedy tend towards bawdy slapstick. The best venues are **Casa de la Comedia**, offering shows at weekends, and Café Teatro Brecht.

Classical Music and Opera

There are two main classical music venues in Havana. The **Teatro Amadeo Roldán**, currently being restored, is home to the National Symphony

The impressive exterior of the Gran Teatro de La Habana

Orchestra, while the Gran Teatro de La Habana (see p86), which has excellent acoustics, hosts opera and other productions.

The lovely Basílica de San Francisco de Asís (see p78) is an atmospheric venue for choral and chamber music concerts. The Agrupación Anfitriona de Música Antigua "Ars Longa" puts on Renaissance and Baroque concerts in the beautiful **Iglesia de San Francisco de Paula**.

Ballet

Classical dance is popular in Cuba thanks to the promotion of the **Ballet Nacional de Cuba**, founded by the international ballet star Alicia Alonso. This institution organizes a biennial international ballet festival and promotes specialist courses for foreign dancers. Performances take place in the Gran Teatro de La Habana (see p86). Visitors are often shocked to discover many performances featuring taped music. The Teatro Mella hosts occasional ballet shows.

La Zorra y El Cuervo – a popular and crowded jazz venue

Folk and Traditional Music

Traditional Cuban music covers a broad range of styles including rumba, guaguancó, son, danzón, bolero and punto guajiro (see pp34–5 and p144).

Some of the best performances are based on Afro-Cuban forms, as perfected by the **Conjunto Folklórico Nacional**, which performs an open-air rumba every Saturday and hosts lessons for Cubans and foreigners. Similar performances are hosted on Sundays at the **Asociación Cultural Yoruba de Cuba**, and at **Rumba**

A traditional *son* band performing on the street

del **Callejón de Hamel** in Centro Habana, one of the city's most popular weekend venues.

Hip Hop, Rock and Jazz

Hip hop is very popular in Cuba. An international festival is held every August in Centro (see p39), where **La Madriguera** hosts live performances in the botanical gardens.

The Teatro Karl Marx is the main venue for big-name rock and pop stars. Rock music is also played and danced to in Playa's **Salón Rosado de la Tropical**, usually referred to as La Tropical. **Río Club** was the most famous rock venue in Havana in the 1970s, when it was called Johnny Club. People still use its old name.

Cubans love jazz, and Cuba's leading jazz musicians are popular the world over. An annual jazz festival is held in venues throughout Havana. Among the best of these is **La Zorra y el Cuervo**, a cramped and smoky basement bar. Cuba's top performers, such as Chucho Valdés, play the spacious **Jazz Café** and the **Café Jazz Miramar**.

Other music venues include **El Sauce**, which puts on everything from salsa to Cuban indie rock, and the basement of the Café Teatro Brecht, which plays host to groups such as Interactivo, a collaborative Cuban jazz-funk band. The intimate bar of the **Centro Asturiano** hosts up-and-coming singer-songwriters and one of the latest hip venues is Vedado's **Fábrica de Arte Cubano**.

Nightclubs and Discos

Salsa is the staple of nightclubs and discos. Havana's hottest salsa venues are the twin **Casas de la Música** in Centro Habana and Miramar, where nightly events don't warm up until after midnight. **1830 Club**, located next to the tunnel to Miramar, is a very popular al fresco salsa venue, as is **La Gruta** on La Rampa. The **Café Cantante**, in the Teatro Nacional, has regular live bands. The **Salón Turquino**, on the top floor of the Tryp Habana Libre hotel, is the classiest salsa spot. As with many Cuban nightclubs, foreigners are likely to be approached by potential partners hoping to have their entrance paid.

Café Concierto Gato Tuerto is famous as home of the blend of Cuban and North American music called *feeling*. This small venue fills quickly, so arrive early. Fans of the *bolero* should head to **Dos Gardenias**.

A live musical performance at one of Havana's many nightclubs

Cabaret

The most exotic of venues, and a long-time Cuban tradition, *cabarets espectáculos* are famous for their extravagantly – and minimally – dressed female dancers in sequins and feathers. The music is first-rate, ranging from salsa to crooners performing traditional boleros.

The most famous is the Tropicana *(see p113)* featuring more than 200 performers. Though expensive, it offers a true spectacular with grandiose choreography, lavish costumes and legendary dancers. The **Cabaret Parisien** is the most important of the hotel shows, while the **Cabaret Salón Rojo** and **Cabaret Copa Room** are among the better small shows.

Bars

The colourful bar-life of pre-revolutionary days is a mere memory today. Nonetheless, most upscale tourist hotels have classy bars (albeit filled with foreigners).

Two bars associated with Hemingway remain among the city's most colourful. La Bodeguita del Medio *(see p69)*, a cramped bar where the author popularized *mojitos*, features troubadors. Famous for its daiquirís, **El Floridita** *(see p76)* exudes a fin-de-siècle ambience. Other hip drinking spots include **Madrigal**, Havana's first private bar, the late-night bar at Tocororo *(see p272)* , **Espacios**, **El Cocinero**, and Fábrica de Arte Cubano.

Bartender preparing one of the famous daiquiris at El Floridita

Dancers at the Tropicana, Havana's most famous and colourful cabaret

In Vedado, the Hotel Nacional's **Bar Vista del Golfo** has served cocktails to the rich and famous for decades. Also in Vedado, head to the top of **La Torre** in Edificio Fosca to enjoy cocktails and an incredible view out over the city.

Cinema

Cuba has a thriving cinema industry. The annual December Festival Internacional del Nuevo Cine Latinoamericano, a major international film festival, is organized by the **Instituto Cubano del Arte e Industria Cinematográfica (ICAIC)**, which presides over the activities of the "seventh art" in Cuba *(see p33)* and also runs the **Cine Charles Chaplin**.

Most of the major cinemas are in the Vedado district. The main one is **Cine Yara**. **Cine Riviera** screens mostly Hollywood action movies, while **Cine La Rampa** shows mainly Cuban and Latin American films. Havana's largest cinema is the multi-screen **Cine Payret**, in La Habana Vieja; it has midnight shows at weekends.

Cultural Centres

For visitors interested in Cuban culture, the Casa de las Américas *(see p104)* has a good library, well-stocked book shop and a fine art gallery. It organizes literary and poetry festivals. High-level cultural events are also held at the **Fundación Alejo Carpentier**, dedicated to the work of the great Cuban writer, and the **Fundación Fernando Ortíz**, specializing in Afro-Cuban studies. The **Asociación Cultural Yoruba**, dedicated to African-derived religions, has a library, exhibits, and lectures.

One of the most active centres is **UNEAC** (Writers and Artists' Union), which hosts musical and literary events at El Hurón Azul – the main spot for Havana's bohemians.

Cultural Tours

Week-long holiday packages are available from Paradiso: Promotora de Turismo Cultural *(see Ticket Agencies)*. The cost includes accommodation in a "4-star" hotel, lunch and dinner in typical Cuban restaurants, transport, guides, entrance to museums and theatres, meetings with Cuban artists and visits to specialist educational centres. The Aché Habana programme focuses on a religious and cultural tour of Regla and Guanabacoa, while "Dancing the Cuban Style" features salsa classes. There are also packages tailored around the city's jazz and ballet festivals.

Children

Cubans adore children and the State takes good care of its young. However, entertainment venues for children are few. The Acuario Nacional *(see p113)* puts on dolphin shows. Donkey rides are offered at **Parque Luz Caballero** in La Habana Vieja, and at Parque Lenin *(see p120)* and **Parque Metropoliano de La Habana**. The **Teatro Guiñol** hosts puppet shows and children's theatre. The **Planetario** and shadow puppet theatre **El Arca** are also popular with families.

DIRECTORY

Ticket Agencies

Paradiso: Promotora de Turismo Cultural
Avenida 5 y Calle 82.
Tel 7204 0601.

Theatre

Café Teatro Brecht
Calle 13, esq. I. **Map** 2 D2.
Tel 7832 9359.

Casa de la Comedia
Calle Jústiz 18, esq.
Baratillo. **Map** 4 F2.
Tel 7863 9282.

Teatro Hubert de Blanck
Calzada 657, e/ Calles A y B.
Map 1 C2.
Tel 7830 1011.

Teatro José Martí
Zulueta, esq. Dragones.
Map 3 D3.
Tel 7866 7152.

Teatro Karl Marx
Avenida 1ra, e/ 8 y 10.
Tel 7203 0801.

Teatro Mella
Línea 657, e/ A y B.
Map 1 C2.
Tel 7830 4987.

Teatro El Sótano
Calle K, e/ 25 y 27.
Map 2 E2.
Tel 7832 0630.

Teatro Trianón
Línea 706, e/ Paseo y A.
Map 1 C2.
Tel 7830 9648.

Classical Music & Opera

Iglesia de San Francisco de Paula
Avenida del Puerto, esq.
Leonor Pérez. **Map** 4 E4.
Tel 7860 4210.

Teatro Amadeo Roldán
Calzada y D. **Map** 1 C2.
Tel 7832 4521.

Ballet

Ballet Nacional de Cuba
Calzada 510, e/ D y E.
Map 1 C2.
Tel 7835 2945.

Folk & Traditional Music

Asociación Cultural Yoruba de Cuba
Prado 615, e/ Dragones y
Monte. **Map** 4 D3.
Tel 7863 5953.

Conjunto Folklórico Nacional
Calle 4 103 e/ Calzada y 5ta.
Map 1 B2. **Tel** 7830 3939.

Rumba del Callejón de Hamel
Callejón de Hamel, e/
Aramburo y Hospital.
Map 3 A2. **Tel** 7878 1661.

Hip Hop, Rock & Jazz

Café Jazz Miramar
Avenida 5, esq. 94.
Tel 7203 7676.

Centro Asturiano
Prado 309, esq. Virtudes.
Map 3 A2. **Tel** 7864 1447.

Fábrica de Arte Cubano
Calle 26, esq. 11.
Map 1 A4.
Tel 7838 2260.

Jazz Café
Avenida 1ra, esq. Paseo.
Map 1 B2. **Tel** 7838 3556.

La Madriguera
Calle Infanta y Jesús
Peregrino final.
Map 2 F4. **Tel** 7879 8175.

Río Club (Johnny)
Calle A, e/ 3ra y 5ta,
Miramar. **Tel** 7209 3389.

Salón Rosado de la Tropical
Avenida 41, esq. 46, Playa.
Tel 7203 5322.

El Sauce
Avenida 9 No. 1201S, e/
120 y 130, Playa.
Tel 7204 7114.

La Zorra y el Cuervo
Calle 23, e/ N y O.
Map 2 F2. **Tel** 7833 2402.

Nightclubs & Discos

1830 Club
Malecón y Túnel, Vedado.
Tel 7838 3092.

Café Cantante
Paseo, esq. 39. **Map** 3 D5.
Tel 7878 4275.

Café Concierto Gato Tuerto
Calle O 14, e/ 17 y 19.
Map 2 F1. **Tel** 7838 2629.

Casa de la Música
Galiano, e/ Concordia y
Neptuno. **Tel** 7862 4165.
Avenida 35, esq 20.
Map 3 C2. **Tel** 7204 0447.

Dos Gardenias
Complejo Dos Gardenias,
Calle 7 y 26, Playa. **Tel**
7204 2353.

La Gruta
Calle 23, No. 111, esq. O,
Vedado. **Map** 2 F2.
Tel 7836 9320.

Salón Turquino
Calle L, e/ 23 y 25. **Map** 2
F2. **Tel** 7834 6100.

Cabaret

Cabaret Copa Room
Paseo y Malecón.
Map 1 B2. **Tel** 7836 4051.

Cabaret Parisien
Calle O, e/ 23 y 19.
Map 2 F1. **Tel** 7836 3663.

Cabaret Salón Rojo
Calle 21, e/ N y O.
Map 2 F1. **Tel** 7833 0666.

Bars

Bar Vista del Golfo
Calle O, e/ 23 y 19.
Map 2 F1. **Tel** 7836 3564.

El Cocinero
Calle 26, esq. 11.
Map 1 A4. **Tel** 7832 2355.

Espacios
Calle 10 No. 513, e/ 5 y 7.
Tel 7202 2921.

El Floridita
Obispo, esq. Monserrate.
Map 4 D2. **Tel** 7866 8856.

Madrigal
Calle 17, no 809 (altos), e/ 2
y 4, Vedado. **Tel** 7831 2433.

La Torre
Calle M, esq. 17, Vedado.
Tel 7832 7306.

Cinema

Cine Charles Chaplin
Calle 23 1155, e/ 10 y 12.
Map 1 C4. **Tel** 7831 1101.

Cine Payret
Paseo de Martí 503, esq.
San José. **Map** 4 D3.
Tel 7863 3163.

Cine La Rampa
Calle 23 111, e/ N y O.
Map 2 F2.
Tel 7878 6146.

Cine Riviera
Calles 23, e/ H y G.
Map 2 E3. **Tel** 7830 9564.

Cine Yara
Calle 23 y Calle L.
Map 2 E2. **Tel** 7832 9430.

ICAIC
Calle 23 1155, e/ 10 y 12.
Map 1 C4. **Tel** 7831 1101.

Cultural Centres

Asociación Cultural Yoruba
Paseo de Martí 615.
Map 4 D3. **Tel** 7863 5953.

Fundación Alejo Carpentier
Empedrado 215 e/
Cuba y San Ignacio.
Map 4 E2. **Tel** 7861 3667.

Fundación Fernando Ortíz
Calle 27 160, esq. L.
Map 2 F2. **Tel** 7832 4334.

UNEAC
Calle 17 351, esq. H.
Map 2 D2. **Tel** 7832 4551.

Children

El Arca
Avenida del Puerto y
Obrapía. **Map** 4 D5.
Tel 7864 8953.

Parque Luz Caballero
Avenida del Puerto y
Chacón, La Habana Vieja.
Avenida 47, Miramar.
Map 4 E1.

Parque Metropol-itano de La Habana
Avenida 47, Miramar.

Planetario
Plaza Vieja.
Map 4 E3.
Tel 7864 9165.

Teatro Guiñol
Calle M, e/ 17 y 19.
Map 2 E1.
Tel 7832 6262.

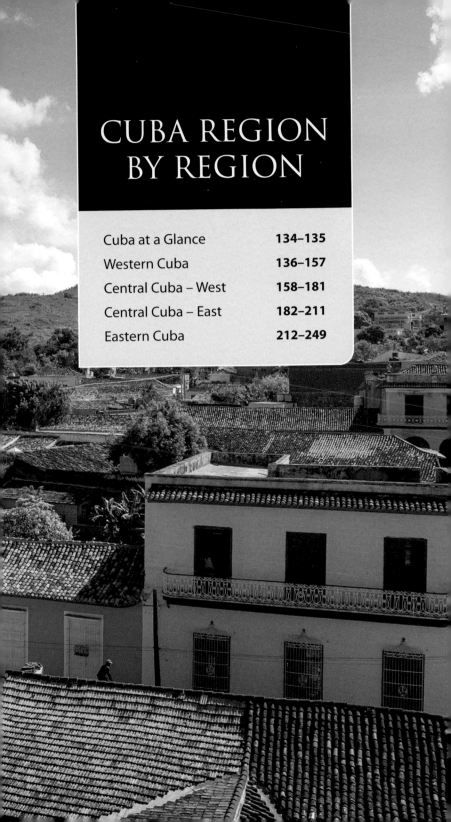

CUBA REGION BY REGION

Cuba at a Glance

The lovely palm-fringed beaches of Cuba, such as those at Varadero and on Cayo Largo, are famous throughout the world, and justly so. But the interior of the island also offers a variety of unexpected experiences, from mountainous scenery to marshland and freshwater lagoons. The towns are full of interest, often with well-preserved architecture. Cuba really has two capitals. Havana is monumental and maritime, modern and colonial, and represents the most European spirit of the country. The second, Santiago, embodies the Caribbean soul of Cuba. For the purposes of this guide, the island is divided into five regions – Havana, Western Cuba, Central Cuba – West, Central Cuba – East and Eastern Cuba. Each area is colour coded as shown here.

Varadero *(see pp166–7)*, known for its clear sea, is a popular holiday resort with sports centres and parks such as the Parque Josone.

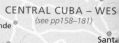

The Valle de Viñales *(see pp146–7)* has spectacular natural scenery with unique outcrops called *mogotes* and many cave formations. The most significant cave is the Cueva de Santo Tomás.

Trinidad *(see pp186–94)* is a beautifully preserved and restored city noted for its colonial architecture. The pastel-washed bell tower of the former Iglesia de San Francisco is the symbol of the city.

Cayo Largo del Sur *(see pp156–7)*, a small island with stunning white sand beaches on the shores of the Caribbean Sea, is a holiday paradise.

Cayo Coco is a natural reserve for flamingoes in the Jardines del Rey archipelago *(see pp202–3)*. The reserve is mostly marshland, but is dotted with white sandy beaches.

Camagüey *(see pp204–7)*, in Central-Eastern Cuba, is full of well-preserved colonial buildings and courtyards, with fine streets and squares such as Plaza San Juan de Dios, seen here.

Baracoa *(see pp246–7)*, the isolated, easternmost city in Cuba, is the only one with traces of the island's first inhabitants. Near the town are remnants of the tropical forest that covered the entire island when Columbus first landed here.

Cayo Coco

Chambas

ancti píritus

Ciego de Ávila

Júcaro

Camagüey

Nuevitas

Manatí

CENTRAL CUBA – EAST
(see pp182–211)

Las Tunas

Holguín

Santa Cruz del Sur

Moa

EASTERN CUBA
(see pp212–249)

Baracoa

Manzanillo

Bayamo

Guantánamo

Santiago de Cuba

Pilón

| 0 kilometres | 90 |
| 0 miles | 90 |

Santiago de Cuba *(see pp226–35)* is a fascinating town built around a bay, with its heart around the Catedral de la Asunción. Every summer Santiago plays host to the liveliest carnival in Cuba, in which the entire local population takes part.

WESTERN CUBA

Pinar del Río · Isla de la Juventud · Cayo Largo del Sur

The western region of mainland Cuba is characterized by swathes of cultivated fields and, at times, extraordinarily beautiful scenery. The main attraction here is the Viñales Valley, where unusual limestone outcrops (called *mogotes*) loom over lush fields of tobacco. Off the coast, scattered islands with stunning white beaches offer a peaceful refuge from the bustle of Havana.

According to the inhabitants of Santiago, Pinar del Río and Artemisa provinces are the least "revolutionary" parts of Cuba. They form the island's most rural region, populated by white farmers who have never been known for their warlike passion, although western Cuba was the scene of several battles against the Spanish in the late 1800s, and in 1958 there was a revolutionary front here.

This part of Cuba was colonized in the 16th and 17th centuries by Europeans mainly from the Canary Islands. Historically, Pinar has preferred to concentrate its efforts on producing what they claim is the best tobacco in the world. Tobacco fields are scattered among the Sierra del Rosario and Sierra de los Órganos ranges, which are barely 600 m (1,970 ft) above sea level – not high enough to be mountains yet tall enough to create a breathtaking landscape. Palm trees mingle with pine trees, and delicate wild orchids thrive where the conditions are right. These low mountains provide excellent walking territory. The Sierra del Rosario is now a UNESCO world biosphere reserve, as is the Guanahacabibes peninsula in the far west. In both areas, the emphasis is placed on conservation-conscious ecotourism.

Ecotourism is less of a priority on Cayo Largo, a long-established island resort with lovely sea and sand, and numerous hotels. This island forms part of the Archipiélago de los Canarreos, in the Caribbean Sea, which is made up of 350 *cayos* or keys. All of these are uninhabited apart from Cayo Largo and Isla de la Juventud (Isle of Youth), a large island with a rich history and second-best dive spot in Cuba.

Soroa waterfall on a sunny day at Pinar del Rio

◀ Thatched hut and *mogote* typical of Valle de Viñales

Exploring Western Cuba

The extraordinary tranquillity and agreeable climate of Western Cuba make it a lovely area for a relaxing break. However, there is also plenty to do. Besides walking and horse riding, there is the provincial capital of Pinar del Río to explore, while tempting coral beaches are easily accessible off the north coast. More effort is required to reach remote María La Gorda, in the far west, but keen divers are attracted to this diving centre. Isla de la Juventud attracts divers and visitors interested in curious attractions, from painted caves to the one-time prison of Fidel Castro. The Valle de Viñales hotels and bed and breakfasts make the best base for a stay in Western Cuba.

Typical street in Pinar del Río, "the city of capitals"

Farmers with typical ox-drawn carts at the foot of a *mogote*

Getting Around

The motorway *(autopista)* connects Havana, Artemisa and Pinar del Río (about a two-hour drive), and another slower, but more picturesque, road follows the northern coastline. From Pinar a road runs southwest to Guanahacabibes. There are one-day tours that start off from Havana and include Soroa, Pinar and Viñales, but not the beaches: information is available at tourist offices. The best way to get to Isla de la Juventud and Cayo Largo is by air from Havana (40 mins). There is also a catamaran service to the former from Batabanó; the trip takes two hours. Excursions can also be booked to the two islands; departures are from Havana or larger towns.

Schools of tropical fish, easily spotted on the sea bed along the Los Canarreos archipelago

Sights at a Glance

Key

═══ Motorway

▬▬▬ Major road

····· Minor road

╌╌╌ Main railway

▬▬▬ Regional border

For keys to symbols see back flap

❶ Sierra del Rosario

Artemisa. **Road Map** A2.

This area of 61,750 acres (25,000 ha) of unspoilt Cuba has been declared a biosphere reserve by UNESCO. Woods consisting of tropical and deciduous trees and plants cover the Sierra del Rosario range, which is crossed by the San Juan river with its small falls. The area is home to abundant, varied fauna: 90 species of bird as well as many different reptiles and amphibians. The walks here are lovely (permission is needed from the resort area), on paths lined with flowers, including wild orchids.

❷ Soroa

Candelaria (Artemisa).
Road Map A2. 🚌
Candelaria. 🛈 Hotel Soroa,
(48) 523 556.

The town of Soroa lies 250 m (820 ft) above sea level in the middle of tropical forest in the Sierra del Rosario region. It was named after two Basque brothers, Lorenzo and Antonio Soroa Muñagorri, who, in around 1856, bought various coffee plantations in the area and soon became the proprietors of the entire territory. One of the estates in the valley, Finca Angerona, was in the 19th century the setting for a legendary love story involving the French-German Cornelius Sausse, who built the farm in 1813, and a Haitian girl, Ursule Lambert.

Soroa, today, is a small town with a hotel (Villa Soroa) and a number of tourist attractions. The most photographed is the **Saltón**, a spectacular waterfall on the Manantiales river, a 20-minute walk from the Villa Soroa. But the major sight here is the **Orquideario de Soroa**, an orchid garden which has been declared a national monument. It has one of the largest orchid collections in the world, with more than 700 species, 250 of which are endemic, in an area of 35,000 ha (86,500 acres). The park, often visited by

A flower in the Soroa orchid garden

Bathing under the falls *(saltón)* of the Manantiales river at Soroa

Hemingway, was founded in 1943 by a lawyer from the Canaries, Tomás Felipe Camacho. He had orchids sent here from all over the world in memory of his daughter, who had died at the age of 20 in childbirth, and his wife who died shortly after.

Outside the town is the **Castillo de las Nubes**, a medieval-like construction built in 1940 for Antonio Arturo Sánchez Bustamante, the

Beaches of the North Coast

An alternative route to the Pinar region from Havana is the road that skirts the coastline at the foot of the Guaniguanico mountain range. The drive from the capital to Viñales, with fine panoramic views and scenery, takes about five hours. From the northern coast there is access to the splendid beaches on some of the small islands in the Los Colorados Archipelago. For the most part, the locals make their living by fishing, but the islands have already attracted some tourism. The sea can be rough and a general lack of facilities makes this area more suitable for visitors who love water sports rather than a place for a relaxing beach holiday.

Cayo Jutías is still unspoilt and frequented more by Cubans than by tourists. The island is an oasis of peace and white sand, populated by many species of local and migratory birds.

Around 3 km (2 miles) from Santa Lucía, which has hotel facilities and connections, is a causeway connecting the mainland with Cayo Jutías.

0 kilometres   15
0 miles   15

landowner of this area. The Castillo boasts marvellous views over the Sierra del Rosario.

🌸 Orquideario de Soroa

Carretera de Soroa km 8. **Tel** (48) 523 871. **Open** 8:30am–4:30pm daily. 🅿

❸ Las Terrazas

Artemisa. **Road Map** A2.
ℹ Las Terrazas, (48) 578 700.

Most of the farmers in the Sierra del Rosario region live in communities founded by a government programme in 1968. The best-known of these is Las Terrazas, whose name derives from the terraces laid out for the hardwood trees that are now a characteristic feature of the area. The 1,000 inhabitants make a living by maintaining the woods and from ecotourism, which has increased since the building of the environmentally friendly Hotel Moka (see p258). The hotel makes a good starting point for guided walks in the reserve, all of which are fairly easy and take no more than two hours to cover. Also open is the restored 19th-century French coffee plantation of Buena Vista, which has a restaurant.

The well-managed pine forest at Las Terrazas

Most of the trails are excellent for birdwatching, with plenty of endemic Cuban birds such as the zunzún hummingbird, the tocororo and the cartacuba (see pp24–5).

The delightful set of natural pools known as the Baños de San Juan, make for another interesting walk along the San Juan river. There are picnic tables, a restaurant and some basic cabin accommodation on the banks of the river, for those wanting to stay the night.

The artificial Lake San Juan at the heart of the Las Terrazas rural community

Cayo Levisa, the best-known island in the archipelago, has a fairly simple tourist village, 3 km (2 miles) of lovely beach and a coral reef with splendid scuba-diving sites.

Cayo Paraíso, whose name means paradise, was the setting for Hemingway's stories Islands in the Stream.

Marina Hemingway, 20 km (12 miles) from the heart of Havana, is a famous tourist spot known for hosting the annual marlin fishing tournament held in honour of the American author. Competitors come from all over the world to participate.

Havana
Artemisa
Pinar del Río

Cayo Paraíso
Palma Rubía
Las Pozas
Playa El Morillo
Bahía Honda
Bahía Honda
Playa San Pedro
Bahía de Cabañas
Cabañas
Orlando Nodarse
Mariel
Playa Baracoa
Marina Hemingway

Mariel was the point of departure for the 1980 marielitos boatlift (see p57) and is now a major container port for the capital.

❹ Cayo Levisa

Pinar del Río. **Road Map** A2. 🚢 from Palma Rubia (1 hr), departures 9am & 10am, return 5pm & 6pm. Excursions from Pinar del Río. 🚺 Havanatur, Calle Osmani Arenado, esq. Martí. (48) 778 494.

This small island, with its white sand beaches, an offshore coral reef and mangroves, is the most geared up for tourists in the Los Colorados archipelago, and the only one with diving facilities. Despite this, it is still unspoilt and is home to several species of bird and the surrounding waters have an abundance of fish, especially marlin.

❺ Parque Nacional La Güira

Los Palacios (Pinar del Río). **Road Map** A2. **Tel** (48) 750 486. 🗺 3,000. 🚗 🚺 Cueva de los Portales: Carretera San Andrès km 14. **Open** 8am–5pm daily. 🚗 📷 Note: fee for photography applies.

At the heart of what was, prior to the Revolution, one of the largest agricultural estates in Pinar del Rio, Parque Nacional La Güira comprises the landscaped grounds and former residence of the landowner Don Manuel Cortina, a successful lawyer and notable politician. This was one of the first properties to be nationalized after Castro's rebel seized power and Cortina was

The entrance to the Cueva de los Portales

The lovely gardens in Parque Nacional La Güira

forced to leave Cuba in 1959, fleeing charges of worker exploitation and ending his days in Miami, where he died in 1970. The large park, though it lay derelict for many years, is still in fairly good shape and includes the ruins of a medieval-style residence and an English garden with a small Chinese temple and statues of mythological figures including sphinxes and satyrs.

About 5 km (3 miles) east of the Güira park is **San Diego de los Baños**, a peaceful village on the slopes of the Sierra de los Quemados, which has retained its colonial atmosphere. The village is a major tourist and therapeutic centre. Springs in the area produce sulphurous water that was said to help cure rheumatism and skin diseases. Unfortunately they have now been closed for several years.

Don Manuel Cortina also owned a nearby cave, the **Cueva de los Portales**, discovered in the 19th century. This old hiding place was used by the natives as a refuge from the massacres that were waged by the Spanish in the early 16th century. During the missile crisis in 1962, the cave became the headquarters of Che Guevara's Western Army, some of whose

personal effects are on display. Plaques indicate where he played chess and slept.

❻ Vuelta Abajo

Pinar del Río. **Road Map** A3.

The small area between Pinar del Río, San Juan y Martínez and San Luís produces very high quality tobacco. Good growing conditions are the result of a series of factors: for example, the Sierra del Rosario protects the plants from heavy rainfall, and the sandy red soil in which the tobacco plants grow is well drained and rich in nitrogen. This is a unique environment; in fact, the former landowners who left Cuba in 1959 have tried in vain to reproduce the miracle in Nicaragua, Honduras, Santo Domingo and the US.

On the road from the provincial capital to San Juan y Martínez, the prestigious Hoyo de Monterrey plantations can be visited. Here plants are protected from the sun by cotton cloth in order to maintain the softness of the tobacco leaves. There are also curing houses, windowless storehouses where the leaves are left to dry on long poles.

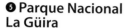

A Hoyo de Monterrey cigar band

Cuban Tobacco

The tobacco plant *(Nicotiana tabacum)* grows from small, round, golden seeds. Cuban tobacco seeds are in demand throughout the world, because their quality is considered to be so good. The plant reaches its full height in the three or four months from November to February. Like cigar-making *(see pp36–7)*, tobacco growing is the result of age-old expertise handed down from generation to generation. Tobacco plants are quite delicate, and need skilful handling. There are two types: *Corojo*, grown in greenhouses, which has the prettiest leaves and is used as wrapper leaves for the cigars, and *Criollo*, which grows outdoors and provides the other leaves.

Criollo **leaves** are separated into three grades: *ligero, seco* and *volado*. The first, which is the best, has the most aromatic leaves, which absorb most sun and are harvested only when completely mature.

Floating cultivation is a technique of experimental hydroculture in which the seeds germinate ten days earlier than those grown with traditional methods.

Tobacco Harvest

Harvesting tobacco is a delicate and laborious operation. The leaves are tied in bunches, hung on horizontal poles and then transported to curing barns. In the case of the Corojo plant, the harvest is carried out in various stages, at intervals of several days.

Poles for transport and drying

Traditional cultivation in rows

Drying takes from 45 to 60 days. The leaves, hung on small poles in storehouses known as *casas de tabaco*, gradually turn from bright green to brown.

Humidification is a hydrating process carried out after the drying so that the leaves do not dry out and become brittle. Once sprayed, the bunches of leaves are suspended in order to eliminate excess water.

By establishing a tobacco monopoly in 1717, the colonial authorities obliged farmers to sell all their tobacco to Spain. Although the Cuban government allows private tobacco growers to have 17-acre (7-ha) plots, the state, along with the UK's Imperial Tobacco, is still the sole manufacturer and distributor of cigars.

❼ Pinar del Río

Road Map A3. 🗺 195,000.
ℹ️ Infotur, Hotel Vueltabajo, Calle
Martí 103, (48) 759 381; Cubanacán,
Calle Martí 109, esq. Colón, (48) 750
178. 🚌 🚂 from Havana.

In 1778, when the Cuban
provinces were founded, the
town of Nueva Filipina was
renamed Pinar because of a
pine grove in the vicinity, on
the banks of the Guamá river.
Nearby, General Antonio Maceo
fought a number of battles in
1896–7 that were crucial to the
Cubans' victory in the third war
of Cuban independence.

Today, the pines no longer
grow here, but the clean air and
colonial atmosphere of Pinar del
Río are unchanged. The town
has long been a centre for the
cultivation and industrial
processing of tobacco. The
most striking aspect about the
historic centre of this small,
orderly and peaceful town is
the abundance of columns:
Corinthian or Ionic, simple
or decorated. Not for
nothing is Pinar del
Río known as the
"city of capitals".

The most important
buildings lie on the
arcaded main street,
Calle Martí (or Real). In
the **Cultural Heritage
Fund** shop, at the
corner of Calle Rosario,
visitors can buy local crafts as
well as art reproductions. In the
evening, the **Casa de la Cultura**
(at No. 125) hosts shows and
concerts of traditional music

A capital with
bas-relief decoration

such as *punto guajiro* (from
guajiro, the Cuban word for
farmer), which is of Spanish
derivation, and is generally
characterized by improvisation.

At Nos. 172, 174 and 176 in
Calle Colón, there are three
unusual buildings
designed by Rogelio
Pérez Cubillas, the
city's leading architect
in the 1930s and 1940s.

🏛 **Palacio Guasch**
Calle Martí 202, esq.
Comandante Pinares.
Museum: **Tel** (48) 779 483.
Open 9am–5pm Mon–Sat,
9am–noon Sun. **Closed** 1 Jan, 1 May,
26 Jul, 10 Oct, 25 Dec. 📷 Note: fee for
photography applies.

This somewhat extravagant
building is a mixture of Moorish
arches, Gothic spires and Baroque
elements. It was built in 1909
for a wealthy physician who had
travelled widely and who wanted
to reproduce in his new residence
the architectural styles that had
impressed him the most. In 1979
the mansion was transformed
into a Museo de Historia Natural
Antonio Núñez Jiménez (natural
history museum) named after
Tranquilino Sandalio de Nodas, a
well-known land surveyor in this
region. The museum illustrates

One of the three eclectic-style buildings on Calle Colón

The Centre of Pinar del Río

① Palacio Guasch
② Museo Provincial de
   Historia
③ Teatro Milanés
④ Fábrica de
   Guayabita
   Casa Garay
⑤ Catedral de San
   Rosendro
⑥ Fábrica de Tabacos
   Francisco Donatién

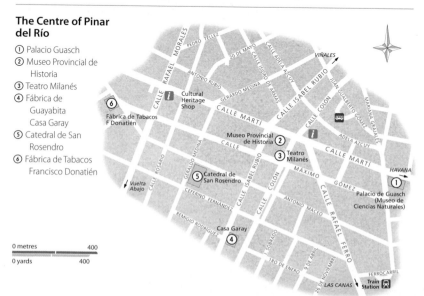

0 metres ⎯⎯⎯⎯ 400
0 yards ⎯⎯⎯⎯ 400

The unusual façade of the Palacio Guasch, Pinar del Río

the natural and geological history of Pinar and has on display stuffed birds and animals, including the tiny Cuban *zunzún* hummingbird, and a crocodile more than 4 m (12 ft) long, as well as rare plants and butterflies. In the inner courtyard are sculptures of prehistoric animals.

Museo Provincial de Historia

Calle Martí 58 e/ Colón y Isabel Rubio. **Tel** (48) 754 300. **Open** noon–4pm Mon, 8:30am–10pm Tue–Sat, 8am–noon Sun. **Closed** 1 Jan, 1 May, 26 Jul, 10 Oct, 25 Dec.

This museum illustrates the history of the province from the Pre-Columbian period to the present. On display is a major collection of 19th-century arms, colonial furniture, works by local painters, including a huge landscape by Domingo Ramos (1955), and mementos of the musician Enrique Jorrín, the father of the cha-cha-cha.

Teatro Milanés

Calle Martí y Colón. **Tel** (48) 753 871. A Neo-Classical gem and the city's pride and joy, this theatre is named after the romantic poet José Jacinto Milanés. It started out as the Lope de Vega theatre, which first opened in 1845 and was then bought in 1880 by one Félix del Pino Díaz. He totally renovated it, modelling it on the Teatro Sauto in Matanzas (*see p162*). Its name was changed in 1898.

This simple but functional structure has a rectangular plan, a linear façade and a portico with tall columns. Its opulent, three-level, U-shaped wooden auditorium has a seating capacity of about 500.

Fábrica de Guayabita Casa Garay

Calle Isabel Rubio 189 e/ Ceferino Fernández y Frank País. **Tel** (48) 752 966. **Open** 9am–5pm Mon–Fri, 9am–noon Sat & Sun. **Closed** 1 Jan, 1 May, 26 Jul, 10 Oct, 25 Dec.

Since 1892 the Casa Garay has produced Guayabita del Pinar, a liqueur based on an ancient recipe. It is made by distilling brandy from the sugar of the *guayaba* (guava), which is grown in this area. Guided tours of the small factory finish up at the tasting area, where visitors can try the sweet and dry versions of this popular drink.

Fábrica de Tabacos Francisco Donatién

Antonio Maceo 157. **Tel** (48) 773 069. **Open** 9am–1:30pm Mon–Fri. **Closed** 1 Jan, 1 May, 26 Jul, 10 Oct, 25 Dec.

This tiny cigar factory, housed in a former 19th-century jail, is open to the public. Visitors can watch the 70 or so workers making Trinidad cigars. These and other cigars are sold in the small shop. The factory is also a training school for *torcedores* (cigar rollers).

⑧ Viñales

Pinar del Río. **Road Map** A3.
🚗 27,000. 🚌

Viñales, whose name derives from a vineyard planted here by a settler from the Canary Islands, was founded in 1607.

This small town, the economy of which has always been based on agriculture, is now the subject of government protection as an example of a perfectly preserved colonial settlement. The main street is named after Salvador Cisneros Betancourt, a 19th-century nationalist and one of the signatories of the 1869 Cuban constitution (*see p48*). It is lined with many colonial houses with characteristic arcades, which make useful shelters from the hot sun and any sudden violent tropical rainstorms.

The town's most important architecture is in the main square, the **Parque Martí**, on which stand the Iglesia del Sagrado Corazón de Jesús (1888), and the former Colonia Española (diplomatic headquarters of the Spanish gentry), which is now the town's Casa de la Cultura.

Viñales also boasts a minor architectural gem, the **Casa de Don Tomás**, built in 1887–8 for Gerardo Miel y Sainz, a rich merchant and agent for a shipping line. The building was blown down in the 2008 hurricane, but then rebuilt true to the original.

Casa de Don Tomás

Salvador Cisnero, e/ Adela Azcuy y Carratera a Pinar del Río. **Tel** (48) 796 300.

The main street in Viñales, with its one-storey porticoed houses

For hotels and restaurants in this region see pp258–9 and pp272–3

❾ Valle de Viñales

A unique landscape awaits visitors to the
Viñales Valley. The *mogotes*, the characteristic,
gigantic karst formations that resemble sugar
loaves, are like stone sentinels keeping watch
over the corn and tobacco fields, the red
earth with majestic royal palm trees and
the farmhouses with roofs of palm leaves.
According to legend, centuries ago some
Spanish sailors who were approaching the
coast thought the profile of the *mogotes*
they glimpsed in the fog looked like a church
organ. Hence the name, Sierra de los Órganos,
given to the network of hills in this area.

A casa de tabaco for curing tobacco near a mogote

0 kilometres 1

0 miles 1

Mural de la Prehistoria
On the face of a *mogote* the Cuban painter Leovigildo
González, a pupil of the famous Mexican artist Diego
Rivera, painted the history of evolution (1959–62), from
ammonites to *Homo sapiens*. The mural, restored in 1980,
makes use of the cracks in the rock to create special
effects of light and colour.

San Vicente •

① Cueva
del Ruiseñor

Sierra
de Viñales

Valle de la Guasasa

Key

△ Peak
═══ Paved road
══ Path
≈≈ River
- - - Underground river

Mogote △
dos Hermanas

△ *Mogote
del Valle*

*Comunidad El Moncada
(Entrance to the Santo Tomás
Cavern)*

Valle de Viñale

Hotel Los Jazmines •

↙ Pinar del Río

Gran Caverna de Santo Tomás
This is the largest network of caves in Cuba and the
whole of Latin America. With its 46 km (29 miles) of
galleries and up to eight levels of communicating
grottoes, the Gran Caverna is a speleologist's
paradise. In the 19th century, the Cueva del
Salón was used by local farmers for festivals.

For hotels and restaurants in this region see pp258–9 and pp272–3

Cueva del Indio

This cave, discovered in 1920, lies in the San Vicente Valley. The first part of the tour here is on foot through tunnels with artificial lighting. Then a small motorboat takes visitors up the underground San Vicente river for about a quarter of a mile.

VISITORS' CHECKLIST

Practical Information
Viñales (Pinar del Río).
Road Map A3. 🗺 27,000.
i Cubanacán Viajes, Salvador Cisneros 63c, Plaza Viñales, (48) 796 393; Infotur, Salvador Cisneros 63c, (48) 796 263. Excursions & tours of the caves: *i* Centro de Visitantes, Carretera a Viñales, (48) 796 144.

Transport
🚌 Salvador Cisneros 63, (48) 793 112; connections with Havana, Cienfuegos, Pinar del Río, Trinidad and Varadero.

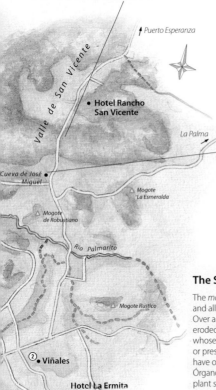

↑ *Puerto Esperanza*

Valle de San Vicente

● **Hotel Rancho San Vicente**

La Palma →

Cueva de José Miguel ●

△ *Mogote La Esmeralda*

△ *Mogote de Robustiano*

Río Palmarito

△ *Mogote Rustico*

② ● **Viñales**

Hotel La Ermita
●

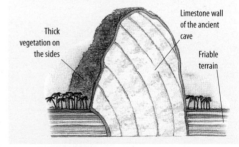

Palenque de los Cimarrones

In the depths of Cueva de San Miguel, past the bar at its mouth, is a spectacular cave that was once a refuge for runaway African slaves *(cimarrones)*. It now houses a small museum and a pleasant restaurant.

The Structure of a Mogote

The *mogotes* are among the most ancient rocks in Cuba, and all that remains of what was once a limestone plateau. Over a period lasting millions of years, underground aquifers eroded the softer limestone, giving rise to large caverns whose ceilings later collapsed. Only the hard limestone pillars, or present-day *mogotes*, were left standing. *Mogotes* generally have only a thin covering of soil, but those in the Sierra de los Órganos are covered with thick vegetation. Some endemic plant species have adapted to life on their craggy crevices; these include the mountain palm tree *(Bombacopsis cubensis)*, and the cork palm *(Microcycas calocoma)*.

KEY

① **Sierrita de San Vicente** is famous for its hot springs.

② **Viñales** still has a colonial feel *(see p145)*. It is a tranquil, pleasant little town, ideal for a short stay.

Thick vegetation on the sides

Limestone wall of the ancient cave

Friable terrain

The jetty at María La Gorda, the departure point for boats taking people to dive sites

⑩ María La Gorda

Pinar del Río. 🛈 Hotel María La Gorda Diving Centre, (48) 778 131, 778 077.

The best-known bathing spot on the southwestern coast owes its name to a sad legend. A few centuries ago, a plump *(gorda)* girl named María was abducted by pirates on the Venezuelan coast and then abandoned here. In order to survive, she was forced to sell herself to the buccaneers who passed by. The place still bears her name today.

The extraordinary beauty of the coral reefs – populated by sea turtles, reef sharks and other rare species of tropical fish – makes these 8 km (5 miles) of coastline with fine white sand and a warm, translucent sea a real tropical aquarium. The reefs are also easy to reach, lying just a short distance from the shore (the coral and fish can even be seen without swimming under water).

From the jetty opposite the diving area, a boat takes divers twice a day to the various dive sites. Areas of particular interest include the so-called Black Coral Valley, a wall of coral over 100 m (328 ft) long, and the Salón de María, a sea cave at a depth of 18 m (60 ft), which is the habitat of rare species of fish.

⑪ Guanahacabibes Reserve

Pinar del Río. 🛈 Estación Ecológica, La Bajada, (48) 750 366. 🗷

The peninsula of Guanahacabibes, named after a Pre-Columbian ethnic group, is a strip of land 100 km (62 miles) long and 6–34 km (4–21 miles) wide. In 1985 it was declared a world biosphere reserve by UNESCO, to protect the flora and fauna. Access to the inner zone, in the vicinity of La Bajada, is therefore limited. Permission to visit is granted by the park rangers at La Bajada, and visits to the park are made in visitors' vehicles and then on foot with a local guide.

A *cotorra*, a species of parrot seen in the reserve

The mixed forest of deciduous and evergreen trees contains about 600 species of plants and many animals, including deer, boar, reptiles and *jutías*, rodents similar to opossums that live in trees. Among the bird species are woodpeckers, parrots, hummingbirds, *cartacuba* and *tocororo (see p22)*.

Cabo San Antonio, the western tip of Cuba, is identifiable by the 23-m (75-ft) high Roncalli lighthouse, built in 1849 by the Spanish governor after whom it was named.

Cabo Corrientes at the southern end of the Guanahacabibes reserve

◀ Harvesting tobacco in the Valle de Viñales

Diving in the Caribbean Sea

The Caribbean Seabeds off the island of Cuba offer some of the most exciting coral reef scenery imaginable. The coral formations lie at a maximum depth of 150 m (495 ft), at an average temperature of about 23° C (73 °F), and never less than 18° C (64 °F). The most fascinating areas for divers are at Jardines de la Reina, María la Gorda, the Archipelago de los Canarreos and Playa Santa Lucía. Qualified scuba-diving centres *(centros de buceo)* take visitors on trips out to the reefs, with live-aboards available at Jardines de la Reina and Isla de la Juventud. In some areas it is possible to see tropical fish and coral simply by snorkelling *(see p285)*.

Sea plume is a type of gorgonia that looks much like a feather.

"Soft coral" results from an evolutionary process during which the hard skeleton turns into a flexible structrure.

The grouper, with its unmistakable colouring, is one of the most common fish in the Caribbean, together with the queen triggerfish and the *Pomacanthus paru* angelfish. Other widespread species are the tarpon, with its silvery colouring, and the barracuda, with its powerful teeth. Sharks are less common.

Sponge

The blue surgeon fish is born with bright yellow colouring that later turns blue.

Coral

The Sea Floor

The coral reef is a rich and complex ecosystem. The Caribbean seabeds are home to numerous varieties of coral and a great many sea sponges and gorgonias, as well as tropical fish, sea turtles and various crustaceans.

Brain coral is one of many types of coral common to the Cuban seas, along with black coral, iron wire coral with its rod-like structure, and elkhorn coral with its flat branches.

Tubular sponges vary in size, the largest ones being 2 m (6 ft) high. If they are squeezed or stepped on they emit a purple dye that will stain your skin for several days. There are also barrel- and vase-shaped sponges.

Gorgonian sea fans (Gorgonia ventalina) are quite widespread on Caribbean seabeds. It is possible to see splendid examples of huge proportions.

⑫ Isla de la Juventud

The naturalist Alexander von Humboldt *(see p189)* described this island as an abandoned place, Robert Louis Stevenson allegedly based his novel *Treasure Island* on it, Batista wanted to turn it into a paradise for rich Americans, while Fidel Castro repopulated it with young people, built universities and changed its name to the Isla de la Juventud (Isle of Youth). With a surface area of 2,200 sq km (850 sq miles) and 86,000 inhabitants, this is the largest island in the Archipiélago de los Canarreos. Comparatively few tourists venture here, but there are a few interesting sights and the diving is excellent.

Ensenada de los Barcos

La Demajagua

Atanagildo Cajige

Mina de Oro

0 km 5
0 miles 5

Hotel Colony

Punta Francés

Ensenada de la Siguanea

Punta Pedernales

Cocodrilo

Nuestra Señora de los Dolores, in Nueva Gerona

Nueva Gerona

Surrounded by hills that yield multicoloured marble, the small, peaceful town of Nueva Gerona was founded in 1830 on the banks of the Las Casas river by Spanish settlers who, together with their slaves, had left countries on the American continent that had won their independence.

The town is built on a characteristic grid plan and the modern outskirts are in continuous expansion. A good starting point for a visit to Nueva Gerona is **Calle 39**, the graceful main street flanked by coloured arcades. Here can be found the local cinema, theatre, pharmacy (which is always open), post office, hospital, bank, Casa de la Cultura and numerous bars and restaurants. This street ends at the Parque Central, Nueva Gerona's main square, where the **Iglesia de Nuestra Señora de los Dolores** stands. First built in

Neo-Classical style in 1853, this church was totally destroyed by a cyclone in 1926 and rebuilt three years later in colonial style.

South of the Parque Central, the former City Hall building is now the home of the **Museo Municipal**. It displays many objects and documents concerning pirates and buccaneers – the main protagonists in the island's history – as well as the inevitable photographs and mementos of the Revolution. Another museum, the **Casa Natal Jesús Montané**, is dedicated solely to the struggle against Fulgencio Batista's dictatorship.

The **Museo de Historia Natural Antonio Núñez Jiménez**, covers the geological and natural history of the island, and there is a fine planetarium here as well, the only one in the world where the North Star can

be seen together with the Southern Cross.

A few kilometres outside of town is the rather forlorn **American cemetery**. In the early 1900s, the Americans declared La Isla part of their overseas possessions; they only relinquished sovereignty in 1925. Ecotur can arrange visits.

The harbour at Nueva Gerona, where fishermen moor their boats

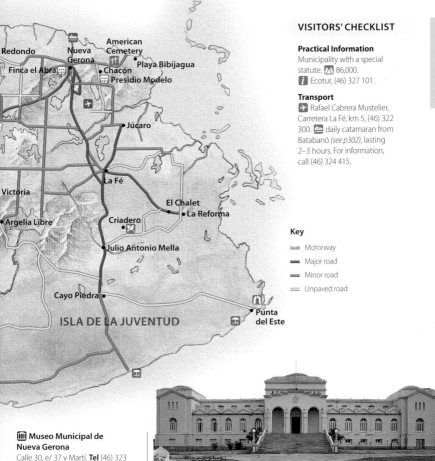

VISITORS' CHECKLIST

Practical Information
Municipality with a special
statute. 86,000.
Ecotur, (46) 327 101.

Transport
Rafael Cabrera Mustelier,
Carretera La Fé, km 5, (46) 322
300. daily catamaran from
Batabanó *(see p302)*, lasting
2–3 hours. For information,
call (46) 324 415.

Key

━━ Motorway

━━ Major road

━━ Minor road

═══ Unpaved road

The austere façade of the Presidio Modelo prison

Museo Municipal de Nueva Gerona
Calle 30, e/ 37 y Martí. **Tel** (46) 323
791. **Open** 9am–4:30pm Tue–Sat,
8am–noon Sun. Note: fee for
photography may apply.

Museo de Historia Natural Antonio Núñez Jiménez
Calle 41, esq. 54, No. 4625. **Tel** (46) 323
143. **Open** 9am–noon & 1–5pm Tue–
Sat, 9am–noon Sun. Note: fee
for photography may apply.

Strolling along the arcades on
Nueva Gerona's Calle 39

Presidio Modelo
4 km southeast of Nueva Gerona,
Reparto Delio Chacón. **Tel** (46) 325 112.
Open 8am–4pm Tue–Sat, 8am–noon
Sun. Note: fee for photography
may apply.

On the road that connects the
capital with Playa Bibijagua, a
popular beach of black sand
frequented by the inhabitants
of Nueva Gerona, is Cuba's most
famous penitentiary. Originally
built by Gerardo Machado *(see
p50)*, it was modelled on the
famous panopticon in Joliet,
Illinois (US), and converted into
a museum in 1967. The prison
consists of tiny cells in the
interior of four enormous
multistorey round cement
blocks. In the middle of each
stood a sentry-box from which

guards could keep a close watch
on all the prisoners. Guards and
prisoners never came into contact with one another. Guards
circulated in underground
galleries, keeping constant
watch over the prisoners above.

It was in the Presidio Modelo
that the organizers of the attack
on the Moncada army barracks
in Santiago, led by Fidel Castro,
were imprisoned in October
1953. They were liberated in
an amnesty in May 1955.

At the entrance to the first
pavilion is cell 3859, where
Castro, despite his isolation,
managed to reorganize the
revolutionary movement,
starting with the defence plea
he made in court, *History Will
Absolve Me (see p51)*.

For keys to symbols *see back flap*

Exploring Isla de la Juventud

Unlike other islands in the Archipiélago de los Canarreos, there are no grand luxury hotels on the Isla de la Juventud. As a result it seems to have a more genuine Cuban atmosphere, and the tourist industry works alongside other island activities without pressure. The island is not new to habitation, unlike other *cayos* which have only recently seen housing development, and retains vestiges of five centuries of Cuban history. The town of Nueva Gerona and its surroundings make a good starting point for a visit, followed by the southern coast. The main hotel is in the southwestern part of the island, while the eastern tip has some fascinating ancient cave paintings by Siboney Indians.

Coral formations on the island's sea floor

🏛 Casa Museo Finca El Abra

Carretera Siguanea km 1.5 (5 km southwest of Nueva Gerona).
Tel 5219 3054. **Open** 9am–5pm Tue–Sat, 9am–noon Sun. 🅿 🔘
Note: fee for photography may apply.

On the edge of the Sierra de las Casas is an elegant villa where, in 1870, the 17-year-old José Martí was held for nine weeks before being deported to Spain for his separatist views. Part of the building is now a museum with a display of photographs and documents relating to the national hero's presence on the island. The rest of the villa is occupied by the descendants of the original owner, a rich Catalan.

Punta Francés

Hotel Colony: **Tel** (46) 398 181. 📠 to the Centro Internacional de Buceo from Hotel Colony daily at 8:30am, return trip around 4:30 or 5pm.

The 56 dive sites between Punta Francés and Punta Pedernales lie at the end of a shelf which gently slopes down from the coast to a depth of 20–25 m (65–82 ft), and then abruptly drops for hundreds of metres. This vertical wall is a favourite with passing fish, which literally rub shoulders with divers. While dives on the platform can be made by beginners, those along the shelf are more difficult and suited to divers with more experience.

Numerous great dive sights are peppered along this stretch; the following are among the most fascinating: La Pared de Coral Negro, which has an abundance of black coral as well as sponges as much as 35 m (115 ft) in diameter; El Reino del Sahara, one of the most beautiful shallow dives; El Mirador, a wall dive among sponges and large madrepores; El Arco de los Sábalos, the domain of tarpons; and Cayo Los Indios, where shipwrecks can be seen on the

seabed at a depth of 10–12 m (33–40 ft).

The low-rise **Hotel Colony** *(see p258)* accommodates almost all of the scuba divers who visit the island. It overlooks Playa Roja, the large, palm-shaded beach named for its spectacular scarlet sunsets. The nearby sea is green and translucent, with a sandy floor that is often covered with swathes of the aquatic plant *Thalassia testudinum*. In the mornings a van takes guests from the hotel to the nearby diving centre, the **Centro Internacional de Buceo**, where all kinds of diving equipment can be

Sign for Hotel Colony

rented (although it is advisable to take a 3 mm wet suit with you). From here boats take visitors to the dive sites. At noon, lunch is served at the jetty next to the stunning beach at Punta Francés.

The boat trip from Hotel Colony to Punta Francés, also known as Costa de los Piratas, is a wonderful excursion. Participants don snorkels, masks and fins to accompany divers exploring a French pirate's cave and then trek to see nesting American crocodiles.

East of Hotel Colony is an area known as **La Cañada**, where Ecotur *(see p153)* can arrange a guided walk through pine, palm and mango forests. The walk passes the "Jacuzzi of the Gods", a freshwater stream where walkers can bathe and ends at the park ranger's house where home-roasted lamb and coffee is served.

The Hotel Colony, surrounded by tropical vegetation

For hotels and restaurants in this region see pp258–9 and pp272–3

White sand and crystal-clear sea at Punta del Este beach

Cocodrilo

86 km (53 miles) southeast of Nueva Gerona. *i* Ecotur, (46) 327 101.

Formerly called Jacksonville, this fishing village was founded in the early 20th century by a small community from the British colony of the Cayman Islands. Even now, a few of the villagers speak English as their first language. The settlers introduced the Round Dance, a typical Jamaican dance, which blended with Cuban music to create Sucu Sucu, a dance very popular among locals.

Criadero Crocodrilo

i Ecotur, (46) 327 101.

This breeding centre is working to protect the endangered Cuban crocodile, and has 46 reptiles on

site. Initially, the intention had been to release the crocodiles back into the wild, but as the hybrid American-Cuban crocodile threatens the Cuban crocodile's distinctiveness as a species, a liberation may never occur.

Pre-Columbian drawings which may represent a calendar, in the Cuevas del Este

Cuevas de Punta del Este

59 km (37 miles) southeast of Nueva Gerona. *i* Ecotur, (46) 327 101, where permits must be obtained in advance (ecotur@iju.mintur.tur.cu).

Punta del Este, on the southeastern tip of the island, has a stunning white sand beach. It is, however, most famous for its seven caves, which were discovered in 1910 by a French castaway who took refuge here. On the walls of the caves are 235 drawings made by Siboney Indians in an age long before the arrival of Christopher Columbus.

The drawings in the largest cave – a series of red and black concentric circles crossed by arrows pointing eastward – probably represent a solar calendar. The complexity of these drawings led the Cuban ethnologist Fernando Ortíz, who studied them in 1925, to call them "the Sistine Chapel of the Caribbean". Protect yourself against mosquitoes – the caves are full of them.

History of the Island

The corsair
Sir Francis Drake

The Taíno and Siboney peoples knew of the Isla de la Juventud long before Columbus "discovered" it in 1494 on his second journey (see p43). The Spanish crown licensed the island to cattle breeders, but in practice handed it over to pirates. Because of the shallow waters, heavy Spanish galleons were unable to approach the island, while the buccaneers' light vessels could land there. This meant that figures such as Francis Drake, Henry Morgan, Oliver Esquemeling and Jacques de Sores were able to exploit it as a hiding place for booty captured from Spanish ships.

After Nueva Gerona was founded in 1830, the island was used as a place of detention for Cuban nationalists, including José Martí. Its use as a prison island continued for 50 years in the 20th century; construction of the Presidio Modelo began in 1926. In 1953 Batista turned the island into a free zone where money could be laundered. The dictator also wanted to turn it into a holiday paradise for rich Americans, but

his plans failed. On New Year's night in 1958, as Castro's *barbudos* were entering Havana, a group of soldiers in the rebels' army took over the island during the opening ceremony of the Hotel Colony, and arrested the mafiosi in the hotel.

In 1966, after a devastating cyclone, the Cuban government decided to plant new citrus groves on the island which would be worked by students from Cuba and around the world. The idea was such a success that in 10 years the island's population grew from 10,000 to 80,000.

An old map of Isla de la Juventud from the Museo Municipal of Nueva Gerona

⑬ Cayo Largo del Sur

This island is a wonderful holiday destination for those who love sun, sea and sand. It is 25 km (15 miles) long and has a surface area of 37.5 sq km (15 sq miles). There are no extremes of climate here. It rains very little, the temperature is 24° C (75° F) in winter and less than 30° C (86° F) in summer. The coast is flat, the sand as white and fine as talcum powder, and the sea is clear and calm. It is safe for scuba diving, and the island offers other sporting activities such as fishing, sailing, tennis and surfing. If you prefer not to swim, you can walk for miles in the shallow water. There are no villages here except those built for tourists, with comfortable hotels, as well as restaurants, bars, discos and swimming pools.

View of Playa Tortuga

★ Playa Sirena
This 2-km (1.5-mile) beach is very tranquil. Sheltered from the wind, the sea is calm all year round.

Isla del Sol · Las Piedras

KEY

① **Playa Lindamar** is a shell-shaped beach, 5 km (3 miles) long and sheltered by white rocks, with hotels and bathing facilities.

② **Playa Paraíso** is very secluded, making nude sunbathing possible.

③ **Combinado** is a marine biology centre which is open to the public.

④ **Marina Cayo Largo** is the point of departure for boat trips to several scuba diving sites. In shallow water there are coral gardens populated by multicoloured fish, and a black coral reef 30 km (19 miles) long. Fishing equipment can be hired in the watersports centre.

⑤ **Playa Blanca**, the longest beach on the island at 7.5 km (5 miles), is surrounded by white rocks and divided from Playa Lindamar by a rocky point.

⑥ **Playa Los Pinos**

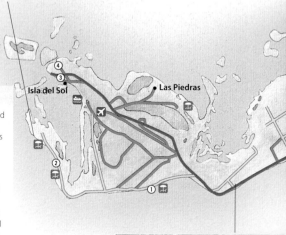

Holiday Villages
Exclusive holiday resorts, with family bungalows and cottages, are concentrated on the southwest coast.

For hotels and restaurants in this region see pp258–9 and pp272–3

★ **Playa Tortuga**
This beach in the eastern part of the island is popular with nature lovers: it is a nesting area for marine turtles and has become a natural reserve for Chaelonidae (species of marine turtle), which are also raised at Combinado.

VISITORS' CHECKLIST

Practical Information
Archipiélago de los Canarreos
(Isla de la Juventud).
Road Map B3. 🚢 500.
ℹ️ Varadero: Cubatur, (45) 667
216; Havanatur, (45) 611 452.
Excursions: from Marina Cayo
Largo: departure in the morning,
return at sunset.

Transport
✈️ Vilo Acuña, (45) 248 141.

Key

▬ Major road

▬ Minor road

═ Unpaved road

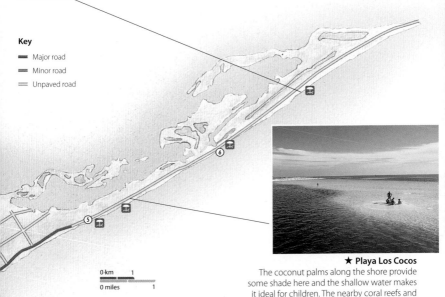

0 km   1
0 miles   1

★ **Playa Los Cocos**
The coconut palms along the shore provide some shade here and the shallow water makes it ideal for children. The nearby coral reefs and shipwrecks attract scuba divers.

An iguana in Cayo Iguana

Visiting the Nearby Islands

The small *cayos* nearby offer many natural attractions. Cayo Rico, an island surrounded by brilliant green water and fringed with beaches of sand as fine as sugar, is only a few minutes away by boat. The seabeds, which are especially rich in lobsters and molluscs, are fascinating and can be admired from glass-bottomed boats. While various species of fish abound at Cayo Rosario, which is a scuba diver's dream, the only inhabitants of Cayo Iguana, just off the western tip of Cayo Largo, are the harmless iguanas, which can be as much as 1 m (3 ft) long. Cayo Pájaro is the craggy habitat of ocean birds, while Cayo Cantiles is rich in flowers, birds and fish.

For keys to symbols *see back flap*

CENTRAL CUBA – WEST

Matanzas · Cienfuegos · Villa Clara

The central-western provinces are the rural heart of Cuba, with cultivated fields and a gentle landscape, even where the plain gives way to the Sierra del Escambray. Apart from Varadero, the famous holiday resort, the main attractions in this region are two lively towns – Santa Clara and Cienfuegos – and the natural scenery of the Zapata peninsula and the Escambray mountains.

In 1509, while circling Cuba, the Spanish navigator Sebastián Ocampo caught sight of a bay on the northern Atlantic coast inhabited by Siboney Indians. Their land was requisitioned almost immediately and assigned to settlers from the Canary Islands. The Indians opposed this injustice so fiercely that the city of Matanzas, which was built in that bay in the 1600s, probably owes its name to the memory of a massacre *(matanza)* of Spaniards by the natives.

Another bay, on the south coast, was sighted by Columbus in 1494. The Jagua Indians living there were later wiped out, but it wasn't until 1819 that Cienfuegos was founded by Roman Catholic settlers from the former French colonies of Haiti and Louisiana, who were granted this territory to counterbalance the massive presence of African slaves. From the mid-1500s to the mid-1700s, both coasts in this region had to face the serious threat of pirate raids, against which the many redoubts, citadels and castles that are still visible along the coastline had very little effect. As a result, in 1689, 20 families from the village of Remedios, not far from the sea, decided to move to the interior to be at a safe distance from the buccaneers' ships and cannons. In this way the city of Santa Clara was founded.

Santa Clara, capital of Villa Clara province, holds a special place in Cuban hearts since it was the setting for heroic acts by Che Guevara and his rebel forces. On 28 December 1958, they captured the area after what was to be the last battle of the Revolution *(see p52)* before Batista fled.

Plaza de la Libertad surrounded by impressive buildings, Matanzas

◀ Varadero, extremely popular with international holidaymakers

Exploring Central Cuba – West

This part of Cuba boasts some exceptional attractions: the beaches of Varadero – perhaps the best and certainly the most well-equipped in Cuba – and the swamp (ciénaga) of Zapata, a nature reserve which is particularly good for fishing and birdwatching. Cienfuegos, Matanzas and Santa Clara are all appealing towns, the latter a must for those interested in Che Guevara's life. A good route for a tour could begin with Matanzas and Varadero, before turning south to Cienfuegos, perhaps via the Península de Zapata. From there it is an easy ride to Santa Clara and beyond to Remedios.

Aerial view of Cayo Libertad, off the coast of Varadero

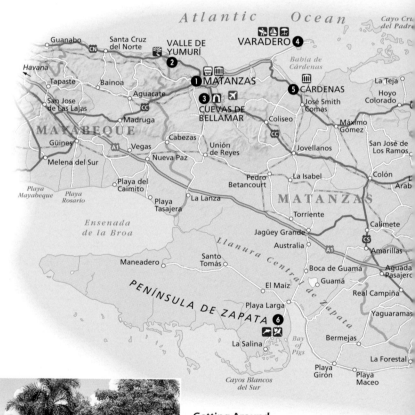

Getting Around

The provinces of Central Cuba – West are traversed by the Carretera Central; although the motorway (Autopista Nacional) which links Havana and Santa Clara is a much faster (though less scenic) road. The railway line connecting Havana to Santiago passes through Matanzas, Mayabeque and Santa Clara, while another links Havana and Trinidad via Cienfuegos. There are also daily return flights from Havana to Cienfuegos and Santa Clara. For visitors with limited time, it may be best to go on an organized tour. These typically cover a province or a few cities, and include visits to parks.

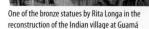

One of the bronze statues by Rita Longa in the reconstruction of the Indian village at Guamá

For hotels and restaurants in this region see pp259–60 and pp273–4

Sights at a Glance

The arcades of the Prado with Corinthian columns in Cienfuegos

Iglesia de San Juan Bautista, the cathedral of Remedios

Signpost at the entrance to the province of Villa Clara

Key

═══ Motorway

━━━ Major road

┄┄┄ Minor road

━━━ Regional border

╍╍╍ Main railway

△ Summit

For keys to symbols *see back flap*

❶ Matanzas

Situated on the shores of a large bay, Matanzas is the capital of the province of the same name. It is a major industrial town, with an important port for exporting sugar. Because of the many bridges over the Yumurí and San Juan rivers, linking the historic centre to the various quarters of Matanzas and its two suburban districts (Versalles and Pueblo Nuevo), the city has been called the "Creole Venice", a match for the no less ambitious "Athens of Cuba". These two names date back to the 19th century, when the artistic and cultural life of the city, the hub of a flourishing agricultural region, outshone that of Havana.

Teatro Sauto in Matanzas with its beautiful wood-panelling

The Centre of Matanzas

The streets in Matanzas are officially indicated by a number, but in practice their colonial names are still commonly used.

The historic centre can be seen in a few hours. A good place to start is **Plaza de la Vigía**, connected to the outskirts by the Concordia and Calixto García bridges. In the square is the statue of an unknown soldier of the wars of independence, and around it stand several of the city's key sights: the Neo-Classical fire station (1898), the Palace of Justice (1826), the Museo Provincial, the Sauto Theatre and Ediciones Vigía.

🏛 Museo Provincial

Calle Milanés, e/ Magdalena y Ayllón. **Tel** (45) 243 195. **Closed** for restoration. Call for details. 🖼 📷

This museum occupies the two-storey Palacio del Junco, a bright blue porticoed building constructed in 1838 for the del Junco family. The collection includes documents and objects concerning the history of the province. The section devoted to the colonial period, with documents on slavery and sugar cane farm tools, is of particular interest. Copies of *Aurora*, the most interesting Cuban periodical of the 19th century, are also on display.

🎭 Teatro Sauto

Calle Magdalena, e/ Medio y Milanés. **Tel** (45) 242 721. **Closed** for restoration work. Call for details. 🖼 📷

The pride and joy of the city, this theatre was designed by the Italian architect Daniele Dell'Aglio, who was also responsible for the church of San Pedro in the Versalles district. On 6 April 1863 the auditorium was opened to the public as the Esteban Theatre, in honour of the provincial governor who had financed the construction. It was later renamed the Sauto Theatre because of the Matanceros' affection for the local pharmacist, Ambrosio de la Concepción Sauto, a passionate theatre-goer. He was famous for having cured Queen Isabella II of Spain of a skin disease, using a lotion he had himself prepared.

A solidly built Neo-Classical structure with several Greek-inspired statues made of Carrara marble, the theatre has various frescoes of Renaissance inspiration, executed by the architect himself. The U-shaped interior is almost entirely covered with wood-panelling.

Because of its exceptional acoustics, the versatile theatre has been the chosen venue for all kinds of shows and great 19th- and 20th-century Cuban artists have appeared here. World-famous performers have included actress Sarah Bernhardt (in *Camille* in 1887), ballet dancer Anna Pavlova and the guitarist Andrés Segovia.

The Danzón

In the 19th century two composers, José White and Miguel Failde, were born in Matanzas, which was at that time a major cultural centre. In 1879 the latter composed *Las Alturas de Simpson*, which introduced a new musical genre to Cuba, the Danzón. This Caribbean and Creole adaptation of European country dancing became the most popular dance on the island for about fifty years. It is still danced in Matanzas, in the Casa Amigos del Danzón, the house where Miguel Failde was born.

Period print of people dancing the Danzón

Bookbinding at the Ediciones Vigía publishing house

🏛 Ediciones Vigía
Calle Magdalena 1, Plaza de la Vigía. **Tel** (45) 244 845, (45) 260 917. **Open** 8:30am–4pm Mon–Fri. **Closed** 1 Jan, 1 May, 26 Jul, 10 Oct, 25 Dec. 📷

This publishing house's beautifully-crafted products are entirely hand-made – duplicated, painted and bound – on special untreated or recycled paper. Visitors can buy books (on poetry, theatre and history) by Cuban and foreign authors, as well as periodicals.

Parque de la Libertad
Calle Milanés, an important commercial street, leads to the city's other large square, Parque de la Libertad, where military parades were held in the 1800s. The square was built on the site of the Indian village of Yacayo. In the middle of the plaza is an impressive statue of José Martí,

surrounded by some attractive buildings: the Liceo Artístico y Literario (1860); the Casino Español, built in the early 1900s; the Palacio del Gobierno; the **Catedral de San Carlos**, dating from the 17th century but mostly rebuilt in the 19th century; and, next to the derelict Hotel El Louvre, the Museo Farmacéutico de Matanzas.

🏛 Museo Farmacéutico de Matanzas
Calle Milanés 4951, e/ Santa Teresa y Ayuntamiento. **Tel** (45) 243 179. **Open** 10am–5pm Mon–Sat, 10am–4pm Sun. 🎫 📷

This fine example of a 19th-century pharmacy, overlooking Parque de la Libertad, was founded on 1 January 1882 by Ernesto Triolet and Juan Fermín de Figueroa and turned into a museum in 1964.

On the wooden shelves stand the original French porcelain vases decorated by hand, others imported from the US, and an incredible quantity of small bottles with herbs, syrups and elixirs. The museum also has a collection of three million old labels, mortars and stills, and advertising posters boasting the miraculous

curative powers of Dr Triolet's remedies. The façade of the pharmacy faces the square.

The shop also serves as a bureau of scientific information, with more than a million original formulae and rare books on botany, medicine, chemistry and pharmaceuticals, in several foreign languages.

The wooden shelves at the Museo Farmacéutico de Matanzas

Matanzas Town Centre
① Plaza de la Vigía
② Museo Provincial
③ Teatro Sauto
④ Ediciones Vigía
⑤ Catedral de San Carlos
⑥ Museo Farmacéutico de Matanzas
⑦ Parque de la Libertad
⑧ Puente Concordia

The lush green undulating land of Valle de Yumurí

❷ Valle de Yumurí

Matanzas. **Road Map** B2.

The Bacunayagua bridge, 7 km (4 miles) west of Matanzas, is a fine work of Cuban engineering. At 110 m (360 ft), it is the highest bridge in Cuba. Built over the Yumurí river in the early 1960s, it offers lovely views of the peaceful, wooded valley below, which can be reached via a road running parallel to the river.

This attractive area of undulating land dotted with royal palm trees is well known for its many centres and clinics specializing in treatments for stress, asthma and high blood pressure. From the Monserrat hill, where the Nuestra Señora

de Monserrat Sanctuary is located, there is a fabulous view of the bay of Matanzas.

Legends vary concerning the origins of the word "Yumurí". The most fantastic of these stories associates it with the lamentation of the Indians massacred by the

A huge limestone formation in the Cuevas de Bellamar

Spanish. Another version came in a letter written by the Swedish writer Fredrika Bremer, who visited Cuba in the late 19th century. According to her, in order to escape from slavery, Siboney Indians used to commit suicide by throwing themselves into the river while screaming "*Yo morí*" (I died).

❸ Cuevas de Bellamar

Carretera de las Cuevas de Bellamar, Matanzas. **Road Map** B2. **Tel** (45) 261 683. **Open** daily. 🏛 🅿 🎫 💻 🚻

Discovered by chance in 1861 by a slave who was surveying the terrain in search of water, the fascinating Bellamar caves lie just 5 km (3 miles) southeast of Matanzas.

Only the first 3 km (2 miles) of these extensive caves have been explored to date, and expert speleologists say there are still many surprises in store. Access to the public, with a specialist guide, is limited to the first 1,500 m (5,000 ft) of the caves. This stretch includes caves and galleries covered with crystal formations in intriguing shapes. The temperature is a constant 26° C (79° F), thanks to the continuous seepage of the cave walls. This impressive tour (available daily) goes 26 m

The Hershey Train

The first stretch of the Hershey rail line, inaugurated in 1916, connected the Hershey sugar factory and the village of Canasí, both near the coast west of Matanzas. The electrical system was one of the first in Cuba. In 1924 there were 38 pairs of trains, though only four covered the full distance between Havana and Matanzas. Today, the Hershey train links Casablanca (*see p115*) and Matanzas (*pp162–3*) via beautiful scenery, covering 89 km (55 miles) in 3 hours 20 minutes, with frequent stops.

The small Hershey electric train

(85 ft) below sea level, and visitors can see marine fossils dating from 26 million years ago. Trained speleologists are allowed to enter a cave that is 50 m (164 ft) below sea level.

At Varadero, guided tours of the Bellamar caves can be booked at the larger hotels.

❹ Varadero

See pp166–7.

❺ Cárdenas

Matanzas. **Road Map** B–C 2.
🗺 145,000.

The linear façade of the historic Dominica building at Cárdenas

On arriving in Cárdenas, 50 km (31 miles) east of Matanzas and 18 km (11 miles) south of Varadero, visitors may feel they are entering another age. This is mostly due to the gigs and one-horse carriages which circulate in the streets.

The town was founded in 1828 as San Juan de Dios de Cárdenas. In the 19th century the town thrived thanks to the sugar industry. Today, however, except for a rum factory near the port, Cárdenas offers only two possible areas of employment: work on a farm or a job in Varadero's important tourist industry.

A closer look at the squares and monuments allows visitors to appreciate the little hidden gems in this town. Parque Colón, one of the two main squares, is dominated by the first statue of Christopher Columbus erected in Cuba, inaugurated in 1862 by Gertrudis Gómez de Avellaneda, the 19th-century Hispanic-Cuban author *(see p32).*

Next to the Iglesia de la Inmaculada Concepción (1846) is a very important monument: the **Dominica** building. In 1850, when it was the headquarters of the Spanish government in Cuba, Cuban nationalist troops led by Narciso López hoisted the Cuban flag here for the first time.

In the second major square, Parque Echevarría, is a fine Neo-Classical building, erected in 1862, which was once the city's district prison. It became the **Museo Municipal Oscar María de Rojas** in 1900, making it the oldest town museum in Cuba. It houses a collection of coins, arms, shells, minerals, butterflies and stuffed animals.

Cárdenas is also famous for being the birthplace of José Antonio Echevarría (1932–57), the revolutionary who was president of the University Students' Federation in Havana. He waged an anti-Batista campaign and was assassinated by the police. The house he was born in is now a museum.

In 1999, five-year-old Elián González was shipwrecked off Miami in a failed escape attempt by his mother. After months of legal tussles between the US and Cuba and an international outcry, Elián was repatriated to his father in Cárdenas. The **Museo a la Batalla de Ideas** is dedicated to this incident.

🏛 **Museo Municipal Oscar María de Rojas**
Calle 13e/ Ave. 4y Ave. 6. **Tel** (45) 522 417. **Open** 9am–6pm Tue & Fri, 8am–5pm Wed, Thu & Sat, 9am–1pm Sun. 🎟 🗋 Note: fee for photography may apply.

🏛 **Museo Casa Natal de José Antonio Echevarría**
Ave. 4e/ 12y 13. **Tel** (45) 524 145. **Open** 9am–noon & 1–5pm Tue–Sat, 9am–noon Sun. **Closed** 1 Jan, 1 May, 26 Jul, 25 Dec. 🎟 🗋

🏛 **Museo a la Batalla de Ideas**
Ave. 6 esq. 12. **Tel** (45) 527 599. **Open** 9am–noon & 1–5pm Tue–Sat 8am–noon Sun. 🎟 🗋

Cárdenas, the city of horse-drawn carriages

❹ Varadero

Cuba's top resort, which occupies the 19-km (12-mile) long Península de Hicacos, is connected to the mainland by a drawbridge, a sign of Varadero's exclusivity. When, in the late 19th century, some families from Cárdenas bought part of the land on the peninsula and built themselves summer residences on the north coast, Varadero became a fashionable beach for the wealthy. After Castro took power in 1959, the area was opened up to all kinds of people, and is now especially popular with Canadians and Europeans, drawn to the white, sandy beaches, clear blue water and good facilities.

Palm trees surrounding the lake in Parque Retiro Josone

Exploring Varadero

The peninsula – which can be toured by hiring a scooter, classic car or one-horse carriage – is a succession of hotels, restaurants, holiday villages, bars, discos, shops and sports centres, all set among lush greenery that includes bougainvillea, royal poinciana, coconut palms and seagrapes.

The main road along the northern side of the peninsula is Avenida Primera (1ra), the eastern part of which is named Avenida Las Américas. It is here that the main luxury hotels, the major marinas and a golf course are located. The Autopista del Sur (motorway) runs along the southern coast.

The Historic Centre

The old centre of Varadero, which has no significant historical monuments, lies around the Iglesia de Santa Elvira and the **Parque de 8000 Taquillas**, in Avenida 1ra between Calle 44 and 46. The oldest hotel of note is Hotel Internacional (at the western end of Avenida Las Américas), which was built in the 1950s, complete with a casino and extravagant swimming pool. It puts on a popular cabaret show.

🏢 Parque Retiro Josone

Avenida Primera y Calle 56.
Tel (45) 667 228. **Open** daily.

This is a beautiful park, with elegant trees, tropical flowers and plants, three restaurants and a small lake where birds gather and tourists hire rowing boats and pedalos. It was established in 1942 by José Iturrioz, the owner of the Arrechabala *ronera*, the rum factory just outside Cárdenas. He named it Josone, a combination of the first syllable of his Christian name and that of his wife, Onelia.

The park is a hit with children, who can enjoy a boat ride, among other attractions.

🏛 Museo Municipal

Calle 57 y Playa. **Tel** (45) 613 189.
Open 10am–7pm Tue–Sun. 🖼 📷
Note: fee for photography may apply.

The Municipal Museum recounts the history of Varadero both as an urban and tourist centre and also has a collection of Indian tools on display. It is interesting primarily because of the building which it occupies.

The white and blue wooden chalet with French roof tiles is characteristic of the architectural style imported from the US and in fashion in Varadero and the Caribbean area in the early 1900s.

The architect Leopoldo Abreu, the original owner of this villa, landscaped splendid gardens which visitors to the museum can still enjoy. One side of the museum faces the sea, and the balcony on the first floor offers a fine view over the splendid beach and the coastline.

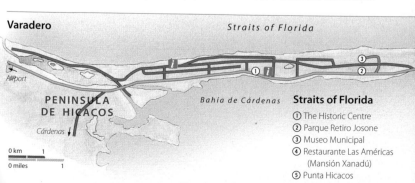

Varadero

Straits of Florida

Bahía de Cárdenas

Airport

PENINSULA DE HICACOS

Cárdenas ↓

0 km — 1
0 miles — 1

Straits of Florida

① The Historic Centre
② Parque Retiro Josone
③ Museo Municipal
④ Restaurante Las Américas (Mansión Xanadú)
⑤ Punta Hicacos

A stretch of the magnificent beach at Varadero

VISITORS' CHECKLIST

Practical Information
Matanzas. **Road Map** B2.
27,000. Infotur, Calle 13 y
Ave 1, (45) 662 966.

Transport
(45) 247 015. Autopista
del Sur y 36, (45) 614 886.

Restaurante Las Américas (Mansión Xanadú)

Avenida Las Américas km 8.5. **Tel** (45) 667 388. **Open** lunch and dinner.

During the years from 1920 to 1950 an American millionaire, chemical engineer Alfred Irénée Dupont de Nemours, gambled a great deal of money by purchasing most of the beautiful Hicacos peninsula from the heirs of the Spanish landowners. At that time there were only a few villas and one hotel here. Dupont then parcelled the land out to Cubans and Americans who, within a few years, had transformed Varadero into a centre for gambling and prostitution.

At the height of his property dealings, Dupont asked the two Cuban architects Govantes and Cabarrocas, who had designed the Capitolio in Havana (see pp86–7), to design a villa for the rocky promontory of San Bernardino, the highest point in Varadero. This sumptuous four-storey building, completed in 1929 and named Mansión Xanadú, was dressed with Italian marble and precious wood. The roof was covered with green ceramic tiles with thermal insulation. The house was surrounded by a huge garden with rare plants and features which included an iguana farm and a golf course. This extravagant construction cost $338,000, an enormous sum at the time.

In 1959, after the Revolution, Dupont escaped from Cuba, leaving the villa to the Cuban government, which, in 1963, turned it into "Las Américas", the most elegant restaurant in Varadero. It specialises in French cuisine, but can be visited without any obligation to eat there. The dining room still has its original furniture. The top-floor bar, with its wide selection of drinks and cigars, is a favourite spot for sundowners.

The golf course offers 18 holes and breathtaking views. Upon request, golf players can book accommodation in the few luxury bedrooms in the villa.

Punta Hicacos

For those interested in wildlife, the most fascinating part of Varadero is the area near Punta Hicacos, which has become a protected nature reserve. Here you can visit several caves, including the Cueva de Ambrosio, with fossils, Pre-Columbian rock paintings, and some quiet, secluded beaches.

The peninsula is also an attraction for scuba divers, who have 23 dive sites, offering both deep and shallow dives, to choose from.

The former Mansión Xanadú, now a bar-restaurant, with its distinctive green roof

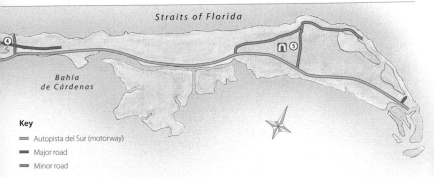

Straits of Florida

Bahía de Cárdenas

Key
— Autopista del Sur (motorway)
— Major road
— Minor road

For keys to symbols *see back flap*

❻ Península de Zapata

This peninsula is named after the landowner who was granted the land by the Spanish crown in 1636. It is one of the least populated areas of the island, and mostly consists of a huge swamp, partly covered by forest. In the past the inhabitants made their living by extracting peat and making charcoal. Zapata is one of the most complete wildlife reserves in the Caribbean, rich in birds and animals, and one part, the area around the Laguna del Tesoro, has been designated a national park, the Gran Parque Natural de Montemar. The Caribbean coast, with its sandy beaches, attracts scuba divers and snorkellers.

A mangrove swamp, characteristic of some tropical coastal areas

Key

━ Major road

━ Minor road

② • Santo Tomás
• Quemado Grande

Maneadero

ZAPATA

The Fauna of the Zapata Swamp

This habitat supports about 150 species of bird, including the *zunzuncito (see p25)*, the Cuban Pygmy owl, the Zapata Rail, a rare type of baldicoot, waterhen, various species of parrot, and heron. Along the coast manatees can be seen (the Caribbean species is over 4 m/13 ft long and weighs about 600 kg/1,320 lbs). The beaches and roads are invaded each spring by crabs leaving the water to mate.

The Cuban crocodile
(Cocodrilo rhombifer) has been protected since the 1960s.

The Cuban Pygmy owl
(Glaucidium siju) is a small nocturnal raptor.

The grey heron lives in the mangrove swamps and feeds on small fish and amphibia.

The zunzuncito *(Mellisuga helenae)* is multicoloured (male) or black-green (female).

KEY

① **The Laguna de las Salinas** is the winter home of many species of migratory bird from November to May and offers excellent bonefishing.

② **Corral de Santo Tomás** is a refuge and observation point for migratory birds. It can only be visited with an official guide (ask at the National Park office).

③ **La Cueva de los Peces** is a natural pool *(cenote)*, 70 m (230 ft) deep, lying along a fault line. It is an ideal spot for scuba diving and snorkelling.

④ **Caleta Buena**, a splendid cove 8 km (5 miles) from Playa Girón, is perfect for snorkelling.

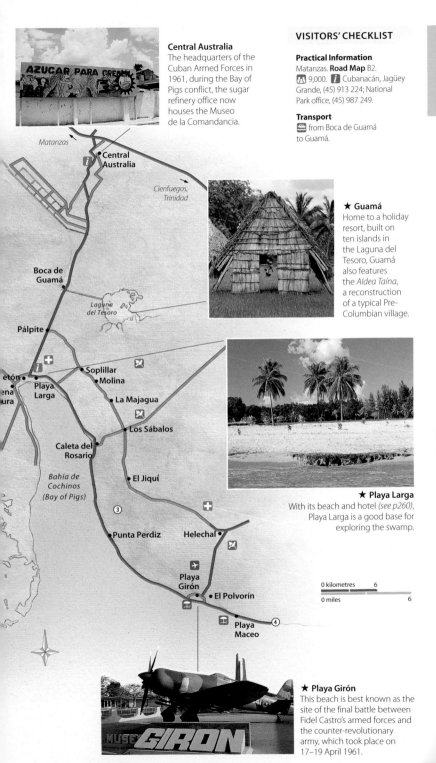

Central Australia
The headquarters of the Cuban Armed Forces in 1961, during the Bay of Pigs conflict, the sugar refinery office now houses the Museo de la Comandancia.

VISITORS' CHECKLIST

Practical Information
Matanzas. **Road Map** B2.
🚏 9,000. 🛈 Cubanacán, Jagüey Grande, (45) 913 224; National Park office, (45) 987 249.

Transport
🚢 from Boca de Guamá to Guamá.

Matanzas

Central Australia

Cienfuegos, Trinidad

★ Guamá
Home to a holiday resort, built on ten islands in the Laguna del Tesoro, Guamá also features the *Aldea Taína*, a reconstruction of a typical Pre-Columbian village.

Boca de Guamá

Laguna del Tesoro

Pálpite

Soplillar
Molina
Playa Larga
etón
ena
ura
La Majagua

Los Sábalos

Caleta del Rosario

Bahía de Cochinos (Bay of Pigs)

El Jiquí

★ Playa Larga
With its beach and hotel *(see p260)*, Playa Larga is a good base for exploring the swamp.

Punta Perdiz
Helechal

Playa Girón
El Polvorín

0 kilometres   6
0 miles   6

Playa Maceo

★ Playa Girón
This beach is best known as the site of the final battle between Fidel Castro's armed forces and the counter-revolutionary army, which took place on 17–19 April 1961.

For keys to symbols *see back fla*

Exploring the Península de Zapata

The Península de Zapata is synonymous with unspoiled nature and luxuriant tropical vegetation. It is a place where visitors can walk among lianas, mangroves and swamp plants, lie in a hammock in the shade of palm trees, observe birds with multicoloured plumage, go fishing, or row a boat on the Laguna del Tesoro. The tranquil Gran Parque Natural de Montemar attracts lovers of wildlife and untouched habitats, rather than adventure seekers. In any case, there is nothing to be feared from the wildlife – there are no ferocious beasts or poisonous snakes on the peninsula.

Statue of Manguanay by the Cuban sculptress Rita Longa, Guamá

Boca de Guamá

Arriving from the north, after passing through Jagüey Grande, which has the largest citrus groves in Cuba, and Central Australia *(see p169)*, the former headquarters of the Cuban Armed Forces, you reach Boca de Guamá. Here a picturesque *ranchón*, a kind of rustic hut, converted into a restaurant, indicates that you are near the **Criadero de Cocodrilos**, or crocodile breeding farm. Visitors can watch and photograph the crocodiles.

Founded in 1962 to safeguard 16 endangered species of reptile, this is the largest crocodile farm in Cuba and includes about 4,000 animals kept in separate pools according to size, age and species.

 Criadero de Cocodrilos
Tel (45) 915 666. **Open** 8am–7pm daily. 🐾 📷 🏛

Guamá

This unusual holiday village in the Laguna del Tesoro (Treasure Lake), measuring 16 sq km (6 sq miles), is named after Guamá, a Taíno warrior who resisted the Spanish conquistadors until he was killed in 1533.

The village consists of 18 huts standing on several small islands in the lagoon. Built of royal palm wood and thatched with palm leaves, the huts provide simple accommodation. However, they are equipped with modern amenities, including air conditioning. Make sure you take adequate supplies of mosquito repellent if you plan to stay here.

The huts are supported on stilts and are connected to one another by hanging bridges or by canoe. In fact, the only way to reach this tourist village is by boat, which takes about 20 minutes to travel along the luxuriantly fringed canal to the lagoon from Boca de Guamá.

This unusual resort also includes a restaurant, a bar, and a small museum, Muestras Aborígenes, which has on display some finds dating back to the Taíno civilization, discovered in the Laguna del Tesoro area.

Also of interest is the reconstructed Taíno village of Aldea Taína, which occupies another of the islands in the lagoon. It comprises four earth *bohíos* (typical Indian huts), a *caney* (a larger round building), and 25 life-size statues of natives by the well-known Cuban sculptress Rita Longa. The figures form the Batey Aborigen, or native Indian square, and represent the few people who lived in the village: a young girl named Dayamí; a crocodile hunter, Abey; Cajimo, hunter of *jutías* (a type of rodent, *see p150*); Manguanay, the mother who is preparing *casabe* (cassava) for her family; Yaima, a little girl who is playing; and the key figure, Guamá, the heroic Taíno warrior.

One of the 18 thatched huts in the Laguna del Tesoro

Playa Larga

At the end of the Bay of Pigs is one of the better beaches along this part of Caribbean coastline, where thick vegetation usually grows down as far as the shore. The coral reef offshore offers magnificent dive sites. Playa Larga's resort area is a popular destination with Cubans; the diving, fishing and birdwatching attract international tourists.

Near the car park, a monument commemorates the landing of the anti-Castro troops in 1961, while along the road to Playa Girón there are numerous monuments honouring the Cuban defenders who died in the famous three-day battle.

Northeast of Playa Larga is an ornithological reserve, and the Centro Internacional de Aves (International Bird Centre) of Cuba.

Cueva de los Peces *(see p169)*, near Playa Larga, ideal for diving

Playa Girón

This beach was named in the 1600s after a French pirate, Gilberto Girón, who found refuge here. It became famous three centuries later, when it was the site of the ill-fated, American-backed landing in 1961. A large sign at the entrance to the beach reads: "Here North American imperialism suffered its first major defeat".

Situated on the eastern side of the Bay of Pigs, this is the last sandy beach in the area, ideal for fishing and diving and also equipped with good tourist facilities.

A must is a visit to the small **Museo Girón**, which covers the anti-Castro invasion using photos, documents, weapons, a tank and the wreckage of aeroplanes that took part in the last battle, as well as films taken during the invasion.

🏛 **Museo Girón**
Playa Girón, Península de Zapata.
Tel (45) 984 122. **Open** 9am–5pm daily. 📷 📹 (with charge).

Playa Girón, the easternmost sandy beach in the Bay of Pigs

The Bay of Pigs Invasion

The long, narrow Bay of Pigs *(Bahía de Cochinos)* became known throughout the world in 1961. On 14 April of that year, at the height of the Cold War, a group of 1,400 Cuban exiles, trained by the CIA with the approval of the president of the United States, John F Kennedy, left Nicaragua for Cuba on six ships. The next day, six US B-26 aeroplanes attacked the island's three military air bases, their bombs killing 7 people and wounding 53.

On 16 April the group of counter-revolutionaries landed on the main beaches along the bay, Playa Larga and Playa Girón. However, they were confronted by the Cuban armed forces, headed by Fidel Castro himself, who were well prepared for the battle and had the support of the local population. The fighting lasted just three days and ended in the rapid defeat of the invaders. In order to avoid an international crisis, which could have escalated into an extremely serious situation, given the Soviet Union's support of Cuba, the US suddenly withdrew its aerial support, leaving the invading forces at the mercy of Cuban troops.

The abandoned invaders, many of whom were mercenaries, were taken prisoner and immediately tried. After 20 months in prison, they were allowed to return to the US in exchange for supplies of medicine, foodstuffs and equipment for Cuban hospitals.

The hostages released by Cuba on their return to the US

❼ Cienfuegos

The capital of the province of the same name, Cienfuegos, a UNESCO World Heritage Site, is a maritime city with a well-preserved historic centre and one of the most captivating bays in the Caribbean Sea, which helped earn the city the name "Pearl of the South" in the colonial era. When Columbus discovered the gulf in 1494, it was occupied by Jagua Indians. In order to defend the bay from pirates, the Spanish built a fortress here in 1745. The first town, called Fernandina de Jagua, was founded in 1819 but, in 1829, it was renamed after the Cuban Governor General of the time, José Cienfuegos.

The "zero kilometre" in the Parque Martí

Parque Martí

The "zero kilometre", the central point of Cienfuegos, is in the middle of Parque Martí, the former Plaza de Armas (parade ground). The vast square, a 200 x 100 m (655 x 330 ft) rectangle, has been declared a national monument because of the surrounding buildings and its historic importance. It was here that the foundation of Cienfuegos was celebrated with a solemn ceremony in the shade of a hibiscus tree, chosen as a marker for laying out the city's first 25 blocks.

Lions on a marble pedestal flank a monument to José Martí, erected in 1906. On Calle Bouyón stands the only triumphal arch in Cuba, commissioned by the local workers' corporation in 1902 to celebrate the inauguration of the Republic of Cuba. One side of the square is entirely occupied by the **Antiguo Ayuntamiento**, now the home of the provincial government assembly, supposedly modelled on the Capitolio in Havana (see pp86–7).

🎭 Teatro Tomás Terry

Ave. 56 No. 2703 y Calle 27. **Tel** (43) 513 361. **Open** daily. 🎫 📷

This theatre was built in 1886–9 to fulfil the last will and testament of Tomás Terry Adams, an unscrupulous sugar factory owner who had become wealthy through the slave trade and then became mayor. World-famous figures such as Enrico Caruso and Sarah Bernhardt performed here in the early 1900s.

The theatre was designed by Lino Sánchez Mármol as an Italian-style theatre, with a splendid U-shaped, two-tiered auditorium and a huge, spectacular fresco by Camilo Salaya, a Philippine-Spanish painter who moved to Cuba in the late 1800s. The austere, well-proportioned façade on the Parque Central has five arches corresponding to the number of entrances. The Byzantine mosaic murals on the pediment, made by the Salviati workshops in Venice, represent the muses.

To the left of the theatre is the Neo-Classical Colegio de San Lorenzo, built thanks to a generous donation by the academic Nicolás Jacinto Acea to ensure that needy children in the town would be educated.

⌂ Catedral de la Purísima Concepción

Ave. 56 No. 2902 y Calle 29. **Tel** (43) 525 297. **Open** 7am–noon Mon–Fri, 8am–noon Sat & Sun. ⛪ 7:15am Tue–Fri, 8pm Sat, 9am Sun.

The cathedral of Cienfuegos, constructed in 1833–69, is one of the major buildings on the central square. Its distinguishing features are the Neo-Classical façade with two bell towers of different heights, and French stained-glass windows depicting the 12 Apostles.

🏛 Museo Provincial

Ave 54 No. 2702 esq. Calle 27. **Tel** (43) 519 722. **Open** 10am–6pm Tue–Sat, 9am–1pm Sun. **Closed** 1 Jan, 1 May, 26 Jul, 25 Dec. 🎫 📷 Note: fee for photography may apply.

The Provincial Museum is in the former Casino Español, an eclectic-style building first opened in1896. The furniture, bronze and marble objects, and crystal and porcelain collections bear witness to the refined taste and wealth of 19th-century families in Cienfuegos.

The mosaic-decorated façade of the Teatro Tomás Terry

Palacio Ferrer, with its unmistakable blue cupola

🏛 Palacio Ferrer
Ave. 54 esq. Calle 25. **Tel** (43) 516 584. **Open** for cultural events.

The palacio that houses the Casa Provincial de la Cultura was built in the early 1900s by the sugar magnate José Ferrer Sirés. Enrico Caruso is said to have stayed here when he performed at the Teatro Tomás Terry.

This building stands on the western end of the plaza and is the most bizarre and eclectic in the square. It is distinguished by its cupola with blue mosaic decoration. It is worth climbing up the wrought-iron spiral staircase to enjoy the fine views over the city.

🏛 Museo Histórico Naval Nacional
Ave. 60 y Calle 21, Cayo Loco. **Tel** (43) 516 617. **Open** 10am–6pm Tue–Sat, 9:45am–noon Sun. 📷

A short walk northwest of Parque José Martí, on the Cayo Loco peninsula, is the most important naval museum in Cuba, housed in the town's rose pink naval barracks. It features a series of documents concerning the local anti-Batista insurrection of 5 September 1957, and an interesting display recording the history of the Cuban Navy.

Paseo del Prado
The liveliest street in town is known for its elegant,

well-preserved buildings and the monuments honouring leading local figures. It crosses the historic centre and goes south as far as Punta Gorda. It was laid out in 1922.

Paseo del Prado, the main street in the historic centre of Cienfuegos

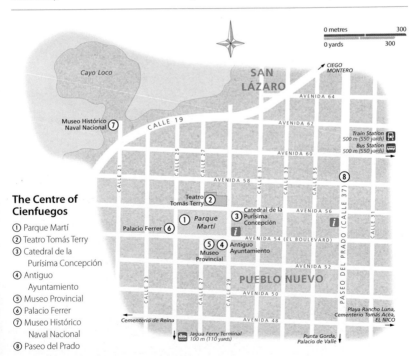

The Centre of Cienfuegos
① Parque Martí
② Teatro Tomás Terry
③ Catedral de la Purísima Concepción
④ Antiguo Ayuntamiento
⑤ Museo Provincial
⑥ Palacio Ferrer
⑦ Museo Histórico Naval Nacional
⑧ Paseo del Prado

0 metres 300
0 yards 300

Cayo Loco

SAN LÁZARO

CIEGO MONTERO

Museo Histórico Naval Nacional ⑦

CALLE 19

AVENIDA 64

AVENIDA 62

AVENIDA 60

Train Station 500 m (550 yards)
Bus Station 500 m (550 yards)

AVENIDA 58

Teatro Tomás Terry ②

Catedral de la Purísima Concepción ③

⑧

Palacio Ferrer ⑥ ① Parque Martí

AVENIDA 56

⑤ ④ Antiguo Ayuntamiento
Museo Provincial

AVENIDA 54 (EL BOULEVARD)

AVENIDA 52

PUEBLO NUEVO

AVENIDA 50

Cementerio de Reina

AVENIDA 48

Playa Rancho Luna, Cementerio Tomás Acea, EL NICO

Jagua Ferry Terminal 100 m (110 yards)

Punta Gorda, Palacio de Valle

For keys to symbols *see back flap*

Exploring Cienfuegos

The presence of the sea at Cienfuegos makes itself felt more and more the further you go from the historic centre towards the Reina and Punta Gorda districts, two narrow strips of land almost entirely surrounded by water. However, for a fuller taste of the sea, go to the mouth of the bay, which is dominated by the Castillo de Jagua fortress with the picturesque Perché fishing harbour. East of Cienfuegos is one of Latin America's most spectacular botanic gardens.

The interior of Palacio de Valle, with its Neo-Moorish decoration

The characteristic wooden houses of Punta Gorda

Punta Gorda

At the southern tip of the bay of Cienfuegos lies Punta Gorda – the aristocratic quarter of the city in the early 1900s – which affords a lovely panoramic view of the bay. A short walk along the seafront takes you past many attractive villas. Various brightly coloured wooden houses can be seen towards the tip of the peninsula. They were modelled on the American prefabricated "balloon frame" homes that were so much in vogue in the early 20th century.

🚌 Palacio de Valle

Calle 37 e/ Ave. 0 y 2, Punta Gorda.
Tel (43) 551 003, ext 830.
Open 10am–10pm daily. 🖉

The most original building in the area, Palacio de Valle was designed by local and foreign architects engaged by the sugar merchant Acisclo del Valle Blanco, one of the wealthiest men in Cuba. It was built as a private house in 1913–17. This two-storey building, which is now a restaurant, is lavishly decorated with Gothic, Venetian and Neo-Moorish motifs, much in the Arab-Spanish style of the Alcázars in Granada and Seville. The façade has three towers of different design symbolizing power, religion and love. The terrace is open to the public.

🚌 Cementerio Monumental Tomás de Acea

Ave. 5 de Septiembre. **Tel** (43) 525 257.
Open 7am–6pm daily. 🖉

This impressive monumental cemetery lies in the eastern suburb of Cienfuegos. Varied in stylistic influences, it was conceived as a large garden with paths and fruit trees. The entrance is a replica of the Parthenon in Athens.

Palacio de Valle, which Batista turned into a casino, now home to a restaurant

For hotels and restaurants in this region see pp259–60 and pp273–4

⊞ Cementerio General La Reina

Ave. 50 y Calle 7, Reina.
Open daily. 🏛

The municipal cemetery of La Reina is located at the western end of the city, and has been declared a national monument. Laid out in the 1830s, this Neo-Classical cemetery includes a famous funerary statue of La Bella Durmiente (Sleeping Beauty).

The statue of Sleeping Beauty in La Reina cemetery in Cienfuegos

⌂ Castillo de Jagua

Poblado Castillo de Jagua. 🚢 **Tel** (43) 965 402. **Open** 9am–5pm Tue–Sat, 9am–1pm Sun. 🏛 📷 Note: fee for photography may apply.

Built by engineer José Tantete, following a design by Bruno Caballero, to protect the bay and the region from Jamaican pirates, the Castillo was the third most important fortress in Cuba in the 18th century and the only one in the central region of the island. The original moat and drawbridge are still intact. According to legend, the citadel was inhabited by a mysterious lady dressed in blue, who every night walked through the rooms and corridors, frightening the guards. It is said that one morning one of the guards was found in a state of shock while wringing a piece of blue cloth in anguish. The unfortunate man never got over this experience and ended up in an asylum.

At the foot of the Castillo is the fishing village of **Perché**, with picturesque wooden houses, in striking contrast to the majestic military structure above. Most visitors arrive by ferry from Pasacaballos hotel (29 km/18 miles south of Cienfuegos), or from the dock in Cienfuegos.

Environs

Cienfuegos province is interesting to eco-tourists. Besides the **Ciego Montero** spa north of the capital, other noteworthy sights are **El Nicho**, to the southeast, which is famous for its waterfalls, and the conservation area of Aguacate.

However the main sight is the **Valle de Yaguanabo**, in the southern region, which is traversed by the river of the same name, which forms small waterfalls and clear freshwater pools. On the slopes of one of the mountains in this valley, populated by mammals such as boar, deer and opossums, is the entrance to the **Cueva de Martín Infierno**. This cave has been a national monument since 1990, because it has one of the largest stalag-mites in the world (67 m/220 ft high) and other rare mineralogical sites such as Moonmilk and Flores de Yeso. About 20 km (12 miles) south of Cienfuegos are the golden sands of **Playa Rancho Luna**. The beach is popular with tourists and local families alike.

Benny Moré

A great source of pride to Cienfuegos is the figure of Maximiliano Bartolomé Moré, better known as Benny Moré, who was born at nearby Santa Isabel de las Lajas on 24 August 1919. Moré inspired many generations of Cubans and foreigners with his supple, unique voice, which enabled him to interpret a variety of musical genres. For this reason the artist was nicknamed *el bárbaro del ritmo* (the barbarian of rhythm). He was self-taught, and when still quite young performed with famous orchestras such as those led by the Matamoros brothers and Pérez Prado (see pp34–5). He died in the early 1960s. For some time Cienfuegos – a city with a great musical tradition and the birthplace of cha-cha-cha – has paid tribute to him with the Benny Moré International Festival. The Cabildo Congo de Lajas in his home town puts on performances of Afro-Cuban popular songs and dances.

The Cuban singer, Benny Moré

❽ Jardín Botánico Soledad

In 1901 Edwin Atkins, owner of the Soledad sugar works 15 km (9 miles) from Cienfuegos, transformed 4 ha (10 acres) of his estate into a sugar cane research centre, and filled the garden with a great number of tropical plants. In 1919 the University of Harvard bought the property and founded a botanical institute for the study of sugar cane and tropical flora. The botanical garden has been run by the Cuban government since 1961, and is one of the largest in Latin America, with a surface area of 94 ha (232 acres) and more than 1,400 different species of plant, including 195 palms. Besides the endemic species there are also huge bamboo trees. Guided tours, made partly on foot and partly by car, reveal the exceptional diversification of the garden.

Medicinal Plants
Indigenous plants with healing properties, such as aloe vera, are grown in this plot.

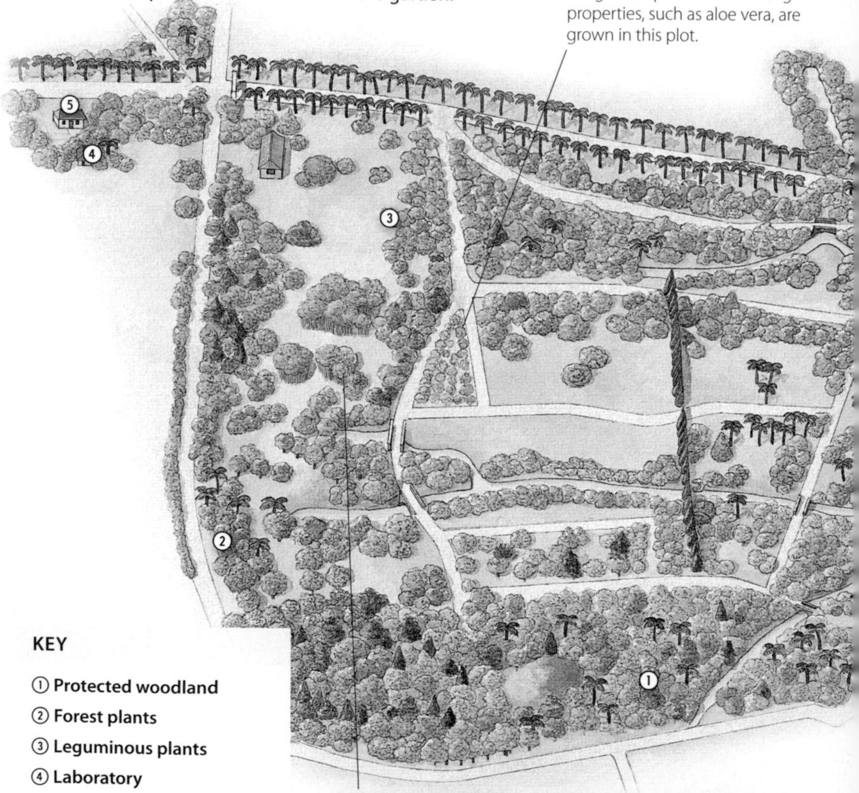

KEY

① **Protected woodland**

② **Forest plants**

③ **Leguminous plants**

④ **Laboratory**

⑤ **Ticket office, library**

★ **Banyan Tree**
Among over 50 varieties of fig in the botanical garden, perhaps the most striking is a huge *Ficus benghalensis* or banyan tree, a species with aerial roots a circumference of over 20 m/65 ft). The roots, trunks and branches form an impenetrable barrier.

VISITORS' CHECKLIST

Practical Information
Calle Real 136, Pepito Tey,
Cienfuegos. **Road Map** C3.
Tel (43) 545 115. **Open** 8am–
6pm daily (last entry 4:30pm).

❾ Santa Clara

See pp178–9.

❿ Sierra del Escambray

Villa Clara, Sancti Spíritus, Cienfuegos.
Road Map C3. ℹ Hotel los Helechos,
(42) 540 330; Centro de Información
de Reservas de Topes de Collantes
(42) 540 117.

Cactuses
Many species of cactus are
housed in this glasshouse.
They are young specimens,
grown after the serious
damage inflicted by
hurricane Lilly (1996).

Water Lilies
The pool near the glasshouse is
entirely covered with water lilies of
different colours: bright pink, white,
dark purple, violet, blue and yellow.

The Sierra del Escambray mountain range, with an average
height of 700 m (2,300 ft) above
sea level, covers a large part of
southern Central Cuba, across
three provinces: Villa Clara,
Cienfuegos and Sancti Spíritus
(see p195). In the heart of the
range is the **El Nicho** nature
reserve, which is of great scientific and ecological value with
its abundant mountain fauna
and varied plantlife. **Pico San
Juan** (1,156 m/ 3,790 ft), dotted
with conifers and lichens as well
as coffee plantations, is the
highest mountain in the Sierra.

A long steep road leads from
the northern side of the mountains up to stunning **Embalse
Hanabanilla**, a large artificial
lake overlooked by a hotel. The
Río Negro path, which skirts the
waterfall of the same name, leads
to a belvedere viewing point from
which one can see the entire lake.

In the village of La Macagua
is the **Comunidad Teatro
Escambray**, an international
theatre school. The school was
founded in 1968 by members of
the Havana Theatre, who used
to rehearse here before touring
rural communities.

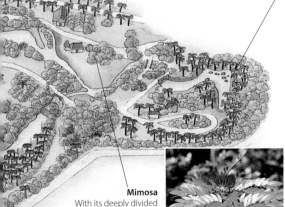

Mimosa
With its deeply divided
leaves, the mimosa
makes a very attractive
ornamental plant.

Palm Trees

For many Cubans, palm trees represent
the power of the gods. A great variety
of species, many of them native to Cuba,
grow throughout the island: the royal palm
(Roystonea regia), the national tree; the bottle
palm *(Colpothrinax wrightii)*, called *barrigona*
(pregnant one), because the trunk swells in the
middle; the sabal, whose fan-like leaves are used
for roofing; the local coccothrinax *(C. crinita)*,
with its unmistakable foliage; and the *corcho*
(Microcycas calocoma).

Royal palm

Bottle palm

Coccothrinax palm

🟡 Santa Clara

Founded on 15 July 1689 by a group of inhabitants from Remedios *(see p181)*, who had moved away from the coast to escape from pirate raids, Santa Clara was for centuries the capital of the province of Las Villas, which included the present-day provinces of Cienfuegos, Sancti Spíritus and Villa Clara. One important historical event has made Santa Clara famous: in 1958 it was here that the last battle of the guerrilla war led by Che Guevara took place, the battle which marked the end of Batista's dictatorship. Santa Clara is now known as "the city of the heroic guerrilla". Today, it is a lively, urbane city and has several interesting sights.

The Teatro La Caridad, where Enrico Caruso performed

Santa Clara's well-tended main square, Parque Leoncio Vidal

Parque Leoncio Vidal

The heart of the city, this charming square with its pristine flower beds, wrought-iron benches and period street lamps has retained its original 1925 atmosphere.

An obelisk stands here. It was commissioned by the rich heiress Martha Abreu de Estévez in honour of two priests, Juan de Conyedo and Hurtado de Mendoza. The heiress also financed the construction of the Teatro de la Caridad, the town's first four public bathhouses, the astronomical observatory, the electricity station, a hospital and a fire station.

There is also a bust of Leoncio Vidal, a colonel in the national independence army who died in battle in 1896, here in this square. The park is also home to a fountain, and a sculpture entitled *Niño de la Bota* (child in boots), purchased by mail order from the J L Mott Company, an art dealer in New York. Until 1894 the square was

partly off limits to black people, who could only walk along certain areas of the pavement.

🎭 Teatro La Caridad

Parque Vidal 3. **Tel** (42) 205 548. Built to a design by the engineer Herminio Leiva y Aguilera for the heiress Martha Abreu de Estévez, this theatre was inaugurated in 1885 and restored from 2009 to 2010. The theatre offered many

An antique vase in a hall in the Museo de Artes Decorativas

additional services – a barber shop, ballroom and gambling room, café and restaurant – with the aim of collecting money to be given to the poor in the city (hence its name, Charity Theatre).

The building has a simple, linear façade, in contrast to the ornate interior, with its profusion of chandeliers and painted panels and a stage with all kinds of mechanical gadgets and draped curtains. The auditorium itself, which has three tiers of boxes with wrought-iron balusters, had folding seats in the stalls right from the start – something completely new in Cuba at the time.

Perhaps the best feature of the theatre is the frescoed ceiling, executed by the Spanish-Philippine painter Camilo Salaya, representing the allegorical figures of Genius, History and Fame.

🏛 Museo de Artes Decorativas

Calle Martha Abreu, esq. Luis Estévez **Tel** (42) 205 368. **Open** 9am–6pm Mon, Wed & Thu, 1–10pm Fri & Sat, 6–10pm Sun. 🎟 🖒

The excellent Decorative Arts Museum, housed in a building dating from 1810, contains 17th-, 18th-, 19th- and 20th-century furniture, as well as furnishings and paintings that belonged to leading local families.

Among the objects on display here, those donated by the Cuban poetess Dulce María Loynaz *(see p33)* are particularly elegant and delightful: five fans, eleven sculptures and two Sèvres porcelain jars, the largest of their kind in Cuba.

The Tren Blindado Monument, a work by José Delarra

VISITORS' CHECKLIST

Practical Information
Villa Clara. **Road Map** C3.
240,000. Infotur, Calle
Cuba 68 e/ E. Machado and
Maestra Nicolosa, (42) 227 557.

Transport
Luis Estévez 323. Carretera
Central km 2.5.

Tren Blindado Monument

Carretera Camajuaní, junction with
railway line. **Tel** (42) 202 758.
Open 9am–5pm Mon–Sat.

On 28 December 1958,
with the aid of only 300 men,
Che Guevara succeeded in
conquering the city, which
was fiercely defended by
3,000 of Batista's soldiers.
The following day Guevara
handed the dictator another
severe setback by derailing an
armoured train that was
supposed to transport 408
soldiers and weapons of all
kinds to the eastern region
of Cuba in order to halt the
advance of the rebels.

Cuban sculptor José Delarra
commemorated this event by
creating a museum-monument
on the spot where it took place,
in the northeastern part of
Santa Clara, on the line to
Remedios. The sequence of
events is recreated using
original elements such as four
wagons from the armoured
train, military plans and maps,
photographs and weapons.
Also on show is the D-6
Caterpillar bulldozer that
was used by the guerrillas
to remove rails and cause
the derailment. The episode
ended with the surrender of
Batista's men.

Parque Tudury

This square, in front of the
Neo-Classical Iglesia de
Nuestra Señora del Carmen
(1756), is also known as Parque
El Carmen. Here stands a
monument commemorating
the foundation of the town of
Santa Clara. It was erected in
1951 around a tamarind tree, on
the spot where, on 15 July 1689,
the first mass was celebrated
in the new city. The monument
consists of 18 columns on which
are carved the names of the first
families in Santa Clara, crowned
by a cross.

The Centre of Santa Clara

① Parque Leoncio Vidal
② Teatro La Caridad
③ Museo de Artes Decorativas
④ Tren Blindado Monument
⑤ Parque Tudury

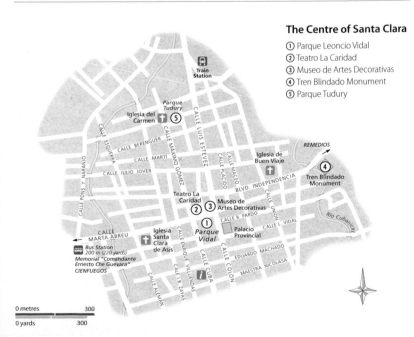

The group of sculptures in Santa Clara, dedicated to Che Guevara

🎭 Conjunto Escultórico Comandante Ernesto Che Guevara

Avenida de los Desfiles, Santa Clara. **Tel** (42) 205 878. **Open** 9:30am–5pm Tue–Sun. 🎭 📷 📹 in the memorial, museum or tomb.

The monument in Plaza de la Revolución was built to commemorate the 30th anniversary of the battle of Santa Clara. It was designed by the architect Jorge Cao Campos and the sculptor José Delarra, and was unveiled on 28 December 1988.

The complex comprises a museum, a memorial and the grave of Che Guevara. Dominating the monument is an impressive bronze statue of Che, with his arm in plaster (he had broken it in a previous battle). Beneath, a bas-relief depicts scenes from the battle, on which are carved the historic words that Che wrote in his farewell letter before leaving for Bolivia.

Under the monument (the entrance is at the back) is the museum, designed by the architect Blanca Hernández Guivernau, which has some of Che's personal belongings on display, together with a chronological reconstruction of his life,

which clearly reveals the evolution of his revolutionary ideas.

Che's personal effects include his pistol holster, his uniform, watch, pipe, the container from which he used to drink *mate* tea, his beret and the telephone he used during the campaign of Santa Clara, along with his binoculars, camera and radio.

The newest construction is the memorial containing the remains of Che and 38 other comrades, found in Bolivia 30 years after their death and transferred to Cuba in December 1998. The tomb is in the shape of a cave and consists of numbers of niches with ossuaries as well as a central brazier where an eternal flame burns. Cubans flock here in order to pay their respects.

Ernesto Che Guevara

When Ernesto Guevara de la Serna was killed in Bolivia upon orders from the CIA, he was only 39 years old. In the summer of 1997 – while Cuba was celebrating the 30th anniversary of the death of the *guerrillero heroico* – the body of Che Guevara was returned to the island. He was one of only two foreigners in the history of Cuba (the other is the Dominican

The photographer Korda with his famous portrait of Che Guevara

general Máximo Gómez) to be proclaimed a Cuban citizen "by birth". Watching his coffin being lowered from the aeroplane to the sound of the *Suite de las Américas* served to remind everyone, especially young Cubans, that Che had died and had therefore really existed; he was not merely a 20th-century legend, but a reality for millions of people who had shared his ideas. Further testimony is given by his children, his widow Aleida March, many of those who fought with him in the Sierra Maestra and in the Congo, and also Alberto Granado, with whom Che made his first trips to Latin America and who, after the Revolution, moved to Cuba on his friend's invitation. Though Che suffered from asthma, he had an iron will, loved books as well as sports, and had a great spirit of sacrifice; he could appreciate beauty and was a perfectionist but had a sense of humour. He was a man of action who also found time to meditate on reality and to write.

SE ASIGNA AL COMANDANTE ERNESTO CUEVARA LA MI. SION DE CONDUCIR DESDE LA SIERRA MAESTRA HASTA LA PROVINCIA DE LAS VILLAS UNA COLUMNA REBELDE

Part of the bas-relief memorial to Che Guevara

Baroque altar at Iglesia de San Juan Bautista, Remedios

⓫ Remedios

Villa Clara. **Road Map** C3. 🏠 16,500. 🚌 🚐 🛈 Infotur, Calle Pi y Margall, (42) 397 227. 🎭 Parrandas (24 Dec).

Founded in 1515 by Vasco Porcallo de Figueroa and given the name of Santa Cruz de la Sabana, this town was renamed San Juan de los Remedios del Cayo after a fire in 1578.

This peaceful place has a small, well-preserved colonial historic centre in the area around Plaza Martí. Overlooking this square is the Iglesia de San Juan Bautista, which is con- sidered one of the most important churches in Cuba. What we see today is the result of restoration carried out in the 20th century thanks to the rich landowner Eutimio Falla Bonet, who revived its original Baroque splendour without touching the Neo- Classical bell tower. Most striking are the lavish Baroque altar and the magnificent decorative ceiling.

Behind the cathedral is the **House of Alejandro García Caturla**. Here, the musical instruments, photographs and some personal belongings of this talented 20th-century

personality are on display. García Caturla was a composer, pianist, saxophone player, percussionist, violinist and singer, as well as a fine tennis player and rower, journalist and art critic.

Also in the square are three other noteworthy buildings. The Hotel Mascotte was the site of an important meeting between Generalíssimo Máximo Gómez and a US delegation in 1899. The former Casino Español, now Casa de la Cultura, and the El Louvre café, founded in 1866, also stand here.

However, Remedios is most famous for the Parrandas, the local festival documented in the fascinating **Museo de las Parrandas Remedianas**. Here, photographs, musical instruments, costumes, sketches, carriages and *trabajos de plaza* – decorated wooden structures – bring to life Parrandas past and present.

Environs
Located north of Remedios, the resort of Cayo Santa María is reached via 48 km (30 miles) of low-lying causeway known as *El Pedraplén*. The resort is made up of hotels set along stunning sandy beaches, as well as a dolphinarium, a bowling alley and a shopping complex.

🏛 House of Alejandro García Caturla
Calle Camilo Cienfuegos 5. **Tel** (42) 396 851. **Open** 9am–noon & 1–6pm Tue– Sat, 9am–1pm Sun. 🎟 📷

🏛 Museo de las Parrandas Remedianas
Alejandro del Río 74 e/ Máximo Gómez y Enrique Malaret. **Tel** (42) 395 448. **Open** 9am–6pm Tue–Sat, 9am–1pm Sun. **Closed** 1 Jan, 1 May, 26 Jul, 25 Dec. 🎟 📷

The Parrandas

A 19th-century print showing people gathering in the square

In 1829 the parish priest of Remedios, Francisco Virgil de Quiñones, had the idea of getting some boys to bang on sheets of tin in order to get the lazier church members out of their homes to participate in the night-time celebrations of the Advent masses (16–24 Dec).

In time this strange concert developed into a fully fledged festival, with music, dances, parades with floats and huge wooden contraptions *(trabajos de plaza)*. The festivity is a sort of cross between Mardi Gras and the Italian Palio horse race, based on the competition between two quarters of Remedios, San Salvador and Carmen.

The Parrandas begin on 4 December with concerts performed with various percussion instruments, and end with a great crescendo on Christmas Eve. The two *trabajos de plaza*, one per quarter, which are made during the year, are left in Plaza Martí during the festivities. They are illuminated at nine in the evening and may have a historical, patriotic, political, scientific or architectural theme. Later on there are fireworks to welcome the entrance of the floats *(carrozas)*, which never occurs before 3am. These *tableaux vivants* move among the crowd.

The most endearing aspect of the Parrandas, enlivened by songs, polkas and rumbas, is that all the inhabitants, of all ages, take part.

Plaza Martí, the tranquil central square in Remedios

CENTRAL CUBA – EAST

Sancti Spíritus · Ciego de Ávila · Camagüey · Las Tunas

This area in the heart of the island presents two different facets. One is colonial, with Spanish traits that are visible in the architecture and local customs, best expressed in beautiful Trinidad, and fascinating, labyrinthine Camagüey. The other aspect is unspoilt nature, the coastline dotted with *cayos* (islands), which now attracts many visitors from abroad.

Trinidad, Camagüey and Sancti Spíritus, the main cultural centres in this region, were three of seven cities founded in the 16th century by a small group of Spaniards led by Diego Velázquez. The 17th and 18th centuries were marked by the threat posed by state-sanctioned pirates and by raids such as that made by Henry Morgan at Camagüey (then Puerto Príncipe) in 1666. At that time Trinidad had political and military jurisdiction over the whole of central Cuba, where the economy was based solely on sugar cane cultivation and the sale of sugar. The great landowners resided in luxurious mansions in these three cities.

In the second half of the 19th century, a period of crisis began with the advent of new technology, for which there was no skilled labour. Slave revolts, the first of which broke out in Camagüey in 1616, became increasingly frequent and violent, while competition from Cienfuegos was becoming more intense. In the late 19th century the major landowners left the cities and as time went on they gradually ceded their sugar factories to American businessmen, who converted them into one large sugar-producing business. Camagüey concentrated on livestock raising, an important resource in the province, while Trinidad engaged in handicrafts and cigar-making. It remained isolated from the rest of Cuba for a long time, since the railway was not extended to Trinidad until 1919 and the road to Cienfuegos and Sancti Spíritus was only laid out in the 1950s. One result of this isolation, however, is that the historic centres of Trinidad and Sancti Spíritus have preserved their colonial atmosphere.

Boulevard with brightly-coloured stores in Ciego de Avila

◀ Panoramic view from Topes de Collantes, just north of Trinidad

Exploring Central Cuba – East

From a cultural point of view, the most interesting place in the area is the delightful town of Trinidad. This small town also has a lovely beach nearby and makes a good base for tours to the Sierra del Escambray *(see p177)* or for excursions to the Valle de los Ingenios. Colonial Sancti Spíritus sees few visitors, while Camagüey is appealing both for its fascinating colonial architecture and as an authentic, vibrant Cuban city. The Atlantic coast in the province of Ciego de Ávila is good for swimming and watersports, especially at Cayo Coco and Guillermo, where there are good tourist facilities.

Playa Prohibida at Cayo Coco, fringed by sand dunes

Key

━━━ Motorway

━━━ Major road

┈┈┈ Minor road

━━━ Regional border

┈┈┈ Main railway

The Salto del Caburní, between rocks and red earth, near Topes de Collantes

For hotels and restaurants in this region see pp261–2 and pp274–5

One of the colonial houses around the peaceful pedestrian square of San Juan de Dios, in Camagüey

Sights at a Glance

1 *Trinidad pp186–94*
3 Península Ancón
4 Valle de los Ingenios
5 *Sancti Spíritus pp198–9*
6 Ciego de Ávila
7 Morón
8 Jardines del Rey
9 *Cayo Coco pp202–3*
10 *Camagüey pp204–7*
11 Sierra de Cubitas
12 Playa Santa Lucía
13 Cayo Sabinal
14 Las Tunas
15 Jardines de la Reina

Tours

2 *Topes de Collantes p195*

Getting Around

There is at least one domestic airport in each province. The cities are linked by road and by trains bound for Oriente. A train from Trinidad tours around the Valle de los Ingenios, but it doesn't always run. Cayo Coco can be reached by air or by car along the causeway, while Jardines de la Reina is only accessible by boat. The most difficult area to travel around is the Sierra del Escambray *(see p177)*, although organized tours now include Topes de Collantes.

For keys to symbols *see back*

❶ Trinidad

This city was founded by Diego Velázquez in 1514, and was declared a World Heritage Site by UNESCO in 1988. The original cobblestone streets and pastel-coloured houses give the impression that time has scarcely moved on since colonial times. From the 17th to 19th centuries, the city was a major centre for trade in sugar and slaves, and the buildings around the Plaza Mayor, the heart of Trinidad, bear witness to the wealth of the landowners of the time. A long period of isolation from the 1850s to the 1950s protected the city from any radical new building and the original town layout has been left largely unchanged. The historic centre has been skilfully restored, down to details like the street lights.

★ **Palacio Brunet**
This mansion is now the Museo Romántico, with a collection of furniture and items that belonged to the wealthiest local families (see p189).

Casa de la Música (p281)

Nuestra Señora de la Popa (p194)

★ **Iglesia y Convento de San Francisco**
This former convent is the home of the Museo de la Lucha contra Bandidos, while the church bell tower, the symbol of the city, offers fine views. The bell dates from 1853 (see p193).

S I M Ó N B O L I V

CALLE HERNÁNDEZ ECHERRI

C A L L E P I R O G U I N A R T

Canchánchara
This typical *casa de infusiones*, housed in an 18th-century building, is known for its namesake cocktail *canchánchara*, made from rum, lime, water and honey. Live music is played here.

CALLE MARTÍNEZ VILLENA

In Plazuela del Jigüe, where an acacia tree (*jigüe*) once stood, Father Bartolomé de Las Casas celebrated the first mass in Trinidad in 1514 (see p193).

Key

━ Suggested route

The Museo de Arqueología Guamuhaya occupies an 18th-century building where the naturalist Humboldt once stayed (see p189).

Iglesia Parroquial de la Santísima Trinidad
The church of the Holy Trinity was built in the late 1800s on the site of a 17th-century church that had been destroyed by a cyclone. It has an impressive carved wooden altar decorated with elaborate inlaid wood (see p188).

VISITORS' CHECKLIST

Practical Information
Sancti Spíritus. **Road Map** C3.
🏠 75,000. 🛈 Cubatur, Calle Antonio Maceo esq. Francisco Javier Zerquera, (41) 996 314; Infotur, Calle Gustavo Izquierdo, (41) 998 258. 🌐 daily.

Transport
🚌 Calle Piro Guinart 224, e/ Maceo e Izquierdo, (41) 994 448. 🚉 Ave. Simón Bolívar 422, (41) 993 348.

The Casa de los Conspiradores, with a wooden balcony on the corner, was the meeting place of the nationalist secret society, La Rosa de Cuba.

La Casa de la Trova, a live music venue (see p282), stands almost opposite the Palenque de los Congos Reales, which also offers music and dance (see p280).

Museo de Arquitectura Colonial
Housed in the beautifully restored Casa de los Sánchez Iznaga, this museum illustrates the main features of Trinidad's architecture (see p188).

PLAZA MAYOR

CALLE MARTÍNEZ VILLENA

CALLE JAVIER

CALLE SIMÓN BOLÍVAR

Casa de la Cultura (p193)

Universal Benito Ortiz Galeriá de Arte
Besides being a fine example of 19th-century architecture, this building has an interesting art gallery with works by local artists, as well as handicrafts (see p188).

★ Palacio Cantero
This Neo-Classical gem was built in the early 19th century and is now the home of the Museo Histórico Municipal, which recounts the history of the region. The tower has a commanding view of the historic centre (see p193).

0 metres   100
0 yards   100

Trinidad: Exploring Plaza Mayor

The museums and buildings facing the main square in Trinidad lend historic weight and depth to the "suspended-in-time" feel of this city. It is worth stopping in the town centre for at least half a day to see the museums, relax on the benches in the shade of the palm trees, enjoy a cocktail at the bar on the steps next to the cathedral, or stroll around the stalls in the crafts market.

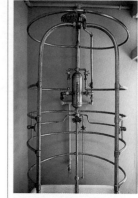

A 19th-century shower in the Museo de Arquitectura Colonial

⛪ Iglesia Parroquial de la Santísima Trinidad

Plaza Mayor. **Open** 11am–12:30pm Mon–Sat.

Completed in 1892, this austere church with a Neo-Classical façade stands at the top of the sloping Plaza Mayor.

The four-aisle interior has a fine Neo-Gothic altar dedicated to the Virgin of Mercy, with a painting by the Cuban painter Antonio Herr on the rear wall. But the real attraction of this church is an 18th-century wooden statue made in Spain, the *Señor de la Vera Cruz* (Lord of the True Cross), which is associated with a curious story. The sculpture, made for one of the churches in Vera Cruz, Mexico, left the port of Barcelona in 1731, but three times in succession the ship was driven by strong winds to the port of Casilda, 6 km (4 miles) from the city of

Trinidad. While preparing to make a fourth attempt to reach Mexico, the ship's captain decided to leave behind part of the cargo, which included the huge chest containing the statue of Christ. The locals regarded the arrival of the sacred image as a sign from Heaven, and from that time on the *Señor de la Vera Cruz* became an object of fervent worship.

The Maundy Thursday procession, which was suspended in 1959 and revived again in 1997, is dedicated to this statue.

Bronze knocker, Museo de Arquitectura Colonial

🏛 Museo de Arquitectura Colonial

Calle Ripalda 83, e/ Hernández Echerri y Martínez Villena, Plaza Mayor. **Tel** (41) 993 208. **Open** 9am–5pm Sat–Thu. 📷 📷 Note: fee for photography may apply.

The front of the 18th-century mansion of the Sánchez Iznaga family, now the home of the Museum of Colonial Architecture, features a lovely portico with slim columns, a wrought-iron balustrade and wooden beams. Originally, the building consisted of two separate houses, both of which belonged to sugar magnate Saturnino Sánchez Iznaga. The houses were joined during the 19th century.

The museum, the only one of its kind in Cuba, covers the different architectural elements seen in Trinidad and illustrates the

building techniques used during the colonial period. There is a collection of various locks, latches, doors, hinges, windows and grilles, as well as parts of walls and tiles.

In one of the bathrooms facing the inner courtyard is a fine example of a 19th-century shower, with a complicated network of pipes supplying hot and cold water.

🏛 Universal Benito Ortiz Galería de Arte

Calle Rubén Martínez Villena y Bolívar, Plaza Mayor. **Tel** (41) 994 432. **Open** 9am–5pm Mon–Sat.

This beautiful mansion with a long wooden balcony, reminiscent of the colonial buildings in La Habana Vieja, is evocative of the city's golden age. It was built in 1809 for Ortiz de Zúñiga, a former slave trader who later became the mayor of Trinidad. The house currently serves as an art gallery.

The first floor has paintings on display (and for sale) by contemporary Cuban artists, including Antonio Herr, Juan Oliva, Benito Ortiz, Antonio Zerquera and David Gutiérrez. Of interest in the gallery itself are frescoes, the great staircase, and, in the upper hall, a ceiling decorated with figures. From the balcony there is a fine view of the entire square.

The statue of Señor de la Vera Cruz (1731), in one of the chapels inside Santísima Trinidad

For hotels and restaurants in this region see pp261–2 and pp274–5

Palacio Brunet, built in the early 19th century and now housing the Museo Romántico

🏛 Museo de Arqueología Guamuhaya

Calle Simón Bolívar 457, e/ Fernando Hernández Echerri y Rubén Martínez Villena, Plaza Mayor. **Tel** (41) 993 420. **Open** 9am–5pm Tue–Sat. 🖼

The building that is now the home of the Archaeological

Alexander von Humboldt

Humboldt in Cuba

The German naturalist Alexander von Humboldt (1769–1859), the father of modern geography, made two trips to Cuba (1800–1801, 1804), which are recorded in a museum at Calle Oficios 252 in Old Havana. The book that followed, *Political Essay on the Island of Cuba*, in which he described Cuba as "the land of sugar and slaves", illustrated its geography, rivers, population, economy, government and slave system. Because of its abolitionist ideas the book was soon banned.

Museum was constructed in the 18th century and was purchased in the 1800s by the wealthy Don Antonio Padrón, who added a portico with brick columns and Ionic capitals.

The Guamuhaya (the native Indian name for the mountainous Escambray area) collection includes Pre-Columbian archaeological finds as well as objects associated with the Spanish conquest and slavery in Cuba, and stuffed animals, including the *manjuari*, an ancient species of fish that still lives in the Zapata swamp.

In the courtyard is a bronze bust commemorating the German geographer and naturalist Alexander von Humboldt, who stayed here as Padrón's guest in 1801, during his travels in the New World.

🏛 Palacio Brunet (Museo Romántico)

Calle Hernández Echerri 52, esq. Simón Bolívar, Plaza Mayor. **Tel** (41) 994 363. **Open** 9am–5pm Tue–Sat & every other Sun. 🖼 📷 Note: fee for photography may apply.

Built in 1812 as the residence of the wealthy Borrell family, Palacio Brunet now contains the Museo Romántico. The decoration of the mansion blends in well with the objects on display, most of which once belonged to Mariano Borrell, the family founder. They were

inherited by Borrell's daughter, the wife of Count Nicolás de la Cruz y Brunet (hence the name Palacio Brunet), in 1830.

The museum's 14 rooms all face the courtyard gallery with its elegant balustrade. The spacious living room has a Carrara marble floor, a coffered ceiling, Neo-Classical decoration, furniture made of precious wood, Sèvres vases and Bohemian crystalware. There are also English-made spittoons, which reveal that the 19th-century aristocratic landowners were partial to smoking cigars. In the dining room the fan windows are a particularly attractive feature.

Other rooms of interest are the countess's bedroom, with a bronze baldachin over the bed, and the kitchen, which is still decorated with its original painted earthenware tiles.

One of the elegant frescoes decorating Palacio Brunet

The Houses of Trinidad

The historic centre of Trinidad has an extraordinarily dense concentration of Spanish colonial houses, many still inhabited by the descendants of old local families. The oldest single-storey buildings have two corridors and a porch parallel to the street, with a courtyard at the back. In the late 1700s another corridor was introduced to the layout. In the 19th century, the houses formed a square around an open central courtyard. In general, the houses of Trinidad, unlike those in Havana, have no vestibule or portico. The entrance consists of a large living room that gives way to a dining room, either through an archway or a *mampara* – a stylized, half-height double door.

Barrotes, small turned wooden columns characterize the 18th-century windows.

Red tile roof

Wooden supports

Wooden beams support the two- or four-pitch sloping roof, which is covered with terracotta tiles. Inside, *mudéjar*-style coffered ceilings can often be found.

Trinidad Façades

The façade of the typical Trinidad house has a large central door, with a smaller door (or doors) cut in it for easy access. The windows, set slightly above ground level, are almost the height of the door. They have strong wooden shutters instead of glass. This house is in Plaza Mayor, next to the Casa Ortiz.

Wrought-iron ornamental motifs

Wooden shutters

The arched windows so characteristic of Trinidad have radiating wooden slats instead of *mediopunto* windows. These allow the air to enter but keep out the sunlight.

The 19th-century iron grilles replaced the wooden *barrotes* and typically have simple decoration at the top and bottom.

The wooden front door is sometimes framed by plaster motifs: flattened pilasters, moulding, half-columns either with simple Tuscan capitals or with upturned bowls at the top.

◄ Ornate façade of a colonial house in Trinidad's historic centre

Trinidad: Around Plaza Mayor

Walking along the streets leading from Plaza Mayor is a fascinating experience even if you have no particular destination. A slow stroll allows time to observe the detail of a window, a small balcony, the irregular cobblestones, or the cannons used as bollards. The centre is more or less free of traffic. In the evening the houses glow in the warm hues of sunset, and music fills the streets: the Casa de la Trova *(see p187)* and Casa de la Música *(see p186)* put on daily concerts by local bands.

The river cobblestones *(chinas pelonas)* used in Trinidad's streets

The frescoed entrance hall in Palacio Cantero and its Italian marble floor

🏛 Casa de la Cultura Julio Cuevas Díaz

Calle Zerquera 406. **Tel** (41) 994 308. **Open** 8am–10pm daily.

During the day, the vestibule is used as exhibition space by local artists (some of whom also have their studios here), selling their paintings. In the evening, performances are held in the rear courtyard: theatre, dance, concerts and shows for children.

🏛 Palacio Cantero (Museo Histórico Municipal)

Calle Bolívar 423. **Tel** (41) 994 460. **Open** 9am–5pm Mon–Thu & every other Sat. 📷 Note: fee for photography may apply.

This 1830s mansion, which belonged originally to Don Borrell y Padrón – one of the major figures in local sugar production – was purchased in 1841 by María de Monserrate Fernández, the widow of a sugar magnate. A year later she married the landowner Cantero, renaming the mansion and transforming it into a sumptuous Neo-Classical residence. The building is now the Museo Histórico Municipal.

From the grand entrance hall, with frescoed arches, the route takes in the dining room, the kitchen, the court-yard and an area for domestic servants.

The history of Trinidad can be traced through exhibits, maps, and monu-ments related to different themes: the Cantero family, piracy, the plantations in the Valle de los Ingenios, the slave trade and the wars of independence. The tower has a viewing platform and a rickety staircase that climbs past fresco-covered walls.

Plazuela del Jigüe

This peaceful little square is rich in history *(see p186)*. El Jigüe restaurant is housed in a lovely porticoed building decorated with panels of painted tiles.

🏛 Iglesia y Convento de San Francisco

Calle Hernández Echerri, esq. Guinart. Museo de la Lucha contra Bandidos: **Tel** (41) 994 121. **Open** 9am–5pm daily. 📷 📷

This elegant church was built in 1813 by Franciscan monks, but it was taken from them in 1848 in order for it to be used as a parish church. In 1895 the authorities transformed the building into a garrison for the Spanish army. Then in 1922, because of the lamentable state of the place, the garrison and part of the church were demolished. Only the bell tower was salvaged, along with adjacent buildings, which were used as a school until 1984, when the complex became the home of the **Museo de la Lucha contra Bandidos**.

The museum illustrates with documents, photographs and exhibits the struggle against the "bandits", the counter-revolutionaries who fled to the Sierra del Escambray after 1959. Fragments of a U2 plane, a boat, a militia truck and weapons are displayed in the building's cloister.

Bell tower of Iglesia y Convento de San Francisco

Beyond Trinidad's Historic Centre

Away from the centre there are more interesting areas to explore. One spot to head for is Parque Céspedes where locals, young and old, gather to listen and dance to live music in the evenings. Or, walking eastwards, Plaza Santa Ana draws people at all times of day. From the hill north of Plaza Mayor there are marvellous views over the valley that are especially beautiful at sunset.

The Cabildo de San Antonio, with votive offerings and sacred drums

Outdoor seating at a restaurant on Plaza Santa Ana

🏛 Ermita de Nuestra Señora de la Candelaria de la Popa

This small 18th-century church on a hill north of the centre is connected to Plaza Mayor by a narrow, steep street. The striking three-arch bell tower loggia was added in 1812, when work was carried out on the church to repair the damage done by a violent cyclone. The complex is being converted into the five-star French-Cuban hotel Pansea Trinidad which will include a restaurant and bar.

Plaza Santa Ana

A short walk from Plaza Mayor, in the eastern part of the city, this square is dominated by the 18th-century Iglesia de Santa Ana, which was partly rebuilt in 1812. The now decaying church is flanked by a royal poinciana tree.

The square is a popular place to gather, and is a favourite with children who come here to play ball games.

🏛 Cabildo de los Congos Reales de San Antonio

Calle Isidro Armenteros 168.
In the picturesque working-class quarter of El Calvario (Las Tres Cruces), in the northern part of Trinidad, is the Cabildo de los Congos Reales, a temple founded in 1859 for the worship of Afro-Cuban divinities. In the 1800s Cuba witnessed the rise of many *cabildos*, cultural centres differentiated by ethnic group, which aimed to preserve the spiritual and musical heritage of the slaves. This Cabildo in Trinidad, dedicated to Oggún – a warrior god whose Roman Catholic equivalent is St Anthony of Padua – is for the followers of the Palo Monte religion *(see p27)*.

Environs

On a rise 1 km (half a mile) northeast of the centre is the **Museo Espeleológico**. Located inside a cave of 3,700 sq m (4,440 sq yds), it can be visited with an expert guide as far as the Salón de las Perlas, a smaller cave where water drops "fall like pearls". According to legend, an Indian girl called Cacubu took refuge (and died) here, escaping from the lecherous Spanish conquistador Porcallo de Figueroa. Karstic fossils gathered from caves near Matanzas are also on show.

Bell tower of Iglesia de Santa Ana

❷ Topes de Collantes

The unspoilt landscape of the Sierra del Escambray *(see p177)*, where pine and eucalyptus grow alongside exuberant trees, ferns and tropical plants, offers extraordinarily beautiful scenery that can best be seen by hiking from Topes de Collantes, a steep 30-minute drive north of Trinidad. On the map below, two tours of the area are suggested, indicated by a letter and colour. Itinerary A consists of a walk of average difficulty through the tropical forest as far as the Caburní falls. Itinerary B is longer but easier and less tiring, and includes a detour to the Batata cave.

Tips for Hikers

Departure points: Topes de Collantes. ℹ Gaviota Reservations Office, (45) 667 864.
Length: Itinerary A: 3.5 km (2 miles); Itinerary B: 4.5 km (3 miles).
Stopping-off point: Parque Codina.

Key

━━ Major road
══ Path
╌╌ Itinerary A
▪▪ Itinerary B

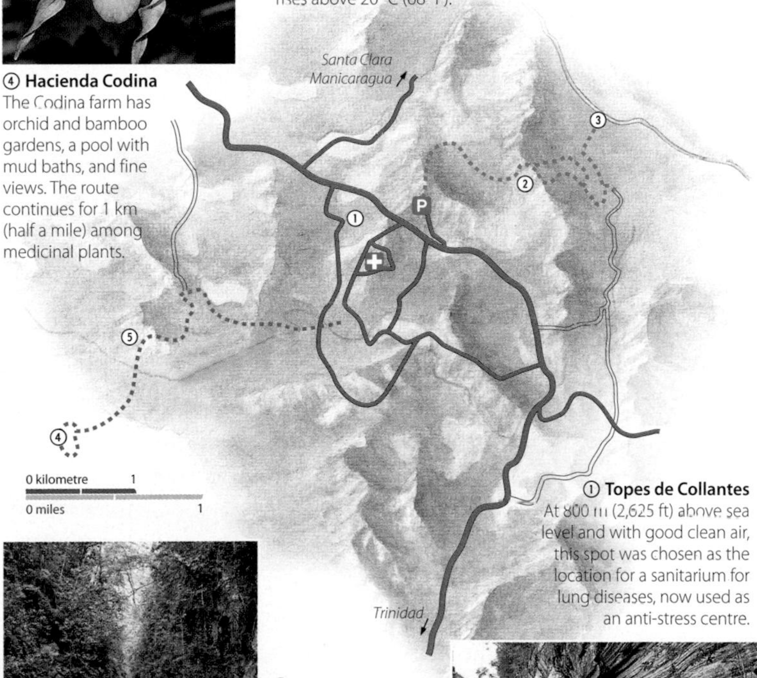

⑤ **La Batata**
This cave is traversed by an underground river, with natural pools at a temperature which never rises above 20° C (68° F).

④ **Hacienda Codina**
The Codina farm has orchid and bamboo gardens, a pool with mud baths, and fine views. The route continues for 1 km (half a mile) among medicinal plants.

Santa Clara
Manicaragua ↗

0 kilometre 1
0 miles 1

Trinidad ↓

① **Topes de Collantes**
At 800 m (2,625 ft) above sea level and with good clean air, this spot was chosen as the location for a sanitarium for lung diseases, now used as an anti-stress centre.

③ **Salto del Caburní**
After a 2-hour walk you will come to a cliff with a steep, plunging waterfall. Water gushes over rocks and collects further down, forming a pool where it is possible to bathe.

② **The Forest**
The path leading to Salto del Caburní crosses untouched tropical forest with curious rock formations.

La Boca beach, shaded by royal poinciana trees

❸ Península Ancón

Road Map C3.

About 10 km (6 miles) south of Trinidad is one of the first coastal areas in Cuba to be developed for tourism, the peninsula of Ancón, where foreign visitors have been coming since 1980. The fine white sand and turquoise water (not as clear here as along the north coast, though) make this promontory a small tourist resort, with a handful of hotels, bars, restaurants and watersports facilities. This area is visited by visitors and locals alike. Cubans head mainly for **La Boca**, 6 km (4 miles) from Trinidad, near the neck of the peninsula, especially on warm Sundays and in summer.

At **Playa Ancón**, 5 km (3 miles) of white sand in the southern part of the peninsula, there are comfortable hotels, a splendid beach and a diving school. From the beach by Hotel Ancón, assorted boat excursions are available to take divers and snorkellers out on the coral reef.

For some fascinating dive sites, divers should take an excursion to **Cayo Blanco**, 8 km (5 miles) off the coast. At the western tip of this small coral island with white sand beaches, is the largest black coral reef in Cuba, where divers can choose from a number of different dive sites. On the rocky coasts near **María Aguilar**, on the other hand, there are pools where swimmers only need a mask to easily spot a great variety of tropical fish.

As with Varadero *(see pp166–7)*, bicycles can be hired and make a pleasant way of getting around the Ancón peninsula.

Opposite the peninsula, across the bay, is the old port of **Casilda**, 6 km (4 miles) from Trinidad, where in 1519 Hernán Cortés recruited the troops that went on to conquer Mexico. Once a prosperous port thanks to the sugar trade, Casilda has long since declined, and is now above all a place that people visit on the way to the local beaches.

❹ Valle de los Ingenios

Road Map C3. 🚌 🚂 Excursions: from Trinidad. 🛈 at railway station, (41) 993 348; Cubatur, Calle Antonio Maceo, esq. Francisco J Zerquera, (41) 996 314.

Leaving Trinidad and heading northeast, along the road to Sancti Spíritus, one can appreciate the beauty of the fertile plain, with the green hills of the Sierra del Escambray forming a backdrop. Only 12 km (7 miles) separate Trinidad from the Valle de los Ingenios, whose name derives from the sugar mills *(ingenios, see pp46–7)* built here in the early 19th century. Today, fields of sugar cane form

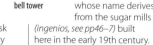

The bell on the Iznaga bell tower

Valle de los Ingenios, from the Mirador de la Loma: green swathes of sugar cane at the foot of the Sierra

The Iznaga estate tower, with a commanding view of the valley

a blanket of green, interrupted only by towering royal palms.

The valley is rich in history with ruins providing evidence of the time when the sugar industry was at its peak. These buildings also help visitors to understand the social structure that was the order of the sugar plantations. The whole zone, which has a surface area of 419 sq km (162 sq miles), includes the ruins of 56 *ingenios*. UNESCO has declared the valley a World Heritage Site.

A good way to visit the area is to take the train that, when working, departs from Trinidad and covers the entire valley.

It stops at the impressive **Manaca Iznaga Estate**, where about 350 slaves lived in the 1840s. The landowner's house survives and has been converted into a bar and restaurant. Also still standing are the *barracones* (slaves' huts), and a monumental seven-level tower 45 m (147 ft) high. Each level is different from the next in shape and decoration: the first three are square, the top four are octagonal. The symbolic meaning of this tower is apparent. It was built in 1830 as an assertion of authority over the valley by

Alejo Iznaga, a rival to his brother Pedro, who was also a major landowner and sugar producer. The tower also functioned as a lookout for supervising the slaves. The top of the tower, which is reached via a steep wooden stairway, today offers lovely, wide-ranging views of the surrounding countryside. At the foot of the tower is the bell that once tolled the work hours on the plantation.

One of the places only accessible by car is the **Mirador de La Loma del Puerto** (6 km/ 4 miles east of Trinidad, on the road to Sancti Spíritus).

This observation point *(mirador)*, 192 m (630 ft) above sea level, offers a magnificent view of the whole valley. There is also an outdoor café where you can sample the drink *guarapo*, sugar cane juice.

Also heading in the direction of Sancti Spíritus, south of the village of Caracusey, is the outstanding, restored **Guaimaro**, built in 1859. Owner José Mariano Borrel y Lemus commissioned Italian painter Daniele Dell'Aglio, who also designed Teatro Sauto in Matanzas, to decorate the walls of the hacienda with European scenes.

Sugar Production in Cuba

For centuries, sugar cane *(Saccharum officinarum)*, which was introduced to the island in 1512 by Spanish settlers, has been the mainstay of the Cuban economy. Sugar extraction takes place in various phases: after being washed, the cane stalks are pressed by special mills and the juice *(guarapo)* is extracted from the fibrous mass *(bagassa)*, which is used as fuel and as livestock fodder. The juice is treated chemically, filtered and then evaporated so as to obtain a concentration of dark syrup that is then heated. This produces crystals of sucrose. The syrupy mass then goes into a centrifuge. Other by-products are obtained from sugar cane, including molasses, a residue of the syrup, which still contains 50 per cent sugar and is used as the basic ingredient in the production of rum *(see p79)*.

Ripe cane is 2–5 m (6–16 ft) tall with a diameter of 2–6 cm (1–3 in). Once cut, the plant shoots again and becomes ripe again in a year. Newly planted cane, grown from cuttings 30–40 cm (12–16 in) long, ripens in 11–18 months.

The *zafra* (harvest) takes place between December and June. Before harvest begins, the cane field is burned to remove the outer leaves, which obstruct harvesting. In the plains cutting is done with machines, while in the hills the *machete* is still used.

Transport has to be rapid to minimize the deterioration of the sucrose in the heat. To this end, in the late 1800s a special railway network was built and steam trains travelled between the cane fields and the sugar works.

❺ Sancti Spíritus

The city of Sancti Spíritus, deep in the heart of fertile agricultural countryside, was founded by Diego Velázquez on the banks of the Tuinucú river in 1514. It was moved to its present site, near the Yayabo river, eight years later. In 1586 British pirates set fire to the town along with all the documents relating to its foundation. The political, economic and military centre of the area, Sancti Spíritus was embellished with elegant mansions throughout the 17th and 18th centuries. Today, its small, attractive colonial centre receives few visitors, despite its "national monument" status.

🚲 Yayabo Bridge

Its medieval appearance and large terracotta arches make this old bridge unique in Cuba, and for this reason it has been declared a national monument. According to one bizarre legend, in order to make the bridge more robust, the workmen mixed cement with goat's milk.

The Yayabo bridge is an important part of the city's street network: it is the only route into town for those coming from Trinidad.

Exploring Sancti Spíritus

The central part of the city can be explored on foot in a few hours. It is pleasant to simply stroll along the attractively restored streets (many of which are for pedestrians only), where brightly coloured colonial houses with wrought-iron balconies are characteristic. The most famous approach to the town is the southern one, across the lovely bridge, built in 1831, over the Yayabo river. The narrow, quiet streets leading up from the bridge to the city centre are the oldest in Sancti Spíritus. They are paved with irregular cobblestones and lined with one-storey houses with shingle roofs.

Calle Máximo Gómez, which leads to the main square, Parque Serafín Sánchez, is lined with 18th- and 19th-century monuments, museums and mansions. These include the **Teatro Principal**, a bright blue porticoed construction built

The Yayabo Bridge, leading to the colonial centre

in 1876 by public donation and restored in 1980; a large 19th-century mansion that is now the Pensamiento bar; the **Casa de la Trova**, also restored in the eighties; a typical bar-restaurant, Mesón de la Plaza; and the Placita, a small square with a statue of Dr Rudesindo Antonio García Rijo, a physician, scientist and illustrious citizen.

🏛 Museo de Arte Colonial

Calle Plácido 74. **Tel** (41) 325 455.
Open 9:30am–5pm Tue–Fri, 2–5pm Sat, 8am–noon Sun. 📷 📷 Note: fee for photography may apply.

This fine building was constructed in 1720 and belonged to the Iznaga family (see p197). It is now an outstanding museum showing porcelain, furniture and paintings.

Parque Serafín Sánchez, the main square in Sancti Spiritus

The interior of the Parroquial Mayor during mass

🏛 Parroquial Mayor del Espíritu Santo
Calle Agramonte Oeste 58. **Tel** (41) 324 855. **Open** 9–11am & 2–5pm Tue–Sat, 8–11am Sun. 🕐 8pm Tue & Thu, 5pm Wed & Fri, 10am Sun.

Using money donated by Don Ignacio de Valdivia, the local mayor, the present church was built of stone in 1680, over the original 16th-century wooden church that had been destroyed by pirates. It is one of Cuba's oldest churches. The simple and solid building is reminiscent of the parish churches of Andalusia, and still has its original, exquisitely worked wooden ceilings. The

30-m (100-ft) bell tower, with three levels, was added in the 18th century, and the octagonal Cristo de la Humildad y la Paciencia chapel, built next to the church in the 19th century, has a remarkable half-dome.

Parque Serafín Sánchez
The heart of the city consists of a tranquil square with trees and a charming *glorieta* (gazebo), surrounded by Neo-Classical buildings. A national monument, the park is dedicated to Serafín Sánchez, a local hero in the wars of independence, whose house is open to the public in the nearby Calle de Céspedes. In the evenings, the plaza is a popular gathering place.

The most notable buildings here are the Centro de Patrimonio, with broad stained-glass windows and Seville mosaics, the large **Biblioteca** (library), and the **Hotel Perla de Cuba**, one of the most exclusive hotels in Cuba in the early 1900s and now a shopping centre. The **Hotel Plaza**, whose bar is popular with locals, is part of a colonial building.

VISITORS' CHECKLIST

Practical Information
Sancti Spíritus. **Road Map** C3.
140,000. Cubatur, Calle Máximo Gómez 7, (41) 328 518.

Transport
Carretera Central, km 2.
Avenída Jesús Menéndez.

Environs
Around 8 km (5 miles) east of Sancti Spíritus, in the direction of Ciego de Ávila, nature lovers and fans of fishing can enjoy **Presa Zaza**, an artificial lake well stocked with trout and black bass. Tours of the lake depart from the Zaza hotel, while the shores are ideal spots for birdwatching. Presa Zaza is Cuba's largest man-made lake but has suffered from low water levels in recent years. Ask at Cubatur for details.

Chatting in the Parque Serafín Sánchez in the evening, a popular pastime

The Centre of Sancti Spíritus
① Yayabo Bridge
② Teatro Principal
③ Museo de Arte Colonial
④ Parroquial Mayor del Espíritu Santo
⑤ Casa de la Trova
⑥ Parque Serafín Sánchez
⑦ Biblioteca
⑧ Hotel Perla de Cuba
⑨ Hotel Plaza

0 metres 300
0 yards 300

Parque Martí in Ciego de Ávila, with a monument to José Martí

❻ Ciego de Ávila

Road Map D3. 145,000. ✈ 🚌
🚍 ℹ Infotur, Calle Honorato del Castillo, esq. Libertad, (33) 209 109.

When Ciego de Ávila was founded in 1538 by the conquistador Jácome de Ávila, it was just a large farm in the middle of a wood, a *ciego*. It only became a bona fide city in 1840. Today, it is a rural town with two-storey houses fronted with Neo-Classical columns, and streets filled with one-horse carriages.

The few visitors who come here are mostly on their way to the *cayos* in the Jardines del Rey archipelago.

Anyone who does stop off should visit the **Teatro Principal** (1927) and the **Museo Histórico Provincial**. This last has four rooms of documents and photographs concerning the history of the province, in particular the story of La Trocha. This line of defence was constructed in the 19th century. It was devised by the Spanish to block the advance of the Cuban nationalists (*mambises*) by cutting the island in half, from Morón, north of Ciego de Ávila, to Júcaro, on the Caribbean coast. Some surviving La Trocha towers, built about 1 km (half a mile) from one another, lie a short distance outside town and are open to the public.

One of La Trocha's redoubts

The multi-ethnic character of the city means that visitors can enjoy both the rural festivals of Spanish origin (*parrandas*), similar to those in Remedios (*see p181*), and merengue and congo dance shows, especially in the quarter where Jamaican and Haitian immigrants live. Ciego de Ávila also has a cycling school which is attended by children from all over the island. At Epiphany the town is the starting point for the month-long Vuelta, a Cuban cycle race much like the Tour de France.

The Cockerel of Morón

"Be careful not to end up like the cockerel of Morón, which lost its feathers as well as its crest." This Spanish saying dates back to the 1500s, when the governor of the Andalusian village of Morón de la Frontera, who lorded it over the local farmers and was known as "cockerel" (*gallo*) for his arrogance and presumptuousness, was punished with a good thrashing and thrown out of town by the angry citizens. The event became well known and to commemorate it, a statue of a plucked rooster was set up in the main avenue. When a community of Andalusians emigrated to Cuba in the 18th century and founded a city they called Morón, to maintain their traditions they put a statue of the rooster at the entrance to the town. It was taken down in 1959, and replaced in 1981 by a bronze sculpture placed next to a tower. At 6am and 6pm daily, a recording of a cock crowing is played here.

The bronze statue (1981) of the legendary cockerel of Morón

❼ Morón

Ciego de Ávila. **Road Map** D3.
67,000. 🚌 ℹ Cubanacán, Hotel Morón, Avda de Tarafa, (33) 504 720.
📷 Cockerel of Morón: end of June.

Morón lies on the road that runs north from Ciego de Ávila (a town with a long-standing rivalry with Morón). The road is known for its occupation in 1896 by nationalist rebels (*mambises*) after they had managed to breach the Spanish defence.

Morón was founded as a villa in 1869 and retains a small, well-preserved colonial centre. The **Museo Municipal** has more than 600 archaeological finds, brought to light in the 1940s

A street in Morón with pastel-coloured houses and arcades

Isla Turiguanó, the unusual "Dutch village" near Morón

a short distance from town, including a famous statuette, the Idolillo de Barro.

🏛 Museo Municipal

Calle Martí 374 e/ Antuña y Cervantes. **Tel** (33) 504 501. **Open** 9am–5pm Tue–Sat, 8am–noon Sun. **Closed** 1 Jan, 1 May, 26 Jul, 25 Dec. 🖼 🎥 🖼

Environs

North of Morón are two freshwater lagoons: the **Laguna Redonda**, which owes it name to its almost circular form and is known for its great abundance of trout, and the **Laguna de Leche**. The latter is called the "Lagoon of Milk" because of its colour, caused by the limestone deposits in the water. It is the largest stretch of brackish water in Cuba, with a surface area of 67 sq km (26 sq miles). It abounds in carp and pike and is a refuge for herons and flamingos.

Immediately north of the Laguna de Leche is the **Isla Turiguanó**, a peninsula with a village of Dutch-style houses surrounded by grazing land for cattle. The animals are also Dutch, having been imported by Celia Sánchez (see p55).

Florencia, about 20 km (12 miles) west of Morón, is the starting point for hikes in the small **Sierra de Jatibonico**. This range can be explored on horseback, along the route followed by Camilo Cienfuegos's column in 1958 (see p52).

The Canal Viejo de Bahamas is used for platform fishing for large tropical fish. There are also hunting reserves: the Coto de Caza de Morón and Coto de Caza Aguachales de Fala.

❽ Jardines del Rey

Ciego de Ávila, Camagüey. **Road Map** D3.

In the Atlantic Ocean, north of the province of Ciego de Ávila, the Sabana and Camagüey archipelagoes, known collectively as "Jardines del Rey", include about 400 small islands, almost all of which are uninhabited.

They were discovered in 1522 by the conquistador Diego Velázquez, who was so struck by them that he dedicated them to the king (rey), Carlos V. They later became a hiding place for pirates and, after the official abolition of slavery, a clandestine landing point for slaves.

A causeway 27 km (17 miles) long, built in 1988 as a link between the archipelago and mainland Cuba, makes it easy for visitors to get to the lovely beaches, the coral reef, and the beach resorts which are currently concentrated on Cayo Coco and Cayo Guillermo (see pp202–3). Visitors must pass a tollgate on the causeway. Cayo Paredón Grande, 6 km (4 miles) long, is the third largest island in the Jardines. Although there are no hotels, it is worth visiting for the lovely beaches, and the coral has some fine dive sites, too. There are good views of the distinctive black and yellow Diego Velázquez Lighthouse, built by Chinese immigrants in 1859.

Although part of the province of Camagüey, Cayo Romano belongs naturally to this archipelago. Its marshy coastline is the habitat of manatees

The lighthouse at Cayo Paredón Grande

Sailing boats at a pristine beach on Cayo Coco island

❾ Cayo Coco

With 22 km (14 miles) of white sandy beaches and 370 sq km (143 sq miles) of partly marshy land abounding in mangroves and coconut palms, Cayo Coco is an important natural reserve for marine birds. Flamingos may be spotted in the lagoon areas near the coast. The name of the island derives from another rare species of bird that lives here: the white ibis, known to Cubans as the "coco". The island is peaceful, and tourist amenities have been built and organized with environmental concerns in mind. The beaches are lovely, with fine sand washed by clear turquoise water. The warm, shallow water makes Cayo Coco particularly suitable for families with children, but the island is also popular among diving and water sports enthusiasts, who can take advantage of the modern sports facilities here.

★ Playa Pilar
Named after Ernest Hemingway's yacht, Playa Pilar sits at the western tip of Cayo Guillermo.

CAYO GUILLERMO

Archipélago de Sabana - Camagüey

CAYO

Cayo Guillermo
Linked to Cayo Coco, this small island is covered with mangroves and palms as well as mahogany, juniper and mastic trees. The Cayo has become a popular centre for kitesurfing.

Key

━━ Major road

══ Minor road

Bahía de Perros

The Pedraplén
A major work of civil engineering, this causeway links the islands with the mainland. It has caused some concern to ecologists, since it blocks the tide and may disturb the ecosystem of the bay.

La Loma

San Rafael

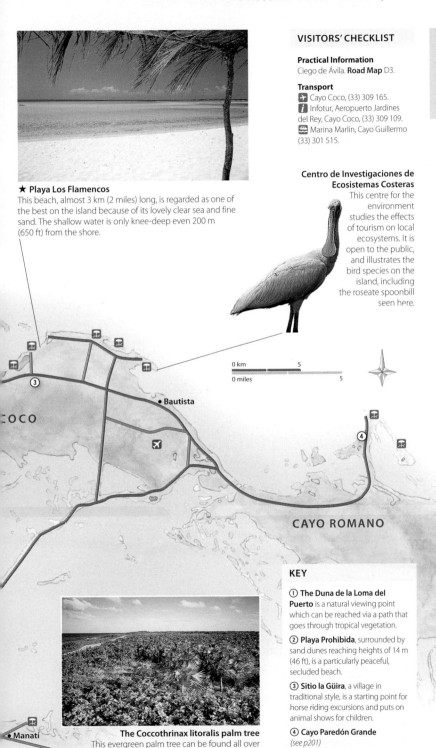

★ **Playa Los Flamencos**
This beach, almost 3 km (2 miles) long, is regarded as one of the best on the island because of its lovely clear sea and fine sand. The shallow water is only knee-deep even 200 m (650 ft) from the shore.

The Coccothrinax litoralis palm tree
This evergreen palm tree can be found all over Cuba, but is particularly common in Cayo Coco.

Centro de Investigaciones de Ecosistemas Costeras
This centre for the environment studies the effects of tourism on local ecosystems. It is open to the public, and illustrates the bird species on the island, including the roseate spoonbill seen here.

VISITORS' CHECKLIST

Practical Information
Ciego de Ávila. **Road Map** D3.

Transport
✈ Cayo Coco, (33) 309 165.
🛈 Infotur, Aeropuerto Jardines del Rey, Cayo Coco, (33) 309 109.
⛴ Marina Marlin, Cayo Guillermo (33) 301 515.

0 km 5
0 miles 5

Bautista

COCO

CAYO ROMANO

Manatí

KEY

① **The Duna de la Loma del Puerto** is a natural viewing point which can be reached via a path that goes through tropical vegetation.

② **Playa Prohibida**, surrounded by sand dunes reaching heights of 14 m (46 ft), is a particularly peaceful, secluded beach.

③ **Sitio la Güira**, a village in traditional style, is a starting point for horse riding excursions and puts on animal shows for children.

④ **Cayo Paredón Grande**
(see p201)

For keys to symbols see back flap

⑩ Camagüey

This city, declared a UNESCO World Heritage site in 2008, lies in the middle of a vast area of pastureland. It is nick-named "the Legendary" for its traditions of heroism and patriotism as well as for its Neo-Classical architecture. There is a large, rich colonial-style historic centre and the city has an active cultural life. Founded in the bay of Nuevitas on the northern coast as Nuestra Señora de Santa María del Puerto Príncipe, the city was moved to the interior to escape from revolts by the Indians, who staunchly resisted Spanish domination in the 1500s, and from pirate attacks. The irregular, intricate street network that distinguishes Camagüey from other Cuban cities resulted from the need to protect itself from raids.

An example of 19th-century Neo-Classical architecture in Camagüey

Parque Agramonte: the equestrian statue and the Cathedral

of the city, was designed by Manuel Saldaña and built in 1735. In 1777 a bell tower was added, but it collapsed a year later. Since then, the church has been through phases of reconstruction, taking on its present appearance in 1864. It now has a monumental façade surmounted by a pediment, and a bell tower crowned by a statue of Christ.

Parque Ignacio Agramonte

The former Plaza de Armas is dominated by an equestrian statue of Agramonte, a Cuban independence hero, sculpted by the Italian artist Salvatore Boemi and inaugurated by Amalia Simoni, Agramonte's wife, in 1912. At the four corners of the small square stand royal palms, planted in memory of a group of nationalists executed here on 24 February 1851. As so often during the wars of independence, the palms were symbolic monuments to the rebels, as the Spanish would never have allowed real monuments to be built.

Buildings of interest on the square include the Palacio Collado (1942), Bar El Cambio, opened in 1909, a colonial building housing the Café de la Ciudad, the **Casa de la Trova Patricio Ballagas** in an 18th-century building with a courtyard, the Biblioteca Julio Antonio Mella and the cathedral. With its benches

and shade from the palm trees, the square is a natural gathering point for the people of Camagüey. During the day old people gather to watch life go by, and in the evenings the young are drawn to the square.

It is also a popular spot for tourists to see the town's famous *tinajones* (clay pots) up close.

🏛 Catedral de Nuestra Señora de la Candelaria

Calle Cisneros 168, Parque Agramonte. **Tel** (32) 294 965. **Open** 2:30–6pm Mon–Fri (also 8–11:45am Wed), 2:30–4pm Sat, 8–11:45am Sun. 🕐 5pm Mon–Fri, 9am Sun.

Camagüey's cathedral, dedicated to Our Lady of Candelaria, the patron saint

The Centre of Camagüey

1. Parque Ignacio Agramonte
2. Catedral de Nuestra Señora de la Candelaria
3. Casa Natal de Ignacio Agramonte
4. Iglesia de la Merced
5. Teatro Principal
6. Iglesia del Carmen
7. Cinco Esquinas
8. Plaza San Juan de Dios
9. Museo Ignacio Agramonte
10. Parque Casino Campestre
11. Casa de la Trova
12. Casa Natal de Nicolás Guillén
13. Iglesia de la Soledad

The courtyard at Casa Agramonte, where concerts are performed

Casa Natal de Ignacio Agramonte

Calle Ignacio Agramonte 459, e/ Independencia y Cisneros. **Tel** (32) 297 116. **Open** 9am–4:45pm Mon–Sat, 9am–2:30pm Sun. **Closed** 1 May. Note: fee for photography may apply.

Near Plaza de los Trabajadores, where a large ceiba tree marks the middle of the old town, is the former home of Ignacio Agramonte. This famous local

Plaque on Nicolás Guillén's birthplace

patriot died in battle in 1873 at the age of 31. The two-storey house dates from 1750 and has a beautiful inner courtyard with old *tinajones*.

The museum has documents concerning the war of independence, the hero's personal belongings, such as his 36-calibre Colt revolver from 1851, and family furniture, including the piano of his wife, Amalia Simoni, reputed to be one of the richest, most virtuous women in the city.

A short walk away is another famous home. The **Casa Natal de Nicolás Guillén** *(see p32)*, birthplace of Cuba's poet laureate who died in 1989, is at Calle Hermanos Aguero 58.

VISITORS' CHECKLIST

Practical Information

Camagüey. **Road Map** D3. 330,000. Infotur, Calle Ignacio Agramonte 426, (32) 256 794. Jornadas de la Cultura Camagüeyana (first half of Feb); Carnival (23–29 Jun).

Transport

Ignacio Agramonte, (32) 261 010. Ave Avellaneda y Finlay, (32) 292 633. Carretera Central km 3, (32) 270 396.

Iglesia de la Merced

Plaza de los Trabajadores 4. **Tel** (32) 292 783. **Open** 8–11am, 4–5:30pm Mon–Fri, 8–11am Sat, 8–10am, 5–7pm Sun. 5pm Mon–Fri, 7am Sat, 9am & 6pm Sun.

The Iglesia de la Merced was built in 1601 but was rebuilt from 1748 to 1756, and now has a Baroque façade with a central bell tower. Inside are striking, almost Art Nouveau-style murals. The choir and catacombs are also of interest. Most famous, however, is the Holy Sepulchre with an 18th-century statue of Christ by Mexican sculptor Juan Benítez Alfonso. It was cast from 23,000 silver coins collected from the faithful by Manuel Agüero, a citizen who, after his wife's death in 1726, became a monk and devoted himself to restoring the church.

Teatro Principal

Calle Pedro Valencia 64. **Tel** (32) 293 048. First opened in 1850 and rebuilt in 1926 after a devastating fire, this theatre is famous as the home of the Camagüey Ballet, one of the leading dance companies in Latin America *(see p280)*.

The Tinajones

These symbols of the city can be seen everywhere – in parks and gardens and especially in the courtyards of the local colonial houses. *Tinajones* are large jars, which may be as much as 2 m (6 ft) tall, made of clay from the nearby Sierra de Cubitas. The jars were introduced by Catalonian immigrants in the early 1700s, and are used today to collect rainwater and to store food.

A *tinajón* in the central square

Exploring Camagüey

The vast historic centre of Camagüey, a complex 16th-century labyrinth of winding alleyways, dead ends, forks and squares, is not easy to navigate. The centre consists mainly of two-storey houses without arcades, pierced by large windows protected by wooden grilles. Each house has an inner courtyard. There are numerous old churches, most of them well attended, whose bell towers jut above the red tile roofs of the colonial houses. As with Trinidad, the well-preserved architecture is the result of the town's geographic isolation: the railway line only arrived in 1903, and the Carretera Central road in 1931.

The Cinco Esquinas (Five Corners), one of the town's more complicated junctions

Other City Centre Sights

Many interesting sights are just a short walk away from Parque Ignacio Agramonte.

Calle Martí runs west from the square up to Plazuela de la Bedoya, a delightful colonial square that has been restored and filled with statues. An old Ursuline convent stands here, as well as a church, the **Iglesia del Carmen**. Although not completed until 1825, it has a distinctly Baroque character.

Calle Cristo leads to Plazuela del Cristo, which is dominated by the Iglesia del Santo Cristo del Buen Viaje and the Cementerio General (1814),

Author Gertrudis Gómez de Avellaneda

the oldest cemetery in Cuba. Back near Parque Agramonte, there is a complex interchange, the **Cinco Esquinas** (five corners), near the top of Calle Raúl Lamar, which is a good example of the intricate layout of the city centre.

Another route to explore runs along or near Calle República, a narrow, straight street that crosses the entire city from north to south. At the northern end, beyond the railway line, is the Museo Provincial Ignacio Agramonte (see p207).

Further south, a right turn at the Hotel Colón leads eastwards across to Calle Avellaneda. Here,

at No. 22, is the birthplace of Gertrudis Gómez de Avellaneda, the 19th-century author of antislavery novels.

Further south, on Calle República, stands the **Iglesia de Nuestra Señora de la Soledad**, built in 1776. It was here that local patriot Ignacio Agramonte was baptized and also married. The façade features pilasters and moulding typical of early Cuban Baroque architecture, but the real attractions here are the decoratively painted arches and pillars and the wooden *alfarje* ceiling inside.

By going south to the far end of this street you will reach Calle Martí, which will take you back to Parque Agramonte.

Plaza San Juan de Dios

Laid out in 1732, this square is also known as Plaza del Padre Olallo, in honour of a priest who was beatified in 2008 because he dedicated his life to caring for the sick in the city hospital.

Today, the totally restored Plaza San Juan de Dios is a quiet, picturesque spot, but also a gem of colonial architecture. Around it are 18th-century pastel buildings, several of which have been converted into restaurants. One whole side of the plaza is occupied by an important group of buildings that include a church and an old hospital, which is now the home of the Dirección Provincial de Patrimonio and

The Iglesia del Carmen, on Plaza del Carmen

the Oficina del Historiador de la Ciudad, a body that takes care of the province's cultural heritage. Construction of the building began in 1728.

Despite its small size, the **Iglesia de San Juan de Dios** is one of the most interesting churches in Camagüey. It still has its original floors, ceiling and wooden choir, and, most importantly, the high altar with the Holy Trinity and an anthropomorphic representation of the Holy Ghost, the only one in Cuba. The church façade is simple and rigorously symmetrical.

The old **Hospital** was used in the 20th century as a military infirmary, then a teacher training school, a refuge for flood victims, a centre for underprivileged children and, most recently, as the Instituto Tecnológico de la Salud (Technological Institute of Health). The square plan with two inner courtyards (clearly of *mudéjar* influence) was modelled on Baroque monasteries. The enclosure walls are thick and plain; in contrast the window grilles and wooden balustrades in the galleries are elegant and elaborate.

One of the cloisters in the old San Juan de Dios hospital

🏠 **Iglesia y Hospital de San Juan de Dios**
Plaza San Juan de Dios. **Open** 7–11am, 2:30–4pm Mon–Sat. **Closed** 1 Jan, 1 May, 26 Jul, 25 Dec. 📷 📸

🏛 **Museo Provincial Ignacio Agramonte**
Avenida de los Mártires 2, esq. Ignacio Sánchez. **Tel** (32) 282 425. **Open** 9am–5pm Mon–Thu & Sat, 9am–8pm Fri, 9am–noon Sun. 📷 📸 Note: fee for photography may apply.

The only military building in town was the head-quarters of the Spanish army cavalry in the 19th century. In 1905 it became a hotel, and since 1948 it has housed a large museum of the history, natural history and art of the city and its province. The prestigious small art collection is second only to that in the Museo de Bellas Artes in Havana, with three works by the famous Cuban artist Fidelio Ponce. There is also a fine collection of books, including some manuscripts by the Canaries writer Silvestre de Balboa, author of *Espejo de*

The Holy Trinity high altar

Paciencia, a poem (1608) regarded as the first literary work in Cuba *(see p32)*.

🌳 **Parque Casino Campestre**
The largest natural park in any Cuban city, the Casino was for a long time used for agricultural fairs, and became a public park in the 19th century. The Hatibonico river flows through it. Besides the many statues of patriots and illustrious figures from Camagüey and Cuba, it has a monument to the Seville pilots Barberán and Collar, who on 10 June 1933 made a historic transatlantic flight from Seville to Camagüey in 19 hours 11 minutes.

Environs
The plains north of Camagüey are cattle country. **Rancho King**, a former cattle ranch, has a restaurant and rooms and offers horse-riding trips and rodeos. It is most easily accessed from Playa Santa Lucía, 26 miles (16 km) to the north.

Plaza San Juan de Dios, known for its well-preserved colonial architecture

A country road north of Camagüey, leading to Sierra de Cubitas

⓫ Sierra de Cubitas

Camagüey. **Road Map** D3.

The range of hills that lies 40 km (25 miles) north of Camagüey forms the largest local reserve of flora and fauna, with over 300 plant species. To date, however, this area has no tourist facilities on any scale.

The main attractions are caverns such as Hoyo de Bonet, the largest karst depression in Cuba, and the Pichardo and María Teresa grottoes, where cave drawings have been discovered. Expert speleologists, on the other hand, can visit the Cueva de Rolando, a cave 132 m (435 ft) long with a subterranean lake 50 m (165 ft) across, the bottom of which has not yet been explored.

In the neighbouring Valle del Río Máximo is the **Paso de los Paredones**, a long, deep ravine with holes caused by water erosion, some as much as 100 m (328 ft) deep and up to 1 km (0.6 mile) wide.

The thick vegetation, through which sunlight penetrates for only a few hours, is home to a variety of native birds (tocororo and cartacuba; see pp24–5) and migratory birds, as well as harmless reptiles and rodents.

⓬ Playa Santa Lucía

Camagüey. **Road Map** D3.
🛈 Cubatur, Ave. Turística, Playa Santa Lucía, (32) 336 291 or (32) 365 303.

The most famous beach resort in the province offers 21 km (13 miles) of fine white sand lapped by turquoise waves. The large coral reef only 3 km (2 miles) from the shore is good for scuba divers (see p285). It shelters the coast from the currents of the Canal Viejo de Bahamas, thus safeguarding calm swimming conditions for adults and children alike, as well as creating a good area for practising all watersports. There are more than 30 dive

sites along the reef, which can be reached with the help of the international diving centres, while Shark's Point offers dives full of romance, exploring the wrecks of pirate and Spanish vessels. For the brave there is also the chance to observe the bull shark, Carcharinus leucas, at close range from February to March and from July to September.

At the bay of Nuevitas, 6 km (4 miles) west of Santa Lucía, near the tiny seashore village of La Boca, is **Playa Los Cocos**. This lovely unspoilt beach has fine white sand and clear water, and is a must for visitors to Santa Lucía.

A beautiful beach on the protected island of Cayo Sabinal

⓭ Cayo Sabinal

Camagüey. **Road Map** D3.

Together with Cayo Romano and Cayo Guajaba, this small island forms part of a protected area. It is the home of deer and the largest colony of flamingoes in Cuba, as well as a nesting area for four species of sea turtle. Cayo Sabinal can be reached via a causeway from

A pier at Playa Santa Lucía, departure point for boats going out to the coral reef

◀ Playa Los Cocos, near Playa Santa Lucía

Playa Santa Lucía, and a planned *pedraplén* causeway will link it with Jardines del Rey.

In the past Cayo Sabinal was home to permanent residents: first the natives, then pirates and Spanish coalmen. Today, the key is visited mostly for its three beautiful beaches, Playa Bonita, Playa Los Pinos and Playa Brava. The Colón Lighthouse dates from 1894.

South of Cayo Sabinal is the Bay of Nuevitas, where the city of Camagüey was first founded. The three small islands in the bay, known as **Los Ballenatos**, are popular destinations for boat trips.

⑭ Las Tunas

Las Tunas. **Road Map** E3. 🚗 198,000. 🚆 🚌 🚕 *i* Hotel Las Tunas, Ave. 2 de diciembre, (31) 345 014; Ecotur, (31) 372 073. 🎭 Jornada Nacional Cucalambeana (end of Jun).

Until 1975, Las Tunas was just one of the cities in the old Provincia de Oriente. Then administrative reform made it the capital of an autonomous province. The town was founded on the site of two native villages that were razed to the ground by the *conquistador* Alonso de Ojeda in the early 1500s. However, the town only really began to develop three centuries later, progressively taking on the character of a frontier town between central and eastern Cuba. The historic centre has some colonial buildings but no major monuments of note. However, the city does have some artists' studios.

The **Museo Histórico Provincial**, in the town hall, has archaeological finds and documents relating to the history of the province. The **Museo Memorial Mártires de Barbados** commemorates a terrorist act against Cuba carried out in 1976: a bomb exploded on a Cubana aeroplane headed for Havana, killing 73 passengers and the entire crew.

Every year Las Tunas springs to life on the occasion of the Jornada Nacional Cucalambeana, dedicated to Juan Cristóbal Nápoles Fajardo, known as El Cucalambé, a farmer and poet born here in 1829. Local and other Cuban artists, as well as foreign scholars, take part in this festival of music and folk traditions.

Environs

Near Las Tunas are many sites linked with the wars of independence. They include the **Fuerte de la Loma**, now a

The town hall of Las Tunas

national monument, built by the Spanish to halt the advance of the Mambí, on the edge of the city of Puerto Padre, the scene of major battles in the Ten Years' War (1868–78).

The best beach here is **Playa Covarrubias**, which is near Puerto Padre, on the Atlantic coast.

⑮ Jardines de la Reina

Ciego de Ávila, Camagüey. **Road Map** D4. 🚢 Júcaro, Embarcadero Avalón, *i* Avalon, Júcaro, 7204 7422.

This archipelago in the Caribbean Sea was discovered by Christopher Columbus and called Jardines de la Reina in honour of the queen *(reina)*, Isabel of Castile. Established as a National Park in 1996, it is one of Cuba's largest protected areas. These islands can be reached by boat from Júcaro.

The great number of unspoilt *cayos*, mangroves and palm groves are rich with fauna including crocodiles, iguanas, turtles, hutias and tropical birds, and the 200-km (125-mile) coral reef which runs the length of the archipelago is a paradise for divers.

Near Cayo Anclita, only about 100 m (328 ft) from the coast, is **La Tortuga**, a floating hotel reserved for fishermen, divers and photographers *(see p261)*. The waters abound with groupers, snappers, barracudas and Caribbean reef and silky sharks, among many other fish. Tours, diving trips and live-aboard accommodation can be booked via Avalon.

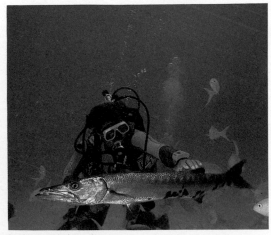
A scuba diver with a barracuda

EASTERN CUBA

Granma · Holguín · Santiago de Cuba · Guantánamo

Cubans refer to the eastern part of Cuba as the Oriente, giving it an exotic, magical appeal. The landscape, stretching out towards Haiti and other Caribbean islands, is varied, with majestic mountains, magnificent coastlines and an area of arid desert unusual in Cuba. The eastern cities, often rich in history, include Santiago de Cuba, host to one of Latin America's most famous carnivals.

From the 17th to the 19th centuries, thousands of black slaves were brought to Cuba from Africa, men and women who became the ancestors of the multi-ethnic mix visible in Eastern Cuba today, part African, but also part Spanish, part French and part Chinese. In this cultural melting pot, African and European, Roman Catholic and pagan traditions are blended, sometimes inextricably.

The area is full of apparent contradictions: there is the combative Oriente, rebellious and indomitable; and yet there is also the laid-back Oriente, an oasis of pleasure; and the sonorous Oriente, the cradle of great musicians. It is true that the people of Eastern Cuba have always fought with great fervour. One example is the Indian chief Hatuey, who was burned at the stake in the 16th century for organizing resistance against the Spanish. Then, in the 19th century, local nationalists led the wars of independence. The citizens of Bayamo even burned down their town rather than hand it over to the enemy. In the 20th century, there were the *rebeldes* (many of whom were from Eastern Cuba, including the Castros themselves), who launched the struggle against Batista's dictatorship by attacking the Moncada barracks in Santiago.

Yet the people of eastern Cuba also know how to have a good time. They adore music, rhythm and dance of all kinds, and each July put on a colourful Carnival and Fiesta del Caribe at Santiago de Cuba; the carnival is one of the most celebrated in Latin America.

Cactuses growing along the Costa Sur, the only arid zone on the island, east of Guantánamo

◀ Basílica del Cobre, location of the venerated black Madonna, Virgen de la Caridad

Exploring Eastern Cuba

The classic starting point for touring the eastern provinces is Santiago de Cuba, a city rich in history, with lovely colonial architecture and sites associated with the 1959 Revolution. To the west rises the majestic Sierra Maestra, also with its own associations with the guerrilla war of the 1950s. The Sierra is most easily reached, in fact, from the north, near Bayamo. To the east, the Parque Baconao has all kinds of attractions, ideal for families with children, while more adventurous souls can head further east, to the province of Guantánamo, famous for its US naval base, and Baracoa, Cuba's oldest city. The province of Holguín, further north, has some fine beaches, and Cuba's most interesting archaeological site.

The small islands of the Bahía de Naranjo national park

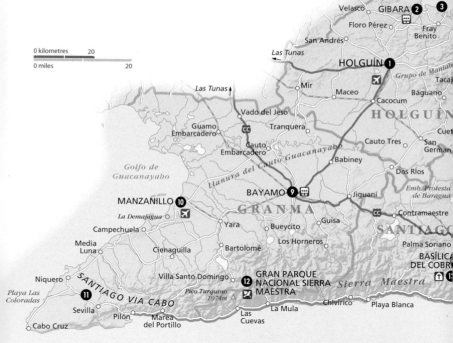

Key

━━━ Motorway

━━━ Major road

═══ Minor road

━━━ Scenic route

┄┄┄ Main railway

━━━ International border

━━━ Regional border

△ Summit

A group of musicians improvising a concert in Parque Céspedes, Santiago de Cuba

For hotels and restaurants in this region see pp262–3 and p275

Sights at a Glance

1. *Holguín pp216–17*
2. Gibara
3. Bahía de Bariay
4. Guardalavaca
5. Chorro de Maíta
6. Banes
7. Mayarí
8. Cayo Saetía
9. Bayamo
10. Manzanillo
12. Gran Parque Nacional Sierra Maestra

13. Basílica del Cobre
14. *Santiago de Cuba pp226–35*
15. *Castillo del Morro pp236–7*
16. *Parque Baconao pp238–41*
17. Guantánamo
18. Costa Sur
19. La Farola
20. *Baracoa pp246–7*
21. El Yunque
22. Río Toa
23. Parque Nacional Alejandro de Humboldt
24. Boca de Yumurí

Tour

11. *Towards Santiago via Cabo Cruz pp222–3*

The *azulejos* decoration in the Colonia Española in Manzanillo

Getting Around

Although sights on the outskirts of Santiago can be reached by bus or taxi, by far the best way to get around Eastern Cuba is to hire a car. Some journeys are among the most picturesque in Cuba, especially the drive to Baracoa via "La Farola" *(see p243)*. Another option would be to fly to the main eastern towns. Various organized tours are also available, starting off from Santiago or from the beach resorts of Holguín province, especially Guardalavaca. These tours can be booked through travel agencies.

A perfectly restored Neo-Classical building in the centre of Baracoa

For keys to symbols *see back flap*

❶ Holguín

Called the city of parks because of its many leafy squares, Holguín is a colonial town with a grid layout, situated between two hills, Cerro de Mayabe and Loma de la Cruz. The people of Holguín took an active part in the wars of independence under the leadership of Calixto García, the famous general who liberated the city from the Spanish in 1872. The house he was born in is now a museum; the square named after him marks the centre of the city and is dominated by a statue of the heroic general.

Interior and main altar of Catedral de San Isidoro

Exploring Holguín

Calle Maceo and Manduley – two parallel streets with shops, hotels, bars and clubs, including the Casa de la Trova – cross three squares: **Parque San José, Parque Calixto García** and **Parque Peralta**. Parque García, always buzzing with people, is the site of the town's chief monuments and museums including **Casa Natal de Calixto García**.

🏛 La Periquera (Museo Provincial de Holguín)

Calle Frexes 198, e/ Libertad y Maceo. **Tel** (24) 463 395. **Open** 8am–noon, 12:30–4:30pm Tue–Sat, 8am–noon Sun. **Closed** 1 Jan, 1 May, 26 Jul, 10 Oct, 25 Dec. 🚫 📷 Note: fee for photography may apply.

This large Neo-Classical building with a courtyard overlooks Parque Calixto García. It was built in 1860 as the private home of Spanish merchant Francisco Roldán y Rodríguez. In 1868, at the beginning of the Ten Years' War (see p48), the building was occupied by the Spanish army and converted into barracks. Hence the building's nickname, *La Periquera*, which translates as "parrot cage", a reference to the brightly coloured uniforms of the Spanish army.

Today, the building is the home of the Museo Provincial de Holguín, where five rooms illustrate the main stages of the cultural development of the

town. Also on display are archaeological relics of the Taíno Indians, who lived here from the 8th to the 15th centuries. The most famous item in the collection is the Hacha de Holguín, a stone axe head carved as a human figure. It was discovered in the hills around Holguín, and has become the symbol of the city.

🏛 Museo de Historia Natural Carlos de la Torre

Calle Maceo 129, e/ Martí y Luz Caballero. **Tel** (24) 423 935. **Open** 9am–noon, 12:30–5pm Tue–Sat, 9am–noon Sun. 🚫 📷 Note: fee for photography may apply.

Holguín's museum of natural history is housed in a brightly painted building with a handsome portico and Spanish tiling throughout. A mildly interesting collection of birds and shells, including *Polymita* snails from Baracoa (see p249), is on display, along with a 50-million-year-old fossil fish, found in the Sierra Maestra.

Hacha de Holguín

🏛 Catedral de San Isidoro

Calle Manduley, e/ Luz Caballero y Aricochea, Parque Peralta. **Tel** (24) 422 107. **Open** 5:30–6:45pm Mon, 7am–noon & 3–5:30pm Tue & Fri, 7am–noon & 3–6:45pm Wed & Thu, 7am–noon & 7–8:45pm Sat & Sun. ✝ daily.

Consecrated as a cathedral in 1979, San Isidoro was built in 1720 on the site of the first mass held to celebrate the city's founding: Parque Peralta. It is also known as Parque de Flores because a flower market used to be held here.

The church contains a copy of the popular Madonna of Caridad, the original of which is in the Basilica del Cobre near Santiago de Cuba (see p225). On 4 April there is a celebration in honour of the Virgin.

Bazar de Artesanía

Two blocks north of Parque Calixto García is Bazar de Artesanía, a charming indoor market selling a range of handmade accessories, carved wooden ornaments and seed and resin jewellery. The pedestrianized street outside the market is a peaceful spot to sit.

Parque Calixto García, with La Periquera; behind, the Loma de la Cruz

For hotels and restaurants in this region see pp262–3 and p275

A panoramic view of Holguín from the top of the Loma de la Cruz

Plaza de la Revolución
Situated east of the city centre, behind Hotel Pernik, this square contains a monument to the heroes of Cuban independence, the mausoleum of Calixto García and a small monument to his mother. The square is the main venue for popular festivities.

Loma de la Cruz
There are marvellous, far-reaching views from the top of the Loma de la Cruz (Hill of the Cross). The engineers who founded Holguín used this site to plan the layout of the town, but it was only much later (from 1927–50) that the 458-step stairway was built to the top. Every year on 3 May, the people of Holguín climb up the hill for the Romerías de Mayo, a Christian celebration of Spanish origin. The top of Loma, about 3 km (2 miles) northwest of Parque Calixto García, is marked by a Spanish lookout tower and by a cross placed there in 1790 by friar Antonio Alegría. During his visit in 2015, Pope Francis blessed the city from here.

Environs
Another more distant viewing point over the city is the **Mirador de Mayabe** on the Cerro de Mayabe, 10 km (6 miles) south-east of the city centre.

From the mirador there is a view of the valley with Holguín in the distance. This spot is also home to an *aldea campesina* (country village), with simple lodgings and a restaurant, as well as an open-air museum, illustrating the lives of farmers living in a small village. Reconstructions include examples of a *bohío real*, a typical rural home with a palm-leaf roof, a henhouse and a courtyard containing jars for transporting water.

Rural village huts, *bohío real*, at a country village outside of Holguín

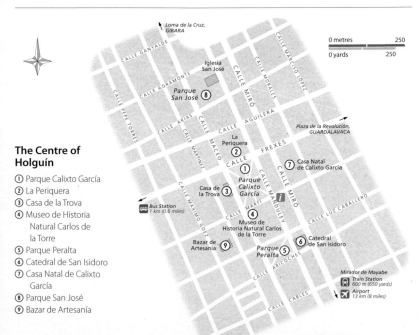

The Centre of Holguín
1 Parque Calixto García
2 La Periquera
3 Casa de la Trova
4 Museo de Historia Natural Carlos de la Torre
5 Parque Peralta
6 Catedral de San Isidoro
7 Casa Natal de Calixto García
8 Parque San José
9 Bazar de Artesanía

For keys to symbols *see back flap*

Gibara, an appealing seaside town with a colonial centre

❷ Gibara

Holguín. **Road Map** E3. 72,000.

South of the bay that Columbus named Río de Mares (the river of seas) is the picturesque town of Gibara, famous for an exten-sive network of caves perfect for exploring on the edge of town. In the 19th century, Gibara was the main port on the northern coast of the province of Oriente, and it has the most important colonial architecture in the area.

The shady Malecón (seafront) has a statue of Columbus shown gazing at the horizon, a restored garrison and views of the small fishing harbour. From here, narrow streets lead to the main square, overlooked by the **Iglesia de San Fulgencio** (1854), and an old theatre.

The **Museo de Artes Decorativas** (Decorative Arts Museum) is housed in a 19th-century manor.

Façade of the Iglesia de San Fulgencio at Gibara

A staircase bordered by marble columns and fine stained-glass windows represent the region's best ensemble of 19th- and 20th-century furniture and objects.

About 2 km (1 mile) from the centre of town are the **Cavernas de Panadernos**, etched with pictographs and home to bats. Cave diving and exploring the system of caves with a guide is possible.

🏛 Museo de Artes Decorativas
Calle Independencia 19. **Tel** (24) 844 687. **Open** 8am–noon & 1–5pm Mon–Wed, 8am–noon, 1–5pm, 8–10pm Thu–Sun. 🖉 🗂
Note: fee for photography may apply.

🏚 Cavernas de Panadernos
Oficina de Monumentos Technicos, Calle Sartorio 7. **Tel** (24) 845 107.

❸ Bahía de Bariay

Holguín. **Road Map** E3.

East of Gibara is a bay with a spit of land in the middle called Cayo de Bariay. Most historians (but not Baracoans, *see p246*) agree that Columbus first landed here in 1492. With its abundant flowers and trees laden with fruit, it looked like paradise to the explorer. In 1992, on the 500th anniversary of Columbus' landing in Cuba, a monument called *Encuentro* ("Encounter"), dedicated to the Taíno Indians, was erected here. The site is relatively remote if travelling by car, but boat trips can be arranged from Guardalavaca (*see p219*). East of Cayo de Bariay is the beautiful **Playa Don Lino**.

Columbus in Cuba

On 28 October 1492, when he first set foot on Cuban land, Columbus wrote in his travel journal: "I have never seen a more beautiful place. Along the banks of the river were trees I have never seen at home, with flowers and fruit of the most diverse kinds, among the branches of which one heard the delightful chirping of birds. There were a great number of palms. When I descended from the launch, I approached two fishermen's huts. Upon seeing me, the natives

Christopher Columbus, explorer of the New World

took fright and fled. Back on the boat, I went up the river for a good distance. I felt such joy upon seeing these flowery gardens and green forests and hearing the birds sing that I could not tear myself away, and thus continued my trip. This island is truly the most beautiful land human eyes have ever beheld."

❹ Guardalavaca

Holguín. **Road Map** F3.

Converted in the mid-1980s into a holiday resort, the beaches of Guardalavaca are among Cuba's most popular holiday destinations. Although the resort is within easy reach of Holguín, which lies 58 km (35 miles) to the southwest along a road through curious conical hills, the location still feels remote.

The 4-km (2-mile) crescent-shaped main beach, enclosed at either end by rocks, is backed by abundant vegetation. The sea is crystal-clear, the sand is fine, and there is a coral reef quite close to the shore. To the west are several developed beaches.

The name "Guardalavaca" (watch the cow) derives from the Spanish word for the cattle egret *(see p24)*, a bird which is common throughout Cuba, and especially prevalent here.

West of the beach is **Bahía de Naranjo**, a natural park that comprises 32 km (20 miles) of coastline and 10 sq km (3.9 sq miles) of woods, with karst hills covered with thick vegetation. There are three small islands in the bay; on one, Cayo Naranjo, there is an aquarium featuring shows with sea lions and dolphins. Boat tours, diving and fishing trips are also organized here.

Skeletons found in the necropolis of Chorro de Maíta

❺ El Chorro de Maíta

Cerro de Yaguajay, Banes (Holguín). **Road Map** F4. **Tel** (24) 430 201. **Open** 9am–5pm Tue–Sat, 9am–1pm Sun. 🎥 📷 Note: fee for photography may apply.

Near the coast, just 5 km (3 miles) south of Guardalavaca, is El Chorro de Maíta, the largest native Indian necropolis in Cuba and the Antilles. At this unmissable site archaeologists have found 108 skeletons and a number of clay objects, bone amulets, funerary offerings and decorated shells.

All this material can be seen from a boardwalk inside the museum. Across the road is an *aldea taína*, a reconstruction of

a Pre-Columbian rural village, built for entertainment, but historically accurate. Visitors can buy souvenirs and sample food that the Amerindians used to eat. In front of the huts are life-size statues of natives.

❻ Banes

Holguín. **Road Map** F4.

This country town, 32 km (20 m) southwest of Holguín, is located in the middle of a vast and rich excavation zone (the province of Holguín has yielded one-third of the archaeological finds in Cuba). Banes is the home of the **Museo Indocubano Bani**, Cuba's most important archaeological museum outside Havana. The museum has over a thousand objects on display, including axes, terracotta vases, flint knives and, most notably, a 4-cm (2-in) high figure of a woman in gold, known as the Ídolo de Oro. It was found near Banes, and dates from the 13th century.

Ídolo de Oro, Museo Indocubano Bani

🏛 **Museo Indocubano Bani**

Calle General Barrero 305, e/ Martí y Céspedes. **Tel** (24) 802 487. **Open** daily (Sun am only). 🎥 📷 Note: fee for photography may apply.

The lovely clear turquoise sea at Guardalavaca

The coves at Cayo Saetía, known for their fine white sand

🟡 Mayarí

Holguín. **Road Map** F4. 🗺 100,000.

Mayarí, 100 km (62 miles) southeast of Holguín, was founded in 1757 and, together with Gibara *(see p218)*, is the oldest city in the province.

Nearby are the **Farallones de Seboruco**, caves where objects left by the Taíno people have been found and the **Meseta de Pinares de Mayarí**, a large forest cloaking the hills up to an altitude of 1,000 m (3,280 ft).

Southwest of Mayarí is Birán, where Fidel Castro was born. His parents' house, **Finca Birán**, is now a museum.

🏛 Finca Birán

Tel (24) 286 102. **Open** 9am–3pm Tue–Sat, 9am–noon Sun (except when raining).

🔵 Cayo Saetía

Holguín. **Road Map** F4.

Lying at the mouth of the Bay of Nipe, this small island covering 42 sq km (16 sq miles), with stunning coves, is connected to the mainland by a drawbridge. It was formerly a private hunting reserve, and in the woods and meadows, antelopes and zebra still live side by side with species native to Cuba. On safaris, led by expert guides, visitors travelling on horseback or in jeeps can observe and photograph the animals. The few tourist facilities on this island are for paying guests only and were designed with every care for the environment. A boat trip to Cayo Saetía from Guardalavaca is a highlight.

🔵 Bayamo

Granma. **Road Map** E4. 🗺 235,000. 🚫 🚉 Saco y Línea, (23) 423 034. 🚌 Carretera Central y Jesús Rabí, (23) 424 036. 🛈 Infotur, Plaza del Himno, (23) 423 468.

The second oldest town in Cuba after Baracoa, Bayamo was founded in 1513 by Diego Velázquez. Until 1975 it was part of the large Oriente province, but after administrative reform it became the capital of a new province, Granma. It is a pasture and livestock breeding area, but has also been the home of nationalists and the cradle of political revolts and struggles.

In 1869, rather than surrender their town to Spain, the citizens burned Bayamo down. As a result, the centre is relatively modern.

Daily life revolves around **Parque Céspedes**, the main square, dominated by a statue of local plantation owner and war of independence hero Carlos Manuel de Céspedes (1955). The square is home to almost all the important buildings in town: the Cultural Centre, the Royalton Hotel, the offices of the Poder Popular, and the historic Pedrito café.

The statue of Carlos Manuel de Céspedes at Bayamo

Adjacent to the main square is **Plaza del Himno** (Square of the Hymn). It gained its name after *La Bayamesa*, the Cuban national anthem, was first played in the church here on 20 October 1868. Marking this event is a sculpture that includes a bronze plaque on which are engraved the words and music by Perucho Figueredo. His bust stands next to the nationalists' flag. In the smaller **Parque Maceo Osorio**,

Relaxing in the shade at Parque Céspedes, in Bayamo

Bayamo "the Rebellious"

Bayamo has a long tradition of rebellion. In the early 1500s, the native Indians, led by their chief, Hatuey, fiercely resisted the Spanish (see p223). A few years later an African slave killed the pirate Gilberto Girón, displaying his head as a trophy in the central plaza. This episode inspired the epic poem *Espejo de Paciencia* by Silvestre de Balboa, the first major work of Cuban literature (see p32). But the most dramatic episode in the history of Bayamo concerns the struggles for independence, during which, on 10 October 1868, a group of local nationalists and intellectuals – Juan Clemente Zenea, Carlos Manuel de Céspedes (see p47), Pedro Figueredo, José Fornaris and José Joaquín Palma – organized an anti-Spanish revolt. They entered the town on 20 October, and declared it the capital of the Republic in Arms. On 12 January, faced with the fact that Bayamo would be recaptured by colonial troops, the citizens decided to set fire to their own town, an act which later led to the choice of *La Bayamesa* as the national anthem.

Interior of the Parroquial Mayor de San Salvador

The monument dedicated to the national anthem, *La Bayamesa*

formerly Parque de San Francisco, north of Parque Céspedes, is the Casa de la Trova Olimpio La O, one of the town's few 18th-century buildings. The courtyard is used by local groups for concerts.

🏛 Casa Natal de Carlos Manuel de Céspedes

Calle Maceo 57, e/ Marmol y Palma. **Tel** (23) 423 864. **Open** 9am–5pm Tue–Fri, 9am–2pm, 8–10pm Sat, 10am–1:30pm Sun. 📷 🎫 Note: fee for photography may apply.

The house where the leading figure in the first war against Spain in the 19th century was born on 18 April 1819 is a handsome, two-storey colonial building facing Parque Céspedes. Architecturally it is the most important building in the city.

The rooms on the ground floor, which open onto a courtyard with a fountain, contain the heart of the

collection, with Céspedes' documents and personal items, including his steel and bronze sword.

Upstairs are several furnished rooms, one of which has a bronze bed with mother-of-pearl medallions, a fine example of colonial furniture. A gallery leads to the old kitchen, which still has its original ceramic oven.

Façade of the birthplace of Carlos Manuel de Céspedes

🏛 Parroquial Mayor de San Salvador

Plaza del Himno, esq. José Joaquín Palma. **Tel** (23) 422 514. **Open** 9am–noon & 2:30–5pm Mon–Fri, 9–10:30am Sun.

When the nationalists of Bayamo chose to burn down their own town rather than leave anything for the Spanish, they put the holy images kept in the Parroquial Mayor (the Cathedral) into safekeeping. That was the plan, at all events. Unfortunately, the only things spared by the fire were the font (which had been used for the baptism of Carlos Manuel de Céspedes) and the Capilla de los Dolores, a chapel built in 1740, which contained an image of the Virgin Mary and a Baroque altarpiece made of gilded wood. The altarpiece has a particularly fine frame decorated with tropical motifs and representations of local fruit and animals, an unusual and very Cuban element in the art of the 18th century.

In 1916, Bishop Guerra commissioned the reconstruction of the old Parroquial Mayor, dedicated to Jesus the Saviour, the patron saint of Bayamo. The original building had been finished in 1613 and in the course of time had been transformed into a large three-aisle church with two choirs, nine altars and a finely wrought pulpit.

The new church was opened on 9 October 1919, with the old image of Jesus the Saviour salvaged from the fire, a new marble altar, a patriotic painting by the Dominican artist Luis Desangles, and plastered brick walls frescoed by Esteban Ferre

⑩ Manzanillo

Granma. **Road Map** E4. ✈ "Sierra Maestra", 8 km (5 miles) south of town. 🚌 🚐 Bayamo, Camagüey, Havana, Pilón, Yara.

Built along the Caribbean Bay of Guacanayabo, Manzanillo is a charming seaside town. It was founded as Puerto Real in 1784, and reached its apogee in the second half of the 19th century, thanks to sugar and the slave trade.

Memories are still strong of the feats of Castro's rebel forces in the nearby Sierra Maestra, especially those of Castro's assistant Celia Sánchez, who organized a crucial rearguard here. She is honoured by a striking monument in the town.

In Parque Céspedes, the central square, a brickwork bandstand for concerts by local

The Glorieta Morisca de Manzanillo, where the municipal band plays

bands was opened on 25 June 1924. The so-called Glorieta Morisca gained its name for its Arab-influenced decoration, designed by José Martín del Castillo, an architect from Granada. Other monuments in town, all near the Parque

Céspedes, include the Neo-Classical Iglesia de la Purísima Concepción, built in the 1920s; the atmospheric Café 1906, the 19th-century town hall, now the Asamblea Municipal del Poder Popular; and the Colonia Española, a social club for

⑪ Towards Santiago via Cabo Cruz

This fascinating route by road to Santiago skirts the high slopes of the Sierra Maestra which, along the south coast, forces the road into the sea in places, especially after hurricanes. The scenery is unspoiled and at times wild, and conceals several places of historical significance. The route can be covered in a long day, but for a more relaxing drive visitors could consider staying in Marea del Portillo or Chivirico.

① La Demajagua
Céspedes's estate still has sugar-making equipment, such as these *calderas* used for making molasses.

0 km   15
0 miles   15

③ Playa Las Coloradas
It was near here that 82 rebels landed aboard the *Granma* in December 1956 *(see p52)*.

• Niquero

Punto Nuev

• Bélic

④ Parque Nacional Desembarco del Granma
This park is rich in local flora, including some extraordinary orchids. There are also various sites commemorating the journey of the revolutionaries following their arrival on the *Granma*.

③
④
⑤
• Cabo Cruz

⑤ El Guafe
This archaeological site has Pre-Columbian finds displayed in caves.

Spanish immigrants that was completed in 1935. The club is located in a building with an Andalusian courtyard and a panel of painted tiles representing Columbus's landing in Cuba.

Environs

10 km (6 miles) south of Manzanillo are the remains of **La Demajagua**, the estate belonging to Carlos Manuel de Céspedes (see p48 and p221). On 10 October 1868, he freed all of his slaves, urging them to join him in fighting the Spanish.

Yara, 24 km (15 miles) east of Manzanillo, is where Céspedes proclaimed Cuban independence, and where the Indian hero Hatuey was burned at the stake. There is a small museum in the central square, Plaza Grito de Yara.

Hatuey's Sacrifice

Over the centuries, the sacrifice of Hatuey acquired great patriotic significance and gave rise to numerous legends, including *La Luz de Yara* (The Light of Yara), written by Luis Victoriano Betancourt in 1875. The author relates that from the stake on which the Indian hero was being burned, there arose a mysterious light that wandered throughout the island, protecting the sleep of the slaves who were awaiting their freedom. This light was the soul of Hatuey. Three centuries later, the wandering light returned to the site of the Indian's sacrifice, and in a flash all the palm trees in Cuba shook, the sky was lit up, the earth trembled, and the light turned into a fire that stirred Cubans' hearts: "It was the Light of Yara, which was about to take its revenge. It was the tomb of Hatuey, which became the cradle of independence. It was 10 October" – the beginning of the war of independence.

The Indian chief Hatuey being burned at the stake

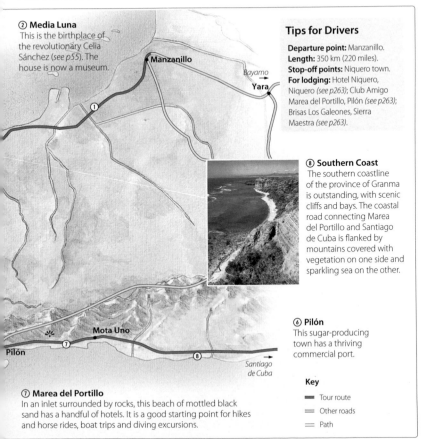

② **Media Luna**
This is the birthplace of the revolutionary Celia Sánchez (see p55). The house is now a museum.

Manzanillo

Bayamo

Yara

Tips for Drivers

Departure point: Manzanillo.
Length: 350 km (220 miles).
Stop-off points: Niquero town.
For lodging: Hotel Niquero, Niquero (see p263); Club Amigo Marea del Portillo, Pilón (see p263); Brisas Los Galeones, Sierra Maestra (see p263).

⑧ **Southern Coast**
The southern coastline of the province of Granma is outstanding, with scenic cliffs and bays. The coastal road connecting Marea del Portillo and Santiago de Cuba is flanked by mountains covered with vegetation on one side and sparkling sea on the other.

Mota Uno

Pilón

⑥ **Pilón**
This sugar-producing town has a thriving commercial port.

Santiago de Cuba

⑦ **Marea del Portillo**
In an inlet surrounded by rocks, this beach of mottled black sand has a handful of hotels. It is a good starting point for hikes and horse rides, boat trips and diving excursions.

Key

— Tour route
= Other roads
= Path

⑫ Gran Parque Nacional Sierra Maestra

Granma, Santiago de Cuba. **Road Map** F4. ℹ️ Ecotur, Hotel Sierra Maestra, Bayamo, (23) 487 006 ext. 639; Flora y Fauna, Santo Domingo, 5356 5349; Villa Santo Domingo, (23) 565 568.

This national park, which covers an area of 38,000 ha (95,000 acres), spans the provinces of Granma and Santiago de Cuba. This is where the major peaks of the island are found, including Pico Turquino (at 1,974 m/ 6,390 ft, the highest in Cuba), as well as sites made famous by the guerrilla war waged by Fidel Castro and the *barbudos*.

The main starting point for exploring the Sierra Maestra is **Villa Santo Domingo**, about 35 km (22 miles) south of the Bayamo–Manzanillo road (there is comfortable accommodation in Santo Domingo).

From Santo Domingo, you can make the challenging 5-km (3-mile) journey – on foot or in a good off-road vehicle – to the **Alto del Naranjo** viewpoint (950 m/ 3,120 ft). With a permit (obtainable from the visitors' office north of Villa Santo Domingo), you can go on to

View from the Pico Turquino, the highest mountain in Cuba

Comandancia de la Plata, Castro's headquarters in the 1950s. Here there is a museum, a small camp hospital and the site from which Che Guevara made his radio broadcasts.

Comandancia de la Plata is accessible only on foot – a one-and-a-half hour's walk through lovely, though often foggy, forest. The area was made into a national park in 1980. The dense, humid forest conceals many species of orchid and various kinds of local fauna. The Sierra Maestra mountains are excellent hiking territory, and also attract mountain climbers. The scenery is spectacular but be prepared for spartan facilities. A limited

The gavilán del monte, common in the Sierra Maestra

number of treks can be organized from the visitors' office, where guides must be hired. Overnight accommodation in the mountains is available either at campsites or in simple refuges. Note, however, that since much of this area is a military zone, lone trekking is not permitted.

At present, it is possible to do a three-day guided trek across the park, beginning at Alto del Naranjo and ending at Las Cuevas, a small town on the Caribbean Sea. Hikers do not need to be expert mountaineers in order to take part in this walking tour, because the path is equipped with ladders, handrails and rock-cut steps. However, it is still advisable to do a certain amount of training beforehand. The final descent from Pico Turquino onwards is fairly strenuous and walkers need to be reasonably fit.

It is important to take proper mountain gear with you: walking boots, thick socks, a sun hat, a sweater, a windproof jacket, and perhaps even a waterproof groundsheet and a good tent. Humidity in the often misty Sierra is very high, and showers are common.

The coast at the southern edge of the Sierra Maestra is spectacular. The coastal road runs close above the waters of the Caribbean Sea and offers excellent views. However, great care should be taken if driving after dark as the road is in need of repair in some places.

The splendid coastline south of Sierra Maestra

⓭ Basílica del Cobre

Santiago de Cuba. **Road Map** F4.
🚌 Carretera Central 21, (22) 346 118.
Open 6:30am–6pm daily. ✝ 10am
Mon, 8 & 10:15am Tue–Fri, 8am Sat,
8 & 10am Sun. 🎺 procession, 8 Sep.

The village of El Cobre, about
20 km (12 miles) west of Santiago
de Cuba, was once famous for
its copper *(cobre)* mines. A great
number of slaves worked here
up until 1807. Nowadays the
village is best known for Cuba's
most famous church, the Basílica
de Nuestra Señora de la Caridad
del Cobre. Here the main attraction is a statue of the Virgen del
Cobre. This black Madonna is
richly dressed in yellow, and
wears a crown encrusted with

The striking façade of pilgrimage destination Basílica del Cobre

diamonds, emeralds and rubies,
with a golden halo above. She
carries a cross of diamonds and
amethysts. The statue is kept in
an air-conditioned glass case
behind the high altar.

It is taken out every year on
8 September when a procession
takes place to commemorate
the Virgin's saint's day. The Virgen
del Cobre was proclaimed the
protectress of Cuba in 1916 and
was blessed and crowned by
Pope John Paul II in 1998 *(see p68)*.
Pope Francis laid a silver vase
with his coat of arms during a
subsequent papal visit in 2015.

This fine three-aisled church, built
in 1926, stands on a hill, the Cerro
de la Cantera, which is linked to
the village by a flight of 254 steps.
The elegant central bell tower

The austere interior of the Sanctuary of the
Virgen del Cobre

and two side towers crowned
by brick-red domes are a striking
sight above the cream façade.

The basilica is the object of
pilgrimages from all over the
island. In the Los Milagros
chapel, thousands of *ex votos*
left by pilgrims are on display.
Some are rather curious, such
as the beards left by some of the
rebels who survived the guerrilla
war in the Sierra; an object
belonging to Castro's mother;
and earth collected by Cuban
soldiers who fought in Angola.
There is a guestbook for visitors
to peruse and sign.

The Virgen del Cobre

The statue of the
Virgen del Cobre

According to legend, in 1606 three
slaves who worked in the copper
mines of El Cobre were saved in the
Bay of Nipe, off the north coast of
Cuba, by the statue of a black Virgin
Mary holding the Holy Child in
her arms. They had been caught
in a storm while out in a boat
and would have drowned had
not the Virgin, whose image
was floating among the waves,
come to their aid. In reality, it
seems that the statue arrived in Cuba by ship from
Illescas, a town in Castile, upon the request of the
governor Sánchez de Moya, who wanted a Spanish
Madonna for the village of El Cobre. Whatever the
truth, in 1612 the Virgen de la Caridad was given a
small sanctuary and immediately became an object
of veneration for the locals, who continued to
attribute miraculous powers to her. The devotion
for this Madonna has always been very strong,
even among non-practising Catholics. Her figure
is associated with the Afro-Cuban saint Oshún

(see p26), the goddess of rivers, gentleness,
femininity and love, who is also always depicted as
a beautiful black woman wearing yellow. Now that
the *Santería* religion is widespread in Cuba, the
sacred image of the Virgin of El Cobre and the
more profane, sensuous image of the beautiful
African goddess are often combined in prayers
and discussion, and set beside each other on
rustic home altars, often without any apparent
awareness of contradiction.

A group of *ex votos* offered by the *barbudos*

⑭ Santiago de Cuba

This is perhaps the most African, the most musical and the most passionate city in Cuba. In 1930 the Spanish poet Federico García Lorca likened it to "a harp made of living branches, a caiman, a tobacco flower". Except for the cars and some modern buildings, Santiago has not altered much. This is a city where the heat – and the hills – mean that people move to a slow rhythm. Yet it is a lively, exciting place where festivities and dancing are celebrated with fervour, never more so than during July's Carnival. Santiago's citizens also take pride in the fact that Santiago is called the "Cradle of the Revolution". Sandwiched between the Sierra Maestra mountains and the sea, this is the second city in Cuba in population size. In 2012, Hurricane Sandy tore through Santiago causing much devastation.

A restored Neo-Classical building in the historic centre

Parque Céspedes

The city centre spreads out in chaotic fashion around Parque Céspedes in a maze of narrow streets. Any visit to the historic centre of Santiago must start in Parque Céspedes, the main square. From here, visitors are inevitably drawn along **Calle Heredia**, the most famous, popular and festive street in the town. Every house bears signs of the city's great passions: music, dancing, carnivals and poetry. At certain times, including the first half of July when the Fiesta del Caribe is held, this street becomes a stage for amateur artists. Traditional son music, on the other hand, can be heard in the courtyard of the Patio de Artex at No. 304,

Calle Heredia, a street focused on music and festivities

while No. 208, the former "Cafetín de Virgilio", became the **Casa de la Trova** in 1968, and local and foreign bands can be heard playing here day and night. Photographs of great Cuban musicians past and present such as El Guayabero and Compay Segundo cover the walls.

West of Parque Céspedes

The picturesque area southwest of Parque Céspedes, called Tivolí, and the deep bay can be seen from the **Balcón de Velázquez**, a wonderful viewpoint situated at the corner of Calle Mariano Corona and Bartolomé Masó. The viewpoint was named after the Spanish conquistador Diego Velázquez, who founded the city in 1515. A small fort was built here in the 16th century to house artillery

Sights at a Glance

① Casa de Diego Velázquez
② Ayuntamiento
③ Hotel Casa Granda
④ Catedral de la Asunción
⑤ Casa de la Trova
⑥ Casa Natal de José María Heredia
⑦ Museo Emilio Bacardí Moreau
⑧ Museo del Carnaval
⑨ La Isabelica
⑩ Museo del Ron

⑪ Balcón de Velázquez
⑫ Steps of Padre Pico
⑬ Museo de la Lucha Clandestina
⑭ Casa Natal de Antonio Maceo
⑮ Cuartel Moncada
⑯ Parque Histórico Abel Santamaría
⑰ Plaza de Marte

VISITORS' CHECKLIST

Practical Information
Santiago de Cuba. **Road Map** F4.
515,000. Infotur &
Cubatur, Ave. Garzón e/ 3ra y
4ta, (22) 652 560. Festival
del Caribe (early Jul), Carnival
(late Jul).

Transport
7 km (4 miles) south of town.
Ave. Jesús Menéndez, esq.
Hechevarría. Ave. de los
Libertadores, esq. Yarayó,
(22) 628 484.

Key

Street-by-Street pp228–9

0 metres   200
0 yards   200

Cementerio de Santa Ifigenia
Plaza de la Revolución
PASEO DE MARTÍ

CALLE MAYIA RODRÍGUEZ (RELOJ)
CALLE VALIENTE (CALVARIO)
CALLE J.M. GÓMEZA
CALLE MONSEÑOR BARNADA
SATURNINO LORA
AVENIDA DE LOS LIBERTADORES

Parque Histórico Abel Santamaría ⑯

Cuartel Moncada ⑮

CALLE MONCADA

Bosque de los Héroes
VISTA ALEGRE

AVE DE (VICTORIANO) GARZÓN

CALLE PADRE QUIROGA
CALLE HERNAN CORTÉS

⑰ ℹ
PLAZA DE MARTE

CALLE HEREDIA
BARTOLOMÉ MASÓ (SAN BASILIO)
CALLE J. CASTILLO DUANY (SANTA LUCÍA)
CALLE CLARÍN
AVENIDA 24 DE FEBRERO (TROCHA)

Calle Padre Pico seen from the top of the steps

to be used in the event of an attack. Today, only fragments of the original walls remain. Inside the viewpoint area itself are some attractive bronze tondos (circular relief carvings) with portraits of Diego Velázquez, Hernán Cortés, Bartolomé de Las Casas and the Indian chief Guamá. Cultural events are sometimes held at the Balcón de Velázquez.

South of Parque Céspedes

Around 100m (330 ft) southwest of the square, the **Steps of Padre Pico** lead to Tivolí, the most authentic, picturesque mixed quarter in Santiago. Here, over the centuries, various peoples have arrived and stayed, including Puerto Ricans, Jamaicans, Arabs, Dominicans and Chinese. In the 1700s a colony of French people from Haiti also settled here, setting up shops, music schools, theatres and hotels.

East of Parque Céspedes

To the east of the square, at the corner of Calle Bartolomé Masó and Calle Hartmann (San Félix), is the **Museo del Ron** (Rum Museum), housed in a late 19th-century building. Displays illustrate how rum is distilled

and matured (see p79), alongside the history of the Bacardí factory, with an exhibition of labels from bottles of rum, new and old.

Another place to visit is Parque Dolores, a leafy square surrounded by buildings with wrought-iron balconies. A small old café on the square's corner, **La Isabelica**, serves excellent coffee.

Customers at La Isabelica, an atmospheric historic café

For keys to symbols see back flap

Street-by-Street: Parque Céspedes

The former Plaza de Armas in Santiago is the heart of the city, both geographically and spiritually. Renamed Parque Céspedes in honour of the nation's founding father *(see p48)*, this square is a place for socializing, relaxing, chatting and celebrating. At all hours of the day and night, the benches are filled with people, young, old, women, children and visitors. No one is alone here for long. Everyone sooner or later gets involved in a conversation or entertainment of some kind, because this square's other role is as an open-air venue where music – live, recorded or improvised – takes the leading role. Restored in Neo-Classical style in 1943, the square consists of four areas divided by lanes.

Casa de la Trova
Live music is performed here daily.

The house where the poet José Heredia was born is a fine 18th-century building around a leafy courtyard *(p231)*.

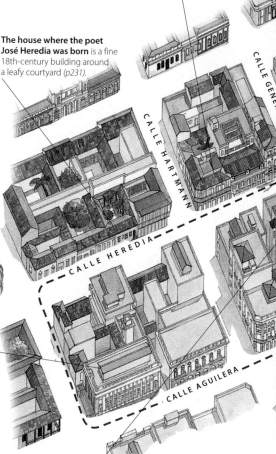

★ **Museo Emilio Bacardí Moreau**
The oldest museum in Cuba, housed in an elegant Neo-Classical building, is also the most eclectic. Items on display range from an Egyptian mummy to mementos of the wars of independence and works by living artists *(p232)*.

Hotel Casa Granda
One of Cuba's historic hotels *(see p263)*, the Casa Granda opened in 1920. Graham Greene *(see p91)* described it in *Our Man in Havana* as a hotel frequented by spies. Its terrace overlooks the park.

Key

 Suggested route

★ Catedral de la Asunción
The Cathedral façade is Neo-Classical, but the original church is four centuries old. It is believed that Diego Velázquez is buried somewhere beneath the building, but there is no proof of this (p231).

CALLE BARTOLOMÉ MASÓ

CALLE FÉLIX PEÑA

CALLE HEREDIA

CALLE MARIANO CORONA

PARQUE CÉSPEDES

Seafront

Balcón de Velázquez
This spacious viewing terrace, built over the site of a Spanish fortress, offers a magnificent view of the picturesque quarter of Tivolí, as well as the port and the bay of Santiago.

★ Casa de Diego Velázquez
Built in 1516–30, the residence of the Spanish conquistador Diego Velázquez is considered by some to be the oldest building in Cuba. Restoration was carried out in 1965 and 2013, and it is now the home of the Museo Ambiente Histórico Cubano (p230).

| 0 metres | 50 |
| 0 yards | 50 |

The Casa de la Cultura Miguel Matamoros, an eclectic building (1919) housing the sumptuous Salón de los Espejos, is a venue for artistic and cultural events.

Ayuntamiento
The Ayuntamiento (town hall), a symbol of the city, was built in 1950 according to 18th-century designs found in the Indies Archive. It was from this building's central balcony that Fidel Castro made his first speech to the Cuban people, on 1 January 1959.

Exploring Parque Céspedes

One of the liveliest squares in Cuba, Parque Céspedes is not only a place for socializing, but also has sites of cultural and architectural importance. Allow half a day to visit three of the most important monuments around the park: the house of Diego Velázquez, the impressive cathedral and the residence of the great 19th-century poet José María Heredia.

The courtyard in the 19th-century wing of Diego Velázquez's house

A room with colonial furniture in Diego Velázquez's house

🏛 Casa de Diego Velázquez (Museo Ambiente Histórico Cubano)

Calle Félix Pena 612, e/ Heredia y Aguilera. **Tel** (22) 652 652. **Open** 1–5pm Fri, 9am–5pm Sat–Thu. 🧳 📷 Note: fee for photography may apply.

This building, constructed in 1516–30 as a residence for the governor Diego Velázquez, is the oldest home in Cuba, according to architect Francisco Prat Puig, who restored the house in 1965. (Other scholars have disputed this assertion, however, and not everyone has praised the restoration.) Whatever the truth, this splendid residence is still a fascinating place to visit.

In the 1600s it was the so-called House of Transactions (the ground floor still has an old furnace in which gold ingots were made). In the 19th century it was joined to the building next door. The upstairs gallery facing the courtyard is closed off by a Moorish wooden blind, to screen residents from the eyes of strangers. Also upstairs, some of the original *alfarje* ceilings survive.

The building now houses the Museo Ambiente Histórico Cubano, covering the history of furniture in Cuba. It contains superb examples from all colonial periods. Among the mostly austere Creole furniture, dating from the 16th and 17th centuries, are a splendid priest's high-backed chair and a finely wrought coffer – two excellent examples of Moorish-style objects.

The basement has 18th-century "Luis Las Casas" furniture, a style peculiar to Cuba which combines English influences and French Rococo motifs. These pieces of furniture are massive, lavish and intricately worked, often finished at the base with feet shaped like claws. The 19th-century section includes a dining room with stained-glass windows and French furniture, including rocking chairs, a console table and a Charles X mirror.

Another important item is a tapestry with the coat-of-arms of the Velázquez family, the only piece in the museum that is directly related to this Spanish *conquistador*.

The 16th-Century Mudéjar-Style House

Considered the oldest private building in Cuba and declared a national monument because of its historic value, the 16th-century section of Velázquez's house is a fine example of the Cuban version of the *mudéjar* (Moorish) style – although much of what is there is the result of restoration.

The courtyard, in *mudéjar* style, is narrow and long and runs around a central well.

Wooden screens protect the gallery and balconies from the sun and public gaze.

Frescoes, known as *cenefas*, decorate the lower part of the walls, but they are not original.

Cedar ceilings with geometric patterns, called *alfarjes*, were common in the 16th century.

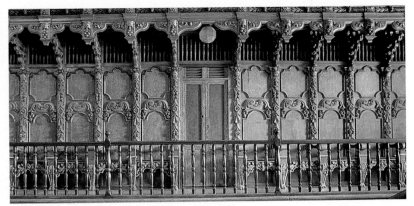

The lovely wooden inlaid choir in the Catedral de Nuestra Señora de la Asunción

⬆ Catedral de Nuestra Señora de la Asunción

Calle Heredia, e/ Lacret y Félix Peña. **Tel** (22) 628 502. **Open** 8:30am–12:30pm, 5–7:30pm Tue–Sat, 8–10am, 5–6:30pm Sun. ⬆ 6:30pm Tue–Fri, 5pm Sat, 9am & 6:30pm Sun.

The cathedral of Santiago, which was extensively restored in 2014, has a basilica layout, with a central nave and four aisles, an apse and a narthex or vestibule at the back. The church was originally built in 1522, but in the 17th century a series of pirate raids caused so much damage that the church had to be built from scratch in 1674. This church was subsequently rebuilt and then destroyed by an earthquake in 1766.

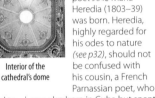

Interior of the cathedral's dome

The existing church, built in 1818, displays a mixture of styles, the result of a series of changes made by the architect Carlos Segrera Fernández in 1922. He added the bell towers, had the interior painted, and also reworked the façade. A marble angel was set over the main entrance and statues of Christopher Columbus and Bartolomé de las Casas were placed in side niches.

The cathedral also has a museum, the **Museo Eclesiástico**, which displays frescoes by the Dominican friar Luis Desangles, liturgical objects, statues and an important collection of ecclesiastical music scores.

🏛 Casa Natal de José María Heredia

Calle Heredia 260, e/ Hartmann (San Félix) y Pío Rosado (Carniceria). **Tel** (22) 625 350. **Open** 9am–noon Mon, 9am–7pm Tue–Fri, 9am–1pm Sun. 🖼 📷 Note: fee for photography may apply.

This is the modest but elegant 18th-century house where the nationalist poet José María Heredia (1803–39) was born. Heredia, highly regarded for his odes to nature *(see p32)*, should not be confused with his cousin, a French Parnassian poet, who was also born in Cuba but spent practically all his life in Europe.

The well-preserved house contains period furniture and objects, wooden ceilings and tiled floors, and is well worth a visit. From the large entrance hall, with a coffered ceiling and paintings of the poet's ancestors on the walls, a large arch leads into the central peristyled courtyard. Here there are wooden columns, a stone well and abundant vegetation.

Other rooms in the house include Heredia's bedroom with its impressive mahogany bed and elegant antique lamps.

Cultural events and poetry readings are often held in the museum's large porticoes. In addition, every year literary seminars and workshops are held here as part of the Fiesta del Caribe, or Fiesta del Fuego. This summer cultural event takes over the entire city of Santiago *(see p39)*.

Entrance hall of Heredia's house, its arch leading to the courtyard

Around Calle Heredia

Running straight along the bottom of Parque Céspedes, Calle Heredia buzzes with the sound of guitars, maracas, percussion and singing. For a performance head to the Casa de la Trova or the Patio de Artex *(see p226)*. The Museo del Carnaval displays musical instruments and costumes from the festivites surrounding Carnival, while the nearby Museo Emilio Bacardí is devoted to Cuban history.

Decorated *tumbadoras (see p35)* in the Museo del Carnaval

Techos de Santiago de Cuba by Felipe González, Museo Bacardí

🏛 Museo Emilio Bacardí Moreau

Calle Pío Rosado (Carniceria), esq. Aguilera. **Tel** (22) 628 402. **Open** 1–4:30pm Mon, 9am–4:30pm Tue–Sat, 9am–12:30pm Sun. 🎟 📷 Note: fee for photography may apply.

The statue of Liberty in the foyer

This is the oldest museum in Cuba. It was founded in 1828 and is a rich source of relics dating from the Spanish conquest to the wars of independence. The objects were collected and organized in the late 1800s and early 1900s by Emilio Bacardí, founder of the famous rum distillery. Bacardí was also a famous patriot and the first mayor of Santiago when Cuba became a republic. His aim was to display the origin and development of the Cuban nationalist movement from a cultural point of view, and he asked the architect Segrera to design a building for the objects and works of art he had collected.

The museum is housed in an eclectic building with a broad staircase and an atrium dominated by large statues of Minerva and Liberty. On the ground floor is a collection of arms used by nationalist heroes such as Antonio Maceo, Máximo Gómez and José Martí. There is also a collection of works by 19th-century Cuban painters, including Felipe López González, Juan Emilio Hernández Giro, José Joaquín Tejada Revilla and Buenaventura Martínez. Twentieth-century artists represented here are Wifredo Lam and René Portocarrero *(see pp30–31)*. The archaeology section includes the only Egyptian mummy in the country.

🏛 Museo del Carnaval

Calle Heredia 303, esq. Pío Rosado (Carniceria). **Tel** (22) 626 955. **Open** 9am–5pm Tue–Sat, 9am–1pm Sun. 🎟 📷 Note: fee for photography may apply.

This lovely late 18th-century building was converted into an elementary school in the mid-1900s, then into an office building, and eventually became the offices of the Carnival Commission. The Museo del Carnaval was opened here on 7 June 1983.The six rooms contain photographs with some explanatory captions in Spanish, chronologies, banners, musical instruments, costumes and papier mâché masks – a survey of the Carnival festivities held in Santiago. Carnival here differs from the traditional Spanish model and combines many African and Franco-Haitian elements.

Every Monday at 4pm, performers, such as traditional music ensemble La Peña Folklórica Raices, play in the museum's courtyard.

🏛 Museo de la Lucha Clandestina

Calle Rabí 1, e/ San Carlos y Santa Rita. **Tel** (22) 624 689. **Open** 9am–5pm Tue–Sun. 🎟 📷 Note: fee for photography may apply.

The Museum of the Clandestine Struggle overlooks a pleasant square in the district of Tivolí, southwest of Parque Céspedes. The building was the headquarters of Batista's police from 1951 to 1956. On 30 November 1956 it was burnt down by revolutionaries, led by Frank País *(see p54)*.

The four rooms in the restored building commemorate the activities of the Movimiento 26 de Julio. The movement was headed in Santiago by Frank País up to 30 July 1957, when the young rebel leader was assassinated by Batista's police.

Part of an elaborate float in the Museo del Carnaval

Carnival in Santiago de Cuba

The roots of the Carnival in Santiago are religious: since the end of the 17th century there have been processions and festivities from 24 June to 26 July in honour of the city's patron saint, Santiago Apóstolo. At the end of the parade, slaves who were members of the *cabildos* – societies that kept alive African languages, traditions and beliefs – were allowed to go out into the streets, where they sang to the accompaniment of drums, rattles and other instruments. These were the forerunners of the *comparsas*, the soul of Carnival: groups of people wearing masks or costumes, dancing to the rhythm of the *conga* and carrying streamers, banners and *farolas* (brightly coloured paper street lamps). In the second half of July the whole town celebrates, every district taking part in the parades, each with at least one *comparsa*.

The young people in each quarter meet every evening except Monday in the focos culturales, places where they prepare for Carnival by rehearsing the dances and music they will perform in July.

Parades go through the streets of Santiago. Some of the *comparsas*, such as the Cabildo Carabalí Izuama *(see p281)*, date from the 19th century.

The type of *tumbadora* used in the conga

The musicians in each group are dressed alike. They are followed by a crowd swaying to the rhythm of the music.

The Conga

The chief dance for Carnival is the conga (also a genuine musical genre). People form a procession and dance through the streets, following a band playing various instruments, including different kinds of drums, and led by the trompeta china, *introduced to Cuba in the late 1800s.*

The *bombo*, a drum with a deep sound

The Tropicana de Santiago joins the procession with the other *comparsas*, and also presents open-air performances in lavish costumes.

Papier mâché masks or *gigantes* are an essential part of a Carnival float. Huge and brightly coloured, they often represent animals or caricatures of human faces.

Beyond Santiago's Historic Centre

Calle Saco (also known as Enramada), Santiago's main commercial street, links the heart of the old city with the port. After passing through a working-class quarter, with early 20th-century wooden houses, the street ends at Paseo Marítimo. Laid out in the colonial era as a seafront promenade for the city's high society, this broad street retains echoes of its former beauty and still has its original 1840 paving, stretching out along the port, where cruisers and yachts are moored. An alternative route to explore is to go in the opposite direction, east of the centre, where there are important historic sites, including the Moncada barracks.

⌂ Casa Natal de Antonio Maceo

Calle Los Maceo 207, e/ Corona y Rastro. **Tel** (22) 623 750. **Open** 9am–2pm Mon, 9am–5pm Tue–Sat. 📷 🎫 Note: fee for photography may apply.

The house where this great general was born on 14 June 1845 (he died near Havana on 7 December 1896; *see p48*) is a modest place. Visitors can see some of the hero's personal belongings and family photographs, including one of his brother José, who was also a general, and one of his mother, Mariana Grajales.

⛪ Cementerio de Santa Ifigenia

Avenida Crombet. **Tel** (22) 632 723. **Open** 7am–6pm daily. 📷 🎫
This monumental cemetery (1868) is the second most important in Cuba after the Colón cemetery in Havana (*see pp108–9*). It was originally laid out with a Latin cross plan and divided into courtyards, the most important of which

The mausoleum of José Martí in the Santa Ifigenia Cemetery

were reserved for those of higher social status. A visit to the Santa Ifigenia cemetery evokes two centuries of Cuban history, past the tombs of such illustrious 19th-century figures as José Martí, Carlos Manuel de Céspedes, Emilio Bacardí and the mother of Antonio Maceo, as well as the 20th-century revolutionaries of the Movimiento 26 de Julio such as Frank País, who was killed in 1957 (*see p54*).

The funerary monuments themselves are fascinating. The Neo-Classical tombs nearest the entrance are the oldest, followed by the eclectic and then Modernist tombs. The Rationalist tombs built from the mid-20th century on include Martí's large octagonal mausoleum.

⌂ Museo 26 de Julio – Cuartel Moncada

Calle General Portuondo (Trinidad), e/ Moncada y Ave de los Libertadores. **Tel** (22) 661 157. **Open** 9am–12:30pm Mon & Sun, 9am–4:30pm Tue–Sat. 📷 🎫 Note: fee for photography may apply.

On 26 July 1953, at the height of the Carnival festivities, Fidel Castro led about 100 rebels in an attack on the Moncada barracks (*see p52*). Capturing Moncada, the second largest garrison in Cuba, built in the 19th century, would have meant securing a large stock of weapons and thus triggering a general revolt. Abel Santamaría was to attack the Saturnino Lora hospital, a strategic site on a promontory overlooking the barracks, and Raúl Castro was to capture the law courts building. This bold attempt failed, but it did succeed in increasing public awareness of the activity of the young revolutionaries. Eight of them died during the attack, while 55 were taken prisoner; some were tortured and executed.

Since January 1959 the barracks, which still bears bullet holes, has housed the Ciudad Escolar 26 de Julio school. Part of the building houses the Museo

The impressive façade of the former Moncada army barracks, now a school and museum

The monument to General Antonio Maceo in Plaza de la Revolución

Plaza de la Revolución

In the northeastern part of Santiago, beyond the Moncada barracks, is Plaza de la Revolución, a large, rather soulless square at a crossroads of three major avenues. The square is dominated by a vast monument executed in the early 1990s by the Santiago sculptor, Alberto Lezcay, representing General Maceo *(see p48)* on horseback, surrounded by 23 stylized machetes. Plaza de la Revolución marks the start of the modern, residential area of the city, where the architecture shows a marked Soviet influence.

26 de Julio, which in fact illustrates the history of Cuba from the time of Columbus, but devotes most space to the guerrilla war of the 1950s. There is a model reproducing the attack on Moncada. There are also possessions which belonged to Fidel Castro, his brother Raúl and Che Guevara when they were waging war in the Sierra Maestra.

🏛 Museo Abel Santamaría Cuadrado – Parque Histórico Abel Santamaría

Calle General Portuondo (Trinidad), e/ Calle Nueva y Ave. de los Libertadores. **Tel** (22) 624 119. **Open** 9am–5pm Mon–Sat. 🐾 📷 Note: fee for photography may apply.

The Moncada barracks, former Saturnino Lora hospital and law court buildings, form part of the Parque Histórico Abel Santamaria. In the 1953 raid, the former hospital was the target of a group of rebels led by Abel Santamaría, who was captured and killed by the police after the failed attempt.

The remaining hospital buildings now house a museum with documents and photographs relating to the trial of Fidel Castro and other rebels, which was held a few days after the attack on the barracks in one of the rooms.

Besides the photographs illustrating the difficult social and economic conditions in Cuba during the 1950s, there is the manuscript of Castro's landmark self-defence in court, later entitled *History Will Absolve Me (see p153)*.

Plaza de Marte

East of Plaza Dolores is the third largest square in Santiago, laid out in the 19th century. It is of great historic importance: here capital punishment was meted out both in the colonial period and under General Machado. At its centre is a 20-m (65-ft) column (1902) celebrating Cuban independence.

🏛 Bosque de los Héroes

East of the centre, behind the unmistakable Hotel Santiago, lies a small, unobtrusive hill. A white marble monument was erected here in 1973 to honour Che Guevara and the comrades-in-arms who died with him in Bolivia. Their names are engraved here.

The column in Plaza de Marte

Vista Alegre

The Vista Alegre quarter has fine eclectic-style buildings constructed in the 1920s and 1930s. The quarter also has two important institutions: the **Centro Cultural Africano Fernando Ortíz**, with African masks, statues and musical instruments on display, and the **Casa del Caribe**, which houses a historical archive, library, alfresco music venue and centre for conferences, workshops and events *(see p282)*. During the Fiesta del Caribe, the Casa del Caribe presents examples of Yoruba, Congo and voodoo rites.

Bosque de los Héroes, honouring Che Guevara and comrades

⓯ Castillo del Morro

At the entrance to the Bay of Santiago, 10 km (6 miles) southwest of the city centre, stands an imposing castle, declared a World Heritage Site by UNESCO in 1997. The Castillo del Morro San Pedro de la Roca combines medieval elements with a modern sense of space, adhering nonetheless to classical Renaissance principles of geometric forms and symmetry. The fortress was designed in 1638 by engineer Giovanni Bautista Antonelli for the governor Pedro de la Roca, who wanted to defend the city against pirate raids. Large enough to house 400 soldiers when it was built, the castle was converted into a prison in 1775, becoming a fortress once again in 1898 during the wars of independence, when the US fleet attacked the city. Today it houses a naval and piracy museum.

A cannon, part of the old battery used to defend the bay

★ **View of the Bay**
The parapets and lookouts on the upper parts of the fortress were used by the sentries to keep watch. Visitors today can appreciate the setting and enjoy a marvellous view over the bay.

KEY

① **Plataforma de la Punta** (*morrillo*, or **bluff**)

② **The stone stairway** on the side of the castle facing the sea is part of an open-air network of steps leading to the upper levels.

③ **Underground passageways** link the various parts of the castle. This one leads to the artillery area.

④ **Artillery area**

⑤ **In the casemates** a display of prints illustrates the history of Santiago's forts.

⑥ **Dry moat**

⑦ **Three separate main structures**, built on five different levels, form the skeleton of the castle. This unusual construction is a result of the uneven terrain of the headland.

Triangular Lunette
Built in 1590–1610 as the main protection for the fortress gate, this structure originally stood separately from the castle. It was later incorporated into the main structure.

Drawbridge
This bridge passes over a dry moat that runs alongside the fortification on the inland side. It is well preserved, and still has the original winch which was used to raise and lower the bridge.

★ Central Square
This square, the nerve centre of the castle, was used as an area for organizing daily activities. The square provides access to the chapel, barracks, garrison and underground rooms.

The Bay of Santiago

About 8 km (5 miles) southwest of the centre of Santiago, at the end of the Carretera Turística, is Marina Punta Gorda. From here ferries cross over to a small island in the middle of the bay.

This is Cayo Granma, home to a picturesque fishing village made up of multicoloured huts and small houses. Many of those on the island's margins are built on piles or pontoons extending over the water. This island is a peaceful place off the beaten track, although there are a few restaurants and cafés. It makes a good place to relax and round off a visit to Santiago de Cuba.

View of Cayo Granma from the Carretera Turística

⑯ Parque Baconao

Lying between the Caribbean Sea and the eastern fringes of the Sierra Maestra, and straddling the provinces of Santiago and Guantánamo, Parque Baconao has been declared a biosphere reserve by UNESCO. The largest and most original amusement park in Cuba (80,000 ha/197,600 acres) combines mountains and beaches with old coffee plantations and an unusual range of attractions. The park was developed in the 1980s thanks to the voluntary work of students and labourers, and has been updated periodically. Unfortunately, the park received a severe battering from Hurricane Sandy in 2012 and has still not entirely recovered. There is limited accommodation.

Gran Piedra
This is an enormous monolith, from the top of which, at an altitude of 1,234m (4,048 ft), you can even see Jamaica and Haiti on clear days *(see p240)*.

Prado de las Esculturas
This sculpture garden, with 20 works by Cuban and foreign artists, was laid out in the 1980s. Following the damage caused by Hurricane Sandy, the park was restored and reopened in 2015.

KEY

① **Granjita Siboney**, once a key operational base for the Cuban rebels, is now a museum of revolutionary artifacts *(see p240)*.

② **Cafetal La Isabelica**, the oldest coffee plantation in the province, has been converted into a museum with a small café *(see p240)*.

③ **Jardín Avenida del Paraíso** *(see p240)*

④ **Exposición Mesoamericana** *(see p241)*

⑤ **Jardín de Cactus (Cactus Garden)**

⑥ **Comunidad Artística Verraco** *(see p241)*

⑦ **The sea bed** in the area between Playa del Indio and Playa Larga is dotted with shipwrecks.

⑧ **Museo Nacional del Transporte** *(see p241)*

Siberia ③

② La Isabelica

Perseverancia

Tres Arroyos

Abel Santamaría • Las Guásimas

Damaiayabo

El Palenque • Siboney •

Juraguá

Playa Siboney is the favourite beach of the citizens of Santiago. Only 19 km (12 miles) from town, it can be reached by regular bus service or taxi.

Laguna Baconao
Boats can be hired for pleasure trips around this lagoon, which is surrounded by mountains.

VISITORS' CHECKLIST

Practical Information
Santiago de Cuba. **Road Map** F4.
Tours in the park: 🚻 Cubatur,
Ave. de las Américas y Calle M
(22) 68 7040.

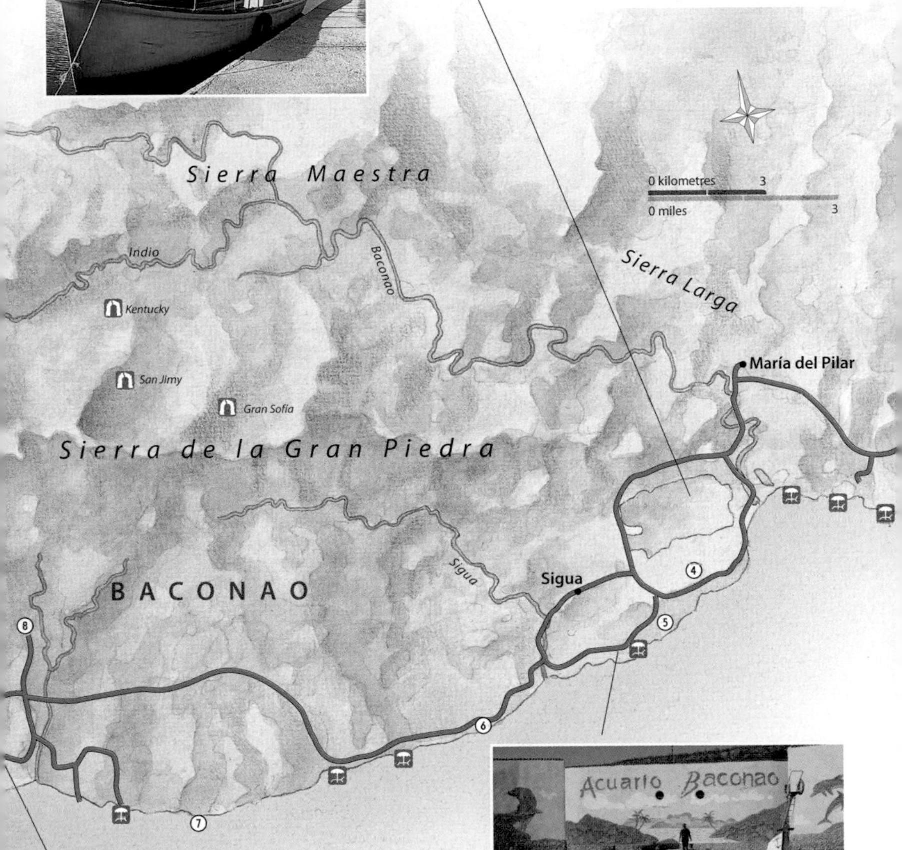

0 kilometres   3

0 miles   3

Sierra   Maestra

Indio

Baconao

Sierra Larga

🏛 Kentucky

• **María del Pilar**

🏛 San Jimy

🏛 *Gran Sofia*

Sierra de la Gran Piedra

🏊 🏖 🏖

B A C O N A O

Sigua

Sigua

④

⑧

⑤

⑥

🏖 🏖

⑦

🏖

Acuario Baconao
This aquarium has a good display of sharks, sea lions and other fish. Dolphins perform a show three times a day in the aquarium's pool.

Valle de la Prehistoria
This children's park features huge sculptures of dinosaurs and there is also a Natural History Museum.

Key

━━ Major road

═══ Path

For keys to symbols *see back flap*

Exploring the Parque Baconao

It is possible to explore the park by car or taxi in a day, although accommodation is available. Heading east from Santiago, along Avenida Raúl Pujol, you will pass the zoo (Parque Zoológico), and, nearby, the Arbol de la Paz (Tree of Peace), a ceiba tree beneath which the Spanish signed the surrender agreement in 1898. The entrance to Parque Baconao is not far beyond the confines of the city. Most of the attractions are suitable for families and can be reached by car, but the peak of the Gran Piedra and the easternmost beaches are only accessible on foot.

A strelitzia in flower at the Jardín Avenida del Paraíso

The spectacular view from the Gran Piedra

🔲 Granjita Siboney

Carretera Siboney km 13.5. **Tel** (22) 399 168. **Open** 9am–5pm daily. 🖼 📷 Note: fee for photography may apply.

By the roadside 16 km (10 miles) east of Santiago, this is the farm rented by Abel Santamaría in 1953 as a base of operations in the run-up to the assault on the Moncada barracks. It was from here, on 26 July, that the young rebels drove into Santiago to launch the attack. Their attempt failed and Granjita Siboney itself was later attacked by Batista's men. The (reconstructed) bullet holes can be seen around the door.

Granjita Siboney is now a museum with the uniforms and some of the weapons that the revolutionaries wore and carried that day. Next door is the Generación del Centenario gallery, with paintings honouring the rebels who died during the attack on the barracks, as well as photographs, documents and the car Castro used in the attack.

🌿 Gran Piedra

Jardín Botánico: **Open** 7am–6pm daily. 🖼

Heading west from Granjita Siboney, you come to a turn-off to Gran Piedra: this 12-km (7-mile) road with hairpin bends provides one of the best panoramas in Cuba with views of the intense green of the tropical and mountain forests. Beyond the **Jardín Avenida del**

Granjita Siboney farm, showing the signs of the July 1953 attack

Paraíso, with its many species of orchid and multicoloured strelitzias (flowers more commonly known as bird of paradise), a flight of 459 steps leads up to the top of the Gran Piedra (1,234 m/4,048 ft above sea level). This gigantic, 25-m (82-ft) monolith rests on the crater of an extinct volcano.

It is best to make the climb in the morning, because the afternoon can bring foggy weather and you may not see far into the distance. However, on clear days the view is simply superb: it stretches from the mountains to the coast, and even as far as Haiti.

🏛 Cafetal La Isabelica

Carretera de la Gran Piedra km 14. **Open** 8:30am–5pm daily. 🖼 📷 📹

There are numerous old coffee plantations around the Gran Piedra, all of which were granted World Heritage Site status by UNESCO. Almost all of the plantations are in ruins, but one exception is the Cafetal La

Isabelica, which can be reached easily via a path from the foot of the Gran Piedra. This plantation belonged to Victor Constantin, a French landowner who, together with many others, fled from Haiti in the late 1800s following a slave uprising there. He brought with him numerous slaves and his mistress, Isabel María, after whom he named his plantation.

The largest structure is the manor house, which has been reconstructed following a fire that burned it down. The ground floor was partly for the labourers and partly used to store tools and implements. The first floor consists of a bedroom, living room, dining room and studio, all with 18th-century furniture and furnishings.

Reproductions of Pre-Columbian objects, Exposición Mesoamericana

Interior of the Cafetal La Isabelica owner's manor house

The house overlooks a terrace where coffee beans were left to dry – actually the roof of a large storehouse. Nearby are the kitchens, behind which is the water tank; the whole area is surrounded by coffee plants. Visitors to the *cafetal* museum are offered a demonstration of how coffee is grown and processed for consumption.

🏛 Museo Nacional del Transporte
Carretera de Baconao. **Open** 8am– 5pm daily. 🖼
This museum houses a fascinating collection of 2,500 miniature cars and an array of old vintage cars, including a local Maya Cuba – a tiny, one-cylinder car. The oldest is a 1912 Model T Ford. There are also vehicles of historical significance, including cars that once belonged to Fidel Castro and Benny Moré.

Comunidad Artística Verraco
Close to the small Playa Verraco, artists, potters and sculptors live and work in is a nascent artists' community. Drop by to watch them at work and to see their small gallery.

🏛 Exposición Mesoamericana
Carretera de Baconao. **Open** daily.
This series of sea caves along the road are showcases for reproductions of Central American Pre-Columbian works of art.

The Origins of Coffee Growing in Cuba

Coffee was introduced to Cuba at the end of the 18th century, by which time it had been a fashionable drink among the European aristocracy and bourgeoisie for some time. The French coffee growers who had fled to Eastern Cuba from Haiti in 1791 were well aware of this: they were the ones who brought the "new" plant to the island. The hills around Santiago and the valleys between Baracoa and Guantánamo were ideal for coffee growing, because they offered both water and shade. Coffee was an immediate success, and demand increased so much that it was planted along the coast too. In 1803 there were 100,000 coffee trees; by 1807 this figure had increased to four million, cultivated on 191 plantations. The French growers became very wealthy, building palatial manor houses on their plantations. As the cultivation of coffee required plenty of manual labour, and there weren't enough workers from Haiti, there was a "boom" in the slave trade in the early 19th century. Cuban archives mention 7,654 "dead souls" at the beginning of the century, and 42,000 in 1820. While this immigration contributed to the economic fortune of the island, it proved to be the end of the landowners. It was not long before the slaves, increasingly numerous and organized, began to rebel against their condition (*see p46*).

Coffee growing beneath the trees in the mountains

⑰ Guantánamo

Guantánamo. **Road Map** F4.
🏛 225,000. 🚉 🚌 🚗 **𝒊** Infotur,
Calle Galixto García el Crombet y
Emilio Giró, (21) 351 993.

If it were not for the US naval
base and the famous song
Guantanamera (girl from
Guantánamo), this town would
probably only be known to
Cubans and music experts.
Its name, in fact, is linked with
the *changuí*, a variation of *son*
music that developed in the
coffee plantations in the
mountains, music made famous
by the musician Elio Revé.

Guantanamera was composed
by Joseíto Fernández in the
1940s almost for fun, drawing
inspiration from a proud local
girl who had not reacted to a
compliment he paid her. Later,
some "literary" verses from the
Versos Sencillos by José Martí
were adapted to the music.

The town of Guantánamo
was founded in 1796 to take
in the French fleeing from
Haiti and developed during
the 19th century. The capital
of a varied province where
desert areas studded with
cactus alternate with green
mountains, Guantánamo has
few sights of note. Principal
Parque Martí is dominated by
the **Parroquial de Santa
Catalina de Riccis** (1863).

Opposite the church is a
statue of General Pedro A Pérez,
sculpted in 1928. Nearby, on
Calle Pedro A Pérez, stands one
of the town's most impressive
buildings, the **Palacio de
Salcines**. Designed by architect
José Leticio Salcines in 1919,

The Parroquial de Santa Catalina de Riccis in the Parque Martí

this building's eclectic architectural style features a decorative
façade of cornices and columns.
A Neo-Classical cupola crowns
the building, on top of which
stands a statue of La Fama –
the messenger of Zeus, in
Greek mythology – by Italian
architect Américo J Chini.
The Palacio is also home to the
Museo de Artes Decorativas,
in which antique furniture and
decorative objects can be seen.

An interesting colonial
building facing Principal Parque
Martí is the old Spanish prison.
It is now the home of the
modest **Museo Provincial de
Guantánamo**, which has a
fascinating room dedicated to
Cuba's first space flight in 1980,
a joint mission with the USSR.

The Plaza de la Revolución is
one of the largest and probably
most austere in the country. The
kitsch 1960s Hotel Guantánamo
dominates the vast, concrete
Plaza Mariana Garajales, which
itself is dominated by a
towering brutalist sculpture,
Monument to the Heroes, which
honours Cuba's independence
fighters, including Frank País.

🏛 **Museo de Artes Decorativas**
Calle Pedro A Pérez 804, e/ Prado y
Aguilera. **Tel** (21) 324 704. **Open** 8am–
noon & 2–5pm Mon–Thu, 8am–noon
& 5–9pm Fri, 5–9pm Sat.

🏛 **Museo Provincial de
Guantánamo**
Plaza Martí, esq. Prado. **Tel** (21) 325
872. **Open** 8am–noon & 2:30–4:30pm
Mon–Fri, 8am–noon Sat. **Closed** 1 Jan,
1 May, 26 Jul, 10 Oct, 25 Dec. 📷 📹
Note: fee for photography may apply.

Environs
Around 20 km (12 miles) east
of Guantánamo, on the road to
Lomas de Yateras, a coffee-
growing area, is an unusual
open-air museum, the **Museo
Zoológico de Piedra**. It was
founded by Angel Iñigo (1935–
2014), a farmer and self-taught
sculptor. Beginning in 1978 he
produced sculptures of about 40
animals in stone, including lions,
boa constrictors, tapirs, buffaloes,
rhinoceroses and gorillas, all of
which are on display.

Some 23 km (14 miles) south
of Guantánamo city is the small
port of **Caimanera**, north of the
US naval base. It used to be
possible to "spy" on the base
from a viewing point, or *mirador*,
on a hill off the Baracoa road, but
this is now closed to the public.
Caimanera is within a Cuban
military zone and is off-limits to
everyone except those who live
there and those with a special
pass. It is relatively straightforward to get hold of one of
these passes, which permits you
to visit by day or stay overnight
at Hotel Caimanera (see p262),
where there are views of the
base through the hotel tele-
scope and a small, interesting
museum. You will need to get
permission from the Ministry of
the Interior and this can be
arranged; with at least 72 hours'
notice, through Izlazul at Hotel
Guantánamo, tel. (21) 381 015.

🏛 **Museo Zoológico de Piedra**
Boquerón de Yateras. **Open** 9am–6pm
daily. **Closed** 1 Jan, 1 May, 26 Jul,
10 Oct, 25 Dec. 📷

Joseíto Fernández, composer of the
song *Guantanamera*

⓲ Costa Sur

Guantánamo. **Road Map** F4.

Travelling eastwards from Guantánamo, visitors will pass through the most barren part of Cuba, where the climate is desert-like because of the hot winds blowing here. This is a unique area on the island where cactuses and succulents are the main vegetation. The coast road, tucked in between the mountains and the blue sea, is spectacular. The rocky coast has tiny coves with pebble beaches, home to an assortment of seashells and *Polymita picta* snails *(see p249)*.

⓳ La Farola

Guantánamo. **Road Map** F4.

Cajobabo – a southern coastal town where José Martí and Máximo Gómez landed to begin the 1895 war against Spain – marks the beginning of La Farola, a spectacular 49-km (30-mile) road that wends its way upwards over the mountains to Baracoa, through vegetation that becomes more and more luxuriant as the coast is left behind.

Until 1959 Cajobabo could only be reached by ship. In order to connect it to the rest of the island, in the 1960s engineers excavated sections of mountainside in the Sierra del Purial in order to create a kind

The American Naval Base

In 1901 the US – the victors, together with the Cubans, in the war against Spain – obliged the Cuban Republic to accept the Platt Amendment *(see p49)*, whereby the latter had to grant the US Navy the right to install a naval base in the bay of Guantánamo. The US was granted a lease of a minimum of 99 years in 1934. For this occupancy, the American government pays $2,000 per year, though it is said that the Cuban government has regularly returned this sum to the US since 1959. In the past the situation has taken on the dramatic overtones of the Cold War and highlighted a difficult state of co-existence. Inside the base, menial jobs are done by Puerto Ricans, the wives of the servicemen do their shopping in supermarkets stocked with food flown in from the US, and there are two English-language radio stations and one TV station. The base, US territory in Cuba, covers 110 sq km (43 sq miles), and has two runways for military planes. The whole area is surrounded by 27 km (17 miles) of fence.

The American base at Guantánamo

of "flying highway". The road acquired its name (*farola* means beacon) because in some stretches it looks like a beam, suspended in air. It is regarded as one of the great engineering feats of recent Cuban history.

This highway and the periodic viewing points offer incredible views of the peaks

of the Sierra Maestra, lush valleys, tropical forests, pine groves, banana plantations, rivers, waterfalls and royal palm trees. The luxuriant vegetation seems to swallow up the road in places. Along the road, people sell local produce such as coffee, red bananas, chocolate and *cucurucho* (*see p267*).

View from one of the observation points along La Farola road

⑳ Baracoa

The oldest city in Cuba lies at the far eastern tip of the island. Its name in the Arauaca language, spoken by the former inhabitants of the area, means "the presence of the sea". Nuestra Señora de la Asunción de Baracoa villa was founded on 15 August 1511, on a curved bay that had been discovered some 20 years earlier by Columbus, and immediately became the political and ecclesiastical capital of Cuba. However, this status was short-lived. In 1515, the city founder Diego Velázquez transferred his residence to Santiago, marking the beginning of a long period of social and economic isolation for Baracoa.

The Cruz de la Parra, originally carved 500 years ago

A street in Baracoa, dominated by lush vegetation

Exploring Baracoa

"Baracoa means nature", the Cubans say, and it is certainly true: enclosed by tropical forest and the sea, for four centuries this town has managed to live by fishing, cultivating cocoa, coconuts and bananas, and by gathering wood. While the isolation has created inconveniences, it has also allowed the locals to maintain their traditions and preserve the ecosystem.

The historic centre of Baracoa is not colonial, but a mixture of styles, with some Neo-Classical and French influences. Thick vegetation towers over the buildings and has even invaded some houses, many of which are built of wood.

The best view of the town is seen from the terrace of an 18th-century fortress on a hill above the town: the **Castillo de Seboruco**, now Hotel el Castillo (see p262). From here you can see the roofs and the bay of Baracoa, dominated to the west by the mountain of El Yunque (see p248).

Parque Independencia

In the main square, overlooked by the cathedral, is a famous bust of the Indian leader Hatuey (see p223). Nearby are the **Casa de la Trova**, the **Fondo de Bienes Culturales**, which exhibits works by local painters, sculptors and craftsmen, and the **Casa de la Cultura**, an eclectic building with colonial elements that hosts evening performances and events.

At No. 123 Calle Maceo is the **Casa del Chocolate**, which serves excellent hot chocolate. Baracoa cocoa is famous throughout Cuba.

🏛 Catedral de Nuestra Señora de la Asunción

Calle Maceo 152. **Tel** (21) 643 352. **Open** 8–11am & 4–7pm Tue–Fri, 8–11am & 5–9pm Sat, 8am–noon Sun. ✝ 9am.

This modest cathedral, built in 1807 and restored in 2012, is most famous as the home of the Cruz de la Parra, a wooden cross that is said to be the oldest symbol of Christianity in the New World. According to legend, the cross was brought to Cuba by Columbus on his first voyage to America, and on 1 December 1492 it was placed on the spot where Baracoa was later founded. It is said that the cross disappeared one day and was then miraculously found under the climbing vine (parra) in a settler's garden, hence its name. The four tips of the cross are now covered with metal sheets, because in the past worshippers used to pull off splinters and keep them as relics. Scientific analysis of the wood proves the cross is some 500 years old, but the discovery that it is made from indigenous Cuban wood disproves the legendary connection to Columbus.

A typical single-storey wooden house in Baracoa

The bay of Baracoa, with El Yanque on the horizon, viewed from the Castillo de Seboruco

Fuerte Matachín (Museo Municipal)

Calle Martí y Malecón. **Tel** (21) 642 122. **Open** 8am–noon, 2–6pm Mon–Sat, 8am–noon Sun. Note: fee for photography may apply.

This small museum, which provides an interesting overview of local history, is housed in a military fortress built during the colonial period to defend the city from pirates. (Piracy was particularly active in the 18th and 19th centuries.) Along the fort walls, a battery of cannons faces seawards.

Statue of Columbus, Museo Municipal garden

The displays start with archaeological finds of the Pre-Columbian era, and are followed by documents, maps, paintings and prints related to Spanish domination, pirates, slaves and the plantations.

There is an interesting natural history section with specimens on display, including the *Polymita* snails *(see p249)*. The museum is also a historical and geographical research centre and fosters initiatives to preserve and develop local culture; city tours are available.

El Malecón

This is the seafront that connects the two 18th-century forts in Baracoa: Fuerte Matachín to the east, and **Fuerte de la Punta** to the west, which is now a restaurant. The Malecón is ideal for a stroll during the week.

On Saturdays a bustling food market is held here in the morning, and in the evening the road is prepared for the *noche baracoesa* – "Baracoan night" – a lively folk festival during which people gather to eat, drink and dance along the seafront.

Museo Arqueológico de las Cuevas del Paraíso

Loma Paraíso. **Open** 8am–5pm daily. Note: fee for photography may apply.

The pre-Columbian history of Baracoa is best explored in this fascinating museum set in a series of caves. The Taíno Indians once used these caves for ceremonies and as funeral chambers. Some of the original archaeological finds are on display, including 3,000-year-old petroglyphs, skeletons and *esferolitas* – burial rite stones

carved into spheres that were used to indicate a person's age and social standing. Replica of relics and models complete the display. The caves are hidden in the lush vegetation of Loma Paraíso. It is also known for its views of the town and the bay.

Visitors at Museo Arqueologico de las Cuevas del Paraiso

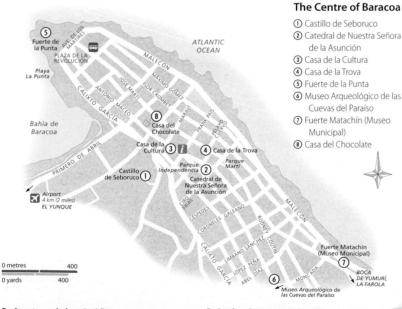

The Centre of Baracoa

① Castillo de Seboruco
② Catedral de Nuestra Señora de la Asunción
③ Casa de la Cultura
④ Casa de la Trova
⑤ Fuerte de la Punta
⑥ Museo Arqueológico de las Cuevas del Paraíso
⑦ Fuerte Matachín (Museo Municipal)
⑧ Casa del Chocolate

The mountain of El Yunque, dominating the bay of Baracoa

㉑ El Yunque

Guantánamo. **Road Map** F4.
ℹ️ Ecotur, Calle Ciro Frías,
Baracoa, (21) 642 478.

A limestone formation, 575 m
(1,885 ft) high, covered with
thick vegetation, El Yunque
was a sacred site for the Taíno
Indians for many centuries.
Later it became a natural
landmark for navigators about
to land at the port of Baracoa.
The Spanish called it "El Yunque"
(the anvil) because of its
unmistakable outline. The out-
crop's shape has led to local
misapprehension that this
was the rock that Columbus
described as "a square mountain

that looks like an island" in 1492.
In fact, he was referring to a
similarly shaped rock at
Bariay near Gibara
(see p218).

The slopes of
the mountain,
which has been
declared a
biosphere reserve
by UNESCO, are
home to botanical rarities,
including two carnivorous plants
and *Podocarpus*, one of the
oldest plant species in the world,
as well as an endemic palm tree,
Coccothrinax yunquensis.

El Yunque is also the habitat
for some endangered species
of bird such as the *carpintero*

real (Campeophilus principalis)
and the *caguarero* hawk
(Chondrohierax wilsonii), as well as
for the smallest amphibian in the
world, the *Sminthillus limbatus*,
less than 1 cm (0.4 inch) long, and
another very ancient species, the
almiquí (Solenodon cubanus), a
rare mammal similar to a rat.

㉒ Río Toa

Road Map F4.

The valley fed by the Río Toa,
Cuba's biggest river, has been
made into a nature reserve,
the **Parque Natural Río Toa**.
Still lacking in roads and
facilities, this park is part of a
wide-ranging project to create
refuges and camping sites that
will not interfere with the local
ecosystems. Local farmers still
use an old-fashioned craft to
travel upstream – the *cayuca*,
a flat canoe of
Taíno origin.
From the river,
visitors can admire
the majestic Pico
Galán (974 m/
3,200 ft) and the
great waterfalls that cascade
into the river from steep cliffs.
Enquire at Ecotur if you are
interested in exploring the area.

Going up the Río Toa in a
rowing boat

Environs
Northwest of Baracoa, 21 km
(12 miles) past the mouth of
the Río Toa, is **Playa Maguana**,

Playa Maguana, one of the unspoilt beaches near Baracoa

Río de Miel, flowing through virtually virgin tropical forest between Baracoa and Boca de Yumurí

the most beautiful beach in the province, with dazzling white sand. The beach's Taíno name refers to the presence of a nearby archaeological site. A 2-km (1-mile) coral reef lies only 500 m (1,640 ft) from the shore. Be warned though that the sea can often be rather choppy in this area.

There is a smart, rustic hotel hidden among the coconut palms, where villas can be rented, but this place is still delightfully unspoilt.

Polymita Snails

A genus endemic to the Baracoa area, the *Polymita* is a snail with a brilliantly-coloured shell. According to the colour, six species of *Polymita* can be

Patterned *Polymita* shells

identified: *P. picta, P. muscarum, P. sulphurosa, P. versicolor, P. venusta* and *P. brocheri*. All these species live on trees and plants, and feed on mushrooms and lichens, contributing to the health of the plants, especially coffee trees. *Polymita* snails can be easily recognized, because the shell with coloured stripes looks as though it has been painted, and stands out clearly against the bright green vegetation.

One of the many legends that explains how the snail acquired its colours tells of a young Indian who had no pearls or jewels to give to his beloved, so he painted a snail shell. He used the yellow of the sun, the green of the woods, the red of the flowers, and the white from the foam of the waves. But when he decided to take the blue from the sky, it was too late in the day, and he had to be content with the black of night. Today this snail, highly prized for its shell, is an endangered species. Selling or gathering *Polymita* is not permitted.

🔞 Parque Nacional Alejandro de Humboldt

Road Map F4.

This mountainous rainforest 56 km (35 miles) north of Baracoa is Cuba's most richly biodiverse park and a UNESCO World Heritage Site. Named after the 19th-century German naturalist and explorer Alexander von Humboldt,

Here you'll find a variety of birds, snails, scorpions, frogs, birds, and the rare Cuban solenodon (*Solenodon cubanus*), which looks like a giant shrew with an extraordinarily long snout. At the edge of the park is the stunning Bahía Taco bay, home to a small group of manatees. The Ecotur office in Baracoa *(see p247)* can help with arranging walks and boat trips in the bay.

🔞 Boca de Yumurí

Road Map F4.

Around 30 km (18 miles) east of Baracoa, this village of *bohíos* (traditional dwellings with palm-leaf roofs) takes its name from the Yumurí river, which flows into the sea here. Its inhabitants live by fishing, but earn a little extra by taking tourists on river boat rides.

A short boat ride across the Yumurí river will take you to an enchanting beach. Another interesting trip is to go upstream, where the river course reaches an impressive canyon with walls as much 180 m (590 ft) high.

The Río Yumurí flows an area interesting ecology. Colourful birdlife abound zunzún, the to cartacuba (s

TRAVELLERS' NEEDS

WHERE TO STAY

Since 1980, when Cuba dramatically expanded its tourism industry, there has been steady state and foreign investment in the hotel industry. Many old historic hotels have been restored and equipped with international standards of comfort, and new infrastructure has been created, often through joint ventures involving the Cuban Ministry of Tourism and foreign companies. Today, visitors can choose from a variety of accommodation, with choices ranging from modern luxury hotels with swimming pools and good sports facilities, to colonial, city centre hotels and all-inclusive holiday villages on uninhabited islands. Cubans are allowed to let out rooms, or even entire apartments, in their own homes; this arrangement has proved to be popular with tourists. The hotel listings (see pp256–63) are arranged by area, and cater to a variety of different budgets.

Sumptuous lobby in the Iberostar Grand Hotel Trinidad (see p262)

Hotel Chains

Most visitors to Cuba come on package holidays, and many hotel chains cater for this type of tourism. All hotels are partially or wholly state-owned, although many are managed by joint ventures with foreign companies.

One chain is the Cuban **Gran Caribe**, whose hotels include the historic Hotel Nacional in Havana (see p102), and the Hotel Plaza (see p85) in Havana's Parque Central. Gran Caribe also manages several more modern hotels, such as the Hotel Riviera in Havana (see p257) and the Hotel Jagua in Cienfuegos (see p259).

Generally, high standards are also guaranteed by the Cuban chain **Cubanacán** and the Spanish **Meliá** and **Iberostar** chains; all of these companies have hotels throughout Cuba. Cubanacán manages good hotels of its own, and others affiliated to international chains, including several good-value three-star hotels, such as the Club Amigo Atlántico in Guardalavaca (see p263). The Meliá chain manages the Meliá Cohiba in Havana (see p258), and a string of beach resorts including the elegant Meliá Buenavista in Cayo Santa María (see p259).

Gaviota, the tourism arm of the military, offers comfortable accommodation in the main coastal resorts, on the cayos and in mountain areas.

The hotels forming the **Islazul** chain are of a lower standard, but are still on an international level, offering basic levels of comfort at lower prices.

Another quite different style is offered by **Habaguanex**, a Cuban company founded under the auspices of the Oficina del Historiador de la Ciudad in Havana, which restores old buildings in Old Havana, converting them into shops, cafés and hotels. Habaguanex hotels include historic buildings such as 18th-century Palacio del Marqués de San Felipe y Santiago Bejucal with a Baroque façade, and the Hotel Santa Isabel in a splendid colonial building facing the Plaza de Armas (see p256).

Grading

Cuban hotels are classified according to the international star system, from one star rising to five stars. However, visitors are likely to find that standards within a particular star rating can vary considerably. Some mid-range hotels may have been good quality in the 1950s, but have since become rundown and not brought into line with modern needs. One-star hotels are generally to be avoided; a better choice would be a private house.

A fountain in the elegant foyer of the Meliá Varadero

Restaurant tables under the arcades of Plaza Vieja, Havana

Prices

Hotel rates in the capital and in the more famous seaside resorts such as Cayo Largo, Varadero, Cayo Coco and Playa Guardalavaca, are more than those in the rest of the country and correspond approximately to international levels.

Whatever the star rating of a hotel, prices will be higher in peak season, which runs from December to April, and from the beginning of July to the end of August.

Tipping

It is customary to leave a *propina* (tip) for the hotel staff at the end of your stay. The amount of the *propina* is at your discretion and will vary according to the type of hotel, how long you stay and the type and quality of service. It is, however, useful to remember that a tip in convertible pesos (CUC) or euros may amount to the equivalent of a month's salary in Cuban pesos (CUP).

Disabled Travellers

Only the more recently-built hotels have rooms purpose-built for disabled people, including bathrooms with wheelchair access.

Unfortunately, the majority of Cuban hotels are not equipped with such facilities. Nonetheless, in general, hotel staff will do everything they can to be of help to disabled clients.

The terrace at Hotel Casa Granda in the heart of Santiago de Cuba *(see p263)*

Booking

It is best to book accommodation well ahead of your visit through a travel agency in your home country or online to ensure that you will get a room and date to your liking. Your tour operator may also be able to offer special package deals. In high season, in particular, when there are special events such as Carnival in Santiago de Cuba, or one of the many cultural festivals in Havana, it may be difficult to find a room.

Holiday Villages

Resorts and holiday villages are ideal for people who want a relaxing, sunny holiday by the beach, with comfortable rooms and all meals and facilities provided.

All-inclusive packages offer a complete deal, with lodging in bungalows or apartments with bathroom, phone, air conditioning and TV. The price includes breakfast, lunch and dinner (usually buffet), and all drinks. Sports activities of all kinds (sailing, snorkelling, scuba diving, swimming, surfing) are provided – some at extra cost. Other options include games rooms, playgrounds and baby-sitting services, freshwater pools for children and adults, car rental service, shops and beach equipment. In some parts of Cuba, these all-inclusive holiday villages are the only option available.

Specialist Holidays

Many tour operators specializing in holidays in Cuba also offer tours for those interested in a particular activity. Many all-inclusive resorts offer diving lessons for beginners, but qualified divers have a wider range of options. Qualified scuba divers need to provide proof of their qualifications and must take out fully comprehensive travel insurance. Some dive sites such as María La Gorda *(see p150)* and Isla de la Juventud *(see p154)* require skill and experience. Keen divers can stay in hotels and tourist villages near dive sites.

The best place to learn salsa is, of course, in Cuba and UK-based **Caledo** arranges all-inclusive with salsa tuition by teachers, and visit best dance venu

Meliá Cayo Coco, beautifully set on an island just off the Atlantic Coast *(see p261)*

The Hotel Moka, in the Sierra del Rosario, a favourite with ecotourists *(see p258)*

Conservation-conscious holidays in unspoiled landscapes are available from a few hotels that operate as ecological tourism centres. These are found in the Pinar del Río area and in the Sierra del Rosario, near Marea del Portillo (in the Sierra Maestra) and Baracoa. Many centres also organize excursions, such as birdwatching and fishing trips.

Camping

Besides some modest camping sites reserved for Cubans, there are other *campismos* (camping sites) run by **Cubamar Viajes**, located in or near nature reserves and along the coast. Despite being described as camping sites, accommodation is in fact in *cabañas* (bungalows). The sites usually have a restaurant and a pool.

The quality of the *cabañas* varies, but they are usually simple and clean. However, this type of accommodation does not suit everyone, and not all sites are open to foreigners. These camping sites often operate more like a holiday village, with daytime and evening recreational activities.

Casual tent-pitching or sleeping out on beaches is not permitted in Cuba.

Private Rooms

Renting rooms in *casas particulares* (private homes) is an excellent arrangement for visitors who want to meet locals and experience everyday Cuban life first-hand. To make the best of the opportunity, it will help to have a smattering of Spanish.

Besides single rooms, small private apartments are also available to rent. You can often find very comfortable living quarters in historic buildings, particularly in old cities like Trinidad and parts of Havana.

The proverbial Cuban hospitality makes this type of accommodation particularly pleasant: after all, living in a private home is the simplest and best way to feel part of a place. Another advantage is that the home owners and their families can offer suggestions on what to see and where to eat.

Numerous *casas particulares* are included in the hotel listings on pp256–63, and are classified here as B&Bs. Try also to get personal recommendations from people you know and trust. On the whole, avoid taking advice from strangers, and do not allow

Romantic, candle-lit pier at the Meliá Buenavista, Cayo Santa María *(see p259)*

someone you have met casually on the street to take you to a private home. They may be an unreliable hustler, who receives commission from the owners; and that commission would be added to the price you pay.

If you are pleased with the accommodation in a private home, ask the owners for recommended addresses in other places that you intend to visit: this should provide some guarantee of similar standards. Houses legally authorized to let out rooms can be recognized by the sticker on the door. When you arrive, the owners will request a passport, as they are obliged by law to register your personal data with Cuban authorities. It is advisable to call ahead to any *casa* you have booked to confirm that you do intend to stay.

The sticker used for *casas particulares* licensed for rental

There are no official lists of home owners offering rooms, but more information can be obtained by visiting www.cubacasas.net.

María La Gorda hotel, particularly popular with divers, Guanahacibibes *(see p258)*

Recommended Hotels

The accommodation options featured in this guide – listed by area and then by price – have been selected across a wide price range for their unique appeal, location or excellent facilities. They have been divided into a number of categories to help you make the best choice for your trip.

Luxury hotels offer five-star service and amenities. They might not match the impeccable standards you'd expect of a top hotel in London or New York, but they guarantee first-rate facilities and an excellent level of comfort.

Private apartments in Havana have become available to rent in the last few years. Most have been furnished to a high standard and offer stylish independent living in the centre of the city with breakfast service offered (at an additional cost), if required.

Cuba has thousands of B&Bs in private homes known as *casas*. You can find rooms in anything from opulent former colonial mansions to dirt-cheap digs in breeze-block apartments. The quality of accommodation in these places varies hugely, as there are no cut-and-dried standards, but the B&Bs listed in this guide are renowned for their charm, well-kept rooms and friendly, hospitable hosts.

A large number of historic hotels can be found throughout Cuba's biggest cities. These are

Classy yet comfortable Casa Concordia, an apartment available to rent, Havana *(see p257)*

usually set in former palaces and town houses built in the 17th, 18th and 19th centuries. Many feature period details such as antique furniture and original floor tiles.

Modern hotels can also be found throughout Cuba. Though these places may lack character, they usually offer a wide range of facilities and great service.

A small number of hotels are found in the countryside in areas of outstanding natural beauty. The locations are not to be missed, but there may be a limited choice of places to stay. The listings on the following pages feature the best accommodation available in these sometimes remote areas.

Beach resorts are found on almost every stretch of Cuba's coast. The majority of these are all-inclusives offering a high standard of accommodation. The listings also feature smaller, more private boutique resorts in stunningly beautiful locations.

When choosing the very best accommodation for your stay, look out for entries marked DK Choice in this guide. These establishments have been highlighted because they are outstanding in some way. They may be set in beautiful grounds, or in a historically significant building. They might offer exceptional value or a romantic ambience. Whatever the reason, the DK Choice label guarantees an especially memorable stay.

DIRECTORY

Hotel Chains

Cubanacán
Calle 23 no. 156, e/ N y O,
Vedado, Havana.
Tel 7833 4090 ext. 251.
W hotelescubanacan.
com

Gaviota
Edificio de La Marina,
Avenida del Puerto 102,
Old Havana. **Tel** 7869 5774.
W gaviota-grupo.com

Gran Caribe
Calle 7 no. 4210, e/ 42 y
44, Miramar, Havana.

Tel 7204 6366.
W gran-caribe.cu

Habaguanex
Oficios 110,
e/ Lamparilla y Amargura,
Old Havana.
Tel 7867 1039.
W habaguanex.ohc.cu

Iberostar
Lonja del Comercio,
Plaza San Francisco,
Old Havana.
Tel 7866 6069.
W iberostar.com

Islazul
Calle 19 no. 710, e/ Paseo
y A, Vedado, Havana
Tel 7832 0571.
W islazul.cu

Meliã
Calle 2 no. 302, e/ 3 y 5,
Playa, Havana.
Tel 7204 5577.
W meliacuba.com

Camping

Cubamar Viajes
Calle 3, e/ 12 y Malécon,
Vedado, Havana.
Tel 7833 2523.
W campismo
popular.cu

Specialist Tourism

Caledonia
Tel (0131) 621 7721 (UK).
W caledonian
worldwide.com

Where to Stay

Havana

La Habana Vieja

El Balcón de Yamelis $
B&B **Map** 4 F3
Calle Jesús María 58, apto. 7, e/ Calle San Ignacio y Cuba
Tel 5331 9498
The friendly and helpful owner of this B&B offers one modern room in a 1950s building. There's a huge balcony with stunning views of La Habana Vieja.

Casa de Humberto Acosta $
B&B **Map** 4 E3
Calle Compostela 611, 2do piso, e/ Sol y Luz
Tel 7860 3264
W casahumberto.com
A light and bright colonial apartment in southern Old Havana offering guests a comfortable room and a large terrace for dining and sunbathing. Very kind and welcoming hosts.

Casa Vitrales $
B&B **Map** 4 E2
Calle Habana 106, e/ Cuarteles y Chacón
Tel 7866 2607
W cvitrales.com
Set in a colonial home in an emerging quarter of Old Havana, this stylish B&B blends modern furniture with Spanish antiques. Breakfast is served on the rooftop.

DK Choice

Chez Nous $
B&B **Map** 4 E3
Calle Teniente Rey (Brasil) 115, e/ Cuba y San Ignacio
Tel 5264 6061
The professionalism of the owner ensures a first-class stay at this elegant first-floor apartment, furnished in handsome Spanish colonial antiques. It is a beautiful place to stay and just one block from stunning Plaza Vieja. There's also a small roof terrace that's perfect for relaxing on.

Estancia Bohemia $$
Apartment **Map** 4 E3
Plaza Vieja
Tel 5403 1568
W havanabohemia.com
This apartment in a restored colonial mansion is a pretty pied-à-terre on one of Havana's most beautiful plazas. The café upstairs is worth trying for its excellent breakfast.

Hotel del Tejadillo $$
Historic **Map** 4 E2
Calle Tejadillo 12, esq. San Ignacio
Tel 7863 7283
W hoteltejadillocuba.com
This large hotel with spacious rooms enjoys an enviable position – it is tucked down a road just off Plaza de la Catedral.

Suite Havana $$
Apartment **Map** 4 E2
Calle Lamparilla 62, altos, e/ Mercaderes y San Ignacio
Tel 5829 6524
W suitehavana.com
This stylish two-bedroom apartment is in an attractive colonial building, with a roof terrace and wrap-around balcony.

Hotel Ambos Mundos $$$
Historic **Map** 4 E2
Calle Obispo, esq. Mercaderes
Tel 7860 9530
W hotelambosmundos-cuba.com
Located in the heart of Old Havana, this is a smart salmon-pink hotel. It is known for its Hemingway connections and its popular rooftop bar.

Hotel Florida $$$
Historic **Map** 4 E2
Calle Obispo, esq. Cuba
Tel 7862 4127
W hotelfloridahavana.com
A grand, restored Spanish colonial mansion on Old Havana's former shopping street. Its piano bar is a popular place for dancing.

Hotel Raquel $$$
Historic **Map** 4 E2
Calle Amargura, esq. San Ignacio
Tel 7860 8280
W hotelraquel-cuba.com
This former textile warehouse retains its original Art Nouveau

---

fixtures and stained glass, which include some poignant references to Jewish culture. A popular hotel in a prime spot with a good kosher restaurant *(see p270)*.

Hotel Santa Isabel $$$
Luxury **Map** 4 F2
Calle Baratillo 9, e/ Obispo y Narciso López, Plaza de Armas
Tel 7860 8201
W hotelsantaisabel.com
One of Havana's most stunning Spanish colonial mansions – the 18th-century former home of the Count of Santovenia – now houses an elegant hotel facing Havana's oldest plaza. The best rooms have terraces overlooking the square.

Palacio del Marqués de San Felipe y Santiago Bejucal $$$
Historic **Map** 4 F2
Calle Oficios, esq. Amargura
Tel 7864 9191
W hotelmarquesdesanfelipe.com
This refined hotel offers comfortable rooms adorned with contemporary paintings. A great location on handsome Plaza San Francisco.

Centro and Prado

DK Choice

Casa 1932 $
B&B **Map** 3 C2
Calle Campanario 63 bajos, e/ San Lázaro y Lagunas
Tel 7863 6203
W casa1932.com
This beautiful 1930s home is furnished with a mix of Art Deco artifacts and 1950s memorabilia. The three rooms are stylish, comfortable and quiet. Breakfast is taken in the resplendent dining room, while coffee and beer can be enjoyed on the patio.

Casa Miriam y Sinaí $
B&B **Map** 3 C2
Calle Neptuno 521, e/ Campanario y Lealtad
Tel 7878 4456
The spacious colonial apartment is complemented with a pretty courtyard for relaxation. Delicious breakfasts and friendly hosts.

Sleek, minimalist decor, with a scattering of Spanish colonial antiques, at Casa Vitrales

Casa Concordia **$$**
Apartment **Map** 3 C2
Calle Concordia, e/ San Nicolás y
Manrique
Tel *5413 4724*
W casaconcordia.net
This stylish three-bedroom
apartment is run by a British-
Cuban couple and is close to
some of the city's best *paladares*.

Hotel Mercure Sevilla **$$**
Historic **Map** 4 D2
Calle Trocadero 55, e/Prado y Zulueta
Tel *7860 8560*
W mercure.com
Decorated in Sevillano tiles,
this striking Moorish hotel
stands tall above Prado. There's
a large pool and a great top-
floor restaurant.

Hotel Terral **$$**
Modern **Map** 3 B2
Malecón, esq. Libertad
Tel *7860 2100*
W habaguanexhotels.com
The glass-fronted Hotel Terral is
a welcome addition to the few
hotels on the Malecón. The
nautically-themed rooms have
balconies and stunning views.

La Maison Cuba **$$**
Apartment **Map** 4 D3
Calle Cienfuegos 207, piso alto, e/
Corrales y Apodaca
Tel *+33 6 11 738397*
W lamaisoncuba.com
A beautifully restored colonial
apartment that blends Spanish
colonial decor with French
antiques. It has a pretty
rooftop terrace.

DK Choice

Hotel Saratoga **$$$**
Luxury **Map** 3 D3
Prado 603, esq. Dragones
Tel *7868 1000*
W hotel-saratoga.com
Havana's top luxury hotel, the
Saratoga is in a fantastic central
location and its rooftop pool
offers great panoramas of the
Neo-Classical Capitolio and
bustling Prado. The opulent
rooms are decorated with
works by Cuban avant-garde
artists. The best rooms for views
are the Capitolio Suites.

Hotel Telégrafo **$$$**
Historic **Map** 4 D2
Prado 408, esq. San Miguel
Tel *7861 1010*
W hoteltelegrafo-cuba.com
Sitting in an enviable location
on the main Parque Central, this
grand colonial hotel features
large, modern rooms.

One of the plush Capitolio Suites in Hotel Saratoga

Iberostar Parque Central **$$$**
Modern **Map** 3 D2
Calle Neptuno, e/ Prado y Zulueta,
Parque Central
Tel *7860 6627*
W iberostar.com
The good service and excellent
buffet breakfast at the Iberostar
make up for the lack in ambience.
Rooftop swimming pools.

Vedado and Plaza

Casa Lilly **$**
B&B **Map** 2 D2
Avenida de los Presidentes 301,
apto. 13, e/ 13 y 15
Tel *7836 1136*
W casalilly.com
This 13th-floor apartment boasts
astounding views, and breakfasts
are sometimes served on the
balcony. The friendly host is happy
to provide the latest tips on
culture and nightlife.

Casa de Mélida Jordán **$**
B&B **Map** 1 C4
Calle 25 no. 1102, e/ 6 y 8
Tel *7836 1136*
This 1950s home is close to the
cemetery and the busy thorough-
fare of Calle 23. There is a great
covered patio for relaxation.

Central Yard Inn **$**
B&B **Map** 2 E2
Calle I, no. 457, e/ 21 y 23
Tel *7832 2927*
This fabulous hotel offers rooms
arranged over two floors, all
opening onto a leafy patio.
The hosts are welcoming and
speak English.

Vedado House Cultural **$**
B&B **Map** 1 C2
Calle 11 no. 702, apto. 4, esq. A
Tel *5243 3686*
Situated in the city's cultural and
nightlife district, this is a well-
ventilated modern apartment.
The owner is very hospitable.

DK Choice

Artedel Luxury Penthouse **$$**
Apartment **Map** 2 E2
Calle 17 no. 260, penthouse, e/ I y J
Tel *7830 8727*
W cubaguesthouse.com
This gorgeous 1950s penthouse,
which has a wrap-around
balcony and small plunge
pool, is a super stylish place
to stay. The huge suite, with
its private terraces, is the
room of choice. Guests can
rent individual rooms or the
entire apartment.

Hotel Habana Riviera **$$$**
Historic **Map** 1 B2
Paseo y Malecón
Tel *7836 4051*
W hotelhavanariviera.com
This 1950s mobster-built high-
rise hotel is a retro fan's dream,
with much of the original interior
having been preserved.

Hotel Nacional **$$$**
Historic **Map** 2 F1
Calle 21 y O
Tel *7836 3564*
W hotelnacionaldecuba.com
Havana's iconic hotel thrives
off its history and style; it has
hosted Hollywood stars and,
during the 1940s, a Mafia
convention. Today sipping
mojitos on the terrace is *de*
rigueur. The lobby is covered
in Sevillano tiles, and the best
rooms are on the executive floors.

Meliá Cohiba **$$$**
Luxury **Map** 1 B2
Avenida Paseo, e/ 1 y 3
Tel *7833 3636*
W meliacuba.com
It might be an ugly modern
high-rise, but Meliá Cohiba is
supremely comfortable. It has
several restaurants and a lovely
pool area.

For more information on types of hotels *see p*

Tryp Habana Libre $$$
Historic Map 2 F2
Calle L e/ 23 y 25
Tel *7834 6100*
ⓦ meliacuba.com
The former Havana Hilton played
host to Fidel Castro in the early
days of the 1959 Revolution. Now
guests come for the location in
the heart of Vedado and for the
cosy rooms with fantastic views.

Further Afield

Casa Bella Vista Havana $
B&B **Road Map** B3
Calle A 312, apto. 9, e/ 3 y 5, Miramar
Tel *7203 7581*
This great *casa particular is*
located close to several good
restaurants. If you like sea views,
ask for the room with a balcony.

Casa de Mileydis y Julito $
B&B **Road Map** B3
Calle 468, no.512, e/ 5ta y 7ma
Tel *7796 0100*
This *casa particular* is located
close to the beach. Rooms are
comfortable and there is one
with disabled access. It also has
a porch and a pretty garden.

Residencia Miramar $
B&B **Road Map** B3
Avenida 7, e/ 44 y 7, Miramar
Tel *7202 1075*
ⓦ habanamiramar.com
This delightfully stylish *casa
particular* is in a classic Miramar
residence. It has a 1950s Miami
feel and a pretty patio garden.

Hotel Atlántico $$
Resort **Road Map** B3
*Avenida de las Terrazas 21, Sta María
del Mar*
Tel *7797 1085*
ⓦ gran-caribe.com
A fun and popular all-inclusive
resort right on the white-sand
beaches of Santa María del Mar.

Villa Casablanca $$
Apartment **Map** 4 F1
Morro-Cabaña Park, House 29
Tel *5294 5397*
ⓦ havanacasablanca.com
Set on the eastern side of Havana
harbour, this apartment is
adorned with Cuban art and
has a gorgeous, wild garden.

Memorias Jibacoa $$$
Resort **Road Map** B3
*Arroyo Bermejo Beach, Santa Cruz
del Norte, Mayabeque*
Tel *(47) 295 122*
An attractive, low-key adults-only
resort, Memorias is set on a beautiful
curve of sand less than an hour's
drive from Havana. A great pool, a
good restaurant and friendly staff.

Western Cuba

DK Choice

**CAYO LARGO: Hotel Sol Cayo
Largo** $$$
Resort **Road Map** B3
Archipiélago de los Canarreos
Tel *(45) 248 260*
ⓦ meliacuba.com
This plantation-style, all-inclusive
resort on the beautiful Playa
Lindarena is made up of
comfortable bungalows built on
stilts. It is popular with families
and sports enthusiasts due to its
diving and sailing activities.
Guests can go for an ecological
excursion from here.

**CAYO LEVISA: Hotel Cayo
Levisa** $$
Resort **Road Map** A2
Carretera a Palma Rubia, La Palma
Tel *(48) 756 5010*
A short journey from the mainland,
this resort is set on its own island.
Location compensates for ordinary
bungalows and basic facilities.

**GUANAHACABIBES: Hotel María
La Gorda** $$
Resort **Road Map** A3
Península de Guanahacabibes
Tel *(48) 778 131*
ⓦ hotelmarialagorda-cuba.com
The *cabanas* at this diving hotel at
Cuba's western extreme are set
at the edge of a forest. Smaller
bungalows are situated on the
beach. Insect repellent is essential.

**ISLA DE LA JUVENTUD:
Hotel Colony** $
Resort **Road Map** A3
Tel *(46) 398 181*
This 1950s hotel is a dive resort for
the spectacular Punta Francés and
its numerous scuba spots *(see p154)*.

**ISLA DE LA JUVENTUD:
Villa Peña** $
B&B **Road Map** B3
*Calle 10 no. 3710, e/ 37 y 39,
Nueva Gerona*
Tel *(46) 322 345*
Two comfortable rooms in this
lovely, family-run B&B just north
of the town centre.

**PINAR DEL RÍO:
Hotel Aguas Claras** $
Countryside **Road Map** A3
Carretera a Viñales km 7.5
Tel *(48) 778 427*
This is an attractive countryside
resort with bungalows scattered
in a garden around a pool. The
neighbouring farm and extensive
grounds make this an excellent
choice for families.

Hotel Atlántico, swimming pool and beach
with palm trees, Playas del Este, Havana

**PINAR DEL RÍO:
La Nonna Máximo** $
B&B **Road Map** A3
*Gómez no.161, e/ Rafael Ferro y
Ciprian Valdés*
Tel *(48) 770 777*
There are three rooms in this
lovely house, each with a private
bathroom. Breakfast is served on
a pretty, plant-filled terrace.

**PINAR DEL RÍO:
Hotel Vueltabajo** $$
Historic **Road Map** A3
Calle Martí 103, esq. Rafael Morales
Tel *(48) 759 381*
Guests at this smart historic hotel
are welcome to swim in the pool
at the nearby Hotel Pinar del Río.

**SIERRA DEL ROSARIO:
Hotel Moka Villas** $
Countryside **Road Map** A2
*Las Terrazas, Autopista Nacional
Habana-Pinar del Río km 51*
Tel *(48) 578 600*
Stay in a pleasant room in one
of the attractive homes that
surround the lake in the eco-
community of Las Terrazas.

DK Choice

**SIERRA DEL ROSARIO:
Hotel Moka** $$
Countryside **Road Map** A2
*Las Terrazas, Autopista Nacional
Habana-Pinar del Río km 51*
Tel *(48) 578 600*
ⓦ hotelmoka-lasterrazas.com
This dramatic hotel with a tree
growing through the lobby is
at the centre of the eco-
community Las Terrazas
(see p141). It makes a great
base for exploring the
mountains of the Sierra del
Rosario, and a dip in the hotel's
pool is most welcome after a
walk in the woods.

SOROA: Villa Soroa $$
Countryside **Road Map** A2
Carretera de Soroa km 8, Candelaria,
Tel *(48) 523 534*
Set in lush gardens, the modern
bungalows and accommodation
blocks of the Villa Soroa circle the
central swimming pool, which is
popular with locals at weekends.

VIÑALES: Casa Oscar Jaime Rodríguez $
B&B **Road Map** A3
Calle Adela Azcuy 43
Tel *(48) 793 381*
Centrally-located, this *casa* has
a great dining room and offers
delicious communal meals.
Helpful and friendly owners.

VIÑALES: Villa el Isleño $
B&B **Road Map** A3
Carretera a Viñales km 25
Tel *(48) 793 107*
This modern house and garden
back onto the Valle de Viñales,
offering a chance to witness
tobacco farming first-hand.

VIÑALES: Villa Haydée $
B&B **Road Map** A3
Chiroles Rafael Trejo no. 139
Tel *(48) 695 200*
This spacious villa, with mountain
views, has five rooms with private
bathrooms. The well-informed
owner can also organize salsa
lessons, tours and excursions.

VIÑALES: Los Jazmines $$
Countryside **Road Map** A3
Carretera a Viñales km 23
Tel *(48) 796 411*
Set high up on a hill, this hotel
offers stunning views of the
valley. The best lodgings here are
the bungalows in the garden. The
swimming pool terrace is perfect
for sipping rum cocktails or a
beer, while watching the sun set.

SAN DIEGO DE LOS BAÑOS: Islazul Hotel Mirador $$
Countryside **Road Map** A2
Calle 23 y Final
Tel *(48) 778 338*
This is a small, simple hotel, in the
tranquil town of San Diego de los
Baños. Guests love to relax by the
hotel's large swimming pool.

Central Cuba – West

CAYO SANTA MARÍA: Villa Las Brujas $$
Resort **Road Map** D3
Cayo Las Brujas, Villa Clara
Tel *(42) 350 199*
This small resort sits isolated on
its own curve of white-sand
beach. Its reasonable prices and

proximity to the marina and
mainland make it very popular.

DK Choice
CAYO SANTA MARÍA: Meliá Buenavista $$$
Resort **Road Map** D3
Punta Madruguilla
Tel *(42) 350 700*
[w] meliacuba.com
One of Cuba's most stylish
resorts, the Buenavista fronts a
stunning stretch of white sand.
The hotel is adults-only and all-
inclusive, and offers extensive
sports facilities, including hire
of snorkelling equipment, and
a climbing wall and tennis
court. Excursions to observe
local wildlife are also laid on.
The Villa Zaida del Río stands
alone, so it is perfect for couples.

DK Choice
CIENFUEGOS: Bella Perla Marina $
B&B **Road Map** C3
Calle 39 no. 5818, esq. 60
Tel *(43) 518 991*
Waldo and Amileidis run a very
professional *casa*, which is
furnished with beautiful antiques,
and is just a short walk from
downtown. The stand-out room
is the suite with a mezzanine,
private balcony and Jacuzzi.
The hosts are eager to share their
comprehensive knowledge
about the city with guests.

CIENFUEGOS: Casa de la Amistad $
B&B **Road Map** C3
Avenida 56 no. 2927, e/ 29 y 31
Tel *(43) 516 143*
The friendly owners of this
charming B&B offer one of the
best welcomes in Cuba. Their
colonial apartment is a stone's
throw from the central park.

CIENFUEGOS: Casa Piñeiro $
B&B **Road Map** C3
*Calle 41 no. 1402, e/ 14 y 16,
Punta Gorda*
Tel *(43) 513 808*
[w] casapineiro.com
An enthusiastic cook and an
astute host, Jorge Piñeiro runs
one of the best-known *casas* in
the city, and is a great source of
information for guests. Booking
is essential.

CIENFUEGOS: Hotel Jagua $$
Historic **Road Map** C3
Calle 37, e/ 0 y 2, Punta Gorda
Tel *(43) 551 003*
The 1950s Hotel Jagua is at the
foot of Punta Gorda, and has
outstanding views of the bay
of Cienfuegos and the Moorish
Palacio de Valle. The location
makes up for the lacklustre rooms.

CIENFUEGOS: Hotel Unión $$
Historic **Road Map** C3
Calle 31, esq. 54
Tel *(43) 551 020*
[w] hotellaunion-cuba.com
This beautiful colonial boutique
hotel is located in the historic
heart of Cienfuegos. The lovely
pool and bar terrace alone would
make a stay worthwhile.

MATANZAS: Casa Alma $
B&B **Road Map** B2
Calle Milanés (C/83) 29008, e/ 290 y 292
Tel *(45) 290 857*
An elegant colonial home, flood-
lit by *vitrales* (stained-glass, half-
moon windows), in the centre
of Matanzas. The owner is very
helpful and knowledgeable.

MATANZAS: Hotel Encanto Velasco $$
Historic **Road Map** B2
*Calle Contreras e/ Santa Teresa y
Ayuntamiento*
Tel *(45) 253 880*
Facing the main park, this19th-
century colonial hotel has a
fantastic restaurant (*see p273*).

Stylish rooms overlooking the sea at Meliá Buenavista, Cayo Santa María

PENÍNSULA DE ZAPATA: Casa Luis $
B&B   Road Map C3
Carretera Cienfuegos, e/ Carretera Playa Larga y Playa Girón
Tel *(45) 984 258*
Luis and Marley serve outstanding shellfish dinners at their *casa* close to Playa Girón. They can also set up diving and *cenote* exploration.

PENÍNSULA DE ZAPATA: Hotel Horizontes Playa Larga $$
Countryside   Road Map C3
Playa Larga
Tel *(45) 987 294*
This is a basic hotel with bungalows dotted across the grounds. It is a lacklustre complex and usually only a base for divers, birders and fishermen.

PENÍNSULA ZAPATA: Hotel Playa Girón $$
Countryside   Road Map C3
Playa Girón
Tel *(45) 984 110*
This austere hotel comprises bungalows scattered across grassland fronting the beach.

REMEDIOS: Villa Colonial Frank y Arelys $
B&B   Road Map C3
Calle Antonio Maceo 43 e/ General Carrillo y Fe del Vall
Tel *(42) 396 274*
W casa-villacolonial.com
This beautiful 1839 colonial home in the town centre is run by the hospitable Frank and Arelys, who are both mines of information.

SANTA CLARA: Casa de Consuelo Ramos y Nelson $
B&B   Road Map C3
Calle Independencia 265, apto. 1, e/ Pedro Estevez (Unión) y San Isidro
Tel *(42) 202 064*
Che Guevara stayed in this modern house in 1959. The host might even serenade you while you enjoy his garden.

SANTA CLARA: Casa Mercy $
B&B   Road Map C3
Calle Eduardo Machado (San Cristóbal) 4, e/ Cuba y Colón
Tel *(42) 216 941*
This *casa* in the centre of town has two rooms – both of which enjoy access to a terrace where cocktails are served.

SANTA CLARA: Hostal Florida Center $
B&B   Road Map C3
Calle Maestra Nicolasa (Candelaria), e/ Colón y Maceo
Tel *(42) 208 161*
W hostalfloridacenter.com
The rooms here are embellished with antiques and open

onto the flower-filled patio. Meals are served by the gregarious owner and his staff.

SANTA CLARA: Hotel América $$
Family   Road Map C3
Calle Mujica, e/ Colon y Maceo
Tel *(42) 201 585*
Located close to all the historic sights, this is a comfortable no frills hotel. Its real appeal is the swimming pool – the only one in downtown.

SIERRA DEL ESCAMBRAY: Hotel Hanabanilla $
Countryside   Road Map C3
Salto del Hanabanilla, Manicaragua, Villa Clara
Tel *(42) 208 461*
This is a basic, modern hotel set in the Escambray mountains. Guests can explore the neighbouring lake and trails.

VARADERO: Beny's House $
B&B   Road Map C2
Calle 55 no. 124, e/ 1 y 2
Tel *(45) 611 700*
W benyhouse.com
Perfectly located, near Parque Josone and the beach, this B&B has three rooms and a neat garden.

VARADERO: Casa Mary y Ángel $
B&B   Road Map C2
Calle 43 no. 4309, e/ 1 y 2
Tel *(45) 612 383*
W casamaryyangel.com
A short walk from the beach, this family home has a patio and terrace for meals and sunbathing.

VARADERO: Casa Menocal $
B&B   Road Map C2
Calle 14 no. 1, e/Camino del Mar y Playa
Tel *(45) 613 164*
With an excellent location on the beach, this is a cheaper option in Varadero and has basic facilities.

An elegant Garden Villa at Meliá Paradisus Varadero

VARADERO: Varadero 60 $
B&B   Road Map C2
Calle 60 y 3
Tel *(45) 613 986*
This great guesthouse is right on the beach, very close to Parque Josone. Guests have the advantage of a good on-site *paladar* but, unusually, breakfast is not offered.

VARADERO: Meliá Península Varadero $$
Resort   Road Map C2
W meliacuba.com
Key-West style buildings dot this family resort. The extensive children's facilities include a splendid themed playground.

VARADERO: Meliá Varadero $$
Resort   Road Map C2
Carretera de las Morlas
Tel *(45) 667 013*
W meliacuba.com
This all-inclusive hotel has a great location right on the best stretch of Varadero beach, as well as a very good buffet restaurant.

DK Choice

VARADERO: Mansión Xanadú $$$
Historic   Road Map C2
Autopista del Sur km 8.5
Tel *(45) 667 388*
W varaderogolfclub.com
This unusual half-board hotel, on a small bluff overlooking turquoise seas, has one of the best addresses in town, and enjoys spectacular views. Part of the golf club, its guest-rooms, dining room and popular terrace bar feel more like a private house – as it once was – than a hotel.

VARADERO: Meliá Paradisus Varadero $$$
Resort   Road Map C2
Punta Francés
Tel *(45) 668 700*
W meliacuba.com
One of the few truly stylish resorts in Varadero, the Paradisus caters for families and couples, offering sports, a spa and a children's club. The two Garden Villas provide total seclusion.

VARADERO: Royal Hicacos $$$
Resort   Road Map C2
Carretera de las Morlas km 15
Tel *(45) 668 844*
W royalhicacosresort.com
This resplendent all-inclusive, couples-only resort is on one of the most secluded sections of the peninsula. Extensive sporting and entertainment facilities.

Guide *see p256*

Central Cuba – East

CAMAGÜEY: Casa Dalgis $
B&B   Road Map D3
Independencia no. 251 (altos) e/
Herrumans Aguero y General Gómez
Tel *(32) 285 732*
Overlooking Plaza Maceo, this
first-floor apartment has dazzling
antique furniture, original floor
tiles and chandeliers, and a
terrace with a stunning view.
Friendly and helpful owners.

CAMAGÜEY:
Hostal Ivan y Lucy $
B&B   Road Map D3
Calle Alegría 23, e/ Ignacio
Agramonte y Montera
Tel *(32) 283 701*
[W] ivanylucy.com
Decorated with Spanish colonial
furniture, this 1940s home has
two rooms on offer. After a day's
sightseeing, relax amid the plants
on the patio.

CAMAGÜEY: Gran Hotel $$
Historic   Road Map D3
Calle Maceo 67, e/ Ignacio
Agramonte y General Gómez
Tel *(32) 292 093*
[W] hotelgran.com
This historic central hotel –
opened in 1938 with its grand
lobby and indoor swimming
pool – is an institution. Rooms
are compact but comfortable.

DK Choice

CAYO COCO:
Meliá Cayo Coco $$$
Resort   Road Map D3
Cayo Coco
Tel *(33) 301 180*
[W] meliacuba.com
The rooms at this adults-only,
all-inclusive resort (one of
Meliá's flagships), are set in two-
storey *casas* straddling a salt
water lagoon. The rest of the
stylish facilities, including
the bars and restaurants,
front the beautiful Las
Coloradas beach. Watersports
are popular here, too.

CAYO COCO: Memories
Flamenco Beach Resort $$$
Resort   Road Map D3
Cayo Coco
Tel *(33) 304 100*
[W] memoriesresorts.com
This modern, all-inclusive
resort is a favourite with
families because of its various
kids' clubs and baby-sitting
services. Some rooms offer
a magnificent view of
the ocean.

A pretty room with views of the lagoon at Meliá Cayo Coco

CAYO GUILLERMO: Meliá Cayo
Guillermo $$$
Resort   Road Map D3
Cayo Guillermo
Tel *(33) 301 680*
[W] meliacuba.com
This all-inclusive hotel on an idyllic
stretch of Cayo Guillermo beach
is popular with both couples and
families because of the wide
range of facilities on offer.

CAYO GUILLERMO: Sercotel
Club Cayo Guillermo Hotel $$$
Resort   Road Map D3
Cayo Guillermo
Tel *(33) 301 712*
[W] sercotelhotels.co.uk/hotels/
cuba/Cayo-guillermo/club-cayo-
guillermo
This low-key resort is on a lovely
stretch of beach and is renowned
for kitesurfing, which attracts
sporty types and thrill seekers.
Guests can choose between
the two-storeyed *casas* and the
wooden cabins overlooking sea.

JARDINES DE LA REINA:
Avalon $$$
Boat   Road Map D4
Jardines de la Reina
This floating hotel offers
accommodation as part of a
fishing or diving package either
on one of their five yachts or
aboard a seven-cabin hotel. It is
a pristine marine environment.

MORÓN: Alojamiento Valor
Morales $
B&B   Road Map D3
Luz Caballero no. 40b e/ Libertad y
Agramonte
Tel *(33) 504 181*
This professionally run household
offers four en-suite rooms. The
amenities include a small pool,
terrace, garden and an on-site
restaurant. The knowledgeable
and helpful owner, Maite, speaks
English and Italian. Paid parking
is available.

PLAYA ANCÓN: Brisas Trinidad
del Mar $$$
Resort   Road Map C3
Península Ancón
Tel *(41) 996 500*
[W] hotelescubanacan.com
Built to resemble a mini Trinidad,
this is the most attractive of the
few resorts on the white-sand
curve of Playa Ancón.

PLAYA SANTA LUCÍA: Hotel
Brisas Santa Lucía $$
Resort   Road Map E3
Avenida Turística, Nuevitas
Tel *(32) 336 317*
This is the most pleasant resort
on Playa Santa Lucía. The rooms
at all-inclusive Brisas are in blocks
facing the white-sand beach.

SANCTI SPÍRITUS:
Hostal Boulevard $
B&B   Road Map C3
Calle Independencia 17, altos sur, e/
Avenida de Los Mártires y E V Muñoz
Tel *(41) 335 120*
[W] hostalboulevard.com
In the heart of the city, this
welcoming B&B has a balcony
overlooking Plaza Sánchez.

SANCTI SPÍRITUS:
Hostal D'Martha $
B&B   Road Map C3
Calle Plácido 69, e/ Calderón y Tirso
Marín
Tel *(41) 323 556*
This professionally-run modern
casa has two bedrooms with
balconies and a terrace with a
majestic view of the mountains.

SANCTI SPÍRITUS:
Hostal Paraíso $
B&B   Road M
Calle Máximo Gómez 11 Sur, e
Honorato y Cervantes
Tel *(41) 334 658*
[W] paraiso.trinidadhosta
This central, stylish 18
decorated with colo
ings. It has two inte

SANCTI SPÍRITUS:
Hostal e Plaza $$
Historic **Road Map** C3
*Calle Independencia 1, esq. Avenida
de los Mártires, Plaza Sánchez*
Tel *(41) 327 102*
A pretty colonial hotel in the city
centre. Its interior courtyard offers
a retreat from the heat, and the
terrace is a popular spot for a drink.

SANCTI SPÍRITUS:
Hotel Encanto Rijo $$
Historic **Road Map** C3
Honorato del Castillo 12
Tel *(41) 328 588*
One of the most attractive hotels
in the country, this 1827 mansion
is embellished in precious woods.
The best rooms have balconies
overlooking the park.

DK Choice

TRINIDAD: Casa Font $
B&B **Road Map** C3
*Calle Gustavo Izquierdo 105, e/
Piro Guinart y Simón Bolivar*
Tel *(41) 993 683*
casafonttrinidad.jimdo.com
The vast 18th-century home
run by the Font family features
beautiful colonial furniture and
heirlooms, with an elegant bed
decorated in mother-of-pearl in
one of the bedrooms. Breakfast
is served in the patio garden.

TRINIDAD: Casa Muñoz $
B&B **Road Map** C3
*Calle José Martí 401, e/ Fidel Claro y
Santiago Escobar*
Tel *(41) 993 673*
w casa.trinidadphoto.com
Hosts Julio and Rosa offer four airy
en-suite rooms in their colonial
home. Julio knows all about the
town's colonial heritage, and he
offers photography tours and
horse-riding trips. A horse is
stabled in the garden.

TRINIDAD: Casa Santana $
B&B **Road Map** C3
*Calle Maceo 425, e/ Fco. J. Zerquera y
Colón*
Tel *(41) 994 372*
The welcoming hosts at this B&B
offer two rooms on the first floor
of their colonial home. The leafy
patio is a bonus.

TRINIDAD:
...tal las Mercedes $
Road Map C3
*...amilo Cienfuegos 272, e/
...Francisco Cadahía*
...3 107
...e the city centre, Las
...s one colonial room
...ern rooms. The patio
...from the heat.

see p256

TRINIDAD: Casa la Casona $$
B&B **Road Map** C3
Calle Frank País 759
Tel *(41) 998 692*
w lacasona759trinidad.com
Perfect for horse lovers, this is a
beautiful ranch-style property, with
bungalows or rooms in the main
house. Guests can ride the owner's
horses, and enjoy a dip in the pool.

TRINIDAD: Iberostar Grand
Hotel Trinidad $$$
Luxury **Road Map** C3
*Calle José Martí 262, e/ Lino Pérez y
Colón, Parque Céspedes*
Tel *(41) 996 073*
w iberostar.com
Facing the leafy Parque Céspedes,
this is a smart colonial-style hotel.
Its buffet-style restaurant is one of
the top eating spots in town. For
guests 15 years and above.

Eastern Cuba

BARACOA: Casa Daniel $
B&B **Road Map** F4
*Calle Céspedes 28, e/ Rubert López y
Maceo*
Tel *(21) 641 443*
A central, modest home with two
comfortable rooms. The host is
very friendly and knowledgeable.

BARACOA: Casa Nilson $
B&B **Road Map** F4
*Calle Flor Crombet 143, e/ Ciro Frías y
Pelayo Cuervo*
Tel *(21) 643 123*
Nilson's *casa* boasts an enormous
en-suite room and a smaller
bedroom. The restaurant with
sea views is a huge draw.

BARACOA: Hostal la
Habanera $$
Historic **Road Map** F4
*Calle Los Maceos 124, e/ Maraví y
Frank País*
Tel *(21) 645 273*
Centrally located, this is a small
historic hotel. Opt for a room

The opulent lobby at the Iberostar Grand
Hotel, Trinidad

with a balcony overlooking the
main street.

BARACOA: Hotel El Castillo $$
Historic **Road Map** F4
Loma de Paraíso
Tel *(21) 645 194*
A converted castle, the Castillo has
panoramic views of Baracoa and
the sea. Rooms in the original
building surround the swimming
pool, while newer, larger rooms are
on a hillside nearby.

DK Choice

BARACOA: Villa Maguana $$
Resort **Road Map** F4
Playa Maguana, km 20
Tel *(21) 641 204*
w villamaguana.com
Four simply furnished rustic
villas sit in their own private
cove just a short walk to the
coconut palms, food shacks and
white sand strip of Maguana
Beach, 20 km (12 miles) from
Baracoa. An unusual retreat for
Cuba – perfect for couples.

BAYAMO: Casa Olga Celeiro
Rizo $
B&B **Road Map** E4
Calle Parada 16 e/ Martí y Mármol
Tel *(23) 423 859*
This welcoming first-floor flat has
a breezy balcony. It is one block
from the main town square and
faces the Casa de la Trova.

BAYAMO: Hotel Encanto
Royalton $$
Historic **Road Map** E4
*Calle Antonio Maceo 53, e/ General
García y José Palma*
Tel *(23) 422 290*
Rooms are small but comfortable
in this pleasant colonial hotel. The
real draw is its fantastic location,
right on the main Parque Céspedes.

CAIMANERA: Hotel
Caimanera $
Modern **Road Map** F4
Loma Norte
Tel *(21) 499 415*
This is one of Cuba's most
extraordinary hotels *(see p242)* –
it is the closest accommodation
to the US Naval Base at
Guantánamo Bay.

CAYO SAETÍA: Villa Cayo
Saetía $$
Resort **Road Map** F4
Cayo Saetía, Mayari
Tel *(24) 516 900*
w cayosaetia.org
These attractive bungalows are
set amid an African safari park,
and close to sands bordered by
boulders and turquoise seas.

GIBARA: Los Hermanos $
B&B   Road Map E3
Calle Céspedes 13, e/ J Peralta y Luz Caballero
Tel *(24) 844 542*
This enormous colonial home has four spacious rooms and a communal patio. Short walk to the sea.

GUANTÁNAMO: Casa Lisset Foster $
B&B   Road Map F4
Calle Pedro A Pérez 761, e/ Prado y Jesús del Sol
Tel *(21) 325 970*
Lisset offers a warm, helpful welcome at her downtown home, with three rooms to rent.

GUARDALAVACA: Club Amigo Atlántico $$
Resort   Road Map F3
Playa Guardalavaca
Tel *(24) 430 180*
[w] clubamigo.gvc.tur.cu
This sprawling, revamped complex is located in front of a great strip of beach. The rooms and the food are basic, but for the price, it cannot be beaten.

GUARDALAVACA: Sol Río de Luna y Mares $$
Resort   Road Map F3
Playa Esmeralda
Tel *(24) 430 060*
[w] melia.com
With games, watersports facilities and a children's club, this large hotel is popular with families. It is set on a stunning beach.

GUARDALAVACA: Hotel Brisas Guardalavaca $$$
Resort   Road Map F3
Calle 2 no. 1, Playa Guardalavaca
Tel *(24) 430 218*
[w] brisasguardalavaca.com
Right next to the larger, busier Atlántico, this is a family-focused hotel. The accommodation blocks huddle around four swimming pools and face the beach.

GUARDALAVACA: Paradisus Río de Oro $$$
Resort   Road Map F3
Playa Esmeralda
Tel *(24) 430 090*
[w] melia.com
This luxurious adults-only resort sits in lush gardens. Private coves dotted along the shoreline make perfect retreats for relaxation. It has a fine Japanese restaurant.

HOLGUÍN: Villa Liba $
B&B   Road Map E4
Calle Maceo 46, esq. Línea, Reparto El Llano
Tel *(24) 423 823*
This 1950s home is a peaceful haven, a short walk from the centre.

Colonial-style decor at Casa Muñoz, Trinidad

Enjoy massages, and the hosts' home-cooked Lebanese food.

HOLGUÍN: Villa Mirador de Mayabe Countryside $
                       Road Map E4
Altura de Mayabe km 8.5
Tel *(24) 422 160*
This simple hilltop hotel offers bungalows in flower-filled gardens just a short drive from downtown Holguín. A peaceful location with views of the palm-studded plain below.

NIQUERO: Hotel Niquero $
Budget   Road Map E4
Calle Martí 100
Tel *(23) 592 367*
A basic town-centre hotel, the Niquero is the only accommodation close to the Parque Nacional Desembarco de Granma.

PILÓN: Club Amigo Marea del Portillo $$
Resort   Road Map E4
Marea del Portillo km 12.5, Pilón
Tel *(23) 597 008*
This remote black-sand resort enveloped by the surrounding Sierra Maestra mountains is popular with vacationing Canadians.

DK Choice

SANTIAGO: Casa Colonial Maruchi $
B&B   Road Map F4
Calle Hartmann (San Félix) 357, e/ Trinidad y San Germán
Tel *(22) 620 767*
A gorgeous Spanish colonial home in the historic city centre, with an internal patio surrounded by flourishing ornamental plants. One room is set up on its own private terrace; the other two face the patio and are furnished with colonial beds and antique lace.

SANTIAGO: Roy's Terrace Inn $
B&B   Road Map F4
Calle Diego Palacios 177, e/ Mariano Corona y Padre Pico
Tel *(22) 620 522*
There are modern rooms across three terraces at this home known for its excellent service and home-cooked meals.

SANTIAGO: Hostal San Basilio $$
Historic   Road Map F4
Calle Bartolomé Masó 403, e/ Carnicería y Porfirio Valiente (Calvario)
Tel *(22) 651 702*
This small, elegant city centre hotel is adorned with 19th-century Spanish colonial furnishings.

SANTIAGO: Hotel Casa Granda $$
Historic   Road Map F4
Calle Heredia no. 201, esq. San Pedro
Tel *(22) 686 600*
Santiago's iconic hotel has a roof garden, perfect for cocktails at dusk, and a parkside terrace.

SANTIAGO: Hotel San Juan $$
Family   Road Map F4
Carretera de Siboney km 1.5
Tel *(22) 687 200*
[w] islazul.cu
This modern hotel with a pool is a short distance from the historic centre. Perfect for those with kids.

DK Choice

SIERRA MAESTRA: Brisas los Galeones $$
Resort   Road Map F4
Carretera Chivirico km 72
Tel *(22) 326 160*
An all-inclusive hotel perched on a bougainvillea-fringed hilltop and set against a mountain backdrop. The small beach is reached by descending more than 100 steps, while the pool area is perfect for relaxation.

For more information on types of hotels *see*

WHERE TO EAT AND DRINK

In traditional Cuban cooking, rice and beans are the staples rather than bread, and the most common dishes are meat-based. Seafood also features heavily with shrimp, lobster and fish dishes found on a large proportion of restaurant menus. Different influences can be seen in Cuban cooking and there are local variations, especially in the east of Cuba. Food is rarely spicy. Besides international dishes, local menus generally feature some specialities of *comida criolla* (Creole cuisine, *see p266*). Places offering food range from state-run restaurants and hotel restaurants (usually comfortable and elegant), to *paladares*, or privately run restaurants (ranging from informal to chic) that serve home cooking. In Havana, kiosks selling pizza, sandwiches and ice creams are now everywhere. The restaurants listed on pages 270–75 are arranged by area and cater to a variety of different budgets.

Restaurants and Cafés

Cuba's state-run restaurants used to have a bad reputation. However, standards have improved in many, particularly in Havana. This is partly due to competition from private *paladares*, and some well-regarded state-run restaurants, for example La Imprenta *(see p270)*.

Some of Havana's most delightful restaurants are housed in colonial buildings. Many have a view or a patio, and live music is often performed.

The restaurants in luxury hotels are usually high-quality and feature international dishes along with a good wine list. As an alternative to formal à la carte dining, many hotels offer buffets, which in Cuba are called *mesa sueca* (smorgasbord), where, for a fixed price, you can eat anything from pasta to roast pork with rice and black beans.

Some of the capital's most famous bars have a separately managed restaurant, such as

Elegant dining room with grand piano, Restaurante de Iberostar, Trinidad *(p275)*

La Bodeguita del Medio and El Floridita in Havana *(see p270)*, and La Terraza de Cojímar *(see p272)*. These are open all day serving snacks and cocktails, and offer a full menu for lunch and dinner.

Paladares

The cheapest and best places offering Cuban cooking are called *paladares*. Traditionally, these are private restaurants offering a fixed price or à la carte menu inside Cuban homes. Dishes are often simple but can be surprisingly good – and often better quality than their state-run equivalents. However, be wary of people who accost you in the street and offer to show you a *paladar*: once there, your helpful guide will receive a commission and your bill will cost a few pesos more. Furthermore, they may ask you to treat them to dinner!

Since Raúl Castro's moderate economic reforms in 2011, the private dining scene in Cuba has been transformed. *Paladares* have become more sophist-icated, and in some cases, have taken over entire apartments. They are now found in beach resorts such as Varadero where, previously, they had been banned. The greatest changes can be seen in Trinidad and Havana. In the capital, entrepreneurs have increased the range of dining options by opening chic dining establish-ments, putting Havana on the

Private Homes

It often happens that private homes offering rooms to let *(casas particulares, see p254)* also provide main meals as well as breakfast. Since the food usually eaten by the home owners is plainer than the food offered to guests, you will be asked to let them know in advance whether

...nsive buffet at the Meliá Paradisus resort in Varadero *(p260)*

Beautiful location at the Castillo del Morro outside Santiago de Cuba (p275)

you intend to eat in or out. In general, the standards of cleanliness in authorized private homes are good. The quality of the food varies quite a lot: you may be lucky and eat extremely well, feasting perhaps on fresh lobster or prawns.

Snacks and Fast Food

All kinds of snacks are widely available in Cuba. Virtually all cafeterías, inside and outside hotels, sell the classic Cuban sandwich with cheese and ham. Another popular choice is a hot dog with mustard, ketchup and chips, to eat in or take away.

There is also an American-style fast food chain, El Rápido. While it's the antithesis of the fine dining, for a few convertible pesos you can buy fried chicken with a side dish of papas fritas (chips), beer or refresco (soft drink). These places also offer perros calientes (hot dogs), hamburguesas (hamburgers), pizza and ice cream.

Along the major roads and on the motorways you will find the equivalent of small motorway cafés selling soft drinks, beer, fruit juice, pizza, ice cream and, sometimes, sandwiches.

The best ice cream is sold at the Coppelia parlours, which are found in many Cuban cities (the one in Havana is an institution, see p102). They are highly popular so be prepared to wait in a queue.

Lastly, you can buy food along the road from people who run small stalls in front of their homes. Papas rellenas (potato balls stuffed with meat), croquettes, home-made pizzas, cakes, coconut sweets, peanut brittle and biscuits are some of the filling and tasty Cuban snacks on offer.

The same foods can be found on sale in the fruit and vegetable markets (agromercados). However, standards of hygiene may vary considerably.

Paying

In many restaurants and paladares, expect to pay in cash with convertible pesos. Only the better restaurants and hotels accept credit cards. At markets or on the road you can pay in Cuban pesos, although convertible pesos would also be accepted (change may be given in Cuban pesos). Restaurant bills may include a service charge.

When to Eat

Desayuno (breakfast) is served from 6 to 9am at most hotels. Lunch is served from noon to 1:30pm, but many restaurants and paladares have adapted to tourists' needs and serve food well into the afternoon.

Dinner is eaten from 7 to 9pm. Do not expect to find a restaurant willing to serve you a meal after 11pm, except perhaps in Havana.

Recommended Restaurants

The restaurants listed in this guide are among the best in Cuba, from simple paladares to decadent fine dining establishments. Whether you are looking for authentic comida criolla, fresh seafood or a range of international options, the following pages offer lots of choice.

Where a restaurant is in some way exceptional – perhaps for its setting, the quality of the food or its good-value menus – it has been highlighted as DK Choice.

Terrace seating at Waco's Club in Varadero (p274)

The Flavours of Cuba

Cuba's *mercados agropecuarios* (farmers' markets) are a cornucopia of fruits and vegetables fresh from the fields. Tomatoes, cucumbers and squash are staples, along with ripe *plátanos*, the humble yet ubiquitous plantain (a relative of the banana). Exotic fruits enliven stalls with their distinctive bouquets and hues. Poultry run around freely until ready for the pot, while home-fed pigs provide pork – the main meat. The government maintains a monopoly on the sale of beef, prawns and lobster, making them hard to find outside the state-run restaurants.

Guava paste and white cheese

A young Cuban farmer displays his harvest of plantains

Comida Criolla

Traditional Cuban *comida criolla* (creole cuisine) is the main cuisine, based mainly on the frying pan and using simple ingredients, with little regional variation – not least due to national shortages of everything. It is a melding of Spanish, African and indigenous, Pre-Columbian Indian influences. Local produce such as *calabaza* (a squash), yucca (cassava) and maize (sweetcorn), tomatoes, potatoes and bell peppers are combined with pumpkin and cabbage introduced by the Spanish. African vegetables include *malanga* (a root vege-table with a delicate flavour), *plátano vianda* (a variety of plantain that is eaten cooked) and *quimbombó* – okra, often called ladies' fingers. Typically flavoured with peppers, onion, oregano and cumin, *criolla* dishes are usually served with boiled potatoes or other root vegetables (*viandas*). Simple salads vary according to the time of year: in winter they might well feature lettuce, tomatoes, white cabbage and, at times, beets; in the summer they may include green beans, carrots, cucumber and avocado.

Custard apple · Plantains · Limes · Watermelon · Pineapple
Mango
Papaya

Some of the tropical fruits that add flavour and colour to Cuban cuisine

Cuban Dishes and Specialities

Cuba's zesty cultural mix has produced some superb national dishes, such as aromatic *ropa vieja*. Pork (*cerdo*) is a Cuban favourite, especially smoked loin (*loma ahumado*) roasted on a spit. The main accompaniment is white rice with black beans (*frijoles*), often cooked together to form *moros y cristianos*, known as *congrí* or *congrí oriental* when the beans are red. Another common accompaniment is fried plantains, which are sometimes mashed and re-fried in patties (*tostones*). Rice dishes, and even succulent roast chicken cooked in orange sauce, are often enlivened ...o, a zesty sauce of garlic, oil and bitter orange. Main ...usually followed by a fruit plate, or a relatively simple ...as flan or a fruit preserve served with cheese.

...ck beans

Filete de pescado grillé may be any grilled fillet of white fish, here served with *tostones* and white cabbage salad.

Fruit and vegetable stall at a Havana farmers' market

The most ubiquitous meat on the island is ham; pork is also served roasted *(cerdo asado),* diced *(masas)* or as thin fillets *(chuletas).* Chicken is usually coated with flour and fried in oil *(pollo empanado),* although it is also occasionally served fricasséed, accompanied by French fries. Fish and seafood, notably lobster and shrimp, is typically served in a tomato sauce *(enchilada)* or fried, grilled or baked with butter and garlic, as with sea bass and mahi mahi, which is almost always grilled. *Camarones* (meaty prawns) are served in many different ways – stewed, grilled, baked or boiled and garnished with mayonnaise. Breakfasts are usually limited to simple omelettes and a fruit plate, perhaps with bread and local white cheese (similar to Greek féta) plus yogurt.

Baracoan Specialities

Baracoan fare, from the far eastern side of the island, revolves around the use of coconut and cocoa, cultivated since Pre-Columbian times by the indigenous peoples.

Cubans fishing in the evening on the Malecón in Havana

Coconut milk flavours *bacán,* a tortilla of baked plantain filled with spiced pork and cooked wrapped in a banana leaf. It is also used as a base in which to simmer spinach-like *calalú.* Red plantains, known as *plátanos manzanos,* are mashed with coconut milk to make *rangollo.* Cocoa forms the base of Baracoa's delicious chocolate and is the key ingredient of *chorote,* an ambrosial drink thickened with cornflour. Mixed with copious amounts of sugar (sometimes with the addition of grated orange peel and nuts), shredded coconut makes a delicious sweet.

ON THE MENU

Coco rallado Grated coconut in syrup, served with cheese.

Cucurucho Shredded coconut with orange, fruits, nuts and honey, pressed in a palm leaf.

Filete uruguayano Pork or fish cutlet stuffed with ham and cheese, then baked.

Frituras de malanga Grated *malanga* mixed with egg and garlic, then deep fried.

Potaje Thick soup made from black or red beans with garlic, onions and herbs and spices.

Ropa vieja Shredded beef marinated and cooked with spices and onion, served with white rice.

Ajiaco consists of vegetables, including plantains, which are simmered with meat and herbs to form a rich stew.

Cerdo asado is roast pork, usually served quite simply with rice and beans and often an orange sauce.

Flan de huevos appears on most menus. It is a typically Spanish dessert, similar to crème caramel but sweeter.

What to Drink in Cuba

A wide range of drinks, both alcoholic and non-alcoholic, are available in Cuba. Imported wine is available in restaurants and *paladares*. To avoid mild stomach upsets and more serious ailments such as dysentery, it is best to avoid tap water and drink bottled water instead. Visitors should be careful, too, about buying drinks such as fruit juice or fruit shakes and ice-cream from street or market stalls. In bars and cafés not up to international standards – especially in eastern Cuba – avoid ice in drinks like cocktails. In such places, it is advisable to stick to pre-packaged drinks, draught beer or rum.

Preparing refreshing *guarapo*, or sugar cane juice

Beer

Beer *(cerveza)* is the most widely seen and popular drink in Cuba. It is drunk very cold and at all hours of the day, as well as during meals. There are excellent bottled and canned Cuban lager beers, such as Cristal, Lagarto, Mayabe and Bucanero, which is stronger and drier – *fuerte* – than the others. A drink similar

to beer is *malta*, a very sweet, fizzy malt-based drink that is popular with all Cubans, including children. *Malta* is sometimes mixed with condensed milk to be used as an energizer and tonic.

Bucanero (strong) and Cristal (light) canned beer

Packaged Soft Drinks

Soft drinks – lemon, orange and cola – called *refrescos*, either Cuban or imported, are sold canned. The Tropical Island range of fruit juices, packaged in cartons, is excellent. All kinds of fruits are used: mango, *guayaba* (guava), pineapple, apple, pear, orange, grapefruit, banana with orange, tropical cocktail, tamarind, peach and tomato. The most common brand of bottled water sold, still *(sin gas)* or sparkling *(con gas)*, is Ciego Montero. San Pellegrino mineral water is also available, but is comparatively expensive.

Hot Drinks

Hotel bars serve coffee or American coffee. The coffee served in private homes or sold on the streets is usually strong and has sugar already added. It is served in a tiny coffee cup. For a dash of milk, ask for a *cortado*; order a *café con leche* for a more milky coffee. *Sin azúcar* means "without sugar".

Black tea is generally not on any restaurant or café menu, nor can black teabags be found in supermarkets. It is best to pack your own. Herbal tea is more readily available; camomile tea *(manzanilla)*, for example, is easy to find.

Spirits

The most widespread and popular spirit in Cuba is rum. There are several different types *(see p79)*: the youngest – *silver dry* and *carta blanca* – are used in cocktails, while the aged rums (*carta oro*, five years old, and *añejos*, at least seven years old) are mostly drunk neat. Besides Havana Club and Varadero, which are known worldwide, there are many other different brands of rum in Cuba. Among the best are Matusalém, an upmarket, aged rum from Santiago with a smooth flavour; and Mulata, which is very popular.

A "poor relation" of rum is *aguardiente*, which is stronger and quite sour, and drunk mainly by locals. *Guayabita* is a speciality of Pinar del Río, made from rum and guava fruit *(see p145)*. In addition, a range of very sweet flavoured liqueurs (such as coconut, mint, banana and pineapple) is available, usually served with ice or in cocktails.

A bottle of aged rum

Fruit Shakes and Squashes

The most common fruit squash is fresh lemonade, made with lime, sugar, water and ice. More nutritious drinks are the *batidos*, which are shakes made from fresh fruit, often mango and papaya. Milk, sugar and *guanábana*, not an easy fruit to find, make a drink called *champola*. Coconut juice with ice is a delicious, refreshing drink. Another typical Cuban drink is *guarapo*, which is made by squeezing fresh sugar cane stalks with a cane crusher. It makes for a refreshing and energizing drink, but it is exceedingly sweet. To tone down the sweetness, Cubans add a few drops of lime or a dash of rum.

Coconut juice served in the shell

Cuban Cocktails

Cuba has been famous for its rum since the 1500s, although the rum the pirates loved so much was not the same as today's, but a bitter and highly alcoholic drink, at times sweetened with sugar and *hierba buena*, a variety of mint common in Latin America. This explosive mixture, jokingly called *draguecito* or "little dragon", is probably the ancestor of the *mojito*, one of the most famous Cuban cocktails. In the early 1900s a Cuban engineer named Pagluchi and his American colleague Cox, while making an inspection near Santiago, mixed rum with sugar and lemon, and named the drink after the place they were in, Daiquirí. In the 1920s, during American Prohibition, Cuba, which had become an "off limits" paradise for drinkers, developed and refined these early cocktails and went on to create others. In parallel, the role of the professional barman *(cantinero)* acquired increasing importance.

Daiquirí frappé is served in a chilled cocktail glass. White rum is placed in an electric blender and mixed with one teaspoon of sugar, five drops of maraschino, lime juice and crushed ice. Hemingway liked to drink this cocktail at El Floridita *(see p270)*.

Mojito comes in a highball glass. White cane sugar is mixed with lime juice and a crushed stem of mint. To this is added white rum, and the glass is then filled with sparkling mineral water and chopped ice and the drink is stirred. The "temple" of the *mojito* is La Bodeguita del Medio *(see p270)*.

Cuba Libre is made from rum and cola mixed with ice and lime juice. The drink was supposedly invented by US soldiers who took part in the Cuban wars of independence (1898). The name, Free Cuba, comes from the nationalists' motto.

Havana Especial is made with pineapple juice, silver dry rum, a dash of maraschino and crushed ice, mixed and served in a tall, slim glass. This cocktail has a very delicate flavour.

The Cantineros' Club

This club for professional barmen *(cantineros)* was founded in Havana in 1924 and sponsored by a group of Cuban distilleries and breweries. By the early 1930s the club had a central office on the Prado. The club's aims remain unchanged today: defence of the interests of its members, professional training for young people (who are required to learn the recipes for at least 100 cocktails), and English lessons. The club also currently promotes the Havana Club International Grand Prix.

The Bodeguita del Medio barman with a *mojito*

Canchánchara is made by the bar of the same name in Trinidad *(see p186)* with rum, lime, honey and water. It is served in an earthenware cup.

Where to Eat and Drink

Havana
La Habana Vieja

DK Choice

304 O'Reilly $
Spanish **Map** 4 E2
Calle O'Reilly, e/ Habana y Aguiar
Tel 5264 4745
This stylish café-cum-restaurant
celebrates crab *empanadillas*,
and fresh *ceviche*. Their outstanding cocktails include the
unusual melon mojitos and
bloody Marys garnished with
octopus. There are a limited
number of tables, so it is best
to book well in advance.

Café Bohemia $
Italian **Map** 4 E3
San Ignacio 364, Plaza Vieja
Tel 7860 3722
Tucked away on the patio of an old
colonial mansion, this café and
delicatessen serves dishes named
after famous Cuban texts. It is a
good breakfast spot.

El Chanchullero $
Spanish **Map** 4 D3
Calle Teniente Rey (Brasil) 457
Tel 7872 8227
A buzzy hole-in-the-wall tapas joint
serving herby sausages, tuna tapas
and other light bites. Arrive early
as they run out of the best dishes.

La Bodeguita del Medio $$
Cuban Creole **Map** 4 E2
*Calle Empedrado 207, e/ San Ignacio
y Cuba*
Tel 7866 8857
This restaurant *(see p69)* has retained
much of the alluring character that
made it popular with the likes of
Ernest Hemingway and Gabriel
García Márquez. The Cuban meat
and seafood dishes are good.

La Imprenta $$
Cuban Creole **Map** 4 F2
*Calle Mercaderes, e/ Lamparilla y
Amargura*
Tel 7864 9851
A surprisingly good state-run
restaurant based in a former printing
works in the heart of the old town.
The *solomillo* (steak) is outstanding.

El Jardín del Eden $$
Kosher **Map** 4 E2
*Hotel Raquel, Calle San Ignacio 103,
esq. Amargura*
Tel 7860 8280
A range of delicious dishes are
served in an elegant dining room

featuring Art Nouveau stained glass
featuring Hebrew symbols. The
borscht and *baba ghanoush* come
highly recommended.

La Mina $$
Cuban Creole **Map** 4 F2
*Calle Oficios 109, esq. Obispo, Plaza
de Armas*
Tel 7862 0216
At the heart of the tourist circuit,
this is a lively place with friendly
staff. The fish, pork and chicken
dishes are surprisingly well priced.

Café del Oriente $$$
Cuban Creole **Map** 4 F2
Calle Oficios 112, esq. Amargura
Tel 7860 6686
An old-world café on Plaza San
Francisco that serves some of
Havana's most sophisticated
cuisine. The menu features rabbit,
beef and plenty of fish. European
dishes are also available.

La Dominica $$$
Italian **Map** 4 E2
Calle O'Reilly 108, esq. Mercaderes
Tel 7860 2918
There's an emphasis on seafood at
this friendly restaurant. Start with the
smoked salmon and follow with the
prawn and lobster pasta. A good
range of Spanish and Chilean
wines. Live music on most nights.

El Floridita $$$
Seafood **Map** 4 D2
*Avenida de Bélgica (Monserrate), esq.
Obispo*
Tel 7867 1299
A plush restaurant located in the
back room of a classic bar where
Hemingway famously sipped
daiquiris. Serves lavish dishes such
as prawns in orange-cream sauce
and Lobster Thermidor.

Price Guide
Prices are based on a three-course
meal for one, including a cocktail,
tax and service.

$	up to $15
$$	$15–$25
$$$	over $25

Ivan Chef Justo $$$
International **Map** 4 D2
Calle Aguacate 9, esq. Chacón
Tel 7863 9697
This place is set in an elegant old
Havana home filled with antiques.
The menu includes pastas, paellas
and good meat dishes.

DK Choice

Paladar Doña Eutimia $$$
Cuban Creole **Map** 4 E2
*Callejón del Chorro 60c, Plaza de
la Catedral*
Tel 7861 1332
This beautifully decorated little
hideaway, tucked away in a
corner of Plaza de la Catedral
(see pp66–7), dishes up superb
Cuban cuisine. Be sure to try
the tasty *ropa vieja* (shredded
beef) stewed in a sauce of
onions, peppers and tomatoes.
A wide selection of wines and
cocktails are available. Reservations are strongly advised.

El Patio $$$
Cuban Creole **Map** 4 E2
*Calle San Ignacio 54, Plaza de la
Catedral*
Tel 7867 1035
A charming restaurant in a
beautiful spot facing Catedral de
San Cristóbal *(see p68)*. Cuban
cuisine is the speciality, but the
menu offers everything from
sandwiches to lobster.

Dining on the covered terrace at seafood restaurant El Templete, Havana

El Templete $$$
Seafood **Map** 4 F2
Avenida del Puerto 12–14, esq.
Narcisco López
Tel 7864 7777
Overlooking the harbour, this
restaurant offers some of the
best fish in La Habana Vieja.
The lobster salad is excellent.

Centro Habana and Prado

Café Arcángel $
International **Map** 3 C2
Concordia no. 57, e/ Aguila y Avenida
de Italia (Galiano)
Tel 7862 6355
Unlike the other frenetic venues
of the city, Café Arcángel has a
refreshingly laid back atmosphere and charming vintage
decor. It dishes up a good
selection of American breakfasts,
coffee, pastries and sandwiches.

Castropol $$
International **Map** 3 C1
Malecón 107, e/ Calles Genios y
Crespo
Tel 7861 4867
This popular restaurant enjoys
spectacular views of Vedado and
the Atlantic Ocean, but it's the
seafood and the lamb ribs you
will savour most. Excellent
service and a good wine list.

DK Choice

Paladar San Cristóbal $$
Fine Dining **Map** 3 C3
Calle San Rafael 469, e/ Lealtad y
Campanario
Tel 7867 9109 **Closed** *Sun*
A first-rate *paladar* set in a
beautiful colonial home
decorated with antiques,
paintings and even a Santerían
altar. The food served up in
these sumptuous surroundings
is always excellent, and the
service is flawless. By Cuban
standards the wine list is
outstanding, with fine wines
available by the glass. Don't
miss the superb *solomillo*
(sirloin steak).

La Terraza $$
Barbecue **Map** 4 D2
Prado 309, esq. Virtudes
Tel 7862 3626
A little-known spot, this
restaurant is set over three
storeys and has a lovely terrace
filled with leafy plants. Tender
barbecued meat and fish dishes
are the specialities. The cocktails
are also excellent – request the
mojito frappé.

Casa Miglis $$$
Scandinavian **Map** 3 B2
Calle Lealtad 120, e/ Animas y Lagunas
Tel 7864 1486
An uber-stylish *paladar* set in a
colonial terraced house. Meatballs,
seafood casserole and grilled fish
are just a few of the tantalizing
dishes available. The trendy bar is
also a great place to enjoy a few
tragos (rum drinks).

La Guarida $$$
International **Map** 3 B2
Calle Concordia 418, e/ Gervasio y
Escobar
Tel 7866 9047
From the outside, it looks like a
semi-derelict building, but climb
the grand marble staircase inside
(and just keep climbing) to find
one of Cuba's liveliest restaurants.
Every dish here bursts with flavour.

Roof Garden Hotel Sevilla $$$
French **Map** 4 D2
Calle Trocadero 55, e/ Paseo del
Prado y Agramonte
Tel 7860 8560, ext. 164
This ritzy gourmet restaurant has
beautiful vaulted ceilings, regal
decor and spectacular panoramic
views of Havana. Good, well
presented food. Try the rum lobster.

Vedado and Plaza

Paladar la Casa $$
International **Road Map** B2
Calle 30 no. 865, e/ Calles 26 y 41,
Nuevo Vedado
Tel 7881 7000
An exceptional family-run *paladar*
in the heart of Nuevo Vedado.
The extensive menu includes
rabbit in mushroom sauce, smoked
salmon, paella and risotto.
Thursday nights feature a
spectacular sushi spread served
by staff wearing Japanese dress.

Paladar Casa Lala $$
Cuban Creole **Map** 1 A5
Calle 24 no. 360, e/ 21 y 23
Tel 7830 1410
This small alfresco restaurant offers
a menu that changes weekly, with
tempting dishes such as battered
sardines, pumpkin soup, grilled
tuna and rabbit – all are cooked to
perfection. Often has a live band.

Paladar Gringo Viejo $$
Cuban Creole **Map** 2 D2
Calle 21 no. 454, e/ E y F
Tel 7831 1946
This sweet little hideaway decorated
with paintings and clocks is in
the basement of the owner's
home. The *ropa vieja* is particularly
tasty. The menu is seasonal and
changes each day based on the
freshest produce available.

Tables set outdoors at the Palador
San Cristóbal

Paladar Mediterráneo Havana $$
Mediterranean **Map** 2 D2
Calle 13 no. 406, e/ F y G
Tel 7832 4894
A great restaurant in a smart Vedado
home serving up exquisite seafood,
fresh pasta and home-made
goat's cheese. The chef and waiters
are friendly and hospitable. The
lunchtime menu is excellent
value and a children's menu is
also available.

El Cocinero $$$
Cuban Creole **Map** 1 A5
Calle 26, e/ 11 y 13
Tel 7832 2355
Housed in an old peanut oil factory,
this restaurant is among the best
in the city. Boasting an exclusive
clientele, it serves a well thought-
out menu featuring duck confit
blinis, goat's cheese and papaya
salad and lobster bisque.

Paladar Café Laurent $$$
International **Map** 2 E2
Calle M no. 257, e/ 19 y 21
Tel 7832 6890
The stunning rooftop views of
Vedado from the smart alfresco
dining terrace are not the only draw
at this penthouse *paladar*. The food
is delicious, the 1950s retro feel is
stylish, service is faultless, and the
lunchtime set menu is excellent
value. The Uruguayan beef is
highly recommended.

Paladar le Chansonnier $$$
International **Map** 2 E1
Calle J no. 257, e/ 15 y Línea
Tel 7832 1576 **Closed** *Sun*
A culinary star on the Havana
dining scene, this chic *paladar*
decorated with the work of Cuba's
contemporary artists, and popular
with expats, tourists and Havana's
celebrity set. Mango and avocado
salads plus succulent duck in
orange sauce are some of the
mouthwatering dishes on offer.

For more information on types of restaurants *see pages 264–5*

Paladar Decamerón   **$$$**
Cuban Creole   **Map** 1 B2
Calle Línea 753, e/ Paseo y Calle 2
Tel *7832 2444*
A pretty little restaurant set in
two small dining rooms and filled
with paintings, clocks and antiques.
Decamerón is a top spot to enjoy
large salads and good-value
ropa vieja. There's also a range
of international dishes on the
menu and an extensive wine list.

Starbien   **$$$**
Fine Dining   **Map** 2 D4
Calle 29 no. 205 e/ B y C
Tel *7830 0711*   **Closed** *Sun*
A stylish, swanky mansion offering
very good Cuban food and a range
of Mediterranean options. The
speciality is *masas de cerdo* (sautéed
Cuban pork), but the tapas, seafood
and other meat dishes are all very
good. Food is beautifully presented
and the service is impeccable.

Further Afield

El Aljibe   **$$**
Cuban Creole   **Road Map** B2
Avenida 7, e/ 24 y 26
Tel *7203 1583*
This huge ranch-style restaurant
serves great *comida criolla*, including
its famous eponymous dish
pollo asado el Aljibe (roast chicken
in delicious Aljibe sauce) the
ingredients of which are top secret.
The friendly staff will keep topping
up your plate at no extra cost.

DK Choice

**Paladar la Corte
del Principe**   **$$**
Italian   **Road Map** B2
Avenida 9 y 74, Playa
Tel *5255 9051*   **Closed** *Mon*
One of Cuba's best Italian
restaurants, located in a quiet
corner of Miramar. The menu of
fresh, authentic cuisine changes
daily and usually includes a
variety of *bruschetta*, seafood,
antipasti and home-made
pasta. A popular place with a
lively, bustling atmosphere.

La Terraza de Cojímar   **$$**
Seafood   **Road Map** B2
Calle Real 161, Cojímar
Tel *7766 5151*
La Terraza trades off its Ernest
Hemingway connections – it was
the author's favourite restaurant
in Cojímar – but it is actually a
good little spot serving up tasty
soups, fish dishes and luridly
coloured desserts. It also offers
an excellent view of the bay that
inspired the author's classic novel
The Old Man and the Sea.

La Divina Pastora   **$$$**
International   **Map** 4 F1
*Avenida Monumental, Parque Morro
Cabaña*
Tel *7860 8341*
With a fabulous view of the old
town and harbour from the
lower ramparts of La Cabaña,
this delightful restaurant co-
operative offers a range of
seafood and meat dishes. A
popular choice is the fish fillet
stuffed with cheese and smoked
ham. Request a table on the
pretty terrace.

DK Choice

Paladar la Fontana   **$$$**
Fine Dining   **Road Map** B2
Calle 3 no. 305, esq. Calle 46
Tel *7202 8337*
La Fontana is part eatery, part
bar and is consistently rated
as one of the best private
restaurants in Havana. Its
grilled meats and seafood
are superb, the ambience is
always spot on, and the
service is exceptional. The
late night bar pulls in local
fashionistas and artists, as
well as foreign visitors.

Paladar Río Mar   **$$$**
Fine Dining   **Road Map** B2
3 y Final no. 11, La Puntilla
Tel *7209 4838*
A glamorous Miramar restaurant
set in a stylish modern mansion
with a fabulous terrace overlooking the sea. Well-executed
dishes include a full range of
shellfish, and Cuban favourites
such as *ropa vieja*.

Tocororo   **$$$**
Cuban Creole   **Road Map** B2
Avenida 3 y 18
Tel *7204 2209*   **Closed** *Sun*
A smart eatery in a fabulously
decorated Miramar mansion. The
emphasis is on Creole ingredients,
particularly lobster. The bar next
door is popular with Cuba's
wealthy creative set.

Western Cuba

**ISLA DE LA JUVENTUD:
El Cochinito**   **$**
Cuban Creole   **Road Map** A3
*Calle José Martí esq. 24,
Nueva Gerona*
Tel *(46) 322 809*
This no-frills Cuban restaurant on
the main street in Nueva Gerona
serves up only one dish – pork
with rice and beans – a classic
Cuban staple.

Place settings at refined Paladar le
Chansonnier, Havana

**ISLA DE LA JUVENTUD:
Paladar El Chévere**   **$**
Cuban Creole   **Road Map** A3
*Calle 37 no. 2417, e/ 24 y 26,
Nueva Gerona*
Tel *(46) 328 326*
A *paladar* in a family home
offering a wide variety of
dishes, including chicken
breast in sauces, fish and lamb
chops. Modest surroundings,
but a warm welcome and very
good food.

PINAR DEL RÍO: El Mesón   **$**
Cuban Creole   **Road Map** A3
*Calle Martí y Comandante Pinares
(antigua calle Cavada)*
Tel *(48) 822 867*
A family-run *paladar* serving
traditional fare to locals and
travellers. The pork chops
and roast pork are the most
popular dishes. Generous
portions and excellent value
for money.

PINAR DEL RÍO: Rumayor   **$**
Cuban Creole   **Road Map** A3
Carretera a Viñales Km 1.5
Tel *(48) 763 051*   **Closed** *Tue*
Rumayor is a huge ranch-like
restaurant offering a range
of popular dishes including
the speciality – smoked chicken.
Later in the evening, the place
transforms into a kitsch cabaret
with dancing acts.

**SIERRA DEL ROSARIO: Fonda
Las Mercedes**   **$$**
Cuban Creole   **Road Map** A3
*Comunidad Las Terrazas, Provincia
Artemisa*
Tel *(48) 578 647*   **Closed** *low season*
Just below Hotel Moka *(see p258)*,
the family-run Las Mercedes
offers beautiful views of the
valley and a range of Creole
dishes, including delicious
ropa vieja.

DK Choice
SIERRA DEL ROSARIO:
El Romero $$
Vegetarian **Road Map** A3
Comunidad Las Terrazas,
Provincia Artemisa
Tel *(48) 578 555*
The only authentic organic
vegetarian restaurant in Cuba, El
Romero is a real find. Engineer
turned vegetarian guru Tito
Nuñez Guda has produced a
delicious menu of bean pan-
cakes, root vegetable burgers
and paella, along with juices
made from local ingredients. The
best tables are on the balcony
overlooking the village.

VIÑALES: Balcón del Valle $
Cuban Creole **Road Map** A3
Km 23 de la carretera a Viñales
Tel *(48) 695 847*
Enjoy the lovely view overlooking
the *mogotes* of the Viñales Valley,
from the tables and chairs perched
under the mango trees.

DK Choice
VIÑALES: Finca Agroecológica
el Paraíso $$
Cuban Creole **Road Map** A3
Carretera Al Cementerio Km 1 ½,
Viñales
Tel *5418 8997*
Along with its incredible
panoramas of the Viñales Valley,
this working organic farm
boasts some of the best *comida
criolla* (Puerto Rican food)
in Cuba. The expertly cooked
dishes are served in a herb
garden where sweet fragrances
envelop diners at dusk. Portions
are very generous.

VIÑALES: El Olivo $$
Mediterranean **Road Map** A3
Calle Salvador Cisneros 89
Tel *(48) 696 654*
Choose from lasagne, pasta
bolognese and fresh salads, or go
for roast lamb with caramelized
onions. Dine alfresco on the tiny
terrace, or in the airy dining room.

Central Cuba – West

CIENFUEGOS: Aché $$
Seafood **Road Map** C3
Calle 38 no. 4106, e/ 41 y 43
Tel *(43) 526 173*
Decorated with the works of local
artists, this ranch-style restaurant
specializes in fish dishes, including
barbecued prawns in garlic and
chilli. Excellent *mojitos.*

CIENFUEGOS: Bouyon 1825 $$
Seafood **Map** C3
Calle 25 no. 5605, e/ 56 y 58
Tel *(43) 517 376* **Closed** *Sun*
A *paladar* known for its grilled
food and shellfish. Opt for the
speciality dish, fish fillet 1825 –
red snapper accompanied by
prawns and baked in a delicious
cheese and garlic sauce.

DK Choice
CIENFUEGOS: Villa Lagarto $$
Cuban Creole **Road Map** C3
Calle 35 no. 4b, esq. Litoral,
Punta Gorda
Tel *(43) 519 966*
Tables face on to the bay of
Cienfuegos from the tip of
Punta Gorda at this family home
turned *paladar* – one of the
very best restaurants in town.
The hard-working staff serve up
a delicious fixed-price menu of
several small starters, a main,
dessert and coffee. The grilled
fish is particularly good.

CIENFUEGOS: El Tranvía $$$
Cuban Creole **Road Map** C3
Calle 37 (Prado) no. 4002, e/ 40 y 42
Tel *(43) 524 920*
A popular and lively tram-themed
paladar, with an antique tram on
the rooftop terrace and staff
wearing tram driver uniforms.
Live music plays most nights in
the colonial dining room.

MATANZAS: El Bukan $$
Cuban Creole **Road Map** B2
Calle 110, e/ 127 y 129, Playa
Matanzas
Tel *5296 3126* **Closed** *Tue*
With amazing views of the bay
of Matanzas, this local *paladar*
offers an excellent selection of
seafood and meat dishes. The
place is immaculately presented
and the staff are professional
and courteous. Book ahead.

MATANZAS: Hotel Encanto
Velasco $$
Fine Dining **Road Map** B2
Calle Contreras, e/ Santa Teresa y
Ayuntamiento
Tel *(45) 253 880*
The Hotel Encanto Velasco
(see p259) was resurrected
from ruins a few years ago,
and dining in the colonial
splendour of the main hall is
a real treat. Delicately prepared
Cuban fare, and friendly,
hospitable waiters.

PENÍNSULA DE ZAPATA:
Complejo Turística
Caleta Buena $
Cuban Creole **Road Map** C3
Playa Girón
Tel *(45) 915 589*
A restaurant that sits next to the
natural pools and sunbathing
decks of Caleta Buena *(see p169).*
A perfect place to take a break
from diving or snorkelling. Serves
a good daily buffet.

REMEDIOS: La Paloma $$
Cuban Creole **Road Map** C3
Calle Balmaseda 4, e/ Ramiro
Capablanca y Máximo Gómez
Tel *(42) 395 490*
Built in 1875, this gorgeous
family home serves up
beautifully prepared pork, lamb,
chicken and fish dishes. Dine
near the fountain in the shaded
courtyard, or in the pretty
dining room filled with paintings
and antiques.

SANTA CLARA: La Aldaba $
Cuban Creole **Road Map** C3
Calle Luis Estévez 61, e/
Independencia (Boulevard) y Martí
Tel *(42)208 686*
A pretty rooftop restaurant at the
top of a lovely restored colonial
home, filled with period details
and antique furniture. Although
primarily a B&B, this place offers
great-value Cuban dishes.

The classic dining hall of the refurbished Hotel Encanto Velasco, Matanzas

For more information on types of restaurants *see pages 264–5*

DK Choice

**SANTA CLARA: Hostal-
Restaurant Florida Center** $
Seafood **Road Map** C3
*Calle Maestra Nicolasa
(Candelaria) 56, e/ Colón y Maceo*
Tel *(42) 208 161*
Angel, the gregarious owner
of this delightful restaurant
and B&B *(see p260)*, has run this
place well for years. Dinner is
served on the garden patio,
which is filled with flourishing
orchids. The huge lobster
dishes are very popular.

**VARADERO: Paladar la Casona
del Arte** $$
International **Road Map** B2
Calle 47, e/ 1 y Playa
Tel *(45) 613 986*
This pretty blue wooden home
close to Varadero's beach is now
a *paladar*. The house speciality
is fish fillet with prawns and
cheese. Dine on the veranda
for the best experience.

**VARADERO: Paladar
Nonnatina** $$
Italian **Road Map** B3
Calle 38 no. 5, e/ 1 y Playa
Tel *(45) 612 450*
This Italian-run pizza and pasta
place is located close to the
beach and is a popular spot to
enjoy thin-crust pizzas, *bruschetta*
and lasagne. It also offers plenty
of vegetarian options.

**VARADERO: Paladar
Varadero 60** $$
International **Road Map** B3
Calle 60 y 3
Tel *(045) 613 986*
A romantic *paladar* with an
extensive menu and a lovely
alfresco terrace. The sirloin steak
comes highly recommended.

Art Deco light fixtures in Restaurante de
Iberostar, Trinidad

VARADERO: Casa de Al $$$
Fine Dining **Road Map** B3
Avenida Kawama
Tel *(45) 668 018*
Said to be the home of Al Capone,
this elegant stone house, situated
on the beachfront, offers a gangster-
inspired menu of dishes such as
Lucky Luciano filet mignon.

VARADERO: Dante $$$
Italian **Road Map** B3
Parque Josone, Avenida 1, e/ 56 y 58
Tel *(45) 667 738*
This place is in an idyllic spot next
to the lake in Parque Josone. It
serves a great selection of thin-
crust pizzas, pastas and salads.

VARADERO: Esquina Cuba $$$
Cuban Creole **Road Map** B3
Avenida 1, esq. 36
Tel *(45) 614 019*
This open-sided restaurant is
dominated by a white and red
classic car and 1950s memorabilia.
Tasty *comida criolla* fare and an
excellent wine list.

**VARADERO:
Mesón del Quijote** $$$
Seafood **Road Map** B3
*Carretera las Américas, Reparto
la Torre*
Tel *(45) 667 796*
This lovely hilltop restaurant has
great views over Varadero and
dishes up excellent lobster and
shellfish. The steak is also superb.

**VARADERO: El Toro
Steakhouse** $$$
Steakhouse **Road Map** B3
Avenida 1, esq. 25
Tel *(45) 667 145*
The lacklustre decor pales into
insignificance when presented
with the real attraction here: first-
rate imported Canadian steaks
cooked to perfection.

VARADERO: Waco's Club $$$
Cuban Creole **Road Map** B3
Avenida 3, e/ 58 y 59
Tel *(45) 612 126*
The son of Olympic rower Roberto
Ojeda González – otherwise
known as Waco – runs this *paladar*
specializing in seafood. The
signature dish is lobster baked with
cream, mushrooms and cheese.

Central Cuba – East

**CAMAGÜEY: La Campana de
Toledo** $$
Cuban Creole **Road Map** D3
Plaza San Juan de Dios
Tel *(32) 286 812*
Boliche mechado (beef garnished
with bacon) served with fries

and *congrí* (rice and black
beans) is the dish of choice
at this restaurant in an 18th-
century townhouse on a
beautiful plaza.

CAMAGÜEY: La Isabela $$
Italian **Road Map** D3
*Calle Ignacio Agramonte, e/
Independencia y Lopez Recio*
Tel *(32) 221 540*
This cinema-themed restaurant
in the centre of town offers
good quality thin-crust pizzas
and pasta. The restaurant,
located at the site of Camagüey's
first movie theatre, has director-
style seats and is a perfect place
for children.

**CAMAGÜEY: Paladar
Restaurant 1800** $$
Cuban Creole **Road Map** D3
Plaza San Juan de Dios
Tel *(32) 283 619*
Shellfish and salads are the
speciality at this pleasant
paladar in a historic building
facing Iglesia de San Juan
de Dios *(see p207)*.

**SANCTI SPÍRITUS:
Méson de la Plaza** $
Wine Bar **Road Map** C3
*Calle Máximo Gómez 34, e/
Honorato y Cervantes*
Tel *(41) 328 546*
Located in the heart of town, this
Spanish *bodega* offers hearty
dishes at its long wooden tables.
Try the beef stewed with corn.

**TRINIDAD: Paladar Sol
Ananda** $$
International **Road Map** C3
Calle Real 45, Plaza Mayor
Tel *(41) 998 281*
The extensive, eclectic menu at
this restaurant features *gazpacho*
and fish cakes alongside Cuban
classics. It is elegantly furnished
with a *mudéjar* ceiling.

DK Choice

**TRINIDAD: Taberna
La Botija** $$
Mediterranean **Road Map** C3
*Calle Amargura 71b, esq. Boca
(Calle Piro Guinart)*
Tel *5283 0147*
This 24-hour *taverna* has a
buzzing atmosphere, rustic
decor and boasts its own
live band.The menu
includes pizzas, pastas and
a wide selection of tapas
dishes, perfect for sharing.
Portions are generous and
prices reasonable. It is very
popular so arrive early to
avoid the queues.

DK Choice

TRINIDAD: Paladar Restaurant Vista Gourmet $$$
Cuban Creole   Road Map C3
Callejón de Galdós 2b, e/ Ernesto V. Muñoz y Callejón de los Gallegos
Tel *(41) 996 700*
Situated on a hill affording spectacular views of the old city, this well-run *paladar* offers tasty Cuban creole fare and superb spicy *mojitos*. Dinner includes a buffet spread of mediocre starters and desserts, but the main à la carte courses shine. The chicken stuffed with *tapenade* and honey is divine. Vista, Gourmet's owner, is a sommelier, so wine aficionados will very much enjoy their visit.

TRINIDAD: Restaurante de Iberostar $$$
Buffet   Road Map C3
Iberostar Grand Hotel Trinidad, Calle José Martí 262, e/ Lino Pérez y Colón
Tel *(41) 996 073*
A decadent buffet-spread in a five-star hotel set in a beautifully renovated colonial mansion *(see p262)*. Savour international cheeses, decent burgers, a smorgasbord of desserts and beef *carpaccio*, a rarity in Cuba.

Eastern Cuba

BARACOA: Paladar el Buen Sabor $$
Cuban Creole   Road Map F4
Calle Calixto García 134 (altos)
Tel *(21) 641 400*
A small family-run *paladar* on a pretty roof terrace with sea views. It is the perfect place to sample Taíno dishes rarely served in other parts of Cuba. Try the hearty *ajiaco*, a filling meat and vegetable soup.

DK Choice

BARACOA: El Poeta $$
Baracoan   Road Map F4
Calle Maceo 159, esq. Ciro Frías
Tel *(21) 643 017*
Lively El Poeta serves up well-made local cuisine in its restaurant, daubed in Cuban poems and graffiti. Tender fish is served in coconut sauce (a local speciality), and the scrumptious coconut ice cream is attractively served inside a coconut shell. To top it all, owner Pablo will craft a poem for you while you eat.

Waco's Club, Varadero, specializing in Cuban seafood dishes

BARACOA: Restaurant Al's $$
Seafood   Road Map F4
Calle Calixto García 158a e/ Céspedes y Coroneles Galano
Tel *5290 3651*
The friendly and entertaining owner, Al, serves up fresh barbecued seafood on his roof terrace, which has uninterrupted views to the sea.

BAYAMO: San Salvador de Bayamo $
Cuban Creole   Road Map E4
Calle Maceo 107, e/ Martí y Mármol
Tel *(23) 426 942*
Set in a historic colonial-style building, this restaurant offers one of the largest menus in Bayamo, with a range of seafood and meat dishes, pastas and pizzas.

HOLGUÍN: Paladar San José $$
Barbecue   Road Map E4
Calle Agramonte 188, e/ Maceo y Libertad
Tel *(24) 424 877*
A centrally located *paladar*, serving excellent grilled food and a range of fresh fish dishes and flavourful meats. The roast lamb is superb.

SANTIAGO DE CUBA: El Barracón $
Afro-Cuban   Road Map F4
Avenida Victoriano Garzón
Tel *(22) 661 877*
Santiago de Cuba's most unusual restaurant has been, somewhat questionably, decked out to resemble slave barracks. However, El Barracón serves hearty Afro-Cuban meat stews at great prices.

SANTIAGO DE CUBA: El Morro $
Cuban Creole   Road Map F4
Carretera al Morro Km 7.5
Tel *(22) 691 576*
The only restaurant at Castillo del Morro offers a fixed-price menu of shellfish or meat accompanied with rice and vegetables, followed by dessert.

SANTIAGO DE CUBA: Paladar Doña Martha $
Cuban Creole   Road Map F4
Calle 3 no. 152, e/ Calle 8 y Avenida Manduley, Reparto Vista Alegre
Tel *(22) 641 177*
In Santiago's smart neighbourhood of Vista Alegre, this popular *paladar* has an appealing ranch atmosphere, and serves excellent grilled meats and seafood.

SANTIAGO DE CUBA: Paladar el Holandés $$
Cuban Creole   Road Map F4
Calle Heredia 251, esq. Calle Hartmann
Tel *(22) 624 878*
Close to the Casa de la Trova, this charming restaurant in a colonial home dishes up a wide range of creole cuisine. Try the pork bathed in salsa, and enjoy live music from the jazz club across the street.

SANTIAGO DE CUBA: El Palenquito $$
Cuban Creole   Road Map F4
Avenida del Río 28, e/ 6 y Carretera del Caney, Reparto Pastorita
Tel *(22) 645 220*
A mini ranch in the back garden of a family home, El Palenquito has a lovely, tranquil setting, surrounded by hibiscus and hummingbirds. The menu comprises good value Cuban food, such as pork fricassee and prawns in garlic.

SANTIAGO DE CUBA: El Zunzún $$
Fine Dining   Road Map F4
Avenida Manduley 159, esq. Calle 7, Reparto Vista Alegre
Tel *(22) 641 528*
El Zunzún is an elegant restaurant in a colonial building in the formerly wealthy suburb of Vista Alegre. Dine in style on seafood and meat in various sauces. Impeccable service and a great selection of wines.

For more information on types of restaurants *see pages 264–5*

SHOPS AND MARKETS

Tourists do most of their shopping in state-run shops, often in the hotels. However, the legalization of limited private enterprise has given a boost to the handicrafts and food markets *(mercados agropecuarios)*. In the past there wasn't much to buy, but now an improving range of souvenirs are available. All the same, Cuba is not the place to look for designer outlets. State-run shops offer goods at fixed prices, which tend to be on the high side, whereas market prices are lower and may be negotiable. Cigars of guaranteed quality are sold only for hard currency in specialist shops. Be very wary of buying cigars – or anything else for that matter – on the black market.

Handicrafts for sale at La Rampa market in Havana *(see p102)*

Opening Hours

Opening hours in Cuba are erratic but as a guideline *tiendas* (convertible pesos shops) are open 9am–7pm in the summer and 9am–6pm in the winter, while small shops open 9am–6pm all year round. On Sundays, shops close at 1pm. The fruit and vegetable markets are open on Sunday mornings, closed on Mondays, then open Tuesday to Friday from 8am to around 6pm. Fast food chain El Rápido *(see p265)* is open 24 hours a day.

How to Pay

Most tourists will not use the local currency, called the *peso nacional* or *peso cubano* *(see p299)*, at all during their stay. Most goods that tourists want to buy, from rum to CDs, are only available in hard currency shops (most of which accept credit cards). In the food markets, the locals use mainly *pesos cubanos* but stall holders will happily accept convertible pesos (change may be in *pesos cubanos*). To buy *pesos cubanos*, go to one of the bureaux de change, called CADECA, found in most city centres and often near the entrance to major food markets.

Where to Go

In the cities and tourist resorts, *tiendas* and supermarkets sell everything from clothes to tinned food, but do not carry the range of items seen in European or North American supermarkets.

The logo of a popular *tiendas* chain

Tourist resorts and larger towns often have shops specializing in clothes. Tourist *tiendas*, especially in hotels, sell T-shirts printed with Cuban images including the inevitable portraits of Che Guevara, as well as *guayaberas*, typical Caribbean cotton shirts.

In the El Rápido chain *(see p265)*, Tiendas Panamericanas general stores and at petrol stations, visitors can buy soft drinks, rum, biscuits, sweets, butter and milk, as well as small household utensils and articles normally found in perfume shops.

Fresh fruit, vegetables and fresh meat are to be found only in the food markets.

Specialist Shops

Cigars should be purchased in the specialist shops, often known as **La Casa del Habano**, which sell cigars direct from the cigar factories (and which may, in fact, be attached to a factory), and keep them at the right temperature and humidity level. Do not buy cigars from people on

An outlet of the hard-currency Tiendas Panamericanas chain

the street, as they are almost invariably fakes made by machine, rather than handmade, or are badly preserved, bear signs of faulty workmanship, or contain banana leaves and other rubbish. In addition, street vendors will not be able to provide you with an official purchase receipt, needed to take goods out of the country.

Branches of the **ARTex** chain stock a good selection of CDs, records and cassettes. Another well-stocked music store is **Longina**, in Calle Obispo, La Habana Vieja. Note that recordings of local music may not be available outside Cuba.

Paintings, sculpture and prints in the art galleries and in the *tiendas* of the Fondo de Bienes Culturales are sold with official authenticity certificates, which are needed for export.

Paintings for sale in the huge Almacenes San José, Havana

Shelves with cigars in a Casa del Habano

La Casa del Habano
Real Fábrica de Tabacos Partagás, Havana. **Tel** 7866 8060;
Ave 1, esq. 63, Varadero. **Tel** (45) 667 843.
Club Havana, Ave 5, e/188 y 192, Playa, Havana. **Tel** 7204 5700.

Tienda ARTex
Ave. L, esq. 23, Havana. **Tel** 7838 3162.

Handicrafts

Cuba does not have a long tradition of producing handicrafts. Today, however, market stalls are found everywhere, selling all sorts of things from wood carvings and ceramics to embroidery, papier mâché objects and musical instruments. In La Habana Vieja there is a daily handicrafts market in the Almacenes San José (*see p73*). Plaza de Armas is the place for the rare Latin American novels and second-hand political tomes. There is also a market on La Rampa in Vedado.

The market in Trinidad, near the central square, is a good place to look for embroidered linen and cotton. Crafts are also sold in state-run shops, in the Ferias de Artesanía and in the Galerías de Arte throughout the island.

Art

Many artists have private studios or sell art through state-run galleries which take a 40 per cent commission. There is quite a lot of interest in Cuban art in the international market because of the political system. The Havana Biennale – which is now held every three years, despite retaining the name 'biennale'. – is popular with collectors from around the world. Once a piece of artwork is bought the artist arranges the export permit of around CUC$5 per work.

Markets

The fruit and vegetable markets (*mercados agropecuarios*) in Cuba are lively and entertaining places to stroll around. Stalls sell fresh fruit and vegetables, pork and sausages, sweets, traditional food and flowers. In Havana, the most central food market is in the Barrio Chino (*see p94*), but one of the best is at the corner of 19 y A in Vedado.

A Souvenir in Front of the Capitolio

Photographer with his old Polaroid camera

In front of the Capitolio (*see pp86–7*) in Havana, visitors can have their picture taken with an original 1930s Polaroid camera, for one convertible peso. The photos develop immediately and the resulting picture, in black and white, looks just like a convincingly old photograph.

Souvenirs at the Trinidad street market

What to Buy in Cuba

Apart from the famous Cuban cigars and excellent rum, there are many other good things to buy in Cuba: gold and silver jewellery, and hand-crafted objects made from local materials: wood, straw, papier mâché, shells, seeds, terracotta and glass. Cuban musical instruments are also popular choices. There are also toiletries and pharmaceutical products that are to be found nowhere else in the world, on sale in the international pharmacies and shops in the airport, where you can also buy books, DVDs and CDs.

Rum
This classic brand of rum can be bought all over Cuba. Bottles are also sold in boxes (especially at the airport) to make them easier to transport.

Bauza
Cigars that do not meet the rigorous standards of the cigar-makers are labelled Bauza. However, they are still of very good quality. They are sold at authorized outlets at very reasonable prices.

A box of Vegas Robaina cigars

Cigars
Packaged in elegant cedar boxes, Cuban cigars make a luxury gift *(see pp36–7)*. Copies, however, can be convincing: make sure that the box has the branded label *"hecho in Cuba totalmente a mano"* (totally handmade in Cuba), the official government seal, a hologram and the "Habanos" band.

Local Handicrafts
Raw material from the Caribbean (bamboo, shells and seeds) is used to make decorative wall hangings and colourful necklaces. Do not buy black coral jewellery: the coral is an endangered species.

A seed necklace

A seed and shell necklace

Musical Instruments
Many traditional Cuban musical instruments *(see p35)* such as *claves, bongós, maracas, güiro,* and *tumbadora* drums are made by craftsmen. They are sold in music stores and markets. Some, such as guitars, can be made to order.

Bongós

Hats and Baskets
Banana leaves and other plant fibres are used to weave typical hats and baskets of various shapes and sizes. These make affordable, classic souvenirs.

Books and Curios

Plaza de Armas in Habana Vieja is known for its second-hand book market (see p73). The stall holders also offer coins, badges, stamps and other memorabilia – cigar cards, wrappers, comic books and Bacardí factory receipts. Collectors will also find a market with similar curios at Fin de Siglo in Calle San Rafael, Centro Habana.

A cedar-wood cigar box

Papier Mâché

The *papier mâché* technique is popular in Cuba. It is used to produce many items including masks, models, toys and knick-knacks. These articles are always painted in bright, decorative colours.

A mask representing the sun

African-style figures

Wood

Cedar and rosewood are used to make small wooden figures that often draw inspiration from African tradition. Carved cedarwood cigar boxes always display elegant craftsmanship. Wooden objects can also be found on sale in the Galerías de Arte.

Doll

Model vintage cars

Perfumes and Medicines

The Suchel Camacho company produces very good perfumes, including spicy Coral Negro, flower-scented Mariposa and elegant Alicia Alonso, as well as quality face and body creams, at reasonable prices. A range of natural remedies and supplements is also available, including spirulina, which is derived from algae. Excellent honey, with royal jelly and propolis (bee-glue), is also available.

Naive Paintings

Markets and the Galerías de Arte sell naive paintings of Afro-Caribbean inspiration depicting landscapes and views of colonial towns, or Afro-Cuban divinities.

Eau de toilette

Moisturizing cream

ENTERTAINMENT

The possibilities for lively entertainment are diverse in a country where there is tremendous love of music, dance and theatrical display. Ballet, theatre, concerts, festivals and sporting activities are in full swing all year round. In most major cities, there are theatres and concert spaces, and even in the smallest towns you will find a Casa de la Cultura or Casa de la Trova, hosting performances of traditional music. Visitors opting for a vacation at Cuba's many all-inclusive beach resorts will find canned entertainment mostly performed by hotel staff. Beyond the resorts, any street corner may easily be turned into an improvised dance floor with just the help of a CD player, and discos abound everywhere.

Restored façade of Teatro La Caridad in Santa Clara

Information and Tickets

Major tourist hotels distribute brochures free of charge, but usually these refer only to the costliest tourist venues, and general information on cultural happenings and locales is scant. A good online resource is Cubarte: The Portal of Cuban Culture at www.cubarte-english.cult.cu; try also www.cubaabsolutely.com. Tickets for major cabarets and inter-national events can be bought at hotel tour desks.

Theatre

Regional theatre is more restrained than in Havana. An exception is Santiago – its more than a dozen theatre companies include several experimental ones that, for years, have boldly sought new forms of expression. These can be seen at the **Van Troi/ Cabildo Teatral Santiago** hall. The **José Martí** theatre is more traditional, while the **El Mambí** presents some shows aimed at children. The modern and prestigious **José María Heredia** theatre is particularly active during the Fiesta del Fuego in July *(see p39)*. The **Teatro Papalote** company, in Matanzas, performs in its own theatre and is acclaimed nationwide. The world-famous **Grupo Teatro Escambray** performs in rural communities. Other major venues include the **Teatro Tomás Terry**, in Cienfuegos; the restored **Teatro La Caridad**, in Santa Clara; and the **Teatro Principal**, in Camagüey.

Ballet and Classical Music

Founded in 1967, the acclaimed Ballet de Camagüey presents world-class classical dance productions in the Teatro Principal *(see Theatre)*. Camagüey is also home to the **Ballet Folklórico de Camagüey**, one of Cuba's foremost troupes. In the Oriente, **Ballet Folklórico Babul** is based at the Teatro Guaso in Guantánamo.

Most provincial capitals have theatres where classical music performances are hosted. Travelling symphonies can be heard at Santiago's **Teatro Heredia**; the more intimate **Sala de Conciertos Dolores** is the seat of the Orquesta Sinfónica de Oriente, as well as a venue for smaller ensembles.

Folk and Traditional Music

Traditional Afro-based music and dance thrives in the provinces and is particularly strong in Oriente and Trinidad, where visitors should look for splendid African-derived per-formances by the Conjunto Folklórico de Trinidad, which also performs Bantu and Yoruba dances outside Cuba, as does Trinidad's Cocoró y su Aché, which performs at the **Palenque de los Congos Reales**. Trinidad holds a *Semana de la Cultura* (Culture Week) each January, when *madrugadas*, songs sung in the streets, are performed. Holguín's *Semana de la Cultura* is perhaps Cuba's most vibrant.

Santiago is the home of the **Conjunto Folklórico de Oriente**. In the courtyard of the **Museo del Carnaval**, rehearsals of

Performance by the acclaimed Ballet Folklórico de Camagüey

A traditional *son* band performing in a Trinidad street

groups preparing for Carnival (*see p233*) are open to the public.

Don't miss the evening training sessions in the various *focos culturales* from Tuesday to Friday. The **Cabildo Carabalí Izuama** rehearses Carnival songs derived from African musical traditions. In the *foco cultural*, founded by Haitian slaves in the late 1700s, 18th-century dances are accompanied by Bantu musical instruments. Here, too, both the **Casa del Caribe** and **Centro Cultural Africano Fernando Ortíz** hold *rumbas* on weekends (*see p282: Cultural Centres*).

Guantánamo is the birthplace of many traditional dance forms, including *changuí*, and is home to the annual June Festival Nacional de Changuí. At other times, *changuí* and its derivative, *son*, are performed by the world-famous Orquesta Revé and other leading local proponents at the **Casa de la Música**, the Casa de la Trova (*see p282: Casas de la Trova*) and the **British West Indian Welfare Center**. Witness Haitian folkloric dance at the **Tumba Francesa**.

The **Casa de la Cultura** in Pinar del Río is known for its *controversias*, a form of song in which two singers pit themselves against each another in creative impromptu verse. The **Casa de la Cultura** in Nueva Gerona is a centre for the local music and dance form known as *sucusuco*, unique to the Isla de la Juventud. And Las Tunas

has an annual **Jornada Cucalambeana** folkloric festival where local songsters perform *décimas*, ten-syllable rhyming songs.

Nightclubs, Cabarets and Discotheques

Most tourist villages and large-scale hotels in Cuba have clubs that open until late. Customers pay in convertible pesos; depending on location, most Cubans cannot afford them, so don't expect to find a broad cross-section of Cuban society.

Outside tourist resorts, most nightclubs are associated with cabarets. The most important are the **Tropicana**, in both Matanzas and Santiago. Varadero also offers excellent *cabarets espéctaculos* at the **Cueva del Pirata**, where shows are held in an atmospheric natural cave. It also now boasts a **Casa de la Música**. Every other major town has at least one cabaret, which turn into nightclubs with dancing once the show ends.

Most discos are based in the tourist resorts, concentrated in Varadero. These are large, modern discos featuring loud music (usually a mix of salsa and other Latin sounds with world-beat), neon lighting and simple decor. The entry fee is in convertible pesos and is usually quite expensive. Several such discos are for hotel patrons only. For these reasons, the majority of the customers are foreigners. However, there is usually a sprinkling of young Cuban couples, as well as wayward singles waiting outside in the hope of partnering with a foreigner for entry (occasional police sweeps occur, when Cubans being too friendly with foreigners are arrested).

The best such clubs in Varadero are **Mambo Club** and **Palacio de la Rumba**. All three are popular with Cubans, who often travel many miles to party until dawn. The most unusual venue is Trinidad's Disco Ayala, deep inside a cave.

You can also listen to modern "música popular" in Casas de la Música in a few major cities. The principal venue, the **Casa de la Música de Trinidad**, hosts concerts by local groups. Several open-air ruins in Trinidad are also used as nightclubs. The **Patio de Artex** in Cienfuegos is also bursting with energy on weekends; and the **Club Benny Moré** is a 1950s-style nightclub with disco following comedy and cabaret.

Santiago's venerable hot-spots are the Patio de Artex, Casa de la Trova and **Casa de las Tradiciones**.

One of the Tropicana dancers in a typically exotic costume

Live music and dancing at an intimate Casa de la Trova

Casas de la Trova

The traditional and intimate Casas de la Trova are clubs where people can listen to live music, dance or just relax over a cocktail. First opened in 1959 in almost all Cuban provincial capitals, these were originally places where older musicians, interpreters of traditional *trova*, could perform and educate younger people in their musical skills. Today, Casas de la Trova are found in virtually every town and even in rural villages and are usually the most important musical venues. Many also organize lectures, conferences, poetry readings and art exhibitions, thus maintaining their original spirit as keepers of tradition.

In some places, such as in Santiago and Trinidad, Casas de la Trova have geared themselves to tourists, with a bar offering different Cuban cocktails, and a shop selling CDs, DVDs, books and souvenirs. Whatever the style, Casas de la Trova continue to be popular with Cubans of all ages and offer plenty of atmosphere.

The most important Casas de la Trova are in **Santiago**, home of *son*, and **Trinidad**, where the classical tradition of the *trova* prevails. The *trova* at **Bayamo** has a faster rhythm and stronger Afro-Caribbean overtones, while **Camagüey** focuses more on melodic tunes. Some Casas de la Trova are associated with venerated musicians, such as Casa de la Trova "El Guayabero" in **Holguín**, where the esteemed

Faustino Oramas "El Guayabero" Osorio performed.

In some towns, traditional *trova* activities are held in the Casas de la Cultura, charged with a more broadly based mandate to preserve traditional culture. In **Baracoa** and **Sancti Spíritus**, for example, they put on performances by *repentistas* (improvisers). The Casa de la Cultura in **Pinar del Río** hosts performances of *punto guajiro*, country-style music centred around improvisation.

A less touristy alternative to the Casa de la Trova is the Casa de las Tradiciones (see *Nightclubs, Cabarets and Discotheques*) in Santiago, a good place to see up-and-coming local groups.

Cultural Centres

The Casa de la Cultura is an institution in every Cuban city. These cultural centres foster various forms of artistic expression: the figurative arts, poetry and music. Trinidad and Santiago are the most active cities culturally.

In Santiago, those interested in anthropology and religion can visit the **Centro Cultural Africano Fernando Ortíz**, dedicated to the African influences in Cuba, and the **Casa del Caribe**, which organizes an annual Caribbean Cultural Festival. The eclectic fare at the **Ateneo Cultural** ranges from poetry readings to rap performances.

UNEAC (National Writers and Artists' Union), with branches in a number of cities, puts on exhibitions, conferences and

concerts. The Holguín and Santiago branches are particularly active and host cultural debates, art shows and music shows, as well as poetry readings.

Children

Cuba has plenty of children's playgrounds, including rather basic fairgrounds in Santiago and other major cities. The most complete fairground is Varadero's basic **Todo En Uno**, which has a tiny roller-coaster, *carros locos* (bumper cars) and other attractions. Nearby, Parque Retiro Josone (see p166) has a miniature train among its attractions for children. At the **Delfinario de Varadero**, daily dolphin shows delight children; swimming with these creatures is also permitted.

Cuba has four other provincial dolphin shows: at **Delfinario de Rancho Luna**, near Cienfuegos; **Delfinario Cayo Santa María**, located near Cayo Ensenachos; **Acuario Cayo Naranjo**, at Guardalavaca; and Acuario Baconao (see p239).

Several cities – notably Santa Clara and Bayamo – have goat-drawn cart rides for children in the main squares.

The **Teatro Guiñol** is a noted children's puppet theatre founded in 1959. All year round, plays and puppet shows are performed, as they are in many other Cuban cities. Holiday villages provide safe play areas for small children, as well as shallow swimming pools and children's activity programmes.

Exterior of Casa de la Cultura in Pinar del Rio

DIRECTORY

Theatre

Grupo Teatro Escambray
La Macagua, Manicaragua.
Tel (42) 491 393.

José María Heredia
Ave. las Américas,
Santiago de Cuba.
Tel (22) 643 190.

José Martí
Calle Santo Tomás,
Santiago de Cuba.
Tel (22) 620 507.

El Mambí
Calle Bartolomé Masó
303, Santiago de Cuba.
Tel (22) 628 713.

Teatro La Caridad
Calle Marta Abreu e/Máximo Gómez y Lorda, Santa Clara. **Tel** (42) 205 548.

Teatro Papalote
Calle Daoíz y
Ayuntamiento, Matanzas.
Tel (45) 244 672.

Teatro Principal
Padre Valencia 64,
Camagüey.
Tel (32) 293 048.

Teatro Tomás Terry
Plaza Martí, Cienfuegos.
Tel (43) 551 772.

Van Troi/Cabildo Teatral Santiago
Calle Saco 415, Santiago
de Cuba. **Tel** (22) 651 866.

Ballet and Classical Music

Ballet Folklórico Babul
Paseo 855 e/ Cuartel y
Ahogados, Guantánamo.
Tel (21) 327 940.

Ballet Folklórico de Camagüey
Calle Pobre esq.
Triana, Camagüey.
Tel (32) 298 512.

Sala de Conciertos Dolores
Santiago de Cuba.
Tel (22) 653 857.

Teatro Heredia
Ave. las Américas, esq.
Ave. de los Desfiles,
Santiago de Cuba.
Tel (22) 643 156.

Folk and Traditional Music

British West Indian Welfare Center
Serafín Sánchez 663,
e/ Paseo y Narciso
López, Guantánamo.
Tel (21) 325 297.

Cabildo Carabalí Izuama
Calle Pío Rosado 107,
e/ San Mateo y San
Antonio, Santiago de
Cuba. **Tel** (22) 651 866.

Casa de la Cultura
Calle 24 esq. 37,
Nueva Gerona.
Tel (48) 323 591.
Marti 65, Pinar del Río.
Tel (48) 752 324.

Casa de la Música
Calixto García e/
Crombet y Gulo,
Guantánamo.
Tel (21) 327 266.

Conjunto Folklórico de Oriente
Calle Hartmann 407,
Santiago de Cuba.

Jornada Cucalambeana
Las Tunas, late June
(see p39).

Museo del Carnaval
Heredia 304, Santiago
de Cuba.
Tel (22) 626 955.

Palenque de los Congos Reales
Echerri 146, esq. Jesús
Menéndez, Trinidad.
Tel (41) 994 512.

Tumba Francesa
Calle Serafín Sánchez
715, Guantánamo.

Nightclubs, Cabarets and Discotheques

Casa de la Música de Trinidad
Calle Rosario 3,
Casco Histórico.
Tel (41) 996 622.

Casa de la Música de Varadero
Ave. Playa e/ Calle
42 y 43. **Tel** (45) 668 918.

Casa de las Tradiciones
Calle Rabí 154, Santiago
de Cuba. **Tel** (22) 653 892.

Club Benny Moré
Avenida 54 2907,
e/ 29 y 31, Cienfuegos.
Tel (43) 551 674.

Cueva del Pirata
Autopista Sur, Km 11,
Varadero.
Tel (45) 667 751.

Mambo Club
Club Amigo Varadero,
Carretera Las Morlas.
Tel (45) 668 565.

Palacio de la Rumba
Hotel Bella Costa, Ave.
las Américas, Varadero.
Tel (45) 668 210.

Patio de Artex
Ave. 16 y Calle 35,
Cienfuegos.
Tel (43) 551 255.
Heredia 304,
Santiago de Cuba.
Tel (22) 654 814.

Tropicana de Matanzas
Autopista Varadero
Km 4.5. **Tel** (45) 265 380.

Tropicana de Santiago
Autopista Nacional
Km 11.5. **Tel** (22) 642 579.

Casas de la Trova

Baracoa
Victorino Maceo
no.149B e/ Ciro Frias
y Pelayo Cuevo.
Tel (21) 641 747.

Bayamo
Calle Martí esq. Maceo.
Tel (23) 425 673.

Camagüey
Calle Cisneros y Martí.
Tel (32) 291 357.

Holguín
Calle Maceo 174 e/ Frexes
y Martí.

Pinar del Río
Gerardo Medina 108.
Tel (48) 754 794.

Sancti Spíritus
Casa de la Cultural,
Zerquera esq. Ernest
Valdes.

Santiago
Heredia 208.
Tel (22) 652 689.

Trinidad
Calle Echerrí 29.
Tel (41) 996 445.

Cultural Centres

Ateneo Cultural
Félix Peña e/ Castillo
Duany y Diego Palacios,
Santiago de Cuba.
Tel (22) 623 635.

Casa del Caribe
Calle 13 154, Santiago
de Cuba.
Tel (22) 643 609

Centro Cultural Africano Fernando Ortíz
Manduley esq. Calle 5,
Santiago de Cuba.
Tel (22) 642 487.

UNEAC de Holguín
Libertad 148.
Tel (24) 474 066.

Children

Acuario Cayo Naranjo
Carretera a Guardalavaca.
Tel (24) 430 132.

Delfinario Cayo Santa María
Carretera Cayo
Santa María.
Tel (42) 350 013.

Delfinario de Rancho Luna
Carretera a Pasacaballo.
Tel (43) 548 120.

Delfinario de Varadero
Autopista Km 11.
Varadero.
Tel (45) 66 8031.

Teatro Guiñol
San Basilio e/ San Felix
y San Pedro, Santiago
de Cuba.
Tel (22) 628 713.

Todo En Uno
Autopista Sur y
Calle 54, Varadero.

SPORTS AND OUTDOOR ACTIVITIES

After the Revolution, the government abolished professional sports (with a reprieve for boxing in 2013), and invested large amounts of money in physical education and amateur sports, and as a result some outstandingly successful sportsmen and women have emerged. Baseball and boxing are by far the most popular sports, but volleyball, basketball, football and athletics are also widely practised. For athletes and fitness fanatics who want to stay in good shape, the state-run Cubadeportes organization makes it possible to experience Cuban sports first-hand by arranging meetings with local athletes and the provision of special courses.

The varied Cuban landscape also allows for a number of outdoor activities. Facilities for a wide range of water sports along the coast are increasingly good, and mountain ranges and nature parks have just as much to offer.

Multi-Purpose Sports Arenas

It is both cheap and easy to see sport in Cuba. All the major stadiums have specially reserved seating areas for foreign visitors and you can usually buy tickets on the day. A new stadium, the **Estadio Panamericano** sports complex, was built in the Habana del Este quarter of the capital for the 1991 Pan-American Games. It is now a major venue for athletics. Cuba has produced some great athletes, including high-jumper Javier Sotomayor, middle-distance runner Ana Fidelia Quirot and long-jumper Iván Pedroso (*see p23*). The centre also has pools for swimming competitions, water polo and synchronized swimming, tennis courts and a velodrome.

The **Sala Polivalente Ramón Fonst** in Vedado specializes in volleyball and basketball, while the **Coliseo de la Ciudad Deportiva** in the Boyeros district hosts national and international volleyball, basketball, boxing and fencing matches.

Baseball

This is the national sport. It has been a passion here for over a century, and today's teams are world-class. The first baseball stadium in Havana was built in 1881 and the first amateur championship was held in 1905.

The official baseball season varies from year to year. Games can be viewed on the **Beisbol Cubano** website. To stream the National Series live, visit the **CiberCuba** site.

Watching a live baseball game is great fun; many families attend and there is always a good atmosphere. Games are played in the **Estadio Latino-americano**, inaugurated in 1946, which has a seating capacity of 55,000.

Boxing

Cuba has won several Olympic boxing titles. The founder of the modern school of boxing is Alcides Sagarra, a trainer who has been active in the profession since 1960, producing

The Cuban national women's volleyball team in action

such greats as Teófilo Stevenson (1952–2012), the Olympic heavyweight champion, who set up his own school.

At the annual Girardo Córdova Cardín tournament, expert boxers fight against emerging ones; this is part of the selection procedure for the Equipo Cuba, one of the best boxing teams in the world.

Fights can be seen at the **Sala Kid Chocolate**, located opposite the Capitolio in Centro Habana.

Volleyball

Cubans are passionate about volleyball and the island has performed extremely well in international competitions, particularly in the women's category. Between 1990 and 2000, the Cuba women's national volleyball won gold medals in three Olympic Games, three World Cups and two World Championships. The men's team won the World Grand Champions cup in 2001. Visitors can sometimes get

Cuba's national baseball team during a game

Beach volleyball at a tourist village on Cayo Largo

tickets to see the national teams in action at the Coliseo de la Ciudad Deportiva. Call in advance of your visit for information on when the teams are playing.

Diving

With 5,746 km (3,570 miles) of coastline and over 4,000 small islands, Cuba is one of the supreme places in the Caribbean for diving enthusiasts. The crystal-clear water (with a temperature ranging from 23–30° C, 70–85° F) and variety of sea beds, in particular, make the Cuban sea a paradise for scuba divers at any time of year. Thanks to the coral reef and numerous offshore islands (cayos), there are no strong currents along the coast and the horizontal visibility under water is hardly ever less than 40 m (130 ft).

There is an abundance of sites along the coral reef for both wall and platform dives. Punta Perdiz, in the Bahía de Cochinos (Bay of Pigs) is a spectacular wall dive. Besides all kinds of coral, on the sea bed divers can see gorgonian fans and sponges, all manner of multicoloured fish (see p151), tarpons, barracuda, sea turtles, large lobsters, beautiful anemones, and even sharks. The Jardines de la Reina is teeming with Caribbean reef sharks, silky sharks and nurse sharks. A family of bull sharks lives in the Boca de Nuevitas (near Playa Santa Lucía), and the area can be visited with the instructors from the **Shark's Friends** diving centre.

There are also fascinating shipwrecks to explore. In the past the island's bays were used as refuges for pirate galleons, and in some areas, such as Playa Santa Lucía, divers can still see anchors and cannons – relics from the 19th century – lying on the sea floor. Military enthusiasts can see Soviet vessels and aircraft among the more recent sunken craft. Underwater tunnels and grottoes add to the attractions.

Tourism has spurred the number of diving centres and the modernization of existing clubs that can be found in every holiday resort. Scuba centres have trained international-level instructors, and offer courses for all levels of ability. Some, such as the Hotel Colony on Isla de la Juventud (see p154), also have decompression chambers. Divers can hire all the equipment they need on site; however, it is advisable to bring along indispensable items such as a depth gauge and a knife.

The most important diving centres (centros de buceo) are **El Colony** on Isla de la Juventud (best suited to experienced divers), **Avalon** at Jardines de la Reina, the **Centro de Buceo María La Gorda** and **Green Moray** at Cayo Guillermo. It is possible to dive from the shore at Playa Santa Lucía and Playa Girón. Other operators can be found at Varadero and Guardalavaca.

The Jardines de la Reina islands are Cuba's most outstanding dive area, although they can

only be reached by sea. Liveaboards take scuba divers to sites with unspoiled sea floors, busy with marine life.

For information concerning diving in general, contact **Marlin Náutica** or Avalon.

Surfing, Windsurfing and Kitesurfing

At the main seaside resorts (Varadero, Guardalavaca, Cayo Largo, Cayo Coco and Cayo Santa María) conditions are ideal for surfing and windsurfing, and at the larger holiday villages all equipment can be hired.

Kitesurfing has surged in popularity and a few outfits now offer lessons in Varadero and elsewhere; contact **Cuba Kiters, Havana Kiteboarding Club** or **Caribbean Riders Kite School**. The **Club Cayo Guillermo** is perfectly sited for catching the wind especially between November and April.

Cycling

Touring the island by bicycle is an excellent way to enjoy the landscape and meet local people. The bicycles offered for rent to tourists are of better quality than those the locals have to use. Cycling is not usually dangerous, particularly outside the towns where traffic is light. Beware, however, of potholes in the road.

Bikes should always be locked or left in supervised places (thefts are common), and remember to wear a helmet. Mountain bikes are best for rough terrain.

A scuba diver exploring a shipwreck off the Playa Santa Lucía (see p210)

Enjoying the sea on a catamaran hired from a tourist marina

Sailing and Motorboats

Thanks to its position at the entrance to the Gulf of Mexico, Cuba makes an ideal stopping-off point for yachts and sailing boats. The tourist marinas, many of which belong to the **Marlin Náutica** chain, provide a series of facilities and services, including motorboats and catamarans for hire and yacht excursions.

Most sailing is done around the Archipiélago de los Canarreos, south of the mainland. The best season for sailing is from December to April, because the climate is mild, the winds are not too strong and storms are infrequent. However, Cuba is surrounded by generally tranquil waters, and there are plenty of bays if shelter is needed.

Fishing

Fishing enthusiasts will be in their element in Cuba. The northwestern coast is marvellous for deep-sea fishing, where the catch might include swordfish, tuna or mackerel, while fish such as tarpon and bonefish can be caught off the southern coast.

Fishing is provided by marinas and holiday villages. Holidays tailor-made for fishermen are organized by Marlin Náutica and **Cubanacán**.

The **Marina Hemingway**, along the north coast west of Havana (see p141), is the venue for the annual Ernest Hemingway International Billfishing Tournament, a competition reserved for expert marlin fishermen held for five days in late May or early June (see p39). The original rules were established by the author, who had a passion for deep-sea fishing.

Tennis and Golf

Almost all the holiday villages and large hotel complexes have tennis courts. Non-residents usually make use of them by paying a fee.

The island also has two good golf courses: the nine-hole **Club de Golf Habana** and the 18-hole **Club de Golf de Varadero**.

The sport is increasingly popular and there are plans to lay out even more golf courses in the main tourist resorts in the near future.

Hikers on a path near Topes de Collantes (see p195)

Hiking, Birdwatching and Other Excursions

Trekking on horseback is another way to see the Cuban landscape. In Havana the only horse riding centre is in Parque Lenin (see p120), but hotels in the main resorts, eco-tourist centres and camping sites can provide horses as well as organized excursions. Both experienced and inexperienced riders are catered for.

The Península de Zapata (see pp168–71) is a particularly good area for birders, as the marshland is a haven for hundreds of different bird species. Further east around Baracoa are the biosphere reserve of El Yunque and the Parque Nacional Alejandro de Humboldt (see pp248–9), both home to rare species.

There are also plenty of opportunities for exploring caves in Cuba. Sites include the Cuevas de Bellamar near Matanzas (see p164), the Cavernos de Panadernos in Gibara (see p218) and the Gran Caverna de Santo Tomás in Valle de Viñales (see p146). Always join a tour or expedition, or go with a knowledgable guide.

Keep in mind also that hikers must be accompanied by an official guide around Viñales, Topes de Collantes and Sierra Maestra (from Alto de Naranjo to Las Cuevas).

For information on nature tours and programmes, contact **Gaviota Tours** and **Ecotur**; the latter organization oversees the upkeep and improvement of the trails.

Varadero's golf course, close to the sea

Hunting

Many Cubans enjoy the thrill of hunting (cinegética) and the island has a number of hunting reserves (cotos de caza), where people are allowed to hunt birds and small animals within rigorously defined limits and under the supervision of the forest rangers. The system is strictly controlled to balance the ecosystem and avoid overhunting.

The reserves are usually sited near lagoons, lakes or cays, and hunting is for wild duck, snipe, guinea fowl and pigeons, among other birds.

In general, it is possible to hire all the equipment needed for hunting at these reserves, although prices can be high. The hunting season is from the end of October until the middle of March.

Cuba's specialist hunting trip agency is **Ecotur**.

DIRECTORY

Multi-Purpose Sports Arenas

Coliseo de la Ciudad Deportiva
Ave. de Rancho Boyeros y Vía Blanca, Havana.
Tel 7648 5000.

Estadio Panamericano
Carretera de Cojímar, Km 4.5 y Ave. Monumental.
Tel 7795 4140.

Sala Polivalente Ramón Fonst
Ave. Independencia e/ 19 de Mayo y Bruzón, Havana.
Map 2 E4. **Tel** 7862 8634.

Baseball

Beisbol Cubano
W beisbolcubano.cu

CiberCuba
W cibercuba.com/tele-rebelde-en-vivo

Estadio Latinoamericano
Calle Zequeira, El Cerro, Havana. **Tel** 7870 8175.

Boxing

Sala Kid Chocolate
Paseo de Martí (Prado) y Brasil, Havana. **Map** 4 D3.
Tel 7862 8634.

Diving

Avalon
Jardines de la Reina, Júcaro. **Tel** 7204 7422.

Centro de Buceo María La Gorda
La Bajada, Pinar del Río.
Tel (48) 778 131.

El Colony
Carretera de Siguanea, Km 41, Isla de la Juventud.
Tel (46) 398 181.

Green Moray
Cayo Guillermo.
Tel (33) 301 627.

Marlin Náutica
Marlin Jardines del Rey, Cayo Coco.
Tel (33) 201 221.
W nauticamarlin.com

Shark's Friends
Hotel Brisa Santa Lucía, Playa Santa Lucía, Camagüey.
Tel (32) 365 182.

Surfing, Windsurfing and Kitesurfing

Caribbean Riders Kite School
W varaderokiteschool.com

Club Cayo Guillermo
W clubcayoguillermo.com

Cuba Kiters
W cubakiters.com

Havana Kiteboarding Club
W havanakite.com

Sailing and Motorboats

Marea del Portillo
Marea del Portillo, Pilón.
Tel (23) 597 139.

Marina Cayo Coco-Guillermo
Cayo Guillermo, Archipiélago Jardines del Rey.
Tel (33) 301 515.

Marina Cayo Largo
Cayo Largo.
Tel (45) 248 213.

Marina Cayo Santa María
Cayo Las Brujas, Cayería Norte de Villa Clara.
Tel (42) 350 113.

Marina Chapelin
Autopista del Sur Km 12.5, Varadero.
Tel (45) 667 550.

Marina Dársena Varadero
Carretera de las Morlas Km 21, Varadero
Tel (45) 614 448.

Marina Internacional Vita
Bahía de Vita, Holguín.
Tel (24) 430 445.

Marina Santa Lucía
Playa Santa Lucía, Camagüey.
Tel (32) 365 182.

Marina Santiago
Ave. 1, Punta Gorda, Santiago de Cuba.
Tel (22) 686 101.

Marina Tarará
Vía Blanca Km 18, Playa Tarará, Havana.
Tel 7796 1509.

Marina Trinidad
Carretera María Aguilar, Playa Ancón.
Tel (41) 996 205.

Marlin Náutica
See Diving.

Fishing

Cubanacán
Carretera Playa Girón, Km 1.5, Matanzas.
Tel (45) 912 825.

Marina Hemingway
Ave. 5 y 248, Santa Fe, Playa, Havana.
Tel 7204 5088.

Golf

Club de Golf Habana
Carretera de Vento Km 8, Capdevila.
Tel 7649 8918.

Club de Golf de Varadero
Ave. Las Américas, Varadero.
Tel (45) 668 482.
W varaderogolfclub.com

Hiking, Birdwatching and Other Excursions

Ecotur
Ave. Independencia 116 esq. Santa Catalina, Havana. **Tel** 7273 1542.

Gaviota Tours
Edificio La Marina, level 3, Ave del Puerto 102 e/ Jústiz y Obrapía, Havana.
Tel 7869 5588.
W gaviota-grupo.com

SURVIVAL GUIDE

PRACTICAL INFORMATION

In the last 20 years Cuba has made great strides in the field of tourism and can now provide visitors with modern, international-level facilities. It is now possible for tourists to move about much more easily on the island, although advance planning is still essential, especially as regards transport around the island. An effective approach is to contact one of the many travel agencies in Cuba, which may have their own offices or be based in the major hotels. The latter also function as tourist offices,

providing practical information and often a booking service. However, although Cuban tourist operators are very good, visitors still need to be adaptable and flexible. The pace of life here is slow, as is the bureaucracy, so be prepared to waste a certain amount of time when trying to get things done. Whatever happens, try and remain optimistic. With a bit of patience and a lot of perseverance *"todo se resuelve"*, as they say in Cuba: a solution can always be found.

One of the Playas del Este at Havana, crowded with tourists and locals

When to Go

Apart from September to November, prime hurricane months, and July and August, when the torrid heat can make touring quite tiring (unless you spend your entire holiday at the seaside), any time of year is good for a visit to Cuba. It is possible to relax on the beach all year round, thanks to the mild climate.

The best period for a visit is December to March, when the climate is warm without being unbearable and there are more cultural events, such as the Festival Internacional del Nuevo Cine Latinoamericano, the international jazz festival and the Festival de Habanos, a massive cigar trade fair.

Winter is also a popular time of year to get married in Cuba. However, be aware that getting married here is bureaucratic and requires that all necessary documents be translated

into Spanish and notarised. Contact the Consultoria Jurídica in Cuba for more information.

Consultoría Jurídica
Tel 7204 2490.

Visas and Passports

To enter Cuba, travellers must have a valid passport, a return ticket, valid health insurance, and a tourist visa *(tarjeta de turista)* issued by a Cuban consulate, or the travel agency or the airline you bought your ticket from. This visa is a form which you have to fill in with your personal data. Visas are valid for one month and can be extended for another 30 days: in Havana, go to the **Vedado Immigration Office**. In other cities, you must go to the local Dirección Provincial de Inmigración. If, however, you are going to Cuba on business or to work as a journalist, you should

apply to the Cuban embassy or consulate in your home country well in advance for a special visa.

The travel ban for US passport holders has been lifted, although restrictions still apply. The situation is currently in flux *(see p300)*.

Vedado Immigration Office
Calle 17 No. 203 e/ J y K,
Vedado, Havana.

Travel Safety Advice

Visitors can get up-to-date travel safety information from the **Foreign and Commonwealth Office** in the UK, the **State Department** in the US and the **Department of Foreign Affairs and Trade** in Australia.

Customs Information

Besides your personal belongings, you are allowed to take into Cuba new or used objects whose overall value is no more than CUC$1,000, plus 10 kg (22 lb) of medicines in their original packaging. Small appliances such as electric razors are allowed; walkie-talkies require per-mission. It is forbidden to import fresh food such as fruit and plants of any kind, as well as explosives, drugs, and pornographic material. Hunters with firearms must present their permits at customs.

If you intend to take more than 50 cigars out of the country you must be able to produce a receipt declaring their purchase at a state-run

◄ A colourful street in Camagüey

shop. If you take out more than 50 you may well need to pay duty when you get home. Visitors can take no more than three bottles of liquor and 200 cigarettes out of the country.

In order to export works of art that are part of the national heritage, you must have official authorization from the Registro Nacional de Bienes Culturales del Ministerio de Cultura.

Rum for sale in a *tienda*, three per person for export

Avoid purchasing items made from endangered species such as tortoiseshell, or bags or belts made from non-farmed reptile skins. These are covered under the Convention on International Trade in Endangered Species (CITES). The import and export of vaccinated domestic animals is allowed.

Languages

The official language in Cuba is Castilian Spanish, which is spoken with a distinctive local inflection and vocabulary (see p327).

English is spoken fairly widely in Havana and in most hotels and resorts.

Forms of Greeting

The most common greeting in Cuba is a kiss on the cheek, while shaking hands is common among men only in formal circumstances. It is polite to use proper titles when speaking to Cubans – *señor, señora, señorita, doctor, ingeniero* (engineer) and *profesor*. The word *compañero* (comrade) is not used as much as it once was and in any case is used only among Cubans, or at the very most with foreigners who are part of volunteer organizations on the island.

What to Wear

The most suitable clothing for tourists is light and generally casual attire. In the winter a cotton or woollen sweater is useful in the evening, and may be useful at other times of year in places with air conditioning. A waterproof may come in handy all year round because of the tropical showers. Sunhats are recommended to protect the skin from the burning sun.

Except for evenings out at cabarets and nightclubs, there is usually no need for evening dress. However, Cubans do appreciate elegance and cleanliness. For a formal meeting or interview, men should not wear shorts or T-shirts, but trousers and a light shirt instead; and women should wear a dress or a skirt and blouse, but nothing too revealing.

Local Customs

Cuba is a tolerant country but attitudes are still rather conservative. Nudism and topless sunbathing are not allowed on most beaches.

Cuban men feel virtually obliged to pay compliments (*el piropo*) to women passing by on the street: it is almost a form of chivalry, a ritual, even if it is not always expressed with good taste. In any case, these kinds of comments should not be misinterpreted or a become a cause for concern; no reaction is seriously expected.

Women travelling alone should not experience problems, although they may be obliged to deal with frequent offers of assistance and compliments from men. The best way to put an end to undesired flirtation without offending is simply to say that you are married; this should be enough for most men to take the hint and leave you alone.

Hitchhiking

The lack of fuel and consequent scarcity of public transport has forced Cubans to resort to hitchhiking (*pedir botella*) both in the towns and in the countryside. Everyone hitchhikes, young and old, to get to work, run errands or travel to other towns and villages, but it is never completely reliable. Students sometimes have to walk for miles and miles to get to their schools.

Although locals are used to picking up hitchhikers, it is not recommended for tourists who are driving to do this. Cubans always pick up their fellow countrymen, but if they offer a foreigner a ride they may be fined by police unless they have a permit. Some drivers may expect payment.

Hitchhiking is a popular form of transport for Cubans in rural areas

Jineterismo

The tourist boom and the economic crisis have given rise to a particular form of hustling and prostitution both known as *jineterismo*, which consists of living off foreign tourists, not only through prostitution proper, but also by selling counterfeit goods (especially cigars), finding rooms for rent or *paladares* and receiving a commission from the owners. The *jinetera* (*jinetero* if male) accosts the tourist, and initiates a relationship that may last a night or several days. To avoid difficult situations, be wary of "chance" meetings, especially outside hotels or in discos in cities and resort locales.

This mainly affects Havana and cities and resorts popular with tourists. Cubans are very friendly people so don't dismiss everyone as a *jinetero*.

Cuban Law

In Cuba camping and sleeping in sleeping bags on the beach, or in areas not specifically used as a camping site, is strictly forbidden.

Cannabis may be offered on the street or outside a disco, but purchasing even a tiny amount of marijuana is illegal and could lead to immediate expulsion from the country.

Tourist Information

The state-run tourist information network **Infotur** and national travel agents such as Cubatur and Cubanacán have offices in major cities, at airports and in many hotels, offering basic information, ticket booking and trips. Maps, guides and brochures are also available. The Cuban publisher Ediciones GEO produces particularly good maps.

Opening Hours

Normal weekday working hours are 8am to 5:30pm; banks open at 8am and close at 3pm. Museum opening hours vary, but in general they are from around 9am to 5pm, with a half-day on Sunday. If a visit is important to you, it is best to telephone ahead.

Colonial building of the United Kingdom's embassy in Miramar, Havana

An entry fee is always charged at museums. Children pay half-price, Cubans pay in national *pesos* and tourists, on average, pay 1–5 convertible pesos. The same amount may be charged for permission to take photos in museums.

Gay and Lesbian Travellers

Historically, Cuba holds a poor record on gay rights. However, after the decriminalization of homosexual relations in 1979, the attitude towards homosexuality has changed significantly. Nevertheless, public display of affection such as holding hands may invite unwanted attention. There are many popular gay bars and clubs on Malecón y 23 in Havana. Santa Clara also has a lively gay culture.

Disabled Travellers

Only major airports, hotels and restaurants have wheelchair access for the disabled. José Marti International Airport is wheelchair-accessible throughout, and is equipped with ramps, lifts, and accessible toilets. A programme is under way to gradually add such facilities to other airports and stations, as well as public buildings, museums, offices and streets.

Electrical Adaptors

The electric current in Cuba is 110 volts AC (the same as in the US), and plug sockets take two flat prongs. For European-type appliances and plugs you will need a voltage converter and an electric adaptor plug, although some of the up-market hotels have sockets that accept round-pin Continental-style plugs and three-pin British plugs. Many modern buildings and hotels also have 220-volt AC current.

Cuban Time

Cuba is five hours behind Greenwich Mean Time (GMT), like the US east coast. As in Europe, there is daylight savings time in summer.

DIRECTORY

Embassies

Canada
Calle 30 No. 518, esq. Ave. 7, Miramar, Playa, Havana. **Tel** 7204 2516. **W** **canadainternational. gc.ca/cuba**

UK
Calle 34 No. 702, esq. 7, Miramar, Playa, Havana. **Tel** 7214 2200. **W** **ukincuba.fco.gov.uk**

US
Calle Calzada, esq. L, Vedado, Havana. **Map** 2 E1. **Tel** 7839 4100. **W** **havana.usembassy.gov**

Travel Safety Advice

Australia
Department of Foreign Affairs and Trade
W **dfat.gov.au**
W **smartraveller.gov.au**

UK
Foreign and Commonwealth Office
W **gov.uk/foreign-travel-advice**

US
US Department of State
W **travel.state.gov**

Tourist Bureau

Infotur
Obispo 524, e/ Bernaza y Villegas, Havana. **Map** 4 D2.
Tel 7866 3333. **W** **infotur.cu**

Websites

General
W **cubatravel.cu**
W **cubaupdate.org**
W **dtcuba.com**
W **oncubamagazine.com/en**

Cuban Culture
W **afrocubaweb.com**
W **cubaabsolutely.com**
W **cubarte-english.cult.cu**

In Spanish
W **cubasi.cu**

Personal Security

Compared with any other part of North, Central or South America, Cuba is a peaceful and safe place to travel in. However, in recent years, the great development of tourism, combined with the economic crisis, has triggered an increase in petty crime, especially in Havana and Santiago. Although the situation is under control, it is wise to take a few precautions: leave your valuables, documents and money in the hotel safe; never carry a large amount of money with you; do not wear showy jewellery; and keep an eye on your camera. If you have a hired car, it is always advisable to park near hotels or pay someone to mind it, and do not leave any belongings open to view in the car.

A traffic policeman

Cuban Police and the Fire Brigade

Policemen in Cuba are usually polite and willing to help tourists. The officials who check passports in the airports, who belong to the Inmigración y Extranjería and wear green military uniforms, do their job slowly and with what might be considered excessive meticulousness, but problems are not common. Tourists' luggage is often not checked, but it is best to adhere to the customs regulations to be on the safe side.

The policemen of the PNR (Policía Nacional Revolucionaria) wear blue trousers and a light grey shirt. Their role is to maintain public order, and they seldom stop foreigners. In some tourist areas such as Varadero and La Habana Vieja, you may see policemen in dark blue uniforms; they belong to a special corps that was created expressly to protect tourists from pickpockets and to check the documents of suspicious

A fire engine at Matanzas

individuals. They speak some English and can also provide information.

Different uniforms are worn by the traffic policemen (policía de tránsito) and firemen (bomberos). Traffic police wear very dark navy blue uniforms, sunglasses and motorcycle helmets. They may stop you for speeding; do not ignore them.

Guards from the relatively new SEPSA organization offer security for banks and tiendas and also see to transporting valuables.

Road sign indicating a dangerous stretch of road

Road Safety

There are not that many cars in Cuba, even though traffic is increasing. While driving in the cities, watch out for cyclists, who do not always observe traffic regulations. The greatest potential dangers while travelling on roads and motor-ways through the countryside (see p305) are the animals grazing on the side of the road, the railway crossings without gates, and the vast areas of unlit roads. The road surface is often bumpy, with sometimes deep potholes, so speeds should be kept down.

When it rains for several days in a row, the roads may easily become flooded.

Theft and Lost Property

To report the loss or theft of personal documents and belongings, either find a policeman, who should take you to the nearest police station, or ask for directions. Once there, be prepared for a long wait to make your report.

Natural Disasters

The greatest natural danger in Cuba is the possibility of being caught in a hurricane. These seasonal storms cause very high winds, high tides and heavy rainfall which can lead to flooding. Hurricane season runs from June to November. The autumn months are when hurricanes are most likely, with most occuring in September. Nowadays hurricanes are forecast well in advance, leaving plenty of time for adequate security measures, so the risk involved should not be that great. Should a hurricane occur, follow the instructions given by hotel staff. You will probably be told to wait in the hotel until it passes, and asked to keep away from windows.

DIRECTORY
Emergency Numbers

Ambulance
Tel 104.

Fire Brigade
Tel 105.

Police
Tel 106.

Health and Medical Matters

Thanks to the good health services, and the absence of most tropical diseases, a trip to Cuba should pose no unusual health risks. All the international hotels have a doctor on 24-hour call, and the first visit, as well as first-aid service, is free of charge. However, owing to the present economic difficulties in the country and the embargo, everyday pharmaceutical items are in very short supply. Normal pharmacies are rarely well stocked, but the well-supplied *farmacias internacionales* – international pharmacies which charge in convertible pesos – are now found in many towns. However, it is best to bring your own supply of usual medicine – pain relievers, fever reducers, antibiotics and stomach treatments – as well as strong sunscreens and insect repellents.

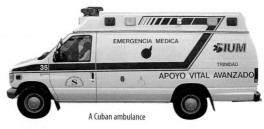

A Cuban ambulance

Vaccinations

No vaccinations or inoculations are required for visits to Cuba and it is quite safe to travel around the entire island. Malaria is no longer a threat thanks to a successful eradication campaign, but there have been recent outbreaks of cholera and dengue fever.

There are restrictive sanitary regulations only for those arriving from countries in which yellow fever and cholera are endemic diseases.

Medical Treatment

Cuban public health care is free of charge, efficient and superior to that offered in any other Latin American country, though it has been put under severe pressure by the US embargo.

The national service is reserved for Cuban citizens. Foreign visitors are treated in international clinics or in public hospitals, where they will have to pay for treatment in convertible pesos. On the plus side, they are given more comfortable rooms.

Health Insurance

Cuba requires that all visitors to Cuba and non-Cuban residents hold a valid health insurance policy. Those who do not may be required to purchase insurance at the airport. This is provided by **Asistur**, Cuba's travel emergency help organisation. US-issued medical insurance policies are not valid in Cuba. Citizens holding these must seek extra cover through **Havanatur Celimar.**

Pharmacies

The national pharmacies are not well stocked and generally reserved for Cubans. Medicines are sold only upon presentation of a prescription. In these pharmacies foreigners can only purchase medicines made from natural ingredients, including syrups, tinctures and vegetable essences, which are made on the premises. They are excellent, effective and cost virtually nothing (they can be paid for in *pesos*). On the other hand, the international pharmacies, which are located in Havana and more tourist resorts, stock various medicines that can be bought with or without a prescription, as well as over-the-counter products not found in the *tiendas*.

Public WCs (Restrooms)

Public toilets are hard to find, and they are often dirty and without water. Toilet paper is limited and it is wise to carry a good supply with you. Be sure to leave a tip for the attendant.

Illnesses

Summer colds are quite common in Cuba and it is a good idea to carry a light sweater or jacket for these occasions.

Asthma sufferers may find that the humid climate could trigger an attack; visitors to Cuba with respiratory problems should always carry their usual medicine (packaged) and an

Entrance to the historic Taquechel pharmacy in Havana *(see p76)*

Wear a hat and use sunscreen to avoid burns and heatstroke

inhaler with them. All the hospitals and *policlínicos* (the neighbourhood out-patient clinics) are well-equipped for these problems.

Another fairly common nuisance in Cuba is diarrhoea, or worse, dysentery. This can generally be prevented by always drinking bottled water, or water that has been purified with tablets; another useful precaution is to avoid food and drinks sold on the street. It is best to avoid ice in cocktails as well.

All these measures should also be enough to ward off giardiasis, a disease caused by a parasite that attacks the intestine and causes dysentery, nausea, fatigue and weight loss.

Rare cases of yellow fever and dengue fever may occur in the summer. However, since these two diseases are spread by mosquitoes, it is advisable to use plenty of insect repellent when planning to tour marshy areas, and to burn mosquito-repellent coils in the evening.

Protection from the Sun

The sun in Cuba is very strong and protection is necessary throughout the whole year. Wear a hat, whether sight seeing in town or lying on the beach, and use a strong sun lotion with a high screen factor. Sunscreen should be reapplied regularly, particularly after swimming. It is also advisable to drink plenty of water to prevent dehydration. High humidity and heat may cause heatstroke, with symptoms of thirst, nausea, fever, and dizziness. If this occurs, keep up fluid intake and take cold baths.

Insects

Mosquitoes are the main irritant in Cuba (and can cause disease). In swampy or lagoon areas, such as the Zapata swamp, pay particular attention to applying insect repellent, cover up in the evening and sleep with the fan or air conditioning on.

Health Tourism

Thanks to its favourable climate, Cuba has long been regarded as an effective sanatorium, popular with an international clientele. By the 19th century, the first hotels had been built near springs of therapeutic mineral water. Beside the spas, there are now international clinics which provide general medical care and also specialize in anti-stress and skin treatments, as well as hospitals for the rehabilitation of alcoholics and drug addicts. These centres are located throughout the country and are in great demand: the waiting lists are not long, the prices are competitive and the results are good. They are run by the state-run **Servimed** organization.

Dermatological treatment in one of the specialist clinics

Communications

The telephone is by far the most widespread system of communication in Cuba. Unlike the inefficient postal service, the telephone network has improved considerably. Today there are public telephones that work with pre-paid phone cards. Although internet usage is still restricted, Cuba took a huge leap forward in 2015 when public Wi-Fi zones were established around the country. Cuba also has five national television channels and a number of radio stations. Many hotels have a satellite dish and broadcast a TV channel especially for tourists. The leading daily newspaper is *Granma*, while *Granma Internacional* is printed weekly in various languages.

Telephone Numbers

If you are calling from abroad, dial the international access code of your country (eg 00 in the UK), followed by the Cuba country code (53), the local area code, and lastly the local phone number you want to reach. The local area codes, which may have one or two digits, are given in brackets in front of all phone numbers listed in this guide. For local calls, there is no need to dial the area code. For Havana numbers, always dial all eight digits. The number of digits of local numbers varies, since the phone network system is in the process of being updated.

Public Telephones

You can make local, long-distance, and international calls from hotels, but while this is certainly the easiest way, since the operator does everything for you, it is also the most expensive. Throughout the country there has been an increase in the number of public telephones that can be used to make direct-dial international calls without the help of the operator. Telephone cards *(tarjetas propias)* with scratch-off codes can be purchased at hotels, post offices and ETECSA telephone centres for $5, $10 and $20. To make a call, lift the receiver and wait for the dialling tone. Either press the button marked 166, or dial 166 and wait for instructions; you will be offered an English-language option if needed. You will then be asked to enter the 12-digit number on your scratch card, followed by the hash (#) key; then dial the number as below.

A few fuctioning coin-operated phones still exist.

Telephone card

These are useful for local calls. You must insert at least one 5-*centavos* coin (also known as a "*medio*"), or use a 20-*centavos* coin (a "*peseta*") to talk for a few minutes.

5- and 20-*centavos* coins

Private Telephones

The only direct-dial calls that can be made from private telephones are to numbers within Cuba; international calls must be made through an operator. Calls to foreign countries are always reverse charge, unless you use an ETECSA telephone with a contract specifying payment in convertible pesos. This type of phone can be found in hotels, in travel agencies, in some public offices and in the homes of foreigners who work in Cuba, rarely in Cubans' private homes. Telephone cards can be used from private lines.

Mobile Phones

There are four main GSM frequencies (Global System for Mobile Communications) in use around the world, so if you want to guarantee that your phone will work, make sure you have a quad-band phone. Tri-band phones from outside the US are also usually compatible. A few US-based service providers have begun offering roaming in Cuba. Contact your service provider to see if they are among them. Also, check your insurance policy in case your phone is stolen, and keep your network operator's helpline number handy.

To use your mobile phone abroad you may need to enable "roaming" for your phone. Keep in mind that rates are high and that you are charged for calls you receive as well as calls you make, and you have to pay a premium for the international leg of the call. Check rates for Internet data usage with your provider as these can be very high as well.

Dialling Codes

• Directory inquiries 113.
• To make a long-distance call via the operator, dial 00.
• To make a reverse charge (collect) international call via the operator, dial 180.
• To dial long-distance within Cuba, dial 01 then the area code, except for calls to or from Havana. For calls to the capital add 0 before the eight-digit phone number; when dialling from it, dial 0, area code and number.
• To make a direct-dial international telephone call from a public telephone with a phone card, dial 119, followed by the country code (Australia 61; Ireland 353; New Zealand 64; UK 44; USA and Canada 1), the area code and then the local telephone number.

Another option may be to purchase a local SIM card – the electronic chip that links your phone to a particular network – that can be topped up with credit and uses the local mobile phone networks. You can only do this if your handset is "unlocked" – some operators lock their phones to specific networks. However, this is not particularly cheap in Cuba, costing CUC$3 a day through the only provider, **Cubacel**. Cubacel works with TDMA and GSM phones. The cheapest international calls start at CUC$1.40 per minute; international texts are CUC$1. For most travellers this will mean using their own phone in Cuba may work out cheaper.

Postal Service

The Cuban postal service is slow, but generally no worse than in any other Latin American country. Stamps *(sellos)* can be purchased in *pesos* in hotels or in post offices *(oficinas de correo)*. Whatever the postage, letters take a long time to arrive; it may help a little to post mail in the *oficinas de correo* postboxes.

The safest, and comparatively the fastest, way to post documents, letters or parcels that are important or urgent is via international courier services: **DHL** or **Cubapack Internacional SA**.

Entrance to a post office *(oficina de correo)* in Havana

Addresses

In Cuba the house number, preceded by "No." or "#", comes after the name of the street or square, followed by *"esq."* *(esquina* = corner) and the name of the cross street, or by

"e/" *(entre* = between) and the name of two streets *(see p122)*. This is followed by the number of the apartment, if it has one, or by *"altos"* (first floor) or *"bajos"* (ground floor) if it is a private house, followed by the name of the *"reparto"* (quarter) or district, and then by the locality.

Radio and Television

There are five main Cuban television channels. Cubavisión broadcasts soap operas, films, news, music and US drama series around the clock. Tele Rebelde specializes in news and sports programmes and airs educational programming during the day and documentaries in the evening, as do Canal Educativo and Canal Educativo 2. Multivisión also screens documentaries. Venezuela's Telesur news channel also broadcasts in Cuba. Each province has its own local channel.

Hotels have a selection of channels such as CNN, Discovery, ESPN, HBO and The Cartoon Network, all of which are not allowed in family homes.

A good radio station is *Radio Taíno*, with music and information in English and Spanish (1180 AM in Havana and 1100 AM in Varadero). *Radio Rebelde* has news, music and sports; *Radio Habana Cuba* broadcasts for an overseas audience; and *Radio Reloj* broadcasts news 24 hours a day.

Newspapers and Periodicals

The only national newspaper in the country is *Granma*, the official organ of the Cuban Communist Party, published in Spanish. The party also publishes a weekly version for foreigners, *Granma Internacional*, in multiple languages. There are also several provincial dailies: *Tribuna de La Habana* in Havana; *Guerrillero* in Pinar del Río; *Girón* in Matanzas; *5 de Septiembre* in Cienfuegos;

Adelante in Camagüey; *Ahora* in Holguín; *Sierra Maestra* in Santiago de Cuba; and *Victoria* in Isla de la Juventud.

Among Cuba's magazines, *Bohemia* is a well-respected cultural weekly. In Havana, the elusive *Cartelera* provides information on the latest cultural events in English.

Most large hotels offer Internet access to foreigners

Internet and Fax

Although the use of personal e-mail is restricted for Cubans, it is being used increasingly in offices. Surfing the Internet is now available to most via public Wi-Fi zones. There are a limited number of such zones, however, the number is increasing. Access is via internet scratch cards for CUC$2 an hour. You can log on in many hotels by buying an ETECSA scratch card for CUC$6 per hour. Some hotels provide the Wi-Fi separately.

Fax services are available in all international post offices in the large cities, as well as in all major hotels.

DIRECTORY

Mobile Phones

Cubacel
W etecsa.cu

Postal Service

Cubapack Internacional SA
Calle 22 n. 4115, e/ 41 y 47, Playa, Havana.
Tel (7) 204 2817, (7) 204 2134.
W cubapack.com

DHL
Calle 26, esq. 1, Playa, Havana.
Tel (7) 204 1876.

Banking and Local Currency

Cuba's currency is the *peso cubano* (CUP), but most visitors primarily use the *peso convertible* (CUC), or convertible peso. You can buy and pay for everything in convertible pesos. The US dollar was valid in Cuba until 2004 when the law changed, and it is now the least desirable major currency to bring to the country as, although exchangeable in banks, it is subject to a 10 per cent surcharge. Credit cards and travellers' cheques issued by US banks are not accepted anywhere in Cuba. Euros are now widely accepted in hotels in Varadero, Jardines del Rey, Holguín, Santa Lucía and Cayo Largo del Sur.

Banks and Bureaux de Change

Banks are usually open from 8am to 3pm from Monday to Friday. Among those that carry out foreign currency transactions the best prepared are the **Banco de Crédito y Comercio** (BANDEC) and the **Banco Financiero Internacional** (BFI), with branches in the major tourist resorts and provincial capitals. Bank commissions on travellers' cheques is 2 or 3 per cent and more at weekends.

Bureaux de change, especially those located in hotels, have longer opening hours than banks. The commission for cashing travellers' cheques is around 4 per cent. The **CADECA Casas de Cambio**, often located near shops or markets, are the only places to buy *pesos cubanos*. Rates at hotel exchange desks are higher than those on the high street. Money can also be

withdrawn using a credit or debit card (VISA or Mastercard), but check with your bank and let them know of your travel plans to avoid any issues. Most Automated Teller Machines (ATMs) accept foreign cards, and can be easily found in cities and near popular tourist destinations.

The logo of the Banco Financiero Internacional

Credit Cards

The vast majority of hotels, some restaurants and many convertible peso-charging shops accept credit cards, though only those issued by non-US banks and never American Express. If you encounter a problem using a credit card, contact the **Centro de Tarjetas de Crédito in Havana**.

In many small towns, and even in some remote tourist resorts, credit cards will be useless, so it is wise to carry cash with you (this is essential outside of the major cities and tourist resorts). Wherever you are, cash will be needed for tips and small purchases.

Currency

The dual economy of the *peso cubano* and the *peso convertible* (convertible peso) can be confusing, especially as both currencies are often referred to as *pesos*. Even the symbol ($) used to denote them is the same. The most

The handsome Neo-Classical façade of a bank in Santa Clara

common terms to differentiate them are *"moneda nacional"* or CUP for the *peso cubano*, and *"divisa"* or CUC for the convertible peso.

There are currently 24 *pesos cubanos* to the convertible peso. Visitors will use the convertible peso almost exclusively, while the *peso cubano* is used mostly just by Cubans. However, it is the only valid currency on local buses, at cinemas and sports stadiums, so it may be a good idea to carry a small amount with you. Plans to abolish the dual currency have been announced but no timeline has been published.

Coins (Pesos Cubanos)

There are 100 centavos (cents) to a national peso. Cuban coins come in 1 centavo ("kilo"), 2 centavos, 5 centavos ("medio" – used for calls), 20 centavos ("peseta", also used for phone calls); and 1 and 3 pesos (the latter bearing Che Guevara's portrait).

3 pesos

1 peso

20 centavos

5 centavos

Bank Notes (Pesos Cubanos)

Cuban bank notes come in units of 1, 3, 5, 10, 20, 50 and 100 pesos. Each note has a different colour. Twenty-four pesos correspond to one peso convertible: be careful not to confuse the bank notes.

5 pesos

10 pesos

20 pesos

Pesos Convertibles (Convertible Pesos)

Bank notes of the peso convertible circulate in units of 1, 3, 5, 10, 20, 50 and 100 pesos. The coins come in units of 1, 5, 10, 25, 50 cents and 1 peso. These pesos convertibles are not valid anywhere outside Cuba.

1 peso convertible

25 centavos

10 centavos

5 centavos

1 centavo

10 pesos convertibles

TRAVEL INFORMATION

The majority of foreign tourists arrive in Cuba by aeroplane. Charter and regular scheduled flights have been landing in Cuba for years from Europe, Canada, Central and South America. In 2016, US commercial flights joined the list. The internal connections within Cuba are good, and there is at least one airport in every Cuban province; 10 are international and 21 domestic. Taxis are available at the airport for hotel transfers, if these have not been previously arranged, or cars may be hired (driving is the most efficient way of getting around Cuba). For the time being, big international rental agencies do not operate in Cuba: car hire firms remain Cuban for now *(see p305)*. On Cayo Largo, one of Cuba's most well-known island resorts, there is an airport with international links, and Isla de la Juventud is linked to the rest of Cuba by a domestic airport as well as by ferries and catamarans.

US Travellers

In December of 2014, US President Obama announced a set of diplomatic and economic changes to chart a new course in US relations with Cuba, including the loosening of travel restrictions for Americans wishing to visit Cuba. This policy change means the **US Treasury Department** no longer requires special tourist licences. Travellers will only have to certify they are visiting in one of 12 categories – educational, religious and humanitarian projects, among others – while pure tourism remains prohibited, for now. To ensure you meet the requirements, travelling through a licensed US travel agent is advisable. Other changes include being able to use US credit and debit cards in Cuba.

Arriving by Air

Cuba is connected to Europe and the rest of the world by flights

Entrance to the José Martí airport in Havana

operated by several major airlines, with scheduled and charter flights. Most arrivals from Britain are charter flights. **Thomas Cook** offers package deals to Cayo Coco, Varadero, Holguín and Cayo Santa María. The Cuban national airline, **Cubana de Aviación**, has regular flights between European cities, including Paris and Madrid, and Havana. **Blue Panorama** flies from Italy.

Most scheduled routes from Britain involve a stopover in a third country, though **Virgin Atlantic** flies direct from Gatwick to Havana. **Air France** flights depart from Heathrow and other UK airports to Havana

CITY	AIRPORT	INFORMATION	DISTANCE FROM CITY OR TOURIST CENTRE
Havana	José Martí	7266 4133	Town centre: 17 km (11 miles)
Varadero	Juan Gualberto Gómez	(45) 247 015	Town centre: 6 km (4 miles)
Cayo Largo del Sur	Vilo Acuña	(45) 248 141	(in the middle of the cay)
Camagüey	Ignacio Agramonte	(32) 261 010	Town centre: 9 km (5.5 miles)
Holguín	Frank País	(24) 462 512	Town centre: 13 km (8 miles)
Santiago de Cuba	Antonio Maceo	(22) 698 614	Town centre: 6 km (4 miles)
Manzanillo	Sierra Maestra	(23) 577 401	Town centre: 8 km (5 miles)
Cayo Coco	Jardines del Rey	(33) 309 165	(in the east of the cay)
Cienfuegos	Jaime González	(43) 552 047	Town centre: 20 km (12 miles)

via Paris. **Air Europa** flies via Madrid; **KLM** via Amsterdam.

From Canada, there are flights with Cubana de Aviación and **Air Canada**. Cubana de Aviación and **Interjet** also operate flights from Mexico – with services departing from Cancún and Mexico City airports. **Avianca** flies from other parts of Central America.

Regular flights have been scheduled by US airlines to all airports across Cuba since late 2016. **American Airlines** and **JetBlue** are among the carriers that operate daily flights to Havana, and a few selected carriers fly to other Cuban cities.

Airports

Cuba has 10 international and 21 domestic airports. The main international airport is José Martí, 18 km (11 miles) south of Havana. Charter flights land at Terminal 2, scheduled flights at Terminal 3, while Terminal 1 is reserved for domestic flights.

Most of the other international airports (other than in Havana) are for charter flights for tourists en route to holiday resorts. Of these, Varadero is the busiest.

Arriving by Sea

British **Thomson** and Canadian **Your Cuba Cruise** both run cruises around the island. **Starclippers** runs from Cienfuegos with port calls on the Cayman Islands.

In 2015 the US government began issuing licenses to American ferry operators for services between Havana and ports in Miami and the Florida Keys. In 2016, the US cruise operator, Carnival Corp made its maiden voyage to Cuba.

With the setting up of suitable terminal facilities, the Cuban government is expected to issue licenses by 2017.

Private yachts are welcome at Cuba's many harbours, including Marina Hemingway in Havana. The following documents are needed: the passports of all those on board, the ownership documents, the name and registration number of the boat, and the customs document *(zarpe)* issued at the last port the ship called at. The *Cruising Guide to Cuba* by Simon Charles is a good source of information.

Organized Tours and Package Holidays

Air fares vary depending on the airline and time of year. The best value is often to buy a package including charter flights from a tour operator; your travel agent can help you decide which is the most suitable for your needs.

Mainstream UK tour operators include Thomas Cook and **The Holiday Place**. Specialist operators, who can help independent travellers plan a tailor-made visit, include **Journey Latin America** and **Esencia Experiences**. Caledonia *(see p253 and p255)* offers arrangements including music and dance tuition.

Special interest holidays, especially those involving diving, watersports and salsa are particularly popular, and eco-tourism is also a developing area *(see p254)*. Among the tour operators offering special interest holidays are **Scuba en Cuba** and **Cubania**.

DIRECTORY

US Travellers

US Treasury Department
Tel (202) 622 2000 (US).
W treas.gov/ofac

Arriving by Air

Air Canada
W aircanada.com

Air Europa
W aireuropa.com

Air France
W airfrance.com

American Airlines
W aa.com

Avianca
W avianca.com

Blue Panorama
W blue-panorama.it

Cubana de Aviación
W cubana.cu

Interjet
W interjet.com

JetBlue
W jetblue.com

KLM
W klm.com

Thomas Cook
W thomascook.com

Virgin Atlantic
W virgin-atlantic.com

Arriving by Sea

Starclippers
W starclippers.com

Thomson
W thomson.co.uk/cruise

Your Cuba Cruise
W yourcubacruise.com

Tour Operators

Cubania
Tel 7207 9888 (Cuba).
W cubaniatravel.com

Esencia Experiences
Tel 01481 714 898 (UK).

The Holiday Place
Tel 020 7644 1770 (UK).
W theholidayplace.co.uk

W esenciaexperiences.com

Journey Latin America
Tel 020 3432 9175 (UK).
W journeylatinamerica.co.uk

Scuba en Cuba
Tel 01895 624 100 (UK).
W scuba-en-cuba.com

An aeroplane landing at Cayo Largo, an international holiday resort

Getting Around Cuba

If your time is limited, one way to get around the island on public transport is by aeroplane, because this is the only really fast means of transport in Cuba. The network of domestic flights is good and connections are made via Cubana de Aviación. Trains are much cheaper, but they are also much slower and very unreliable. Tourist coach services, on the other hand, are a good option. They are numerous, comfortable and provide services to all the tourist resorts and provincial capitals.

years pay only 33 per cent of the normal fare.

The aeroplanes are not always new, the domestic flight safety record is dubious, and the service may lack frills, but the staff are experienced and reliable.

Ships and Ferries

If time is not an issue, it is possible to travel to Isla de la Juventud by sea rather than by air. Departure is from the port of Batabanó, on the southern coast, 60 km (37 miles) from the capital. Nowadays a catamaran built by Damex Shipbuilding & Engineering does the journey in about two and a half hours. Tickets for the catamaran can be bought at the quay or as part of a combination ticket at Havana bus station. Book ahead at all times.

In the cities of Havana, Santiago and Cienfuegos, you can also find waterbuses or ferries called *lanchas* or *lanchitas*, which operate around their respective bays, linking towns or providing a crossing to the opposite side.

Small ferries connect the coast north of Pinar del Río with the island of Cayo Levisa and the mainland outside Santiago de Cuba with Cayo Granma.

Nueva Gerona national airport, Isla de la Juventud

Booking and Check-in for Domestic Flights

There are flights from Havana to Baracoa, Bayamo, Camagüey, Cayo Coco, Cayo Largo, Cienfuegos, Guantánamo, Holguín, Las Tunas, Manzanillo, Moa, Nueva Gerona, Santa Clara and Santiago de Cuba.

It is not necessary to go in person to the **Cubana de Aviación** airline offices to book a domestic flight; any travel agency will contact these airlines for you and make your reservation without any extra charge. However, bear in mind

that you should book very early, especially for flights in high season. Check-in is 60 minutes before take-off, and the maximum luggage weight allowance is 20 kg (44 lbs).

Domestic flights cost about twice as much as trains or coaches,

A Cubana de Aviación plane for domestic flights

but if you book one together with an international flight with Cubana, there is a saving of 25 per cent. Children under the age of two travel free of charge, and young people under 18

Trains

Cuba has 4,881 km (3,030 miles) of public railway lines, serving all the provincial capitals. Over time, the service has severely deteriorated and the carriages

A *lanchita*, a waterbus connecting the various towns around the bay of Havana

are by no means modern and clean. Refreshments may not be available, so take supplies.

There is at least one train per day on each of the main lines, but do not count on it arriving on time.

The trains known as "especiales", which cover long-distance routes such as Havana-Santiago, have air conditioning (though it may not always function as it should), reclinable seats and a refreshment service.

Information on timetables and tickets (tourists have to pay in convertible pesos) can be obtained at the **Agencia de Reservacion La Coubre** agency, which sells tickets to foreigners. It is open for business from 8am to 3pm Monday to Friday.

The advantage in travelling by train is that it is almost always possible to find a seat without booking in advance, even in high season. If you have time, patience and are on a tight budget, railway travel can be an interesting and sociable way of travelling around Cuba.

Façade of the railway station in Morón

Coach Services

The modern coaches operated by the **Víazul** company provide transport to the main cities and towns and tourist resorts in Cuba. They connect Havana with Santiago (passing through Santa Clara, Ciego de Ávila, Camagüey, Las Tunas, Holguín and Bayamo), Varadero, Trinidad and Viñales. There is also a direct service between Varadero and Trinidad, and a daily link between Santiago and Baracoa.

On the positive side, Viazul coaches are very comfortable and arrive on time – the disadvantage is that, at least on

A minibus for tourists

the stretch between Havana and Santiago, the frequent intermediate stops in all the provincial capitals make for rather a long journey. The seats can be reclined, and there are toilets for passengers (but be sure to bring some toilet paper with you). The air conditioning is always turned on full, so that if you do decide to use this means of transport, always carry on board a sweater or jacket.

Now that Cubans use this service, demand, especially in high season, is great. Always book in advance during these times. In July in Santiago, up to a week's advance booking is required.

Cubanacán also runs Conectando Cuba, which is a similar service to that offered by Víazul with the addition of a hotel door to hotel door service, although destinations are limited. Ask about booking this at your hotel tour desk.

Travel agencies also supply hotels with minibus shuttle services to take guests to nearby tourist resorts.

Tickets can either be booked in advance from a travel agency or bought on the day from a bus station.

DIRECTORY

Cubana de Aviación

Baracoa
Calle José Martí 181.
Tel (21) 645 374.

Camagüey
Calle República 400.
Tel (32) 291 338.

Holguín
Calle Libertad esq. Martí.
Tel (24) 468 149.

Santiago de Cuba
Calle Enramada, esq. San Pedro.
Tel (22) 651 578.

Varadero
Ave 1ra e/ 54 y 55.
Tel (45) 611 823–5.

Agencia de Reservacion La Coubre

Havana
Estación La Coubre, Ave. del Puerto esq. Egido, La Habana Vieja. **Map** 4 E4. **Tel** 7860 3165.

Víazul

Havana Main Office
Ave 26 y Zoológico, Nuevo Vedado. **Tel** 7881 1413 or 7881 5652. W viazul.com

Santiago de Cuba
Ave de los Libertadores, esq. Yarayó. **Tel** (22) 628 484.

Varadero
Calle 36 y Autopista.
Tel (45) 614 886.

A Víazul line coach

Travelling by Car

The best way to see a lot of Cuba's hinterland is to travel by car. With a car it is possible to discover places and scenery that it would be difficult to see on an organized tour, and even more so if you travel by air. It is best to plan an itinerary and stopovers in advance, and a good road map is essential. A few precautions should be taken. Keep speed down and always park in supervised car parks. In summer, because of the heat, it is advisable to travel early in the morning. You will see many people hitchhiking on the road. Although this is a normal way of life in Cuba, it it not recommended for tourists to pick people up *(see p291)*.

Example of a new road sign seen outside cities

A lorry picking up hitchhikers on the Autopista Nacional (motorway)

The Highway Code

In Cuba traffic drives on the right. The speed limits for cars are 20 km/h (12 mph) in parking areas, 40 km/h (25 mph) near schools, 50 km/h (30 mph) in town, 60 km/h (37 mph) on dirt roads and in tunnels, 90 km/h (55 mph) on asphalt roads and 100 km/h (62 mph) on the motorway.

Every so often on the *Autopista* (motorway) you will see signs telling you to reduce your speed to around 50 km/h: do not ignore these instructions, as they are often followed by road blocks. In general, the police are quite tolerant with tourists, but speeding may invalidate car hire insurance.

In town, headlights should be kept dipped. Seat belt use is both recommended and compulsory.

The road signs, of which there are very few, are the usual international ones, but there are also others on the country roads that warn drivers they are approaching a junction or a stretch of dangerous road *(see p293)*.

The Road Network

The carretera central is an old, narrow and not particularly comfortable road linking Pinar del Río to Guantánamo, via all the provincial capitals. The only motorway in Cuba is the Autopista Nacional, or "Ocho Vías"; it goes from Pinar del Río to Jatibonico, near Sancti Spíritus (the Holguín–Santiago de Cuba stretch is under construction) and is toll-free. It is in good condition but should be used as if it were an ordinary road, without exceeding the speed limit, because every so often the road is crossed by unmarked railway lines or wandering animals.

The worst roads, with potholes and bumps, are found in Eastern Cuba, but the surfaces of city streets are by no means perfect either.

Petrol

Fuel is distributed through the many Servi-Cupet and Oro Negro service stations throughout the island. They sell petrol for convertible pesos and are open 24 hours a day. However, there are fewer stations outside the towns, so keep the tank topped up, just in case.

Ask the car hire company for a free *automapa*, which shows where the Servi-Cupet service stations are located across the island.

Road Maps

A good road map is essential. The *Guía de Carreteras* published by Limusa is very informative but unfortunately not widely available. **Infotur** in Havana and some car rental companies may stock copies.

Maps and brochures are also distributed free of charge by Infotur, in travel agencies and by car hire companies.

A hire car at a Servi-Cupet service station

Number Plates

Cuban car number plates have changed from the collectable colour-coded ones to long, thin white ones with a letter system to denote the type of ownership. Those beginning with A belong to the state; T for tourist car; C, D and E for diplomats; F for the military; and M for the Ministry of the Interior. The rest of the private vehicles are identified with the other letters of the alphabet.

Recently-issued number plate

Road Safety

The most serious danger on Cuban roads is posed, in fact, by slow, unlit vehicles: carts and carriages, tractors and cyclists tend to occupy the middle of the road, and before overtaking them it is a good idea to sound the horn.

It is also a good rule of thumb to sound the horn before making a sharp turn or when passing a lorry (they often do not have rear-view mirrors).

It is forbidden to keep your car lights on during the day, unless there is heavy fog. It is advisable not to drive outside town at night unless absolutely necessary, because of poor visibility and lack of road signs. Roads are not lit and you may run into animals, pedestrians

and even cyclists, whose bicycles are rarely equipped with front lights and rear reflectors.

At any time of day, take extra care after rainy weather, because road surfaces may become flooded (see p293). In mountain areas there may be some danger of falling rocks.

Tourists on a scooter

Car Hire

In order to hire a car in Cuba visitors must have a valid driver's licence from their own country or an international licence, be over 21 years of age, and have a valid passport to show to the car rental company. The three main agencies are **Havanautos**, **Cubacar** and **Vía Rent a Car**. Cars from Havanautos and Cubacar can be booked through the website of Transtur. Chauffer-driven cars are available from **Rex**. These have their own offices, and a number of branch offices in hotels throughout the island and in Servi-Cupet service stations.

Cars can also be picked up and dropped off at most of the airports, but it is advisable to book them well in advance, especially in high season, when the smaller and cheaper models are very much in demand. Note that cars with automatic transmission cost more than those with manual transmission.

Payment is made in advance, and you must either leave a cash deposit (which is refunded) or leave an imprint of your credit card. You must also pay a minimum of CUC$10 insurance

per driver per day. A car may be dropped off at a different office from the one where it was hired, but there will be a surcharge.

A penalty will also have to be paid if the contract for car hire is lost. There are two kinds of optional insurance for hire cars. Plan A covers accidents but not theft, and Plan B covers all risks except for loss of a tyre. In the event of an accident you must obtain a copy of the police report that states that you are not culpable (if you are not); this should then be handed over to the car hire company.

For exploring certain parts of the island, including the extreme west and far east, it may be best to hire a four-wheel drive (off-roader) to negotiate the pitted roads.

Larger groups of visitors can rent a minibus from **Transtur**. It is also possible to hire scooters.

DIRECTORY

Road Maps

Infotur
Obispo 524, e/ Bernazay Villegas, Havana. **Map** 4 D2.
Tel 7866 3333.
w infotur.cu

Car Hire

Cubacar
Calle 3rd y Paseo, Vedado, Havana. **Tel** 7833 2164.

Havanautos
Hotel Sevilla, Prado e/ Animas y Trocadero, La Habana Vieja, Havana. **Tel** 7866 8956.

Rex
5 ta Avenida y 92 , Playa.
Tel 7204 2214.

Transtur
3 y Paseo, Vedado, Havana.
Tel 7833 2164.
w transturcarrental.com

**Vía Rent a Car
(Transgaviota)**
Calle 98 e/ 9na y 11.
Tel 7206 9935.

A hired four-wheel drive: a good choice of vehicle for the road conditions in Cuba

Getting Around Havana

In Havana, road traffic is on the increase but is still nowhere near the levels of a normal European or American city. Getting around using public transport can be a major undertaking, unless you use the local tourist bus service, HabanaBusTour, or collective taxis. On the other hand, there are plenty of private taxis, which offer a safe and fast way of getting around town. In La Habana Vieja and Centro Habana, the most pleasant way to explore is to hire a bicitaxi or to stay on foot.

HabanaBusTour, the best and cheapest way to explore Havana

A bicitaxi near the Capitol building

Walking in Havana

Havana is an immense city and every district *(municipio)* extends for miles. However, if you are staying in the city centre (the area described on pages 60–109) then it should be quite feasible to do most of your exploring on foot. Besides, walking along the Malecón seaside promenade, or through the tree-lined streets in the Vedado quarter, or the old colonial section of town, is a very pleasant experience. Visitors have the chance to discover hidden corners and details of buildings that would not be noticed from a car.

Should you begin to tire, it's easy enough to flag down a taxi or bicitaxi *(see opposite)*; there are more of these on the streets since the government eased the rules limiting self-employment. The best places for hailing taxis are the main arteries such as Calle 23 in Vedado. Should you get lost, ask a local passer-by for help; Cubans are usually very courteous and helpful with foreign tourists.

Bus Services

Travelling by bus in the city can be something of an adventure. However, it is made easier by the hop-on/hop-off air-conditioned tourist bus service, HabanaBusTour, with two different routes around town. Route 1 starts in Parque Central and travels west to Plaza de la Revolución; Route 2 heads east to Playas del Este. A daily ticket costs five convertible pesos for Route 1 and three convertible pesos for Route 2.

Take the local buses to visit the areas not covered by the tourist buses, but be prepared to devote plenty of time and patience to each journey. The ability to speak Spanish will help, and be sure to make a note of the number of the bus you have to take as well as its route, because there are no route maps at the bus stops to indicate the various stops. At any bus stop you must generally ask who is the last *(último* or *última)* in line for the *ruta* (destination) you want. There is a queue even though you may not be aware of it, which will re-form in an organized way once the bus arrives.

Passengers get on the front of the bus, where the conductor or driver should be paid the fare in small change in national *pesos*. The cost is usually 40 Cuban cents, though you can also pay 5 centavos convertibles per journey. Buses are usually very crowded, so you are privileged if you find an empty seat. The heat can often be suffocating. Allow plenty of time to get out, because passengers tend to block the exit door. Hold wallets and bags close to deter pickpockets.

The metrobus service has now replaced the old *camellos*. The buses are more comfortable and run more often.

The modern Metrobus has replaced the old *camello*

Taxis

Certainly the safest and most comfortable way of getting about in Havana is by taxi. There are many cars bearing the word TAXI, but not all of them are authorized to pick up tourists. Official taxis can be recognized easily because they are new and well-kept, comfortable, and usually have air conditioning. Avoid illegal taxis, which have no accident insurance and may be more expensive. The official taxi company is **Cubataxi**.

Taxis can be summoned by phone or hailed in the street. Taxi ranks are found in front of hotels, at the airport and in the following two places in La Habana Vieja: by Plaza de Armas behind el Templete, and at the corner of Calle Empedrado and Tacón. A quirky alternative is to hire an old American convertible car, which are also official taxis; easily recognisable because they have the Taxis Cuba sign and logo on both sides. These can be found outside the Hotel Nacional (see p257) and around Parque Central (see pp84–5).

Tourists can also legally ride in local taxi *colectivos* – old American cars, which bear the sign TAXI in the window. Each journey within Havana costs 10 Cuban pesos. Foreigners may pay in convertible pesos and will be given change in *moneda nacional*.

Cocotaxis

An original and unusual means of transport is the *cocotaxi*, an egg-shaped yellow scooter that can carry two passengers

Look out for the Cubataxi logo, found on all official state-owned taxis

as well as the driver. It costs more than a taxi and doesn't have a meter. The driver does not give receipts, however, it is very useful for short rides.

The yellow *cocotaxi*, an unusual three-seater scooter

Horse-Drawn Vehicles

In La Habana Vieja it is possible to go on an enjoyable sight-seeing tour in a horse-drawn carriage – either a perfectly restored old cart or a colonial-style carriage, quite unlike those used by Cubans outside of town.

These carriage tours are not cheap, but can be a romantic and picturesque introduction to the city. Tours last from one to two hours. The carriage and gig rank is located in the square between Calle Empedrado and Calle Tacón.

Bicitaxis

A more environmentally friendly but slower alternative to taxis is to use bicycle rickshaws, known as bicitaxis in Cuba. These are used by Cubans and tourists for short rides in the centre.

They circulate in La Habana Vieja and Centro, or can be found outside hotel entrances.

Driving in Havana

People who are used to heavy traffic in big cities will not find driving in Havana too difficult. But it is important to stay alert at all times and watch out for the many cyclists, pedestrians and even dogs, which often run free in the streets. Keep speeds low in order to be able to spot and avoid the many potholes and bumps. The road signs and markings are reasonably good.

In the city centre there are three tunnels. Two pass under the Almendares river, connecting Vedado and Miramar (see p113). The other, which begins in Plaza Mártires del 71, behind the Castillo de la Punta, takes you rapidly to the other side of the bay and the Morro and Cabaña fortresses (see pp114–15). The latter is especially useful for those heading for the beaches in Playas del Este (see p117). The alternative is the long, winding port road, though it is easy to get lost.

DIRECTORY

Taxis

Cocotaxi
Tel 7873 1411.

Cubataxi
Tel 7873 8752.

Taxis Cuba
Tel 7883 1587.

A horse-drawn carriage in Calle Obispo, La Habana Vieja

General Index

Acknowledgments

Fabio Ratti Editoria would like to thank the following staff at Dorling Kindersley:

Map Co-Ordinator
Dave Pugh.

DTP Manager
Jason Little.

Managing Editor
Anna Streiffert.

Managing Art Editor
Jane Ewart.

Director of Publishing, Travel Guides
Gillian Allan.

Publisher
Douglas Amrine.

Dorling Kindersley would like to thank all those whose contribution and assistance have made the preparation of this book possible.

Main Contributor
Irina Bajini, a scholar who specializes in Hispanic-American languages and literature, lives in Milan and Havana. Among her publications are a conversation handbook, a Cuban-Italian dictionary published by Vallardi, and a book on the santería religion: *Il dio delle onde, del fuoco, del vento* (The God of the Waves, Fire and Wind), published by Sperling&Kupfer. She has also translated a number of Cuban books.

Other Contributors
Alejandro Alonso, an expert in Cuban art, is a journalist and critic who has published essays and curated exhibitions in Cuba and abroad. The former deputy director of the Museo de Bellas Artes, Alonso now heads the Museo Nacional de la Cerámica (National Ceramics Museum) in Havana, which he founded in 1990.

Miguel Angel Castro Machado, the second *historiador de la ciudad* of Baracoa, teaches Hispanic-American literature at the University of Santiago de Cuba.

Andrea G Molinari is executive director of Lauda Air Italia airline and a passionate smoker of, and expert on, Cuban cigars. He is the author of *Sigaro. La guida per l'apprendista fumatore di sigari cubani* (Cigars. A Guide for Newcomers to Cuban Cigar Smoking), published by IdeaLibri.

Marco Oliva is a diving instructor and an expert on diving in the Caribbean. He holds various specialist licences, including those for underwater photography, scuba-diving on wrecks, and marine biology.

Francesca Piana, a journalist and specialist on Latin America, has written numerous travel articles as well as guides to Greece, Mexico, Ecuador and Chile for the Touring Club.

Revisions Team
Louise Abbott, Monica Allende, Alejandro Alonso, Claire Baranowski, Marta Bescos, Rohan Bolton, Julie Bond, Claire Boobbyer, Ernesto Juan Castellanos, Conrad van Dyk, Alice Fewery, Emer FitzGerald, Juliet Kenny, Sumita Khatwani, Walfrido La O (Academia de la Historia de Cuba, Havana), Kathryn Lane, Leena Lane, Maite Lantaron, Jude Ledger, Carly Madden, Hayley Maher, Fiona McAuslan, Alison McGill, Matt Norman, Catherine Palmi, Susie Peachey, Naomi Peck, Helen Peters, Adrian Potts, Rada Radojicic, Marisa Renzullo, Lucy Richards, Ellen Root, Juan Romero Marcos, Mary Scott, Ankita Sharma, Akanksha Siwach, Susana Smith, Stuti Tiwari, Helen Townsend, Vinita Venugopal, Laura Walker, Penny Walker, Sophie Wright.

Proofreader
Stewart J. Wild.

Special Thanks
Archivo fotográfico e histórico de La Habana; Archivo ICAIC; Laura Arrighi (Lauda Air Italia); Bárbara Atorresagasti; Sandro Bajini; Freddy L Cámara; Casa de África, Havana; Aleida Castellanos (Havanatur Italia); Pedro Contreras (Centro de Desarrollo de las Artes Visuales, Havana); Vittoria Cumini (Tocororo restaurant, Milan); Juan Carlos and José Arturo de Dios Lorente; Alfredo Díaz (Tocororo restaurant, Milan); Mariano Fernández Arias (Gaviota); Cecilia Infante (José Martí publishers, Havana); Jardín Botánico del Parque Lenin; Lien La O Bouzán; Manuel Martínez Gomez ("Bohemia" archives); Adrian Adán Gonzalez (Tocororo restaurant, Milan); Guillerma López; Chiara Maretti (Lauda Air Italia); Stefano Mariotti; François Missen; Annachiara Montefusco (Cubanacán Italia); Jorge A Morente Padrón (Archipiélago); Orencio Nardo García (Museo de la Revolución); Eduardo Núñez (Publicitur); Mariacarla Nebuloni; Oficina del Historiador de la Ciudad, Havana; Sullen Olivé Monteagudo (Arcoiris); Angelo Parravicini (Lauda Air Italia); Milagros Pérez (Havanatur Italia); Alicia Pérez Casanova (Horizontes); Josefina Pichardo (Centro de Información y Documentación Turísticas); Richard Pierce; Poder Popular de Isla de la Juventud; Carla Provvedini (Ufficio Turistico di Cuba, Milan); Quinta de los Molinos, Havana; Gianluca Ragni (Gran Caribe); Celia Estela Rojas (Museo de las Parrandas de Remedios); Federica Romagnoli; Aniet Venereo (Archipiélago); Yoraida Santiesteban Vaillant; Lucia Zaccagni.

The Publisher would like to thank Andrea G Molinari in particular for the enthusiasm and willingness with which he supported the preparation of this guide.

Picture Sources

Geocuba, Havana; Habanos SA.

Reproduction Rights

The Publisher would like to thank all the museums, hotels, restaurants, shops and other sights of interest for their kind assistance and authorization to photograph their premises.

Specially Commissioned Photos

Drinks: Paolo Pulga, courtesy of the Tocororo restaurant, Corsico (Milan).

Additional Photography

Julie Bond, Ernesto Juan Castellanos, Maite Lantaron, Ian O'Leary, Tony Souter, Daniel Stoddart.

Picture Credits

key: a = above; b = below/bottom; c = centre; l = left; r = right; t = top

Works of art have been reproduced with the permission of the following copyright holders: Augustín Cárdenas *Figure 1953* © DACS, London 2011 99c; Wifredo Lam *Third World* 1966 © ADAGP, Paris and DACS, London 2011 30c.

Alamy Images: 1bestofphoto 297cra; Arterra Picture Library 2-3, 85cra, 288-9; John Birdsall 267tl; Ian Bottle 194cla; Michele Burgess 271tr; City Image 208-9; dov makabaw Cuba 180t, 282br; Adam Eastland 129clb; Fabienne Fossez 244-5; Forget Patrick/Sagaphoto.com 277tr; ImageBroker 258tr; Andrea Innocenti 164t; isifa Image Service s.r.o. /PHB 216tr; Rosemary Harris 12crb; Hemis 18; Tommy Huynh 110; Mike Kipling Photography 128br; LOOK Die Bildagentur der Fotografen GmbH / Holger Leue 206tr; Chris Lewington 190-1; Melvyn Longhurst 217cr; MARKA 11tr, 14br; B. O'Kane 78bl; Sergio Pitamitz 129tr; Norman Pogson 307tr; Prisma Bildagentur AG 148-9; Robert Harding Picture Library Ltd 14tr /Bruno Morandi 202tl; Antony Souter 247cr; villorejo 273br.
Alejandro Alonso, Havana: 97cl, 99c.
Archivio Mondadori, Milan: Andrea and Antonella Ferrari 157tl.
Archivio Radamés Giro, Havana: 34br, 34bl.
Pierfranco Argentiero, Somma Lombardo: 36bl (all the photos), 37br, 37b, 278cla, 278clb.]
AWL Images: Danita Delimont Stock 250-1.

Marco Biagiotti, Perugia: 23bl, 31cl, 91tl, 95c, 114c, 143c, 143clb. **Claire Boobbyer:** 135cra, 206bl, 239crb; 242tr, 279tl, 305cla. **British Embassy, Havana:** Sixto Martinez 292tc.

Capital Culture: James Sparshatt 129br.
Casa Concordia: 255tr.
Casa De África, Havana: 44bl, 46–7c, 46cl, 46bl, 77b.
Casa Muñoz: 263br.
Casa Particular Cuba: 254c.

Casa Vitrales: 256bc.
Centro Documentazione Mondadori, Milan: 50tr, 51clb, 53tr, 53tl, 56bl, 91br, 118cl, 118cr, 118b, 121bl, 171b.
Centro Histórico de La Ciudad de La Habana, Havana: 32c, 32br, 33tr, 44, 45, 47t, 48, 49, 50clb, 51b, 52tr, 52br, 53bl, 54cl, 63b, 155clb, 223cra.
Gianfranco Cisini, Milan: 61bl, 84tr, 115br, 169b, 177tl, 178cla, 179tl, 192cl, 225clb, 235c.
Corbis: Atlantide Phototravel 8-9; Ernesto Mastrascusa. epa 128cla; Chris Parker/Design Pics 11cr; Reuters/ Claudia Daut 130bl; Reuters/Mark Wilson 243cr; Jane Sweeney/JAI 229br.
Raúl Corrales, Havana: 54–5c.
Cubanacán, Milan: A Cozzi 395b.

Dreamstime.com: Absente 277bl; Mira Agron 94bl; Marcel Berendsen 225tr; Evgenia Bolyukh 182; Kian Yung Chua 193br; Ovidiu Craciun 19b; Roxana Gonzalez 113cl; Pablo Hidalgo 183b, 198b; Patricia Hofmeester 13tr; Irishka777 63cr; Kmiragaya 13bc, 64, 82, 135tl; 136; Konstik 137b; Amanda Lewis 12tl; Bastian Linder 132-3; Klemen Misic 107tr; Roberto M Machado Noa 280cla; Marek Slusarczyk 159b; Aleksandar Todorovic 15tr, 70bl; Tupungato 11bl, 15bc, 194br; Alvaro German Vilela 100; Victor Zastol'sliy 10br.

Martino Fagiuoli, Modena: 28cra, 28clb, 55tl, 90cr, 186tr, 224bl, 228cl, 229tl, 229tr, 229cr, 231br, 230br, 233cla, 233c, 233br, 237bc, 238cl, 240tr, 240br, 246cla, 246br, 247t.
Farabolafoto, Milan: 53cr, 54tr, 55tr, 56tr, 56br, 61tl, 70cl.
Flickr: Stephan Mittas 112cla.

Getty Images: Photogapher's Choice/Louis Quail 266cla.
Paolo Gonzato, Milan: 22c, 24crb *(aura tiñosa)*, 24crb (ox), 33c, 34tr, 35tr *(claves)*, 35tr *(güiro)*, 57clb, 79br (all the photos), 167tl, 176br, 177cb, 177bl, 177br, 184b, 186clb, 188tr, 188c, 192cra, 192clb, 192crb, 192b, 193tr, 196b, 198cra, 205br, 217tl, 224tr, 235tl, 238tr, 240cla, 252b, 269clb, 281br (all the photos), 296c, 306tr, 306br.
Grazia Guerreschi, Milan: 27ad, 27bd, 41as.

Robert Harding Picture Library: Walter Bibikow 73br; Michel Renaudeau 212; P. Schickert 58-9; Michael Thornton 189tc.
Hotel Plaza Cuba: 85br.

Iberostar Grand Hotel Trinidad: 252cla, 262tr, 264ca, 274bc.
Icaic, Havana: 31bl, 33br, 41b.
Image Bank, Milan: 25 clb (flamingo); L Abreu 219b; C Ansaloni 160bl, 169ca, 170tr, 170b; G Bandieri 62cra; A Cavalli 20c, 22t, 25tra, 27bd, 27bl, 57cb, 62cla, 63tr, 71tl, 85cr, 92tr, 106tl, 117br, 120tr, 138cl, 156cla, 157cr, 158, 161tr, 174b, 180c, 181tr, 196tl, 197tl, 220tl, 239bl, 279cl, 290cla; M Everton 286bl; GW Faint 130tr; L King

295tl; A Mihich 286tl; A Pistolesi 25cra, 152br, 154c, 215br, 248b, 249t; GA Rossi 24tr, 24cra, 61tr, 62br, 69br, 76tr, 76cr, 79clb, 89ca, 89b, 91bl, 109cb, 114t, 115bl, 119tr, 119bl, 134bc, 156tr, 156br, 160tr, 167crb, 172cl, 202cl, 236tr, 237c, 285cla, 301bc; E Vergani 117t, 169cr.

Lonely Planet Images: Doug McKinlay 267cb.
Hoan Luong: 166cla.

Stefano Mariotti, Milan: 36br.
Meliá Cuba Marketing & Publicity: 253bl, 254tr, 259br, 260bc, 261tr, 264bl.
Wilder Llanes Méndez: 176tr.
Museo Nacional De Bellas Artes, Havana: 30, 31tr, 31cr, 42, 96, 97, 98, 99.
Paolo Negri, Milan: 84cla, 84b, 152cl, 154bl, 268tr, 269b, 269br.
Marco Oliva, Milan: 79cla, 93cra, 138bl, 140crb, 141tr, 141cl, 141clb, 142tr, 142bl, 150t, 151 (all the photos), 154tr, 177tr 195cla, 211bl, 236cl, 254b, 285br.
Olympia, Milan: 23tr, 57tc, 68bl, 284tr, 284bl.

Paladar Le Chansonnier: 272tr.
Prensa Latina, Havana: 32tr, 34bc, 35tl, 35bl, 35bc, 40c, 51tr, 54bl, 55br, 55bl, 56c, 175b, 206c, 242bl.

Reuters: Oswaldo Rivas 280br.
Lucio Rossi, Milan: 22bl, 24cla, 24clb (woodpecker), 24clb (cartacuba), 24bl, 25tl, 25trb, 25clb (gavilán), 25crb (zunzuncito), 25crb (lizard), 25bl, 25 br, 26cla, 26clb, 27tl, 29br, 39tr, 63clb, 76tl, 76br, 91crb, 102cla, 113b, 135tr, 135b, 140tr, 140c, 143tl, 146tr, 146cl, 147tl,

150c, 150bl, 157bl, 168tr, 168bl (all photos), 169tl, 171tr, 171c, 184tr, 196c, 197b (all photos), 201t, 201c, 202tr, 202b, 203cra, 203b, 213b, 214br, 222bl, 224c, 226tr, 228tr, 233cra, 234b, 241cl, 241bc, 243b, 246tr, 248tl, 248c, 249cb, 253tr, 254tl, 287cla, 293bl, 307bl.

Alberto Salazar, Havana: 35c.
Hotel Saratoga: 257tr.
Studio Falletti, Milan: 37tr, 37cla, 37cr, 37clb, 142cr, 143tr, 143crb.

El Templete: 270bc.

Waco's Club: Raciel Cepero 265bc, 275tr.
Wikipedia, The Free Encyclopedia: NASA 40bl.

Front Endpapers
Alamy Images: Tommy Huynh Lca. Dreamstime.com: Evgenia Bolyukh Rcra; Kmiragaya Rbl, Lbr, Lbc; Alvaro German Vilela Lbl. Robert Harding Picture Library: Michel Renandeau Rbr. **Image Bank, Milan:** Rtc.

Cover Images
Front and spine: **Alamy Stock Photo:** Bill Bachmann.

All other images © Dorling Kindersley.
For further information see:
www.dkimages.com

Phrase Book

The Spanish spoken in Cuba is basically the same as the Castilian used in Spain with certain deviations. As in the Spanish-speaking countries in Central and Southern America, the "z" is pronounced like the "s", as is the "c" when it comes before "e" or "i". Among the grammatical variations, visitors should be aware that Cubans use *Ustedes* in place of *Vosotros*, to say "you" when referring to more than one person. Some Indian, African and English words are also commonly used in present day Cuban Spanish. This basic phrase book includes useful common phrases and words, and particular attention has been paid to typically Cuban idioms in a list of Cuban Terms.

Cuban Terms

apagón	apagon	black-out, power cut
babalawo	babala-wo	a priest of Afro-Cuban religion
bohío	bo-ee-o	traditional rural house with palm leaf roof
carro	karro	car
casa de la trova	kasa deh la troba	club where traditional music is played
batey	batay	village around sugar factory
cayo	ka-yo	small island
chama	chama	child
criollo	kr-yo-yo	Creole (born in Cuba of Spanish descent)
divisa	deebeesa	convertible peso (slang)
guagua	gwagwa	bus
guajiro	gwaheero	farmer
guarapo	gwarapo	sugar cane juice
ingenio	eenhen-yo	sugar factory complex
jama	hama	food, meal
eva	eba	woman
jinetera	heenetaira	prostitute, or female hustler
jinetero	heenetairo	male person hustling tourists
libreta	leebreta	rations book
moneda nacional	moneda nas-yonal	pesos ("national currency")
moros y cristianos	moros ee krist-yanos	rice & black beans (Moors & Christians)
paladar	paladar	privately-owned restaurant
puro	pooro	authentic Cuban cigar
santero	santairo	santería priest
tabaco	tabako	low-quality cigar
tambor	tambor	Afro-Cuban religious musical feast
tienda	t-yenda	shop that only accepts convertible pesos
trago	trago	alcoholic drink
tunas	toonas	prickly pears
zafra	safra	sugar cane harvest

Emergencies

Help!	¡socorro!	sokorro
Stop!	¡pare!	pareh
Call a doctor	Llamen a un médico	yamen a oon medeeko
Call an ambulance	Llamen a una ambulancia	yamen a oona amboolans-ya
Police!	¡policía!	poleesee-a
I've been robbed	Me robaron	meh rrobaron

Communication Essentials

Yes	sí	see
No	no	no
Please	por favor	por fabor
Pardon me	perdone	pairdoneh
Excuse me	disculpe	deeskoolpeh
I'm sorry	lo siento	lo s-yento
Thanks	gracias	gras-yas
Hello!	¡hola!	ohlah
Good day	buenos días	bwenos dee-as
Good afternoon	buenas tardes	bwenas tardes
Good evening	buenas noches	bwenas noches
Night	noche	nocheh
Morning	mañana	man-yana
Tomorrow	mañana	man-yana
Yesterday	ayer	a-yair
Here	acá	aka
How?	¿cómo?	komo
When?	¿cuándo?	kwando
Where?	¿dónde?	dondeh
Why?	¿por qué?	por keh

How are you?	¿qué tal?	keh tal
It's a pleasure!	¡mucho gusto!	moocho goosto
Goodbye, so long	hasta luego	asta lwego

Useful Phrases

That's fine	está bien/ocá	esta b-yen/oka
Fine	¡qué bien!	keh b-yen
How long?	¿Cuánto falta?	kwanto falta
Do you speak a little English?	¿Habla un poco de inglés?	abla oon poko deh eengles
I don't understand	No entiendo	no ent-yendo
Could you speak more slowly?	¿Puede hablar más despacio?	pwedeh ablas mas despas-yo
I agree/OK	de acuerdo/ocá	deh akwairdo/oka
Certainly!	¡Claro que sí!	klaro keh see!
Let's go!	¡Vámonos!	bamonos

Useful Words

Large	grande	grandeh
Small	pequeño	peken-yo
Hot	caliente	kal-yenteh
Cold	frío	free-o
Good	bueno	bweno
Bad	malo	malo
So-so	más o menos	mas o menos
Well/fine	bien	b-yen
Open	abierto	ab-yairto
Closed	cerrado	serrado
Full	lleno	yeno
Empty	vacío	basee-o
Right	derecha	dairecha
Left	izquierda	isk-yairda
Straight	recto	rrekto
Under	debajo	debaho
Over	arriba	arreeba
Quickly/early	pronto/temprano	pronto/temprano
Late	tarde	tardeh
Now	ahora	a-ora
Soon	ahorita	a-oreeta
More	más	mas
Less	menos	menos
Little	poco	poko
Sufficient	suficiente	soofees-yenteh
Much	mucho/muy	moocho/mwee
Too much	demasiado	demas-yado
In front of	delante	delanteh
Behind	detrás	detras
First floor	primer piso	preemair peeso
Ground floor	planta baja	planta baha
Lift/elevator	elevador	elebador
Bathroom/toilet	servicios	sairbees-yos
Women	mujeres	moohaires
Men	hombres	ombres
Toilet paper	papel sanitario	papel saneetar-yo
Camera	cámara	kamara
Batteries	baterías	batairee-as
Passport	pasaporte	pasaporteh
Visa; tourist card	visa; tarjeta turistica	beesa; tarheta tooreesteeka

Health

I don't feel well	Me siento mal	meh s-yento mal
I have a stomach ache headache	Me duele el estómago la cabeza	meh dweleh el estomago la kabesa
He/she is ill	Está enfermo/a	esta enfairmo
I need to rest	Necesito decansar	neseseeto dekansar
Drug store	farmacia	farmasee-ya

Post Office and Bank

Bank	banco	banko
I want to send a letter	Quiero enviar una carta	k-yairo emb-yar oona karta
Postcard	postal tarjeta	postal tarheta

Stamp	**sello**	se-yo
Draw out money	**sacar dinero**	sakar deenairo

Shopping

How much is it?	**¿Cuánto cuesta?**	kwanto kwesta
What time do you open/close?	**¿A qué hora abre/ cierra?**	a ke ora abreh/ s-yairra
May I pay with a credit card?	**¿Puedo pagar con tarjeta de crédito?**	pwedo pagar kon tarheta deh kredeeto?

Sightseeing

Beach	**playa**	pla-ya
Castle, fortress	**castillo**	kastee-yo
Cathedral	**catedral**	katedral
Church	**iglesia**	eegles-ya
District	**barrio**	barr-yo
Garden	**jardín**	hardeen
Guide	**guía**	gee-a
House	**casa**	kasa
Motorway	**autopista**	owtopeesta
Museum	**museo**	mooseh-o
Park	**parque**	parkeh
Road	**carretera**	karretaira
Square, plaza	**plaza, parque**	plasa, parkeh
Street	**calle, callejón**	ka-ye, ka-yehon
Town hall	**ayuntamiento**	a-yoontam-yento
Tourist bureau	**buró de turismo**	booro deh tooreesmo

Transport

Could you call a taxi for me?	**¿Me puede llamar a un taxi?**	meh pwedeh yamar a oon taksee?
Airport	**aeropuerto**	a-airopwairto
Train station	**estación de ferrocarriles**	estas-yon deh fairrokarreeles
Bus station	**terminal de guaguas**	tairmeenal deh gwagwas
When does it leave?	**¿A qué hora sale?**	a keh ora saleh?
Customs	**aduana**	adwana
Boarding pass	**tarjeta de embarque**	tarheta deh embarkeh
Car hire	**alquiler de carros**	alkeelair deh karros
Bicycle	**bicicleta**	beeseekleta
Insurance	**seguro**	segooro
Petrol/gas station	**estación de gasolina**	estas-yon deh gasoleena

Staying in a Hotel

Single room/ double	**habitación sencilla/ doble**	abeetas-yon sensee-ya /dobleh
Shower	**ducha**	doocha
Bathtub	**bañera**	ban-yaira
Balcony	**balcón, terraza**	balkon, tairrasa
Air conditioning	**aire acondicionado**	eye-reh akondisionado
I want to be woken at…	**Necesito que me despierten a las…**	neseseeto keh meh desp-yairten a las…
Warm water/ cold	**agua caliente/ fría**	agwa kal-yenteh/ free-a
Soap	**jabón**	habon
Towel	**toalla**	to-a-ya
Key	**llave**	yabeh

Eating Out

What is there to eat?	**¿Qué hay para comer?**	keh I para komair?
The bill, please	**la cuenta, por favor**	la kwenta por fabor
Glass	**vaso**	baso
Cutlery	**cubiertos**	koob-yairtos
I would like some water	**Quisiera un poco de agua**	kees-yaira oon poko deh agwa
Have you got wine?	**¿Tienen vino?**	t-yenen beeno?
The beer is not cold enough	**La cerveza no está bien fría**	la sairbesa no esta b-yen free-a
Breakfast	**desayuno**	desa-yoono
Lunch	**almuerzo**	almwairso
Dinner	**comida/cena**	komeeda/sane-er
Raw/cooked	**crudo/cocido**	kroodo/koseedo

Menu Decoder

aceite	asayteh	oil
agua mineral	agwa meenairal	mineral water
ajo	aho	garlic
arroz	arros	rice
asado	asado	roasted
atún	atoon	tuna
azúcar	asookar	sugar
bacalao	bakala-o	cod
café	kafeh	coffee
camarones	kamarones	prawns
carne	karneh	meat
congrí	kongree	rice with beans & onions
cerveza	sairbesa	beer
dulce	doolseh	sweet, dessert
ensalada	ensalada	salad
fruta	froota	fruit
fruta bomba	froota bomba	papaya
helado	elado	ice cream
huevo	webo	egg
jugo	hoogo	fruit juice
langosta	langosta	lobster
leche	lecheh	milk
marisco	mareesko	seafood
mantequilla	mantekee-ya	butter
pan	pan	bread
papas	papas	potatoes
postre	postreh	dessert
pescado	peskado	fish
plátano	platano	banana
pollo	po-yo	chicken
potaje/sopa	potaheh/sopa	soup
puerco	pwairko	pork
queso	keso	cheese
refresco	refresko	drink
sal	sal	salt
salsa	salsa	sauce
té	teh	tea
vinagre	beenagreh	vinegar

Time

Minute	**minuto**	meenooto
Hour	**hora**	ora
Half-hour	**media hora**	med-ya ora
Monday	**lunes**	loones
Tuesday	**martes**	martes
Wednesday	**miércoles**	m-yairkoles
Thursday	**jueves**	hwebes
Friday	**viernes**	b-yairnes
Saturday	**sábado**	sabado
Sunday	**domingo**	domeengo
January	**enero**	enairo
February	**febrero**	febrairo
March	**marzo**	marso
April	**abril**	abreel
May	**mayo**	ma-yo
June	**junio**	hoon-yo
July	**julio**	hool-yo
August	**agosto**	agosto
September	**setiembre**	set-yembreh
October	**octubre**	oktoobreh
November	**noviembre**	nob-yembreh
December	**diciembre**	dees-yembreh

Numbers

0	**cero**	sairo
1	**uno**	oono
2	**dos**	dos
3	**tres**	tres
4	**cuatro**	kuatro
5	**cinco**	seenko
6	**seis**	says
7	**siete**	s-yeteh
8	**ocho**	ocho
9	**nueve**	nwebeh
10	**diez**	d-yes
11	**once**	onseh
12	**doce**	doseh
13	**trece**	treseh
14	**catorce**	katorseh
15	**quince**	keenseh
16	**dieciséis**	d-yeseesays
17	**diecisiete**	d-yesees-yeteh
18	**dieciocho**	d-yes-yocho
19	**diecinueve**	d-yeseenwebeh
20	**veinte**	baynteh
30	**treinta**	traynta
40	**cuarenta**	kwarenta
50	**cincuenta**	seenkwenta
60	**sesenta**	sesenta
70	**setenta**	setenta
80	**ochenta**	ochenta
90	**noventa**	nobenta
100	**cien**	s-yen
500	**quinientos**	keen-yentos
1000	**mil**	meel

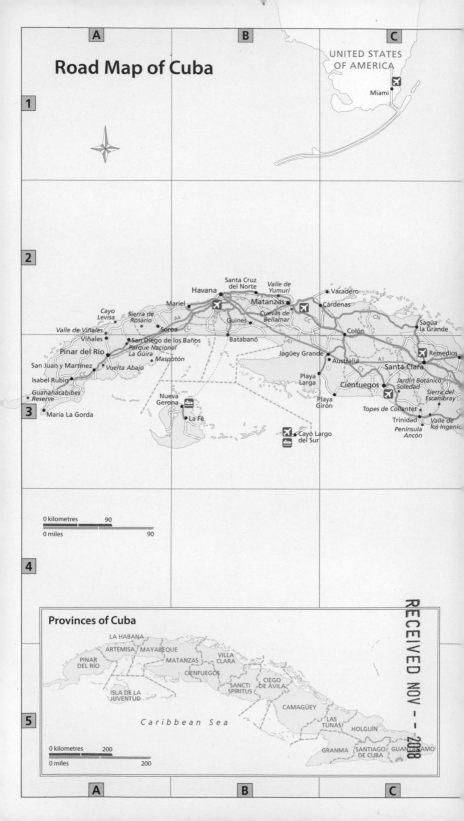